Markets from Networks

Markets from Networks

~~~~~~~~~~~~~~~~~~~~~~~~~~~~~~

Socioeconomic Models
of Production

Harrison C. White

PRINCETON UNIVERSITY PRESS

PRINCETON AND OXFORD

Published by Princeton University Press, 41 William Street, Princeton,
New Jersey 08540
In the United Kingdom: Princeton University Press, 3 Market Place,
Woodstock, Oxfordshire OX20 1SY

Second printing, and first paperback printing, 2005
Paperback ISBN 0-691-12038-2

THE LIBRARY OF CONGRESS HAS CATALOGED THE CLOTH EDITION

OF THIS BOOK AS FOLLOWS

White, Harrison C.
Markets from networks : socioeconomic models of production /
Harrison C. White.
p. cm.
Includes bibliographical references and index.
ISBN 0-691-08871-3 (alk. paper)
1. Market segmentation—Mathematical models. I. Title.
HF5415.127 .W5 2002
658.8—dc21   2001027841

British Library Cataloging-in-Publication Data is available

This book has been composed in Berkeley

Printed on acid-free paper. ∞

pup.princeton.edu

Printed in the United States of America

3   5   7   9   10   8   6   4   2

To Lynn A. Cooper

~~~~~~~~~~~~~~~~~~

BELOVED HELPMEET
AND FELLOW SCIENTIST

Contents

List of Figures

~~~~~~~~~~~~

List of Tables

Preface

~~~~~~~~~~~~~~~~~~~~

Results from work spread over twenty years have been integrated in this manuscript over the past four years, in response to the resurgence of institutionalism in economic sociology as well as in economics. The original model of the individual market is generalized in several ways and then enriched by extending it to network populations of markets. Markets are taken to be tangible, and they are theorized as interactive social constructions.

Social construction is a perspective that is even more radical than it seems from present expositions, as in that by Berger and Luckman, which do not reach to the infrastructure and contingent processes required to effectuate their phenomenology. Interpretive understanding must precede, but also then should lead to, explicit modeling. Structural equivalence and connectivity dynamics in social networks here bridge theory to explicit modeling, which provides a general, flexible, and yet simple description of arrays of settings. These are settings for commitments by producers in markets that add value to their downstream flows by incorporating inputs purchased upstream.

The goal is to explain how firms minimize uncertainty by forming a market as a collection of niches based on signals observed in their commitments. Firms do indeed seek to maximize profits, but only as they find quality niches in recognized lines of business sustained as joint social constructions. These markets are thereby established as distinct identities seen within everyday discourse as sources of action. Firms fit into three critical market roles—supplier, producer, and purchaser—one more role than commonly assumed involved in market decisions. Each market has a specific but flexible orientation, facing either upstream or downstream.

Reaching the goal thus requires market models adaptable to a wide range of contexts across this network population of firms and markets. The goal becomes using the minimum number of parameters to the greatest effect. The models will help elucidate well-known phenomena that are at present inadequately explained along with revealing new implications and particulars for markets. Finally, this book will use these models to explore some consequences for the future both of markets and of the science of markets.

This book is a tangible specification of part of the vision in my theory book of 1992, *Identity and Control*. Both aim to present a quite different way of conceiving social situations, a way that brings out their multiplicity in structural levels as well as interpretive realms, together with their combination of intricacy in mechanism and sheer spread in social space-time.

I thus address this book to disparate—and mutually contentious—audiences. Anthropology provides foundations, along with sociology and economics. The more specialized audiences are economic sociologists, business school faculty, and, within economics, microeconomic theorists and econometricians as well as Industrial Organization practitioners.

Institutional, organizational, and discourse analysts—as well as system modelers from natural science and engineering and those interested in ethnography and case studies—will find here new ways to conceive how actors emerge and get sited in and exert influences upon their surrounding contexts and processes. Each specialist will note the crudities—substantive and mathematical—of this new synthesis as regards his or her own line of expertise. Improvements are welcome, but some patience is warranted to see if these simplifications across an array of paradigms permit both deeper insight and explicit computations.

History still lurks in the background here. All of us pay deference—wave our hands to the historical, so to speak—but there is little theory of how histories actually build. There are suggestions, such as by my colleagues Karen Barkey, Peter Bearman, Allan Silver, David Stark, and Charles Tilly. The test will be envisaging what is in the course of being born as well as generalizing about what has been born across millennia.

Derivations are kept transparent and elementary, even at some cost in added length. The few sections of text that use mathematics extensively are marked by asterisks. Many technical details have been pruned and some shunted to the appendix, which includes a set of numerical tables. The glossary explains symbols used across chapters.

Acknowledgments

~~~~~~~~~~~~~~~~~~~~~~~~~~

T rying to acknowledge each source of stimulation and help over the twenty-five-year gestation of this book has led to unwieldy and yet still incomplete lists of persons (many of them already cited in the references), but I remember all with gratitude.

Guidance, stimulation, encouragement, and chiding from other researchers, as well as from colleagues and students, were indispensable to sticking out the anxious process of revising this manuscript over the past year. Peter Bearman impelled me toward the very last drafts. Excellent guidance came from a review by Randall Collins and from reports from Wayne Baker and Joel Podolny, referees for Princeton University Press. Valuable suggestions came from memos from Neal Caren and from the group of Dottores, attending my course with Professor Giulio Bolacchi at AILUN-Nuoro, Italy. My final draft was significantly improved through the editing of Madeleine Adams, working with Ian Malcolm of Princeton University Press, and the copyediting of Richard Isomaki.

For guidance on the preceding few drafts I am especially indebted to Scott Boorman, Neil Fligstein, Emmanuel Lazega, Richard Nelson, Richard Swedberg, Charles Tilly, and Christopher Winship. And I am indebted to others who over the past two or three years have led me to include a wider range of perspectives: in particular to Karen Barkey, Martin Gargiulo, Szabolcs Kemeny, and David Stark. They all kept insisting also on improvements in clarity and force. I should add that many others who were exposed to versions of this book in workshops or courses of mine have shaped and enlarged my views with their questions and commentary.

Support and facilities for this recent phase of work came largely from the Paul F. Lazarsfeld Center for the Social Sciences at Columbia, where I was director, aided greatly by the wit and wisdom of its administrator, Debi Gilchrest, and of political scientist Robert Y. Shapiro, codirector. I am also indebted for partial support to a grant from the National Science Foundation, jointly with Ann Mische, and to a grant from the Behavioral Sciences Research Council of Citicorp, jointly with Kathryn Neckerman. Financial support and facilities over the early years at Harvard were provided under grants from the National Science Foundation.

Persistent probings by David Gibson, an interdisciplinary fellow of the Lazarsfeld Center, by postdoctoral fellow Ann Mische, and by Shepley W. Orr led to substantial improvements in both content and structure of a draft in late 1996, as did meticulous critique of earlier versions by another interdisciplinary fellow, Holly Raider.

It was a 1996 *journée* on my early markets paper (1981a), organized by economist Olivier Favereau, reinforced by his own astonishingly lucid presentation there, that suggested to me that I should write this book. Lynn Cooper supported this project, and a series of joint workshops ensued at the Nanterre research venue FORUM, and at Maison Suger, both during my 1996 sabbatical leave and again during subsequent visits in May–July 1997 and 1998. I owe much to Alain Degenne for being my research host as Directeur of LASMAS (CNRS), and I am also indebted to Directeur Maurice Aymard of the Maison des Sciences de l'Homme and to Directeur Jean Luc Lory of Maison Suger (MSH) for my appointments and facilities in Paris during research leaves and visits.

Let me add just a few words on the earlier years. I failed to deliver a chapter for colleague Daniel Bell's prescient volume, *The Crisis in Economic Theory* (1981), but the request encouraged me to develop theoretical implications of early models, and so this book may be seen as a long-postponed fulfillment. The dual model now reported in chapter 9 derives from a paper presented at the September 1981 conference at the University of Edinburgh to honor Tom Burns on his retirement, but never published. It was touched on in a 1988 chapter requested by Barry Wellman and Stephen Berkowitz to relate markets to their overview of network process (republished 1995). In 1987 and then again in 1994 I participated in sessions on the New Institutional Economics in a continuing international workshop organized in Wallerfangen, Saarland, by Erik G. Furubotn, Rudolf Richter, and Ekkehart Schlicht (see White 1995a). But I was no longer keeping up with economic sociology in 1988 when Richard Swedberg of Stockholm University interviewed me for one of a dozen chapters in his book (1990) contrasting views expressed by economists with views expressed by sociologists. That got me restarted, together with a follow-up seminar sponsored by the Russell Sage Foundation and chaired by Mark Granovetter along with Swedberg. Throughout my Columbia years, Siegwart Lindenberg of Groeningen University contributed a cognitive perspective on market modeling, in annual cross-Atlantic research workshops that we cohosted. Ronald Burt, who as chair of the Department of Sociology brought me to Columbia University in 1988, encouraged my market modeling in his Stamer Workshops, which also introduced me to his own stream of research that culminated in a 1992 monograph whose influence will be apparent in the pages that follow.

My collaborator over the past two years, Matt Bothner, has assisted as much with trenchant advice as with programming and calculations. He has explored new directions of his own, which are being published separately. Eric Leifer earlier moved this project forward, as shown in solo and joint publications. Leifer brought a sociopsychological and Bothner a pragmatist perspective otherwise missing. In between, Bob Eccles pulled the modeling toward problematics of organization and control. We are by no means always in agreement with one another, yet in this book "we" or "us" are not royal usage but rather are invoking them as well as reaching out to you, the reader.

I made final revisions and proof corrections during sabbatical leave in Paris, and I am grateful to INSEAD and to Columbia's Institute for Scholars at Reid Hall for providing office space and research support, overseen by Natalie D'Abroville and Mihaela Bacou. And my insight was sharpened by joint research on the Languedoc wine industry with a team from INRA-Montpelier: Fabrice Dreyfus, Jean Marc Touzard, and Yuna Chiffoleau.

CHAPTER 1

~~~~~~~~~~~~~~~~~~~~

Introduction

An increasing number of markets are something more than sites for direct transactions between buyers and sellers. These markets are mobilizers of production in networks of continuing flows. Firms continuously and jointly construct their market interface, which provides a measure of shelter from the uncertainties of business. These mobilizer markets induce and adapt flows in production and service, of various sizes and quality, through networks of relations that spread through a production economy.

Producers become individually established in a line of business as together they constitute a recognized industry or some analogous grouping of producers or processors. Having developed specialized facilities and organization, each member firm commits, period after period, to a definite flow of products for placement downstream.

In exactly what does this "production market" consist? Is this joint construction of a market by constituent firms a set of roles among positions? Is this market an integral actor, a chorus, or an agglomeration? Is it an ideal, a figure of speech, or a legal framework that acts as a guide to members? Is the market a by-product of signals that the actors read from each other's actions or from the actions of like markets?

There is also a larger view, in which each market is a by-product of dependencies of its own flows on actions around origin and destination markets. For more than a century, the social sciences have groped through a fog of custom that grew around and with this new institutional system centering on a new species of market.

Each such market coordinates its producer firms in commitments to pumping downstream product flows into which procurements from upstream have been incorporated. This sequence of transformation, controlled by producer commitments, fundamentally distinguishes the production market mechanism from earlier market genres of exchange well theorized by earlier economics. Resulting streams of differentiated goods or services from the market get split among diverse buyers as equally good options: The market discipline centers on product quality.

What is the mechanism by which production markets work, and, equally crucial, how do markets embed among dispersed and heterogeneous networks of relations? The following chapters propose and apply a family of mathematical models in answer. Many varieties of the mechanism are distinguished; therefore the modeling provides usable approximations to confused

and shifting realities that are affected by processes and institutions—technological, political, cultural, and social—that lie partly outside the modeling
field.

The mechanism is adaptable to variety in upstream and downstream contexts (and a dual form oriented upstream is laid out in chapter 9). These
contexts for individual firms and their embedding as a market must also
reflect how this particular market as a whole fits in among other markets. In
the overlapping evolutions of these markets and firms, common business
usages and forms of discourse emerge and spread so that there are some
common framings in terms of quality and monetary value, terms in which to
express the mechanism and the context.

Each market reproduces itself as a social construction by virtue of some
form of signaling within a shared frame of perception among its firms. This
frame disciplines producers' strivings to maximize the gap between procurement costs and sales revenue, vis-à-vis buyers who hold out for equally good
deals across producers with differentiated outputs. The models have roots in
orthodox economic theory but insist on the realities of continuing profitability for firms and of local path dependence. They are models of interactive social constructions being carried out around us.

More concretely, what array of prices do firms maneuver each other into as
such a market? The empirical focus for this question will be twentieth-cen-
tury production markets in the United States. To get at price, one has to
examine individual markets, each with particular firms as members, interacting to comprise a line of business reaching across cities and states. One can
employ a host of intensive case studies of markets. These range from U.S.
light aircraft and the dozen and more in Scottish knitwear (see chapter 4)
through worldwide markets for oil tankers (Zannetos 1985), U.S. markets for
accounting and advertising services (Han 1995; Baker, Faulkner, and Fisher
1998), markets for the latest products such as personal computers (Bothner
2000a)—and even investment banking (see chapter 12). Also relevant are
studies of less glamorous markets—for example, cotton waste for cleaning
machine rooms—and markets still traditionally local, such as for concrete
blocks. One expects, and the case studies document, widely different levels
and sensitivities of market outcomes in volume, quality, and price.

The aim of this book is to penetrate not one but all of these disparate
examples, and to view them together across networks. Production markets
are flexible and are able to persist because they are constructed in and from
widely shared mores. A flexible mechanism can accommodate the intercala-
tions of processes and perceptions in all of them. The model derives from
and illustrates a more general theory of social construction, rooted in network, identity, and control and triggered by exposure to the uncertainties in
ordinary business.

Network ensembles of such markets constitute ecologies with firm, market, and sector levels. Implications for control properties are derived from and point toward devolutions into other forms, subject to additional institutions of finance and ownership. The array of models offers a basis for prognostications about the broader economy.

In this book, we trace some evolutions of identities in interaction with strategic moves, in order to explore degrees of freedom for entrepreneurial action. These market models presuppose human flexibility and scope in the actors, without which there would be no patterns of generalized exchange. So potentialities of maneuvering and disruption are inherent in the formulation.

A key source for the mechanism mathematics was work by the economist Michael Spence on signaling (see chapter 5). He interpreted each outcome, however, as a profile of control over a population of atomized individuals, whereas here the profile is of a joint interactive construction among a handful of players, which then is embedded in networks of other industries but also is subject to disruption and maneuvering.

This introductory chapter now turns to vignettes, accompanied by historical and theoretical framing, that point up key questions about production markets sketched in following sections. In later chapters, existing standard treatments, largely from economics, will be shown either to overlook these aspects or to merely accommodate them through ad hoc additions to their models. These models, such as pure competition, amount to suppression of markets (chap. 11). This introductory chapter ends with a road map of the rest of the book, following sections introducing motivational, contextual, and network aspects of the market mechanism.

FROM LOCALISM TO GENERALIZED EXCHANGE: AMERICAN VIGNETTES

How do firms establish their outputs in each production market? Which firms are in which markets? How does one market relate to others?

Early on, production was more local and less systemic than in today's production markets. Let's begin with colorful just-so stories as a starting point for contrast with standard treatments. Pittsburgh has had several lives as a center of the production of heavy metals. Early in the twentieth century, fierce competition among rapidly growing iron and steel producers blanketed its steep river valleys with smoke. At the same time a trust blanketed much of the competitive action in the steel market. By midcentury, the smoke had thinned and turned apricot-hued as advanced steels came in, along with renewed, although cautious, competition. Across Pennsylvania, to the east in the Lehigh Valley, comparable early scenes out of Tolkien's Mordor were transformed in similar ways, as Bethlehem Steel became intimately connected in networks of business with Pittsburgh steel companies. Since then, Pittsburgh, more than Bethlehem, has spawned and regrown in markets around

newer technologies and the commercialization of specialized services hitherto done in-house if at all. The trust organization was loosened by these
commercial and technological developments as well as by government antitrust actions.

Chandler (1977) gives a broad overview of the history of industries in
America, drawing on rich local, regional, and national materials. He describes interrelated massive changes in institutions of credit, information,
and transport among cities that accompanied the emergence of large firms
and the decline of localism. Inquiry into the mechanism of the accompanying production markets calls for further probes. This whole section could be
preceded by still older developments in New England industry, which offer
examples of markets constrained through the co-optation of state government by cabals of elite industrialists. The American economy soon grew too
large, too fast for such easy derailment of incipient market mechanisms.
Such interventions are not the focus of this book, but later chapters (especially chapter 12) sketch how they may affect predictions from the market
mechanism.

Farther down the river from Pittsburgh lay Cincinnati, another city old by
Midwestern standards, with a very different industrial history but a similar
concentration of wealth and local power in magnates. Consumer goods, soft
and sticky, generated huge receipts in Cincinnati, but receipts mostly direct
from wholesalers and retailers. As in Pittsburgh, there was local concentration, but also measured competition developed between these locals, notably
Procter and Gamble, and parallel consumer-goods giants elsewhere. Minneapolis was similar but larger and more diverse than Cincinnati, embracing
packaged foods, lumber, office supplies, and more, again in a mixture of
competition and elite control.

By the 1920s Pittsburgh Plate Glass (PPG) had emerged along with production market mechanisms for glass industries, with Owens Illinois (initially Owens Bottle) as one peer, located further west. During the genesis of
PPG, several clusters of small local producers across Ohio and Pennsylvania
were struggling with confusing, yet appealing, new circumstances in which
one could ship to—and even buy from—remote localities and new sorts of
industry downstream in production flows. From well before the 1920s,
Corning Glass in upstate New York was developing more sophisticated products and methods in glass, protected by patents. And still other clusters
across the nation became involved.

PPG came to see that Corning was selling more higher-end glass products
to customers no longer committed by relative closeness to upstate New York,
just as PPG and Owens Illinois were coming to sell huge amounts of average
glass products for buildings in booming metropolises, even metropolises
nearer to Corning's plants. It was under such pulls that congeries of small,
traditional, local glass producers, not just in Ohio—and not just in glass—

either disappeared from major commerce or folded into one or another among the producers with size sufficient to seek niches as peers in a national market. The law of large numbers helped ensure that there was indeed demand for regularly repeated outputs from an industry differentiated enough to cater across an array of buyers.

Enter the transposable genus of production market that is central to this book. The focus is on one theme in these just-so stories: changes in structures of visibility, and thence influence, among actors in networks of business relations common across a production economy. The heart of the claim is that producers' attention was pulled away from habitual ties to local suppliers and distributors, whether in Pittsburgh or Minneapolis. Producers' horizon of opportunity opened up; they paid attention to a much larger and more diverse set of connections. In this enlarged world, producers became aware of a much greater range of contingencies and were exposed to more and more intricate influences that were harder to assess by habitual rules of thumb or by focus on a few predominant ties. This was especially true with respect to buyers. Even the largest buyer (perhaps some wholesaler or large building developer, in the case of glass) did not loom large on a national canvas. Markets in very different products came to be akin in mechanism, a mechanism transposable because adaptable to a great many diverse contexts—though by no means all, as we shall see in chapters 3 and 4.

The lure of market formation often was the prospect of gaining increasing returns to scale, which thus must be a main option in any believable modeling of the market mechanism, pace orthodox economics. The irony is that with such larger reach, the distinctive new signaling mechanism of this market was feasible only among a limited number of producers. So long as producers watched each other for cues and clues as each adapted its products for a niche, they could count on continuing in lines of business together as an industry.

Many other industries necessarily were getting together in the same period. A partition into markets imposed itself among networks of flows among firms. Tracing an industry within this interacting array of evolutions could permit us to estimate also the fungibility of products from different industries somewhat parallel in the underlying networks, such as, in the case of glass, translucent sheets or ceramic pots.

The long-term outcome was a production economy with networks of intermediate products and services. This supplanted more episodic economies among localities with self-contained producers and final consumers, mediated only by merchants of various sorts. But, like the system it supplanted, the production market could also routinely generate net profits for many or all producers. Chapter 15 develops this historical sketch further.

Figure 1.1 is a schematic rendering around one industry of flows and nodes in the new system. It is aptly characterized as generalized exchange

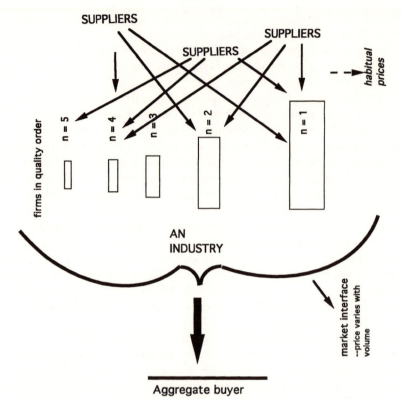

FIG. 1.1 Generalized exchange: configuration of flows across firms for one market in a production economy

because final uses usually require acquisitions originating from many sources through many steps of intermediate processing and service. Here, complementary flows of money and thus a complementary fiscal system are assumed, but anthropology and sociology offer many examples of generalized exchange, such as in kinship systems, that do not require money.

PRODUCTION COMMITMENTS AND KNIGHTIAN UNCERTAINTY

The basic distinction intrinsic to every market in a production economy is between upstream and downstream. This distinction is introduced often in economic theories and business analyses, but casually and without considering the necessary implications. Unlike familiar markets of haggle and exchange, actions in markets for production necessarily implicate not two but three roles for firms: supplier, producer, and purchaser. They are activated as a trio in sequences of interacting decisions that cross market interfaces.

Actions in these input-output networks of a production economy depend not only on sequence but also on timing. Occupancies of the supplier and purchaser roles with respect to that market will be multiple and subject to switching in and out. The producer role is the one entailing specific commitment to future flow, which presupposes investment in specific facilities and organization for that product. For simplicity we will continue to refer to producer firms as in an industry, but the analytic model is equally applicable to markets for services and other markets where the actors commit to process, not product flow. Nor is large size, in firm or market, necessary for applicability.

A producer has to commit its facilities in advance to obtain a level of production for a period, a level to which both its peers in the market and various possible occupants of the other roles adapt their choices. So commitment and uncertainty are the twin themes in production markets. From their interaction spins out the asymmetry among the three roles and all the other distinctive features of production markets.

What counts is that there be commitments visible as signals to induce and support market interfaces shaped by both upstream and downstream context. One can trace this social construction to uncertainty facing alert actors seeking secure footing as well as continuing profitability in networks of flows. Packaging as an industry offers producer firms long-term positions in niches, positions that help to mitigate the vital uncertainties that surround commitment and evaluation in a competitive environment. If we regard the firms as atoms, the market is a molecule.

Producers learn and are pressured to huddle together as an industry such that their key cues come from their fellow producers who face the same opaque diversity of buyers and who offer differentiated products filling distinct niches. Firms and industries thus interleave as actors, operating through this distinct genus of production market. Each of these markets is a social construction hammered out amid the flow of ongoing business life, as Marshall (1930), the first real theorist of industry, argued long ago. Appearances to the contrary, such social constructions all are cousins under their thick skins, since all derive from repeated relations in social networks under exposure to risk. This is what must be modeled.

Just What Are Producers Afraid Of?

The analysis in this book derives from three interwoven distinctions. The first is that between upstream and downstream. The second, also discussed in the previous section, is that between the role of making commitments and the roles of adapting. The third is that between perceptions and subsequent interpretation as signals. Producers' fear reflects the second and engenders the third distinction. All three distinctions fit together in the basic asymmetry in operation of production markets.

Producers' fear traces to the distinction between risk and assessable uncertainty, which was proposed eighty years ago by the economist Frank Knight. In Knight's words: "The problem of profit is one way of looking at the problem of the contrast between perfect competition and actual competition. . . . The key to the whole tangle will be found to lie in the notion of risk or uncertainty and the ambiguities concealed therein. . . . Our main concern will be with the contrast between Risk as a known chance and true Uncertainty. . . . At the bottom of the uncertainty problem in economics is the forward-looking character of the economic process itself. . . . The most fundamental feature of the economic system [is] *production for a market*" (Knight 1971, 19, 21, 237, 241).[1]

One implication to be derived (for it is not obvious) is so basic that if it is invalidated the argument of this book is contradicted: *Each market exhibits an orientation either upstream or downstream.* Producers are not just embedded in a market, as the sociologist Mark Granovetter (1985) would argue; they actually constitute the market's interface in, and as the set of, their perceptions and choices. They constitute the interface vis-à-vis the direction in which risk is perceived to originate.

This book will refine these three basic distinctions by introducing detailed stipulations and specifications of possible contexts for embedding markets. The forms of the mechanism interdigitating market and firms thereby can be arrayed in a space according to parameter values specifying embedding and thus substantive context (chaps. 3, 7). Shape and outputs from a market vary greatly with location in this market space. Orthodox theory of markets offers no such framework for discriminations. Why is this?

In fact, there is a space for each orientation of market molecule, according to the present model. Each of the two spaces splits into the same half-dozen regions defining major varieties of market. Market outcomes prove very different according to orientation, such that in some regions markets seem likely to have one orientation and in other regions the other orientation (chap. 9). But also the orientation of a given market may switch with external incident or internal provocation. Striking changes are predicted in market outcomes from switches. Standard views of markets make no such predictions and do not even distinguish orientation. Again, why is this?

Standard economics does offer various attempts at realistic modeling of a production market (as will be shown first in chapters 2 and 5). While economics has infiltrated common sense over a long period, economic theory itself starts from and borrows from commonsense views. So standard economics views, even though they ostensibly derive from models, often remain close to commonsense views.

But when it considers production markets in a realistic environment of flow networks, orthodox economic theory abandons any realistic or commonsense model and reverts to the fiction of markets with pure competition (as will be elaborated in chapter 11). One great cost of this orthodoxy has been the unacknowledged infiltration of notions of pure competition into practical economists' research. This will be illustrated in a section of chapter 11 on the otherwise outstanding microeconometric work of Nerlove (1965). But it can also be seen in qualitative analysis: for example, in the work of Lazonick (1991), whose aim, ironically, is to challenge the "myth of markets"! Another great cost is the glibness with which economic theorists offer policy advice, such as in recent years for postsocialist economies.

Orthodox economic theory has yet to deal effectively with the three roles in upstream-downstream flows. This blinds it to the relevance of Knightian uncertainty and thereby also to polarization of market orientation and its possible switches. That is not so for the new evolutionary economics, sketched in chapter 14 and presaged by the Flaherty article discussed early in chapter 11, but even these do not take seriously the network spread and embeddings previewed in the preceding and in the next sections.

Like orthodox economics, standard sociology has been reluctant to build up from analysis of particular markets to overall critiques and assessments of economic influences in social process. But then it has not been so charged in the academic division of labor. Because the market is a tangible social construction opaque to tools familiar to economists, and because sociologists by and large have not looked, the market has remained a mystification—much as field anthropology has usually asserted. Developments from these sociological and anthropological traditions will be melded with insights from economics, as is traced explicitly in chapters 10 and 14.

The task of this book is to develop an explicit yet flexible framework for modeling any market in a production economy. The modeling is as applicable to the heavy chemical as to machine tool and other sectors. It is as applicable for Britain or Germany, say, as for the United States (and indeed there may be smaller divergences between countries than between sectors within a country). In Britain and Germany, production markets emerged earlier and later, respectively, than in the American Midwest. But in both European countries, the middling firms, as contrasted with American behemoths, predominated.[2] The production market mechanism is applicable also to analogous processes on a still smaller scale. One can even model barbershops, say, but with the handicap that business journalists and analysts will not furnish much of the investigative material needed to estimate the model, at least until their attention comes to be drawn, for example, to "rationalization" into franchised organizations (Bradach 1998).

MOLECULAR MARKETS IN THEIR NETWORK SETTING

What properties enable a market interface to constitute a foil against Knightian risk for its members? Market transactions deal with repetitive rather than one-shot production; so the size of flows committed becomes one possible form of signal among the producers as to coming commitments to the market. Each can orient to a niche by the size that is appropriate to the market's assessment of its quality compared to that of its fellows, who also are orienting to niches: the market as joint social construction.

The venerable term *quality* suggests judgments of products in themselves, judgments made even of each product separately. The production market mechanism, however, relies on standings that, in contrast, emerge from interactions among judgments by both producers and buyers. Thus, it is dual notions of differential quality, referent both to product and to producer, that become established as the core around which a set of market footings for producers can reproduce itself as footings in a joint market profile. The two sides, buyers and producers, exert contending pressures on the shape of this profile, pressures that correlate with their respective discriminations of quality.

In actual business life, quality meanings become jointly imputed to properties that have gotten bundled together as a "'product," even though these properties may seem to an observer various and somewhat arbitrary. This bundle is perceived with respect to the product market as a whole, the source to which everyone turns for that bundle. Particular producers seek and realize differentiation in appreciation—the quality index—for their particular versions of that market product. And indeed, there often will be a cluster of variants by size, color, and so forth of that firm's product shipments, so that there is bundling at the firm level also.

Choices interact to influence and calibrate the repeated commitments of flows in production and in payment. Think of these markets as molecules. Although the atoms are business organizations rather than individuals, they are making choices of commitment levels. The bonding is competitive rivalry, somewhat analogous to the bonding of atoms in molecules according to the proportions of time orbital electrons spend around one or another atomic nucleus.

This interaction of choices presupposes prior establishment of comparability. A linear order of precedence is perhaps the simplest way to achieve comparability; it is analogous to a linear array of atoms in space within a molecule. Hierarchic inequalities of rank and rewards are pervasive among humans, and indeed, dominance or pecking orders are common among vertebrates of all sorts (Wilson 1979).

Reputation in invidious array is the coin of discipline for production markets. It is hard to sustain the mutual discipline of a pecking order when there are more than a handful or a dozen participants because of limits on perception and cognition (Chase 1974, 2000). Such limits are especially constraining for firms building a market molecule through signaling.

The standard view in economics is starkly different. Any number of firms can fit into a market; indeed, the more the better. The small number of members, the extensive engrossment of the market by its top members, the rarity of ties in precedence order—none of these come as entailments of standard models. And yet all are widely observed and can be found pasted like Band-Aids, by empirical investigators, onto orthodox economic models.

One can note already that the quality or precedence orderings in a market have less load of social ordering to support than do pecking orders in self-contained groups. It is as if the insides of the small world of a pecking order of wolves were opened out and some of the influences, constraints, and signalings transpired outside the small world in network connections that spread out more in time, with less direct feedback, and thus are more visible to observation—and hence to analysis. Such markets are in some senses simpler than closed small worlds, but as parts of a spread-out system of generalized exchange, they also face Knightian uncertainty of a different order.

Because each market is tripartite—suppliers, producers, and buyers—it has two distinct possibilities for a market interface. These are an upstream orientation toward suppliers and a downstream orientation toward consumers. Producer firms establish themselves in niches within their jointly constructed interface only if and as their identities are reshaped within an emerging order by quality, as seen up- or downstream as well as by fellow producers in their market. Chapters 4 and 5 explore the etiology of quality, and chapters 6 and 7 generalize it by parameterizing the substitutability between markets that parallel one another in the production streams of an economy.

The necessary involvement of other markets and firms upstream and down adds complications; it also can justify signaling other than by volume (chap. 4, last section), and modeling larger linear arrays (chap. 5, third section). Network context is how production markets can be distinguished from vertebrate flocks, which fit into some general ecology but not into a long-range pattern of flows among other markets and firms in generalized exchange (fig. 1.1). And at the other extreme, market networks are also not analogous to hydraulic pumping networks, whether biological (within cell, plant, or animal) or technological. The phenomenology is different: Choices are made and changed by actors.

These human actors are oriented to their local contexts, and yet also more indirectly and abstractly they coordinate through common forms held across larger scope. Culture and discourse are not antithetical; indeed Greg Urban argues, "Culture is localized in concrete, publicly accessible signs, the most important of which are actually occurring instances of discourse" (1991, 1; see also chapter 15 below). Culture and discourse support dual flows of money as the generalized medium of exchange (chaps. 12 and 15).

The use of stream as a metaphor misleads if it suggests definite successions

of markets along fixed branches of the stream. That was the vision of Leontief (1966). There is some analogy between market orientation upstream or
down and polarization of a molecule by alignment of the spins of its electrons in an external magnetic field (chap. 9). But here, *upstream* and *downstream* are construed as purely relative terms that describe role relations with
respect to a focal industry. An explicit theory of decoupling can be inferred
from, and will also help to explain, the existence and nature of the two
options of orientation for the market mechanism (chap. 10).

Nine Known Phenomena to Be Explained Jointly

So much for introduction and rationale. Now let's turn to the goals of this
modeling. New theory uncovers and predicts phenomena, but it can well
begin with well-known phenomena that are not yet adequately explained as
a set by any coherent scheme. The reader can check, as the book unfolds,
that the model indeed embraces them all and goes on to others set at a larger
scale.

1. *Small number*. Recognizable lines of business are constituted in and by
some modest number of firms, typically fewer than twenty. The enduring
legacy of transaction cost economics (Williamson 1975) is to have drawn
attention to this.

2. *Identity*. This recognition comes as and through a long-continuing production market in the outputs of these firms, a market with an identity
marked by a special register of discourse concerning its affairs: witness news-
paper business pages or investor tip-sheets.

3. *Inequality*. A pecking order among the firms is marked by their unequal
shares in gross output and profit of the market.

4. *Profit*. Businesses operate for and thus routinely incur profit, sometimes
displaced by losses. They do not, as orthodox economic theory would have
it, routinely operate with net returns of zero.

5. *Increasing returns*. When conditions in their continuing markets induce
firms to increase production volumes, it is commonplace for them to expect
unit costs to decrease.

6. *Perverse returns*. In many lines of business, accolades for higher quality
in a firm's product accompany a cost structure lower than that of any peer
judged of lesser quality.

7. *The rareness of monopoly*. Even in economies where monopolies are not
subject to legal penalties, they are so rare as to be unnatural, despite frequent
invocations of the peril of monopoly (especially by economists).

8. *Product industry life cycle*. Long-term observers (Lawrence and Dyer
1983) as well as the transactors in a given market typically expect to find,
and formulate rules of thumb about, some secular trend in performance:

sometimes improvement, as with a learning curve improvement effect on costs, and other times degradation analogized to senescence.

And finally, a regularity at a more abstract level:

9. *Decoupling.* Rather than supply and demand, local variabilities and path determine market aggregates, which are historical, not accounting outcomes.

What is important about these nine phenomena is that all are explainable in terms of each other, brokered by a model that is operationalized around specific parameters.

MECHANISM AROUND PRODUCTION COMMITMENTS

To "model" is to give explicit mathematical form to the phenomenology summarized in a mechanism. To a sociologist, "'mechanism' . . . gives knowledge about a component process . . . thereby increasing the suppleness, precision, complexity, elegance, or believability of the theory at the higher level . . . without doing too much violence to what we know are the main facts at the lower level. . . . The mechanisms must produce interesting hypotheses or explanations at the higher level *without* complex investigations at the lower level" (Stinchcombe 1988, 1).[3]

The production market mechanism must guide and yet also emerge from the choices of market actors who pay attention to an array of signals. It derives from the social construction of a quality order that producers as well as buyers recognize and regularly reinforce by their commitments. The fundamental idea is co-constitution of footings for firms through the interaction of their competitive strivings for acceptance in that line of business.

Our goal in this book is specification of a mechanism for the production market with a general yet detailed model using parameters that are explicit but widely applicable. Such a theory can with a single mechanism accommodate a variety of markets in their interactions. The formulas derived are to be interpreted richly, but they also must be kept sufficiently simple to permit the tracing of causal patterns.

The mechanism is necessarily a social construction, since there are no gods, no Walrasian imps, no Maxwell demons available to orchestrate patterns of choices in markets (putting aside, for now, the state and other political intrusions). Orchestration must emerge out of interactions. Yet the custodial discipline for markets, economics, has in general slid away from this issue of mechanism.

The present economy has grown up around production by firms that make commitments, period after period, within networks of continuing flows of goods and services. Markets evolved as mechanisms that spread the risks and uncertainties in placing these successive commitments with buyers. Firms shelter themselves within the rivalry of a production market.

Consider a mechanism for such a market. Guided and confirmed by the signals it reads from the operations of its peers, each producer firm can maneuver for position along a rivalry profile sustained out of the commitments of all the rival firms. These are repeated commitments rather than one-shot participation as by individuals at lawn sales. The increase in scale from persons to firms goes with a decline in the number of actors from individual to industry sort of market.

Some dozen or so firms are the players in a production market, the choosers who, period after period, commit to levels of output. Buyers come from a much larger pool across an economy, but most will be corporate firms, whether in manufacturing or other processing, including service. Competition by producers for interaction with buyers can sustain and reproduce a joint interactive profile in revenue for volume.

Call the total revenue received the *worth* of that volume of shipment: designate the volume as y and worth as $W(y)$.

Figure 1.2 is a graph of such pairs. Producers must interpolate through the particular set of observations to estimate a market profile. This is possible for figure 1.2, as is shown by drawing a line through the set of points. This is a smooth curve, easily estimated by the business analysts as a guide to a viable profile across them. Such a profile can discipline the commitments each producer makes to production volume in search of optimal results in revenue over cost.

Quality ordering becomes reflected in this profile of producers' revenues versus volumes, and it does so without requiring any explicit indexing of quality by market participants. Everyday attributions of market footings tend to become assimilated into a quality ordering that is transitive in the domain and network of that market's discourse. Existing network ties become folded into and supplanted by relations within a quality ordering, which comes to be perceived in terms of prestige that combines quality for consumption with competitive relations of rivalry.

The signaling mechanism can come to generate continuing commitments to production by all producers that can get reproduced as a set. Establishment of comparability among producers in each other's eyes is what induced and required establishment of a new relation among a market's producers as peers. Formally, comparability is most complete within a full linear order such as can be represented by a quality index. Substantively, comparability in such a pecking order becomes taken for granted and so all the more effective in framing perceptions.

Firms' exertions as reflected in their cost structures tend to be reflected in differential valuations by buyers in aggregate; otherwise they would not be a set of producers that survived as a profile mechanism emerging within patterns in structural equivalence among production flow networks. This correlation provides the basis for an array by perceived quality, a coherent linear

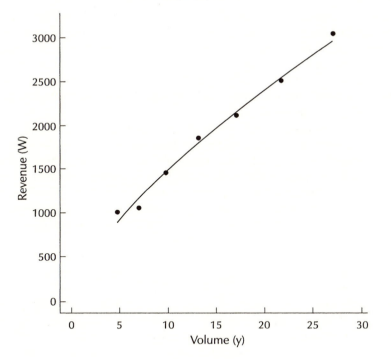

FIG. 1.2. A revenue-against-volume profile

array sufficient to support market profile. The quality index is just a specification by the observer of such an array.

Let's develop the notion of what y means to the buyer by turning from a focus on firms as buyers to individual persons, a scope that can also be accommodated by this market mechanism. Sometimes, a large y connotes higher quality, as in the soda pop industry, but at other times, lower quality, as in the wine industry. So the frequency with which buyers encounter a producer's output (the verb *encounter* is especially apropos for nondurable goods) can signal different things across different shapes of profile. As some goods monopolize shelf space, wealthier suburban mothers, like wealthy East Siders in Manhattan, shy away from them, since they are what the average person is buying. For other goods that receive high exposure in advertising, that's precisely what these shoppers buy. After all, the fact that everyone else is buying it confirms that it's the best.

Quality array comes out of particularities of historical process such that a producer's position on the quality index meshes its reputation as a firm with assessments of its product. Each of these two sides is affected by, and in, particular relations obtaining between the producer and other firms upstream and down. But the key to market formation is that these meshings be ordered with respect to those of other like producers who are structurally equivalent as peers in the market established. The market profile succeeds in reproducing itself only if these various bundlings are such that products together with their producers are seen both inside and outside that market as falling into an array by quality, which often carries invidious overtones. Thereby, roles for firms in market networks are meshed with relative assessments of particular product flows.

Flows of information are central to the mechanism that steers and reproduces a production market. Terms of trade always have evolved through some form of exchange of information among the various parties to any market. Information desired by and useful to one party to the market need not, however, correspond with information as formulated by others. When it is possible for actors to make use of information read from the doings of others, let's call this information a *signal*. Fulfilled prior commitments are themselves the signals read off as profile by the producers.

SOME SEE MARKETS, SOME SEE FIRMS

From this same general mechanism derive many varieties of market. Constraints and opportunities for choices by the three roles—supplier, producer, and purchaser—differ among these market varieties, but all are calibrated by the sizes of flows being committed. Competing firms cluster to form a market through signals that then sustain dispersions in quality and cost, with respect to volume, as perceived either downstream or upstream.

Instead of one emanating from the other, quality and identity produce each other across the set of firms in interaction. Distinctive to the present model is its conception of the etiology of quality as a subtle social construction rather than an evident attribute. Just how this develops establishes the distinct identity of a market within its variety. Our model predicts a continuum of achievable identities for each variety in terms of parameters for context, with each variety of market embracing different ranges on these parameters.

Parameters capture and measure market context as sensitivities both to the volume of flows and to variabilities in quality for these flows. Parameter ratios then define a state space array, a plane that discriminates among varieties of markets and specific identities within varieties. Outcomes predicted by the model, in revenue and market share and the like, will be shown to correlate with and influence the outcomes of other markets that lie downstream, upstream, and parallel.

Recognize that distinct levels of identities are intrinsic to the mechanism. Markets are being constituted as a separate species of actor—molecular with respect to firms as actor atoms—through the reproduction of disciplines of competition for quality niches, yet also as shaped by larger context. The array, the plane for contexts of a given market, is more analogous to the periodic table, which discriminates among the elements according to their atoms' electronic structures, than it is to an arbitrary index such as for books in a library. It is a map or topology across which to predict variation in performance.

This market plane already caught the attention of a group of French social scientists who had independently developed an economics of convention coordinated with substantial observation of several industries in European contexts. This group had identified four regimes of quality that seem to correspond to the most distinctive regions of contexts in the market plane predicted by the signaling mechanism. Their approach distinguishes business cultures.

Production markets evolved together with larger and more complex groupings of the initial entrepreneurial agents along networks of commerce. The historical background, noted earlier, is that networks of commercial connections sustained new, private sorts of bureaucracies called firms that induced and intermeshed with the new sorts of markets. These firms were by no means free-standing, by no means masters individually of their fates. Patterns of investment were crucial, and more than one format for systems of firms has appeared. Such evolution into firms came to include all sorts of coalitions and side arrangements. The most prominent avatar is the multidivisional firm (MDF) (Fligstein 1990), which builds exactly around the production market mechanism.

The boundaries are confusing. Business journalists usually report on individuals as acting from and within particular firms, but they report on prices acting within markets. The two framings direct attention differently. Each obscures some phenomena and brings others into focus. Those active in business switch in their discourse, unaware, between these idioms. A main goal of economic sociology is to integrate the two framings and thereby achieve a more complete realism.

This is difficult. Indeed, theories of economists, who take markets as fundamental, still lack effective characterizations of the process and structure through which particular firms actually constitute a market. So they largely pass over particular *firms* by settling for a stylized story of pure competition. But, analogously, analysts of firms, examining history or strategy as well as structures, usually pass over particular *markets* and focus on various relations among and orientations by firms. The really big firms are seen as together constituting a social field (Fligstein 1990; Mintz and Schwartz 1985; Mizruchi and Schwartz 1987; Useem 1982), and smaller firms are most often pictured in networks, in trade associations, or in attribute categories (Scherer 1970; Scherer and Ross 1990; Uzzi and Gillespie 1999).

Neither the economists' approach nor the firm analysts' has been able to provide a plausible mechanism for the market, because neither explains how markets and firms interdigitate as they evolve together. That is the task of this book. The market mechanism proposed is robust across different kinds of organization within the individual producer firm, including the large divisionalized firms (MDFs hereafter) predominant in the present economy as a hybrid between market and firm. My prediction is that even the newest forms of production organization that have been heralded for some years now (e.g., Powell 1990; Powell and DiMaggio 1991) can be modeled in ways consistent with this same market mechanism.

Roadmap, with Conundrums and Devices

Known phenomena will be accounted for, and new phenomena will be uncovered. The core of the basic model of a market is laid out in regular prose in the last section of chapter 3, following upon careful buildup and technical analysis in chapters 2 and 3 (the most technical sections in these and later chapters are marked by asterisks). Markets in networks are theorized in chapter 10, which wrestles with conundrums of theory for these models that combine determinism with room for agency. The distinct new level of actor produced by embeddings is accompanied by decoupling. Thus chapter 10 is a culmination of the first three parts and points to the exploration of wider realms in part 4.

Each successive part adds, layer by layer, to the preceding minimal version of the model. Additional parameters are introduced only as the scope is enlarged. Each successive cumulation of chapters, such as 2–3, or 2–5 and then 2–8, can stand on its own as a coherent account without reference to subsequent generalization. But of course each new parameter has been foreshadowed at its neutral value in earlier chapters, just as the interpretive themes and constructs new to a part have been assumed implicitly in earlier chapters.

Part 1 fleshes out the sketch of the market mechanism. Chapters 2 and 3 lay out and solve equations for market profiles. Predictions require descriptions for each member firm in its business setting both upstream and down, but chapter 2 reduces the complexity through a simplified specification of market context—that is, of the two valuation schedules—relying on an ordering of producers indexed by quality. This permits a plane map in chapter 3 to differentiate ranges of market operation. This plane applies, no matter the particular locations on a quality index or the number of firms in the market.

Chapter 4 goes on to probe phenomenology and agency. The nature of signaling is broadened in several reconstruals in chapter 5. This chapter draws comparisons with the seminal work of Spence on market signaling, which suggest an addition to the plane of market varieties. Chapter 5 ends with an analysis of monopsony and subcontracting evoked in response to Spence's account.

Part 2 places a focal market in competition with parallel markets. Chapter 6 situates this market of differentiated producers within interactive substitution that involves markets in parallel positions within the system of generalized exchange.

The chapter 3 plane map is seen in chapter 7 to be but one of a sheaf of parallel maps that are laid out as a three-dimensional market space. These chapters establish the molecular nature of the market as an actor distinct in level from its differentiated set of constituent firms. Chapter 7 goes on to trace the close correspondence between present findings and those of the French economics of convention.

Formulas to guide fittings of index values and parameters from observed outcomes in particular markets are then developed in chapter 8 for all parameters; Chapter 8 also ventures to derive predictions for values of two key parameters in terms of network contexts.

Then part 3 theorizes and expands on just how $W(y)$ markets site themselves in networks and across sectors. Chapter 9 articulates and specifies an alternative polarization for the market molecule, facing upstream. It thus uncovers and explains the hitherto little-noted bipolarity in the siting of a production market molecule. Predictions are made concerning circumstances inducing one market polarization over the other. Chapter 10 examines closely the embeddings and decouplings involved, both along stream and at edges.

Chapter 11 turns again to putting-out practices discussed at the end of chapter 5, by which markets may, when they erode, reconstitute themselves in contractual forms. Some kinship is shown with the pure competition theorized by orthodox economists and modeled by econometricians. This pure competition is related to asymptotic limiting forms of the $W(y)$ mechanism, and thereby kinship is shown also with induction of internal hierarchy out of a market context.

Part 4 explores change over time in wider institutional realms and multiple levels of actors. Strategic action again becomes the focus in chapter 12, as it was in chapter 4, along with related maneuvers. But now these are seen as exogenously rooted in financial markets, rather than as endogenously rooted in the roles and mores of the production market. Firms can come to sprawl across distinct markets, but still be disciplined by their profiles. The correlative struggles for increase of investment engender a new level of competition, which may still be modeled by analogues to the $W(y)$ mechanism.

Chapter 13 offers sketches for modeling dynamics directly rather than from successive cross sections of comparative statics. In this chapter, interventions and mobilizations—which shade into one another—together are the dynamics to be assessed from tracks and predicted from trajectories in market space. We could have justified allocating still more pages for chapters 12 and 13 because they are key to the pragmatics of using the models, but instead I refer the reader to applications to be published separately by Matthew Bothner.

Chapter 13 ends with a possible scenario for evolution of the American economy, compared with a scenario consistent with the new evolutionary economics theory. Then in chapter 14 the latter is discussed and compared with $W(y)$ along with a sheaf of other pragmatic approaches to business study.

"The" market, being always observed in some sort of network system, is marked, as anthropologists say, by its subcultures and linguistic registers. Practice and subculture together frame the commitments chosen in markets that in turn frame the identities of participants in a line of business. Chapter 15 explores this constitution of business culture in a feedback loop with business practice. Economics itself results from variants of this process.

Chapter 16, the conclusion, explains some melding of economics and sociology in the analysis, summarizes some findings, and points to challenges that remain.

These chapters all together frame markets in a multilevel role system. Shifts in idiom accompany this interpretive account. Whereas the initial chapters construe the market mechanism as interrelated mores, the idiom becomes network ecology in later chapters. Because markets embed into, but also decouple from, networks of economic relations, every chapter works with identities at two distinct levels: firm and market.

This interpretive voice is twinned with mathematics as a voice in most of these chapters. Mathematical modeling is essential to clarity and definiteness, but getting the basic phenomenology straight is the core. We draw on this tradition for mathematical modeling in sociology and allied social sciences, notably on Coleman 1964, Rapoport 1983, and Simon 1957; see, for early overviews, Fararo 1973 and Leik and Meeker 1975.

The succession of mathematical derivations is marked by intricacy, and many distinct aspects of modeling must be fitted together within a consistent computational framing. Yet the modeling also must be coordinated with the interpretive scheme. This calls both for simplicity of components in the mathematical model and for as much explicitness in constructs as possible in the interpretive track.

The modeling voice switches back and forth between mathematical form and numerical computations according to which best captures relevant interpretive themes. And the numerical examples can make the mathematics more transparent. We have taken pains to make the present account accessible even to readers with limited mathematical background. Asterisks at the beginnings of sections denote concentration on exact formal statement in equations. Most of the essential points from the modeling are, however, sketched nearby in other sections of text.

The resulting models can index predictions of market equilibria to a range of historical paths, which do not derive just from geography or technology. The crux of the mathematical modeling, for us, is effective characterization by parameters of contexts for the market. This is a distinctive feature of this model as compared to alternatives. Parameters are on a level with theoretical constructs (White 2000b). Both are designed for stability and interpretability, to permit tracing complex webs of causation. Simulation of what can happen becomes as important as poking at particular data sets on what did happen.

Firms in particular markets often are targets for, or sources of, maneuvers in larger realms of business and of state intervention, but these larger realms, explored for example by Fligstein (1990; 2001) and in Campbell et al. 1991, are only touched on in the present book. The $W(y)$ parameters that site the market mechanism in context reflect degrees of responsiveness in relations among firms themselves. Help in estimation of these parameters can come from sociolinguistic studies of reflexive indexicality, as discussed in chapter 15, so discourse registers and styles that characterize interaction around particular markets should be a focus of research.

There is some scholarly duty to give an account of relations to other writings, in this case from several disciplines but most especially from sociology and economics. Such accounts are woven into the most relevant sections of the chapters to follow. By comparison with most approaches in economics, the present model is most distinctive in its derivation from Knightian uncertainty together with its focus on asymmetry. Conventional microeconomic theory remains mute on market polarization and has slid away from its earlier emphasis on discrimination of quality. And yet microeconomics does contribute crucial tools and perspective toward analyzing the social construction of the market mechanism around quality order and asymmetry in flow. Altogether six related strands in economics are sketched in chapters 2, 5, 11, and 14.

The references from anthropology are primarily in regard to linguistics, but the emphasis on social construction is rooted in that literature as well as in sociology. Although the overall focus is on the market mechanism, organization analysts will find relevant sections in almost every chapter. Issues of perception and its framings are central in the model, but the only primarily cognitivist chapter is the second, which comes most directly from economics.

To model a mechanism for markets requires, we argue, drawing on economics only as fused with both anthropological and sociological ideas and perspectives (e.g., Strathern 1971; Burt 1992; Granovetter 1985). Optimization and rational choice are indeed important, but they are disciplined within and subsidiary to a joint social construction, a market. The central idea is the emergence of the market as an identity, which is also a source of action: embedding together with decoupling, as is elaborated in chapter 10. Tracking the undoubted turbulence and disarray of socioeconomic action seems by comparison a mere diversion for theory, though the new evolutionary economics argues differently (see chapter 14).

The reader can expect to wrestle with five conundrums:

1. *Action vis-à-vis role.* This conundrum of agency begins in chapter 2, with the play-off between path measure k and profile. It is developed around unraveling in chapter 4, reemerges in subsequent chapters, and is then again central to chapters 12, 13, and 14.
2. *Historicity.* This is the first conundrum seen in different light. Indeterminacies such as here of market profiles and networks lead the new evolutionary economics (see sections of chapters 5 and 14) to introduce explicitly stochastic features into their modeling.
3. *Network vis-à-vis molecule.* This conundrum is at the center of parts 3 and 4. It melds with the existence of distinct levels of actors with their niches and embeddings. But neither the network nor the molecule metaphor emerges unchanged in the $W(y)$ modeling, nor are any simple notions of boundary supportable.
4. *Self-similarity.* The same architectonics reappear again and again at different scopes, both in scale or extension (chap. 6) and in the two polarities (chap. 9). This ties to the previous conundrum.
5. *Mixed languages.* Optimization figures centrally, for example, but it is subordinated to imperatives of economic survival under Knightian uncertainty, which induce framings of market situations as joint social constructions that are costly—if also enticing—to evade: costly because enforced by taken-for-granted mores built into the accustomed discourse of a market sector (chap. 15).

The sixteen chapters meld several distinct arguments and address diverse constituencies, none of which will be entirely comfortable with the resulting synthesis of approaches. Historical view comes to the fore in dissecting quality (chap. 4). The language of state space is ubiquitous (chaps. 3, 7) and accommodates alternatives to $W(y)$ (chaps. 5, 11). But social network analysis pervades this book—readers unacquainted with it are referred to Degenne and Forsé (1999) as a comprehensive introduction for scientists.

Two devices in this book have proved central to obtaining explicit models. One is quality array (pecking order), dissected in chapters 2 and 4. The other device is the representative firm, which is central to the formulation in chapters 2 and 3. Only with chapters 6–8 (part 2) does there appear an explicit set of firms, such as are reported numerically in the appendix tables A.1–A.5 and descriptively in text accounts of particular industries such as light aircraft manufacturing (chap. 4).

The two devices presuppose and dovetail with each other. The quality array is a precursor to the search for optimality. The representative firm is an anticipation of the self-consistent field approach, which is spelled out in chapter 8 for estimation of parameters in market networks, and, a level below, for analysis of the set of firms in a market in terms of the quality index values of the member firms. This is a marvelous illustration of the self-similarity conundrum.

Part ONE

Firms Embed into a Market

These four chapters flesh out the market mechanism as an interactive construction among some set of producers who process procurements to deliver goods or services. Predictions prove to be tied to both the evolutionary path of the mechanism and the context for enacting it. This basic model is summed up at the end of chapter 3.

Chapters 2 and 3 lay out and solve equations for market profiles. Predictions require descriptions of each member firm in its business setting both upstream and down, but chapter 2 reduces the complexity through a simplified specification of market context—that is, of the two valuation schedules—relying on an ordering of producers indexed by quality. This permits a plane map in chapter 3 to differentiate ranges of market operation. This plane applies, no matter the number of firms in the market or their particular locations on the quality index.

Agency is dealt with first in chapter 4, around quality, and again in chapter 5. Each chapter extends the range of contexts and actors considered for markets. In chapter 5, the original modeling of signaling by Spence and others is shown both to construe market and quality quite differently and to induce an additional market half-plane, labeled PARADOX, that can be adjoined to the original market plane of chapter 3. The market plane is the central construct.

CHAPTER 2

Profiles for a Market

Production market forms around and thus consists in a joint interface between producers confronting uncertainty from the other side of the interface. This interface is energized by rivalry among its peer producers, all seeking buyers for their continuing streams of production in amounts optimal for their individual cost structures. The producers have come to signal each other through a profile across their production commitments: that is the market mechanism.

The profile shapes itself in response to competing pressures on a diverse set of producers who gauge one another's performance. By this means, the profile controls the interface. Pressures are local, in time as well as network location, and the comparisons are relative, so that not one but many histories can stabilize a market, leading to any one of a predictable array of profiles, a family of similar shapes.

This chapter lays out a market profile that spreads across the production commitments of that set of competitors. The profile dovetails expectations enforced by buyers in aggregate with commitments, with each producer committing to that level of production optimal for it, given anticipated costs of producing from out of procurement flows from upstream. This mechanism depends on emergence of two lineups, each observable and each generally accepted.

An ordering of producers by cost is paralleled by their ordering by buyers in terms of satisfaction with transactions. This chapter offers simple but flexible specifications of underlying valuation schedules, one of cost with volume and one of satisfaction with volume. These are calibrated in terms of a *single* quality index underlying both orderings. After derivation of a menu of profiles, the viability of each profile is tested. Finally, contrasts are drawn with microeconomics.

PRODUCTION COMMITMENTS AND SIGNALING

Producers of most lines of goods or services commit to a volume of output as they arrange inputs needed for the next period. These commitments, which especially focus on volume, must be made period after period. Each choice of production volume is responsive to the costs expected, and these commitments of producers to a line of business become reflected in their investments in specialized infrastructure and equipment, which are not easily changed (Scherer 1970). The payment subsequently received by a producer will depend not only on this volume but also on how buyers downstream in aggregate assess its product's quality and thus the market valuation of the worth of this producer's flow relative to those from other producers.

The market profile invokes rivalry because rivalry requires and generates comparability among rivals. The producers find and signal distinct footings along a market profile only when they have come to be seen, by both sides, as offering varieties of that product line that are reliably differentiated within an array of standings across them. Observed outcomes then can be strung together as a *market profile* such as that portrayed in figure 1.2. My claim is that such a curve not only reports outcomes in a period but also offers a framing of information that the producers use in deciding their commitments for the subsequent period.

Thus, market profile is a mechanism as well as a report. A producer cannot expect a public announcement of a market schedule it faces, much less descriptions of all other producers' situations on cost and demand sides. So producers turn to evidence of actual payments by volume, which define for them positions in the market. My claim, to repeat, is that this rivalry profile guides each producer to its optimizing choice and continues to guide its subsequent choices and those of its peers, subject to the earlier choices having been accepted by the downstream side of that market. So the profile controls the commitments in the market.

The main feature of this mechanism is simplicity, which is the goal of business even more than that of analyst. But is the mechanism feasible? When does it fail? When a firm estimates the spread across all its peers—on revenue received versus volume shipped last period—as a scattering such as in figure 2.1, there is no profile to guide a market.

By contrast, for some other set of seven producers, figure 2.2 graphs a profile like that in figure 1.2 earlier, through their revenue, volume pairs.

To confirm feasibility, two general pressures must be satisfied, each of which is to be assessed in the particular factual context of that market. One pressure is from producers, as each seeks a distinctive niche along an observed profile that confirms optimum profit relative to its own cost from its choice of volume. Designate by $C(y, i)$ the schedule of *cost* versus volume of producer labeled i. For each possible volume, a unique cost is envisioned; so, in mathematical jargon, $C(y)$ is a single-valued function, just like a market profile. Figure 2.3 repeats figure 2.2 and then adds cost curves for seven producers to this schematic diagram. These seven distinct cost schedules could respectively induce the volume commitments of the seven firms shown in figure 2.2. Each producer is likely to have plants and other infrastructure of different scope, age, and location, so that this first pressure implies differentiated niches.

But there is a counterpressure from the other side of the market. Substi-

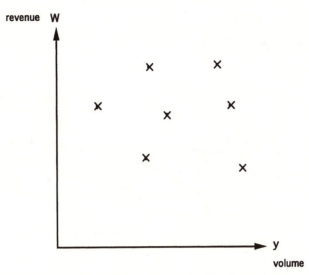

FIG. 2.1. Terms of trade not sustainable as a market profile

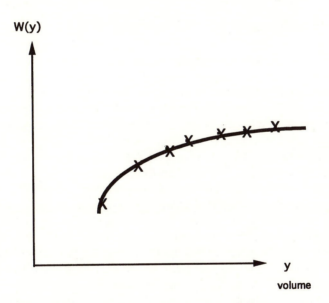

FIG. 2.2. Terms of trade that fit a market profile

tutability of transactions with one producer for those with another, as judged by the buyers in aggregate, generates the second pressure. This is pressure exerted on the market profile as a whole curve or, more precisely, as a set of points. It is pressure from buyers for satisfaction. Define degree of *satisfaction*

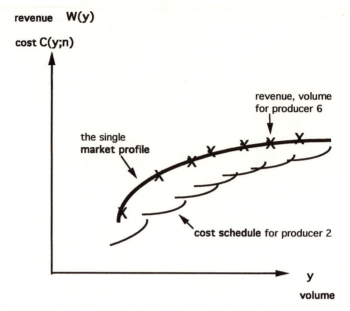

FIG. 2.3. Cost schedules supporting profile of fig. 2.2

by a monetary schedule for each producer's output. Parallel to the cost, designate satisfaction by $S(y, i)$ for volume y of flow to buyers from producer i. S is a statement cast in quantitative terms so that if $S(y, i) = S(y', j)$, one is assured that bundle y from source i is substitutable for bundle y' from source j.

Such a schedule also could be drawn in for each of the seven product sources in figure 2.2. But, unlike W, S is not perceived by the peer producers. The schedules S are constructs of the observer with which to characterize real pressures felt, but not directly discriminated, by the producers, whereas each producer perceives some cost schedule C for itself.

Each producer in each period commits to a volume of production that is keyed to procurement of supplies and labor as well as to marketing and distribution. As noted in the previous chapter, this product flow to which the producer commits is taken in the model to be a single number, designated by y.[1] Of course, several distinct subflows typically issue each period from a given producer. These might be distinguished, for example, according to separate sizes of the product or separate densities, colors, and the like. What the $W(y)$ model asserts is that variation in the relative sizes of such subflows can be neglected when reporting and assessing the commitment level y in volume of a producer competing to maintain a footing in that market. The model also does not attempt to distinguish among different buyers for the given producer, but instead aggregates across them.

A signal is an observable, and a market builds only around observables.

Volumes shipped and revenues received are prime candidates for signals.[2] These are the stuff of managerial conversations, business gossip, and business socializing, through which firms' positions in the market are constituted and recognized. This talk is fueled by newsletters and surveys generated both within and without the industry. Each firm can freely choose a volume to which to commit. Each is motivated to choose the volume that will maximize the net benefit to itself.

This market mechanism can be seen as a self-validating signaling system. The signaling takes place primarily among the producers as they, rather than some auctioneer, enact a profile in rivalry. Each producer concentrates on those who are generally accepted as its peers, seeking to learn how they are doing. Their locations on the $W(y)$ profile are the signals. For more than a dozen participants or perhaps a score, this mutual observation would be difficult.[3]

A particular market profile translates present indefiniteness from across the market into a definite menu based on the most recent commitments from a well-known set of peers, commitments that have been fulfilled and have been accepted by the buying side. The market profile of worth by volume supplies sufficient basis for predictability of further commitments and acceptances, as each participant sifts its options. The original indeterminacy, the Knightian uncertainty, has triggered the evolution of a profile in rivalry that is reproduced jointly between sides and severally among the producers.

Each producer is capable of estimating this profile from just its own network of observations and of accepting it as a discipline. Such a simple social mechanism in market profile can act as a substitute for endless efforts to estimate how actors on the buying side will react. There need be no dependence on, and thus no feedback loops with, actions of specific others downstream, as there surely were in the outwork mode of production organization that preceded the industrial mode.

All transactions in the problematic downstream direction are treated as homologous, with a producer's attention being focused on comparison with its peers' outcomes rather than looking through the profile at particular continuing ties with counterpart firms and industries as buyers. But then there is a seeming paradox (to be explored fully only in chapter 10). From the perspective of the buyers on the other side of that profile, these same transactions are seen as lying in continuing ties at habitual terms, as part of *their* cost structures. On *their* unproblematic or "back" side, producers do not perceive and act in terms of profiles being constituted for markets back there. They instead repeat transactions at established terms with counterpart actors in particular firms in other industries. Yet their own problematic side, across which they perceive their own market profile, necessarily is, in its myriad detail, produced from what other markets perceive as their own back sides.

The seeming direct conflict can in part be resolved into aggregate versus disaggregate points of view. The aggregate buyer is indeed a price-taker. *Price-taker* means that you accept the given price for whatever volume you take, but, of course, only if you take it. From the other side of the profile, a processor as supplier need not track subtotals of flows to just a particular downstream firm or even industry unless it engrosses a predominant share.[4]

QUALITY ARRAY FOR VALUATION SCHEDULES

Just how does this signaling mechanism reconcile—that is, act as broker between—the producer and buyer sides of a market interface? Market phenomenology must come to center around differentiation in product and relative standing among producers, as Chamberlin (1962) argued seventy years ago. Underlying the array of producers by their profile choices, their volume/price pairs, is the emergence of an ordering in status that cues their various identities. This ranking, and its believability among the producers themselves, does not refer to firms considered as isolates but rather to firms as filling niches of quality within that industry, perceived as a market setting. Such rankings carry invidious overtones for many of those involved directly or as observers.

The point is that this status ordering of producers must be compatible with their ordering in quality of product as perceived by buyers—that is, by the nesting of satisfaction schedules. Achieving believability with and satisfaction for the buyers, taken in aggregate, constrains, via perceived quality, the market profile along which a fulfillable set of selling terms can lie. Producers thus take positions in a viable market profile with respect to buyers just to the extent that the standings of products conform with standings of firms, quality with prestige. Yet no explicit indexing of quality by market participants themselves is required.

Explicit analysis does, however, require some indexing that is consistent with this market phenomenology. Figures 1.2 and 2.2 illustrated a market profile as a single-valued smooth function along which lay the worths $W(y)$ assigned by the market to the various volumes offered by its producers. Then $C(y, i)$ was designated as the schedule of variation in cost with y of the producer identified by integer i, just as $S(y, i)$ was the corresponding volume schedule of valuation by buyers, their aggregate satisfaction schedule. Figure 2.3 went on to add an illustrative array of cost schedules that could help sustain the profile in figure 2.2 and permit its reproduction. From figure 2.3 one sees that the cost schedules of the firms lie nested in a series that validates the market profile. The obvious step is to assign the integer labels in that order, so that they constitute an index rather than the merely arbitrary order that was designated by i in the previous section.

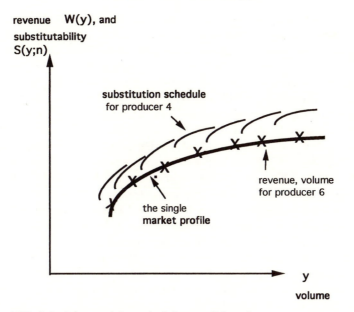

FIG. 2.4. Substitutability schedules paralleling fig. 2.3

Now turn to the satisfaction schedules. The producers are equilibrated through substitutability when the revenues paid to each are in the same ratio to the corresponding satisfactions gained by the buyers in aggregate. This implies that the S schedules nest in the same order as do the set of C schedules such as were shown in figure 2.3. Define this common ordering as one of "niceness" and thus replace the label i for index by the label n. *Hereafter, quality will be designated by this index n.* It applies to both C and S, and the label i is discarded (until chapter 8).

Figure 2.4 is a schematic rendering of satisfaction schedules for the same market profile, figure 2.2, as is accompanied by the cost schedules of figure 2.3.

The nesting of schedules in this figure is consistent with that in figure 2.3: Both suggest that higher-volume producers are of lower quality and hence have lower schedules both on cost and on satisfaction (what later will be called an ORDINARY market).

This common ordering by quality derives from and also induces a distinctive identity of the market as such, the market as a molecular formation on a different level from firms as its atoms. This emergence of an identity for a market is not necessarily a matter of size. Manufacturers of staples may be tiny with respect either to their suppliers of metal or to their customer office supply houses, but nonetheless the staple line of business is their concern. The manufacturer of staples is necessarily committing to a volume of production for the next period with or without the benefit of information or attention from outsiders, big or small. This is a commitment in the present, among other present commitments by its peers.

The most important conclusions are qualitative. First, such a feedback-loop mechanism for market can work across a wide variety of circumstances. Second, and equally important, if there is one, there will prove to be a whole pack of market profiles, of offer curves that each, if a path of events thrusts it up, could confirm and reproduce itself. Inspection of the figures will make it intuitively plausible that if one profile will balance out between cost and substitutability pressures, so will others. Each such profile would induce a somewhat different set of worth and volume pairings, $W(y)$, for that given set of producers. No two of these $W(y)$ curves will be exactly parallel, since it is really the differing curvatures that spread out the producers' volume choices in consistency with buyer pressure. This very flexibility is what makes trial-and-error searches plausible as the path by which a market pro-file gets established. The following mathematical derivation will confirm this second conclusion, that if one worth schedule $W(y)$ can, then a whole host of other profiles also could validate themselves with both sides of the market.

The mechanism presupposes that firms have shaken down into market memberships in such a fashion that rankings of producers by cost and by buyer assessment are consistent, yielding a common ranking n. No attempt will be made to trace particular episodes in such sortings out. Each consists in maneuvers by producers with responses by buyers, out of which a profile emerges as the self-confirming structure of commitments that together build niches for all producers in that market set. Into these positions on a rivalry profile have been folded results from any number of idiosyncratic expe-dients. These can include ad hoc charges for particular shipments in the flow of products constituting that line of business, with varying choices for mo-mentary volumes and the like. Such histories will differ from one industry to another and also may be triggered afresh from time to time in a given indus-try. A historical constant k will be used to designate which particular profile emerges from a particular history from among the host of profiles that could sustain themselves in subsequent sets of commitments.

One-Way Mirror

The core is producer commitments both in pragmatics of volume and in identities recognized by both sides. One metaphor for this market mecha-nism is a one-way mirror. The set of producers' commitments fills out and sustains the one-way mirror. This is a special window through which the producers cannot see the miscellaneous buyers, even though these buyers can see the producers. The one-way mirror is opaque to the producer and shows it the reflection of its comparable peers.

The mirror is flexible, as if made of plasticene, with a shape adapting to the distribution of competing pressures from the two sides. Relatively few producers—a handful or a score—are jointly searching for terms of trade with a variegated and possibly numerous other side. The given market need not figure importantly to this other side, need not in the eyes of buyers stand out among the whole production flow network of inputs and outputs among producers and customers—who typically both are firms.

The proper analogue to the other side is not fans in the bleachers already committed to baseball. Instead, a proper analogue is the urban population scanning street kiosks that display many genres of magazines. One genre is directed to bookworms, others to health buffs, the fashion conscious, off-road bikers, and so forth. In this analogy, market corresponds to genre and particular magazine corresponds to producer.

Market profiles, to repeat, get established through various particular histories of trial-and-error searches. Trial-and-error search is a complex process of interaction between successive provisional choices and false starts by various of the producers both in terms of responses they start seeing from the other side of the market over various periods and in terms of their perceptions of the choices being made in much the same fashion by their peers. Explicit modeling of this process would be difficult, but the results can become outcomes in equilibrium, which will be modeled explicitly.

SPECIFYING CONTEXT BY PARAMETERS

A huge array of descriptive material is called for to determine cost and satisfaction schedules with volume for every producer. It would, in fact, be difficult to gather reliable estimates for detailed schedules of perception by and interaction among such disparate actors as make up any particular production market. Simplification of schedules eases the task. Additional simplification helps also in deriving findings and interpreting conclusions from the model of mechanism.

Two simplifications are involved. The first is the recognition, discussed in the previous section, that nesting has to be in the same order for substitution schedules as for cost schedules. That yields the common order indexed by n in both schedules: $C(y, n)$ and $S(y, n)$. The second simplification is to approximate the shape of each class of schedules, C and S, as a power of y. The resulting shapes smooth over such irregularities and humps as would appear in the schedules for particular firms for a particular era in a market.

The fitting functions for cost and substitution schedules are thereby specialized sufficiently to permit tracing long chains of causation and spread within a large system. Model S as a power of y with exponent labeled a, call it *saturation*:

Formula S The valuation perceived by the buyers, their aggregate satisfaction, $S(y, n)$, is y raised to the power a times some calibration number for that producer with quality index n.

Model the cost schedule for each producer in exact parallel:

Formula C $C(y, n)$ is a calibration number times y raised to the power c.

The model being derived is intended as a base armature subject to redesign and transposition to new uses by others. The market as a small molecule is an idealization. So is reporting production volume and revenue as single numbers. So is use of a single power in y and a single index n. Subsequently further simplifications appear. Ingenuity in application can, however, in application sidestep some of the simplifications.

Now comes a useful generalization: move from integer to metric index for this overall joint ordering of niceness in quality and cost. Hereafter, n will designate the quality index in this metric form. Its variable spacings can reflect participants' views of quality more accurately than an index restricted to integer values.

Hereafter, n will be the only information about individual producers that is required by the model of market mechanism. So the market will be characterized in two parts: first by the parameters of schedules that are common to all its firms and second by the particular set of locations on quality for its member firms.

Since $S(y, n)$ correlates positively with quality, one could for convenience calibrate this metric n such that the S schedules observed for firms in the market are proportional to n. However, it will prove useful to develop a more symmetric, dual calibration of n. Let's bring all the assumptions and simplifications together into a complete specification of schedules.

The Producer Side

The cost schedule for variation of producer cost with volume and across an industry will be characterized by just two principal parameters, the exponents c and d:

$$C(y, n) = q \cdot y^c \cdot n^d. \tag{2.1}$$

Put in words, $C(y, n)$ equals calibration constant q, times y to power c, times n to power d. Quality level affects the scale of cost through this last factor. The parameter d by itself can distinguish between whole markets.

Producers' cost schedules differ in line with their quality niches. The multiplication by n^d shifts the cost curve differently according to the particular firm's position on the quality index n. This is the observer's view. The observer has split the idiosyncratic constant that for a given producer multiplies its output raised to power c, split into a presumed dependence on a quality index n, times a residual factor q, which is merely a numerical scaling factor common across all the firms. Put another way, as long as d is not equal to zero, the n values are coefficients that introduce (empirically realistic) differences in marginal costs, across firms in the industry (Leifer 1985).

A host of distinctions are folded into perceptions of effects and causes of quality on cost. Depending on the particular market, these can include variations in prestige of upstream suppliers, in plant technologies, in wage rates, in advertising, in innovation, in age as a firm or in that particular line of business, and so on.

There likely will be a great many suppliers, from an array of different industries, being fitted into the internal stream of processing by the given producer. The producer, while taking prices from these upstream suppliers as given, is choosing the particular varieties and quality to suit its own equipment and operational routines. The producer in buying may wish to scan further back up the procurement chain beyond its immediate supplier.

Industrial producers often experience increasing returns to scale, which is to say, unit costs decreasing with total volume produced. Standard microeconomics discounts the feasibility of such markets, which is related to its having no agreed model for differentiated products such as the $W(y)$ model. In formula C, the format for producers' cost schedules $C(y, n)$ is flexible enough to represent, according to choice of exponent c,[5] increasing returns to scale for the producer, $c < 1$; or decreasing returns to scale, $c > 1$; with both being seen in contrast to constant returns, $c = 1$.

As far as the producer is concerned, its cost curve is a power function in y times an arbitrary constant measured from its own records. But note that in equation (2.1), dependence on quality takes the same simple form as dependence on volume. In this familiar approximation, called Cobb-Douglas in economics (Cobb and Douglas 1928), the two dependencies interact only as multipliers. Powerful assumptions are being folded into each such schedule; for generalizations see Charnes, Cooper, and Schinnar (1976) and Nerlove (1965), which latter is prominent in chapter 11, below.

Indexing Quality

The quality variable is to reflect spacings between firms due to differences in quality. Because these may appear very unequal, index values tend to come out as decimal numbers rather than integers. Now market profile together with particular firms' outcomes are affected by quality n, not only through cost schedule C, but also through the buyer's valuations of schedule S. But a numerical indexing for the spacing between successive cost curves need not agree with that for spacings perceived by buyers for these producers and products. So two distinct indexings in decimal numbers for quality could have been offered, one for cost schedules and one for valuation schedules.[6] Instead, the same index n is used, but it is cast in different functional forms in the two schedules. The two forms signal the differential sensitivities of cost to n from that of satisfaction to n. The sensitivities will be represented as distinct powers to which n is raised. One is d.

Buyer Side

The buyers perceive the various producers' products as being from the same industry, and therefore comparable. Buyers' assessments thus can be translated into valuation functions of quality and volume for the different firms, each aggregating reactions by the same buyers to the output from just that one among the comparable firms. The valuation of a flow volume of size y, from a producer indexed by n, on the part of buyers in aggregate is still designated by $S(y, n)$, their aggregate satisfaction level. Define a parameter b for the saturation with quality index of buyers' valuation that is exactly parallel to the saturation d of producer's cost with quality index n in the formula for C.

$$S(y, n) = r \cdot y^a \cdot n^b. \tag{2.2}$$

Here, r is a numerical scaling factor common across all the firms and products, the analogue of q. The formula (2.2) is exactly parallel to formula (2.1) in its dependence upon y and in the resulting multiplicative interaction. Note that the illustrative figure 2.4 for S parallels figure 2.3 for cost. Of course, the satisfaction schedules lie above rather than below the profile $W(y)$ of payments to producers.

The S in the notation $S(y, n)$ can be thought of as standing for substitutability or even sales as well as for satisfaction. It also can be thought of as standing for shadow, shadow of the cost functions seen by firms in some markets downstream—developed further in the next-to-last section of chapter 8. Those downstream markets are of course valuing the flows they are buying in the focal market only so as to reap their own profits over and above what they are willing to lay out themselves as cost. A key feature of the market schedule $W(y)$, to which we return in a later section, is that it decouples at the same time as it enacts such open-ended chains of contingencies in purchases.

The buyers in aggregate enforce a $W(y)$ schedule. Buyers react to, rather than make, production commitments and so are able only to insist on as good a deal from one producer as from another: that is, as good a trade-off between volume and quality desired. This is why S can be interpreted as a stand-in for substitutability among products of that market.

Express this criterion in a ratio designated by theta, θ. And let $y[n]$ designate the volume commitment from the producer of quality n. The index value n has replaced the designation by integers in the first section. The buyer side insists upon equal markup theta on each producer, corresponding to the equation

$$S(y[n], n) = \theta W(y[n]),\qquad (2.3)$$

holding for each n. So theta can be described as the deal criterion.

OVERVIEW

Figure 2.5 sums up the interaction of such buyers'-side determinations with producers' choices made along the market profile of terms of trade that was illustrated in figures 2.3 and 2.4.

It does *seem* clear that simple schedules such as these for C and S can only be approximations. For example, there is no provision for changing curvature (saturation exponents a and c) according to range of volume, and yet for large-enough volume, curvatures surely will change. But these issues are only in part technical matters of social scientists' modeling, because they also involve what framings guide managerial choices.

Use of the same index n both in S and in C entails the powerful assumption that firms lie in the same qualitative rank order when judged by product quality as when their production cost schedules are nested. This hypothesized index n of quality is a modeling construct that is not synonymous with quality as seen by either side separately, producer or buyer. Use of the two exponents b and d quantitatively differentiates variability with demand from variability with cost.

Establishing viability of market profile for some particular case study need not be subject to such constraints as in equations (2.1) and (2.2). The resulting ad hoc profile can be viable as the mechanism for a particular market whose context need not be describable by functional forms. Yet there will not be the guidance given by a complete mathematical solution on what to look for in parameters and in outcomes.

Explicit mathematical solutions only come from empirical framings with standard forms. Solutions for a single alternative specification of schedules (also simple: see equations (5.2–5.3)) will be reported in chapter 5. And these results are striking parallels with a case reported using the neat nestings in functional forms that have been stipulated by equations (2.1, 2.2). Working up such ad hoc schedules and resulting profiles could be effective in the case study of a particular industry or market. The most important flaw with such ad hoccery is being cut off from scans across variety in market contexts and outcomes from a whole economy. Those scans depend on replacing ad hoc schedules for C and S by specific families of functions that can approximate a host of contexts for each of many varieties of markets.

Specification of arrays of contexts are needed to guide understanding of the multiple actor, multiple relation, and multiple level interactions, whose feedbacks will be traced in the chapters that follow. (In this direction of greater generality, see also Charnes, Cooper, and Schinnar 1976.) Very gen-

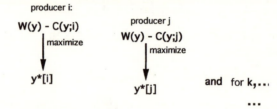

producer i:

$$W(y) - C(y;i)$$

$\downarrow$ maximize

$y*[i]$

producer j

$$W(y) - C(y;j)$$

$\downarrow$ maximize

$y*[j]$

and   for k,...

...

where $y*[i]$ > $y*[j]$ >   ...

But at the same time, buyers insist on

$$\frac{W(y*[i])}{S(y*[i])} = \frac{W(y*[j])}{S(y*[j])} = \frac{W(y*[k])}{S(y*[k])} = \cdots$$

which then **restricts the shape of W(y).**

This mutual searching can lead to a market only among a set of firms whose cost schedules C(y) nest in the same order as the satisfaction schedules S(y) nest inside one another. Once the indexes i,j,k, . . . are represented as a variate for quality n, parallel to volume y, eq. (2.10) shows the shape of W(y) that results.

FIG. 2.5. Summary account of the market profile mechanism

eral functions could be proposed to describe prototype markets, thereby subsuming ad hoc cases more general than allowed here. The flaw is that little in the way of explicit solutions would be obtained, since invoking general functional forms usually leads toward empty practice of mathematical rhetoric. The price paid in constraint for adopting the simplified specifications in equations (2.1–2.2) is more than made up for by the ability to derive explicit formulas for how market profile is shaped by its context and history approximated with parameters and constants in standard forms.

*OUTCOME FOR REPRESENTATIVE FIRM

Why carry along the whole set of index values for quality of producers in a market? The market profile describes footings for any firm and thus for the representative firm; so, regard the quality index as an unspecified variable, *n*, that characterizes a hypothetical representative firm. Depth in mathematical derivation thereby becomes more accessible, and a different slant is provided on producers' views. Designate this the representative-firm approach to deriving the formula for market profile.[7]

Equation (2.3), which derives from imposing the same buyer deal criterion theta for every product flow, is the key to deriving viable shapes for the market profile. *The derivation proceeds backward.* Suppose a curve labeled $W(y)$ is indeed a viable market profile for a given context, yielding an accepted set of terms of trade. Then one can derive what its shape must be. Taking up just *one* firm exemplar for the index value $[n]$ proves to be enough to permit teasing out an explicit specification of the shape. This specification will be in terms of standard mathematical shapes (available for centuries as tabulations in handbooks, and now in computer software programs) interpreted for the parameter values of a particular context.

The volume y from this producer designated by quality index $[n]$ is such that the gap between $W(y)$ and the cost curve is maximum; so their slopes must be equal at that volume:

$$\text{at } y = y[n], \tag{2.4}$$

$$dW(y)/dy = dC(y, n)/dy. \tag{2.5}$$

Then compute the right side of equation (2.5), by differentiation of (C), to yield

$$\text{at } y = y[n],$$

$$dW(y)/dy = c \cdot C(y, n)/y = cqy^{c-1}n^d. \tag{2.6}$$

The approach here is to scan just one small continuous numerical region for n at a time, anywhere along the scale, disregarding what particular set of firms is in a market.

One cannot just integrate this apparently simple differential equation to find the shape of $W(y)$ as a formula in known functions. Such integration would be over neighboring values of y each of which must imply a slightly different level of n, in accord with $y[n]$. That is, one needs to allow for how n must move as $y[n]$ shifts. Somehow equation (2.6) must be transformed so as to eliminate n from its statement.

Turn back to equation (2.3) and substitute into it the formula for S, equation (2.2). It follows that

$$n = [\theta \cdot W(y)/r \cdot y^a]^{1/b}. \tag{2.7}$$

(where complexities of bracketings are now suppressed). The resulting formula for n can then be substituted in equation (2.6). Thus, one obtains a more complex differential equation that *expresses how $W(y)$ must shift with y when one allows for n having to change in step.*[8]

This issue is central: According to the model, at each separate value of n, a producer will choose a distinctive (optimal) volume. But this means that *along the market profile, n will be neither a parameter nor a constant index* value. Thus n can be thought of as a function of y, designate it $n\{y\}$, within equation (2.6). (Thus there will be another—and as yet unknown—function of y in equation (2.6), nested within the cost function that appears there.)

Then, using equation (2.7), equation (2.6) can be regrouped as

$$W^{-d/b} \cdot dW(y) = cq(\theta/r)^{d/b} \cdot y^{c-1-(da/b)}dy. \qquad (2.8)$$

A market profile $W(y)$ has allowable shape *only* if it satisfies this differential equation.

Equation (2.8) is simple enough to be integrated by a standard calculus formula, yielding:

$$W(y) = \{[q(\theta/r)^{d/b}(1 - d/b)/(1 - [ad/cb])]\ y^{a[(c/a)-(d/b)]} + k\}^{1/[1-(d/b)]}. \qquad (2.9)$$

This solution contains, on the right, a so-called constant of integration, whose value is undetermined by the parameters. Any number, positive or negative, can be entertained for this k. Formally, k is being specified from within a cross-sectional model, but substantively one can interpret k as summarizing the particular path in mutual jockeyings of trial and error that resulted in that market profile getting established.

The previous qualitative analysis concluded that if there was one, there was likely to be a host of profiles. This reflected dependence on the actual history of interactions that settled out as the profile. So it makes sense to refer to k as a historical constant. Profiles $W(y)$ will prove to be viable for a range of values of k that depends on the context as defined by the parameters of C and S schedules plus theta from equation (2.3).

Inspection of $W(y)$ shows that four of the parameters appear in two ratios, which are, respectively, a/c deriving from volume y, and b/d deriving from quality index n. Three other measures of context also appear: namely, θ together with the scaling factors r and q.

$$W(y) = [(K/gf)y^g + k]^f \qquad (2.10)$$

by substituting into equation (2.9) the abbreviation

$$K = cq(\theta/r)^{d/b};$$

together with

$$g = (bc - ad)/b; \qquad (2.11)$$

$$f = b/(b - d). \qquad (2.12)$$

This formula for $W(y)$ consists in adding the historical constant k to the product of some constant with a fixed power g of y, and then raising the whole to yet another fixed power, f—with the product of these two powers included as a discount within the constant multiple of y^g.

Consider some particular examples of profile. Keep just one parameter, say a, unspecified numerically. Take first a context, later to be labeled ORDINARY, for which equation (2.10) becomes a double reciprocal in y:

$$W(y) = 1/\{1.33(1/y^{0.85a}) + k\}, \qquad \text{(profile i)}$$

which, when $k = 0$ and $a = 2/3$, reduces to W being proportional to approximately the square root of y.

Note that when g is negative, f must also be negative, and so on, to avoid W decreasing as y increases. Revenue W must, of course, grow with volume y. So, for those contexts where the power to which y is raised is negative, the possibilities are that either the whole expression in brackets on the right of equation (2.9) is also inverted, and/or the power to which y is raised is negative. A mathematical formula that has many parameters has many alternative paths to meet a given requirement such as W growing monotonically with y.

Moreover, a real quantity such as revenue, W, cannot be represented by a negative number. Nor can it be the root of a negative number. And so on. Practical sense supplies many such restrictions. But again there are many twists between the mathematical guise formula W takes and corresponding observable shape of profile interpolated by producers.

In a context of a different sort, to be labeled UNRAVELED in chapter 4,

$$W(y) = \{0.833y^{0.75a} + k\}^2, \qquad \text{(profile ii)}$$

so that the profile curves upward, depending on the size of k, somewhat less than the square of y.

For an example from a third sort of context, to be labeled ADVANCED in chapter 3, set $k = 0$,

$$W(y) = 4y^{0.33a}, \qquad \text{(profile iii)}$$

such that the profile decelerates upward as the cube root of y, if $a = 1$.

Figure 2.6 reports curves corresponding to the first two of these examples.

Where along any such profile will a given firm appear? This derives from its index value on quality. Subsequent figures 3.4 and 5.3 will exhibit examples of market profiles that have been transformed in this way.

In contrast with the other measurable constants and parameters, which each has a single numerical value corresponding to a given context and history for the resulting market profile, the index value $[n]$ is, in fact, standing in for a whole set of numbers, the quality index values for the whole set of producers. Pause to notice the wheels within wheels concerning functions in this derivation. The $y[n]$ identified from a market profile is not an independently measurable curve, as a cost schedule is: rather it is a function that must be derived, just as $W(y)$ is derived.

*Viable Contexts

Viability of a $W(y)$ profile for producers must be confirmed by tests with substantive interpretations. First, each producer must be motivated to choose

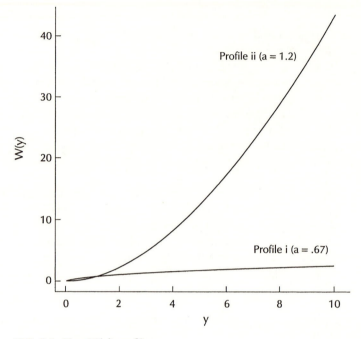

FIG. 2.6. Two $W(y)$ profiles

a distinct (and finite) volume at which it optimizes its net revenue, $W - C$. And second, at this volume chosen the net revenue must be positive. The mathematical version of the second test is easy, but in the model the version used for the first test is awkward and sometimes misleading.

The *second mathematical test* is to check an inequality, namely that $W > C$. At volume $y[n]$, the producer requires positive cash flow.[9] The general statement is

$$W(y[n]) > C(y[n], n\{y\}). \tag{2.13}$$

(The notation $n(y)$ is used here to remind us that in actual fits to data the quality index is likely to be chosen to yield best fit to observed volume of given firm.)

Now, the *first mathematical test*. Optimality is enforced in two parts. The initial part is that a peak has a flat top; that is, the first derivative of $(W - C)$ is zero at the volume y chosen for each quality n. This initial part is easy, since this was built into the derivation of the W formula through equations (2.4, 2.5). The second part is checking that the second derivative is indeed negative there, thus confirming a peak rather than a valley from this difference in slopes. In short, equation (2.5) was only a necessary condition for $y[n]$ to be yielding the maximum of $W - C$, so that now another condition must be added on to establish sufficiency, namely, that at $y = y[n]$, which is the extremum identified by equation (2.5),

$$d^2[W(y) - C(y)]/d^2y < 0. \qquad (2.14)$$

From equations (2.14) and (2.13) respectively one derives the following explicit inequalities:

$$[cb/ad] \cdot [(a/c) - 1]/[(b/d) - (a/c)] \cdot q(\theta/r)^{(d/b)}y^{c-(ad/b)} > (-k) \quad (2.15)$$

$$\{[(a/c) - 1]/[(b/d) - (a/c)]\} \cdot q(\theta/r)^{(d/b)}y^{c-(ad/b)} > (-k). \qquad (2.16)$$

These two inequalities follow from substitution of equation (2.9).

According to these tests, parameters from the C and S schedules, together with the deal ratio theta, determine viability of the rivalry profile $W(y)$ through two inequalities with the historical constant k. Each inequality can yield, even with a given value specified for k and given values for parameters, a whole continuum of inequality statements, one for each conceivable value that y may assume along the specified rivalry profile.

For some combinations of parameters, no market can be viable when k is positive, because there are no values of y for which both conditions are satisfied; and similarly for other combinations when k is negative. There are some combinations, some contexts, for which any value of k yields a viable profile. Anywhere in the range of market contexts, a given value of k may restrict the range of volumes y allowed, whether by setting a ceiling or by setting a floor.

Of course, the only constraints activated are for the values of y chosen corresponding to values of n that characterize firms actually in the given market. The next chapters will develop the mapping of y to n that remains implicit in equation (2.7). Until then, viability only of the market profile as a function in y is considered, not the viability of the set of locations of firms.

The issues are just what the range of k is and, for given k, what any boundaries on y are that correspond to profiles viable for markets in a given range of context for markets. Note the interaction of conceptions of range at three different levels—of y for a firm, of k for a profile, and of parameterized context for a market mechanism; so the term *boundary* has also been used, especially for volume y, to lessen confounding.

Establishment of a market, just because it is a matter of trial and error, is more likely the broader the range of viable options, that is, of profiles. Each k yields a profile. So, a range for k translates into a range of market profiles. One thus should emphasize the range of k allowed for a set of parameter values, a, b, c, d, and theta, rather than the particular value of k and the particular profile that turn up. In the real world of mixed signals and noise and confusion, it is reasonable to see the range of k that is feasible for a given context, a given point within a market range, as a measure of the likelihood of a market getting itself established—or of recovering from disruption.

From these two formulas (2.15, 2.16) for inequalities that must be satisfied, one can compute the range of k values each of which yields a viable profile for the given context as specified by parameter values. The two inequality formulas take on different configurations for various combinations of sign and relative size among the parameters, so that examination is postponed until the next chapter. Whether constraints (2.15) and (2.16) are satisfied will be found to depend primarily on the sign found for the historical constant k. The viable range of k remains the same across whole swaths of combinations of values for parameters. The next chapter develops a representation of these swaths.

Microeconomic Traditions and $W(y)$ Models

Consider briefly how producers would maneuver for places along a rivalry profile that proves sustainable across them, such as in figures 2.2 and 2.6. Such a profile likely is an outcome of a trial-and-error search, as just discussed. This outcome is indeterminate beforehand within some range as to shape and scale. Yet once established, acceptance from buyers downstream of a rivalry profile does embargo any unilateral price hike. And, as microeconomists have always argued (see Schmalensee and Willig 1989, especially chapters 6, 8, 17), price *cuts* by producers are discouraged by anticipation of potential countermoves by their peers. But whereas these microeconomists construe firms' settings of prices on differentiated products in terms of very numerous pair comparisons, the present model instead sees firms as playing against the rivalry profile as a gambling house enforcing payoff outcomes.[10]

Economists have sought, for more than a century, to model a production market instead as interacting sets of conjectural variations. Augustin Cournot introduced such sets in order to analyze the duopoly, the industry consisting of just two firms. Cournot argued that each duopolist would choose an optimal quantity on the basis of the volume conjectured to be coming from the sole competitor. His compatriot and critic Bertrand in 1883 argued that producers would instead conjecture about and choose prices, not quantities. Then, since 1933, when Edwin Chamberlin established that product differentiation was central to market formation, economic theorists have tried again and again to meld his differentiation with various combinations of Cournot and Bertrand.[11]

Key ideas from this line in economics are synthesized in the present model of markets.[12] More precisely, this model can be seen as a compromise between Cournot and Bertrand derived from a principled explanation of Chamberlin's differentiated markets via the signaling theory of the economist Michael Spence (1974a), which is central in chapter 5 below. But each of these approaches from economics is being both reinterpreted and generalized as social constructions sited in networks. The goal remains a general theory.

The importance of quality in market assortation was worked out more than a quarter century ago by Rosen (1974), and there are commonalities with the formulation by this $W(y)$ model. But instead of quality being a unitary social ordering at the center of a self-enacting market mechanism, in that Rosen paper quality becomes the multidimensional basis for cognitive assessment of prices. As can be seen from his title, Rosen was concerned with consumers to the neglect of intermediate goods.[13] He was able to examine tendencies toward market segregation from the interactions between particular sorts of buyers and particular producers, but at the cost of sidestepping the issue of market mechanism, because he did not examine social construction of quality. Much the same contrast is taken up again in chapter 11, in discussion of an econometric measurement approach by Nerlove that has significant commonalities with Rosen's theoretical model.

On the other hand, accounts by institutionalist economists, along with some of the contributions from economic sociology, tend to dissolve into a welter of diversity, with the critique of pure competition being the only unifying feature. Neoclassical and institutionalist accounts thus sustain each other's inadequacies. Each focuses on weaknesses in the other's account as sufficient justification for its own account. (For a similar assessment, which also emphasizes the importance of Knightian uncertainty, see Beckert 1996.)

Consider, for example, this assessment in an otherwise excellent institutional history of governance in the U.S. auto industry: "The propensity of car buyers to develop brand loyalties further reduced the allocative effectiveness of price signals" (Scherrer 1991a, 212). He is presupposing a neoclassical model of market pricing as a foil to make interesting his own folk account of brand loyalties. The present model instead subsumes (in chapter 4) particular folk conventions such as these brand loyalties within a generic account of the market mechanism.

Even rich institutionalist accounts of market process thus can, in juxtaposition, come to seem scattered and arbitrary. And, once it moves beyond pure competition, microeconomics itself appears scattered and arbitrary because there is no general mechanism supplying context and embedding to the market interface. Even so, microeconomics does provide some theoretical scaffolding for Industrial Organization, a data-oriented subdiscipline of economics that provides sensible observations on industries and their doings.[14] Yet much-used measures for industries, such as concentration ratios, still have little basis in microeconomic or any other theory of market mechanism. And, conversely, economic theorists are astonishingly ignorant (see discussions of work by Baumol in chapter 12 and by Arthur in chapter 14) of the insights earned in studies of business strategy and Industrial Organization (also see chapter 14).

Proper theory should address questions about major observed phenomena. Why are unequal profit rates ubiquitous along with unequal market shares? How is it that industrial markets with increasing returns to scale can remain viable? And, especially, what signals to a firm that it is indeed in an industry, together exactly with firms that are neither its suppliers nor its buyers? How is it that these other firms become peers instead of just noisome busybodies? And these questions arise again for markets vis-à-vis other markets.

Derivations of patterns of structural equivalence from network models can be the basis for answers to these last questions, which straddle the domain of macroeconomics. Like microeconomics, existing macroeconomic theory largely ignores how such network connectivities can affect predictions of equilibria. One has to turn to other sociological investigations such as Burt 1988a; Burt and Carlton 1989; Baker 1990; Baker and Faulkner 1991; and Baker, Faulkner, and Fisher (1998), as well as to part 2 below. Even so, macroeconomic insights on financial networks do provide important additional context to the $W(y)$ models (see chapter 12).

The disastrous truth is that the microeconomic tradition failed to come up with any viable characterization of monopolistic competition, which is to say, realistic competition. I say "disastrous" because the consequence is that economic theory generally has to build on a false foundation, and this distortion sets a pernicious example for all social science. These considerations are so important that all of chapter 11 is devoted to them. Perhaps the most compelling case made there is in the section on Nerlove's econometrics.

~~~~~~~~~~~~~~~~~~~~~~

CHAPTER 3

Market Plane

This chapter continues modeling just for a representative firm, but the results nonetheless characterize whole markets. Market outcomes, rather than depending on supply and demand pressures from far away, instead depend on matchings of local dispersions. Specifications of local context for a representative firm are sufficient to frame outcomes for market varieties. These can be arrayed as a market plane that is applicable for more or for fewer firms in a given concrete application. The chapter next calibrates revenues according to quality and exploits these to estimate aggregation over an economy. In the last section, I sketch the principal results.

This representative firm is a device for encompassing a continuum of possible quality values. For each firm, labeled by quality n, besides the volume $y[n]$, and worth $W(y[n])$, one seeks to determine the cost $C(y[n], n)$, plus some further spin-off measures. I use square brackets to denote dependence on n. This convention not only clarifies notation but also signals that solving for this nested dependence is much more difficult than solving for the profile $W(y)$ itself, as was done in the previous chapter. Numerical solutions and various devices of approximation will come into play alongside some tidy algebraic solutions such as appeared in chapter 2. Despite complexities, the overall pattern of outcomes, of market performances, can be made clear through this plane map, which lays out contexts in a plane and groups them.

FOUR REGIONS IN TWO DIMENSIONS

Market action is affected and thence market profile is determined by the choice frames used in producing and buying. These frames are reflected in the model by schedules $C(y, n)$ and $S(y, n)$ from the two sides—producers and aggregate buyer. The general formula $W(y)$ reports the shapes of market profile that broker the pressures from the two sides; see equation (2.9) with pendant illustrations, profiles (i–iii). Each profile depends on the path of evolution taken, on history. This is indexed within the formula in part by the two evolutionary indexes for the interface: the displacement k and the buyer deal criterion theta, defined in equations (2.9) and (2.3). Also appearing in the formula, of course, are the numerous parameters of the C and S schedules (a, b, c, d, r, q), which together define context.

Let's review the solution thus far. Where each producer lands along a market profile—which is to say, the output volume it will commit to—is determined by its value on n, the label for index of quality. This is an index value within an array of such across all its peer producers. The index, in fact, reflects a twofold niceness. The array of n values summarizes interacting assessments both by the particular set of producers and by the buyers in that market.

We turn now to explore how to think about and array the schedule parameters to best bring out varieties in markets and their operation. Our application centers on tests of viability for market profiles. Market operation identifies firms with their niches in quality, but instead of individual locations on the quality index n, this and the previous chapters deal only with two measures of dispersion across quality in valuation.

These two measures are b and d, the exponents of discount of valuation with declining quality by, respectively, taste of consumers and cost of producers. We intuit that these two parameters, in interaction with the like parameters for dispersion across production volume in valuation, control the viable shape of profile—revenue versus volume—for that market. Even without knowing quality index values, one can estimate the impact on cost and buyer valuations from shifts in quality and can report these shifts as functions of the d and b parameters. Similarly, in a and c one can report valuations of shifts in volume produced.

The general formula (2.9) for revenue $W(y)$ devolves into distinct families of computational formulas representing this smooth curve of market profile, depending on ranges of parameters and, in particular, on d. The parameter d, as an exponential power, gauges responsiveness of cost valuation across whatever particular range of n brackets member firms in a market.

Many combinations of ranges for the several parameters must be surveyed. We seek simplification. The idea throughout this book is to use a scheme of approximations simple enough to allow a comparative inventory of markets in terms of numerical settings for a few parameters. Even four exceeds scanning capacity, but the parameters a, b, c, d, unlike the quality indexes n, need not be examined one by one.

Let us think of the problem abstractly. Separating "inputs" from "outputs" is the wrong way to proceed; it misses the cascading of product flows through successions of markets as intermediate goods. It also elides local variabilities; and a tangible mechanism for the market can only be grounded in these. The mechanism throws up a lasting configuration, a market profile, out of feedbacks around continuing flows of product among distinct actors. From the beginning, one must build in such a way as to represent within one figure the sorts of spreads among participating actors that can support such a market mechanism.

Spread must be allowed for on each side of a transaction interface, and yet each descriptor laid out must be construed also as a trace of a compound social actor with internal dispersions, a market as interface. Otherwise, one bypasses the social interactions and reproductions responsible for the flow of production through markets.

Characterization of the mechanism should be by descriptive parameters that combine and compare aspects of the receiving and of the sending sides of transactions. Each such descriptor must integrate design features with measures of the environment. These descriptors are neither reports on geography and technology nor prescriptions from a consultant. But each must integrate exogenous with endogenous aspects that have interacted in concrete sociohistorical paths of experience.

It is not only acceptable, it is vital to simplify and approximate the various spreads that are involved. We seek to characterize market mechanisms by locations in a plane. One descriptor axis should measure the size of production flows. Another should measure differentiation in products flowing within that market. Each descriptor must further calibrate such volume and quality measures in terms of valuations as perceived by the two sorts of participants, shippers and receivers.

Intuition suggests that it is primarily ratios that should matter. The $W(y)$ schedule is, after all, the mediator of that market. Let's return to the explicit model. On the one side there are producers' optimization searches over curvature c (see figure 2.3). These searches face from the other side buyer's veto inspection in terms of curvature a (see figure 2.4). One can make a two-by-two array of all four power exponents a, b, c, and d by whether they characterize the producers' (cost) or the buyers' (need, taste, or the like) perspective, and with regards to variation of valuation with volume or with quality index. See table 3.1.

Which ratios give most insight?

Two ratios of parameters, taken across the rows in table 3.1, can yield effective characterization. Each is a ratio of saturation exponents, with buyer side in the numerator and producer side in the denominator. One ratio is for valuations concerning volume, the other for valuations concerning quality.

Make these two numerical ratios the axes of a plane, as shown in figure 3.1. Each single point in this planar space represents a stack of characterizations that yield the same ratios, a/c and b/d. These points come arrayed as if in rows and columns: *This state space is as much like a library of case studies that are cross-referenced as it is like a geologist's topography.*

TABLE 3.1
Cross-Tabulation of Parameters

	Buyer Need	Producer Cost
Volume sensitivity	a	c
Quality sensitivity	b	d

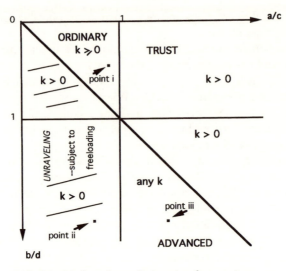

FIG. 3.1. Market plane, designating four regions, three locations

Profiles (i) and (ii) in figure 2.6 graphed particular profiles for markets located at the points indicated in figure 3.1 by arrows pointing to these roman numerals that also correspond to the example formulas for profiles that were written earlier near figure 2.6.

To designate the plane of figure 3.1 a state space for the market mechanism is to claim that the context for the mechanism in all these competitive markets can be summed up by just two ratios of parameters. Each location characterizes a market within its larger environment, upstream and down. We will establish that viabilities of profiles can be calculated, along with outcome variables like revenue, from these ratios. One can inventory variations in the production market mechanism in terms of just these two axes, these two numerical ratios.

Designate regions of this map for varieties of market according to ranges of parameter. Designate the map itself as the market plane—although, strictly speaking, this is a map just of the market mechanism for a representative firm rather than for a market with its array of firms. Figure 3.1 is a plane with *b/d* as one axis (running vertically from zero to plus infinity), and *a/c* as the other axis (running horizontally (from zero to plus infinity).

This array brings out by its clusterings both similarities and differences in contexts that predict market profiles and outcomes. The plane is split among regions, four of which will figure large in this book. Each region is distinguished primarily, as we shall see, by the range of values of the historical constant *k* for which profiles are viable. Each region may exhibit quite different profile shapes, but even when profiles are not dissimilar, they nonetheless are configured differently with respect to underlying valuation schedules and therefore shift differently with shifts in parameters, which fix these schedules.

In figure 3.1, the regions are divided by the lines $a/c = b/d$ and $a/c = 1$. Location in ORDINARY will come to be seen as very—perhaps most—common, and it is the region easiest to relate to microeconomic analyses. ADVANCED, by contrast, is furthest from microeconomics because its locations exhibit increasing returns to scale.

The other two regions will get less attention in this chapter. TRUST also shows increasing returns to scale, but with what will turn out to be involuting rather than innovating tendencies. TRUST will figure prominently only in chapter 9, along with UNRAVELING, which will be introduced in chapter 4.

Further technical analysis of this map of ranges is needed, but first consider its substantive significance. Each producer gains a footing as a distinguishable identity only as and if the jointly constructed market also becomes recognized as a distinct entity, with a separate market identity that guides actions. Each producer's identity is indexed by level of quality, n, but the set of these index values is *not* sufficient to characterize a market. State space is needed for that.

The central point is that the $W(y)$ market mechanisms construct themselves socially so effectively that each production market becomes perceived and discussed as an actor in its own right with a distinct *identity*. This further level of economic actor and action is distinguishing itself exactly by the embedding ratios a/c and b/d for footings for its constituent firms. And, conversely, the footings that supply identities for constituent producer firms also support, by the pattern of their embeddings, a distinct identity for that market as a whole. These embeddings are described by the points in the *abcd* space, as chapters 5–7 will develop further. So there is reciprocal identity formation, which is to say, identity co-construction across levels:

firms → market, together with market → firms.

The viable range of the historical constant k, determined by the procedure in chapter 2 around inequalities (2.15) and (2.16), is the same throughout each of the several ranges into which the market space is partitioned in figure 3.1. Table 3.2 reports, using the labels given in that figure, the corresponding allowed ranges of k.

Note the intricacy of the variation in pattern of constraints with shifts of parameter, different for the different regions. These applications of the two inequalities requires care in derivations that are intricate rather than deep. To save space, two further abbreviations have been used in table 3.2 beyond those given in equation (2.10):

$$k' = (\{ck\}/K) \, |[(b/d) - (a/c)]/[1 - (a/c)]|, \text{ and } e = g/c, \qquad (3.1)$$

TABLE 3.2
Viability Constraints by Region in Market Space

Region			
ORDINARY	$e < 0 < b/d < a/c < 1$: no constraint for $k > 0$, since	**max:** $-(1/y^{c|e|}) < (ad/bc)\,k'$, so that for $k > 0$, all y, **pos:** $-(1/y^{c|e|}) < k'$, so that for $k > 0$, all y,	whereas for $k < 0$, $y < y_{max}$, where $y_{max} = (bc/ad)^{1/c|e|} y_{pos}$; and for $k < 0$, $y < y_{pos}$, where $y_{pos} = (1/|k'|)^{1/c|e|}$	and thus for $k < 0$, unraveling can occur, since $y_{max} < y_{pos}$.
UNRAVEL	$e > 0$, $a/c < b/d$, $a/c < 1$: no profiles for $k < 0$, since	**max:** $y^{ce} < (ad/bc)\,k'$, so that for $k < 0$, no y, **pos:** $y^{ce} < k'$ so that for $k < 0$, no y;	whereas for $k > 0$, $y < y_{max}$, where $y_{max} = (ad/bc)^{1/ce} y_{pos}$; and for $k > 0$, $y < y_{pos}$, where $y_{pos} = (k')^{1/ce}$,	and so for $k > 0$, profile subject to unravel since $y_{max} < y_{pos}$.
ADVANCED	$b/d > a/c > -1$, $e > 0$: no constraint for $k > 0$, since	**max:** $-y^{ce} < -(ad/bc)\,k'$, so that for $k > 0$ all y, **pos:** $-y^{ce} < -k'$ so that for $k > 0$ all y,	whereas for $k < 0$, $y > y_{max}$, where $y_{max} = (ad/bc)^{1/ce} y_{pos}$; and whereas for $k < 0$, $y > y_{pos}$, where $y_{pos} = |k'|^{1/ce}$,	and thus for $k < 0$, the profile NOT liable to unravel, since $y_{max} < y_{pos}$.

TRUST	$a/c > b/d$; $a/c > 1$; $e < 0$: no profiles for $k > 0$, NO unravel for $k > 0$, since	**max:** $y^{ce} < (ad/bc)\, k'$ so that $k < 0$, no y; $k > 0$, $y > y_{max}$, and **pos:** $1/y^{c|e|} < k'$ so that $k < 0$, no y; $k > 0$, $y > y_{pos}$, where $y_{max} = (bc/ad)^{1/c|e|}\, y_{pos}$, so that $y_{max} < y_{pos}$.
PARADOX	$d < 0 < e$: $a/c > 1$, no profile since	**max:** $k > 0$, no y; $k < 0$, $y < y_{max}$; and yet **pos:** $k > 0$, $y < y_{pos}$, $k < 0$, no y.
	But with $\underline{a/c < 1}$,	**max:** $k < 0$, all y—but $k > 0$, $y > y_{max}$; and **pos:** $k < 0$, $y > y_{pos}$—but $k > 0$, all y;
		so profile with $k < 0$ never unravels, whereas profile for $k > 0$ may unravel.

Note: See text formulas (2.15, 2.16) for inequalities called **max** (maximum), and **pos** (positive). Abbreviations: $e = 1 - (ad/bc)$; and $K = cq\,(\theta/r)^{d/b}$, and in turn $k' = (ck/K)\{[(b/d) - (a/c)]/[1 - (a/c)]\}$. Upright bars ‖ denote absolute value, that is, taking the positive sign. Note that y_{pos} and y_{max} may be either upper or lower bounds on y.

where ‖ is the standard notation for taking the absolute value, that is, taking the positive sign.

Intuition does not give sufficient guidance. Let's trace out the entry in table 3.2 for the ADVANCED region. For $k < 0$, the maximization inequality (2.15) sets a lower bound on the y that a firm will choose, and the positive profit inequality (2.16) also sets a lower bound, one that is higher and so is the binding constraint on choice of y for negative values of k.

By contrast, for any and all values $k > 0$, and also for $k = 0$, there are no constraints on the y values for which one or another firm might opt, for any context in the ADVANCED region.

Entries in table 3.2 for other regions are explicated in chapters 4 and 5, and also chapter 9. Note that table 3.2 already incorporates some further and finer distinctions in parameter ranges anticipated from later sections and chapters.

Intuition by itself would suggest, for example, that when c is small, costs rise so slowly with volume that each producer is lured not into picking a distinctive quality position for itself but rather into producing as much as possible, destroying the viability of any market profile, whatever its k. However, the differentiated market profile proves to be viable even for large a/c, as will be developed in chapter 7, which introduces a context still larger than that for table 3.2.

*REGIONS AND RAYS

The state space of figure 3.1 offers three distinct forms of guidance as to varieties of production markets. One is the regions. The same bounds on k values for viable markets apply throughout each region. As shown by the headings in panels of table 3.2, the regions are bounded by straight lines. Across one of these polygonal regions the formulaic expression $W(y)$ will be the same, but, as will be shown in chapter 7, these profiles can, despite their similar shape, generate substantially different aggregate revenues.

The second kind of guidance is to performance achieved by producers, in profit ratio and market share. This second form of guidance picks out not the region but *rays,* which designate those lines in the state space that pass through the point $(1, 1)$ within the market plane of figure 3.1. Rays through this special anchor point accommodate locations of markets that tend to have similar measures of relative performance. One key ray is a boundary between regions: *designate it the diagonal,* the diagonal along which the two ratios are equal, $a/c = b/d$. In contrast is the boundary ray at the opposite edge of the ORDINARY region to the diagonal, namely the vertical line, $a/c = 1$, in figure 3.1.

The term *ranges* is used for general reference. It can be parsed in terms of regions or alternatively in terms of rays. *Range* has the connotation of more or less ordered variation in the specimens under study and therefore is more appropriate than a botanical term such as *variety*. The range of quality encountered in a given market is affected by its setting, which is being summarized in parameters for context. The previous chapter suggested that markets located, for example, near the diagonal ray through the point (1, 1) in state space would tend to be markets with limited dispersion in quality between their members. Additional examples are suggested by both this chapter and the next. So measurement of quality is not divorced from measures of context.

To find outcomes, such as the revenue W, for a representative firm, the first requisite is the production volume y for that firm. The distinctive identity of the firm derives from n as a fixed index attribute rather than from the value of the dependent variable, volume, which adapts to context. Outcomes have to be referred to the fixed index of quality n to be of predictive value. So, what is needed is a formula for $y(n)$, volume for any given n.

Begin with equation (2.7) and then substitute for $W(y)$ from equation (2.9). The resulting equation is

$$n^{b-d}r/\theta = \{q[1 - (d/b)]/(1 - [ad/cb])\}y^{c-a} + k \cdot (r/\theta)^{d/b} \cdot y^{a[(d/b)-1]}. \quad (3.2)$$

Unfortunately, except when $k = 0$, this equation can only be inverted to find $y[n]$ through numerical computations. These yield only the particular outcome for each particular value of k and θ and the context parameters, whereas the goal is a function $y[n]$ specifying volume for the representative firm.

Path dependence, the existence of a whole range of viable profiles as indexed by k, thus is a major barrier to theoretical exploration. It comes on top of having to deal with a large set of constants and parameters (two are yet to be introduced, in chapter 6). Numerical calculations for markets, such as are reported in the appendix tables, are hardly sufficient for understanding patterns and elaborating theory. So guidance is needed from special cases that permit analytic, closed-form solutions for revenue of the representative firm, and thence also of market aggregates, to be addressed in chapters 6 and 7. When the value of k is zero, not only are the outcome formulas for revenue and volume much more tractable, but computational results are easier to interpret.

The market map of figure 3.1 indicates the allowed range of k for each region, computed from inequalities (2.15) and (2.16). Zero is in the middle of the range allowed for k only for one region, ADVANCED. In fact, only this and ORDINARY, the two regions running lower right to upper left, include zero in the range of k for which profiles are known to be viable whatever the particular dispersion of producers on quality n. In consequence, explicit predictions for the other two areas UNRAVELING and TRUST will appear only with further technical development in chapters 4 and 9.

Let's turn to the full solutions where $k = 0$. Reconstitute these two regions of the market plane that do allow $k = 0$ into a set of rays through the key point $(1, 1)$. This anchor point is included in each boundary line between all pairs of regions in the market plane. Important aspects of firm and market performance will turn out to be constant along these rays.

In the special case of $k = 0$, an explicit formula for y derives from substitution of equation (2.9) into equation (2.7), and then solving for y:

$$y_0[n]^{(c-a)} = (r/c\theta q)n^{(b-d)}[bc - ad]/(b - d). \tag{3.3}$$

Then revenue W, for $k = 0$, can be expressed in terms of n by substitution of the resulting $y_0[n]$ formula into equation (2.9) for the profile $W(y)$. This profile becomes, in full detail,

$$W_0(y)^{(1-d/b)} = q(\theta/r)^{d/b}(b - d)c/(bc - ad)\, y_0[n]^{(bc-ad)/b}, \tag{3.4}$$

from which an explicit formula for $W_0[n]$ can be obtained.

The important point is that the same formula holds for all values of n, and thus also for the aggregate revenue in that market. The explicit formulas require tedious manipulation and detail and will, like those for aggregates, be reported only for the more general setting of chapter 7.

In this same special boundary case, $k = 0$, similarly straightforward, if tedious, calculation yields a formula for the producer costs C that is exactly parallel to that derived for W in equation (3.4). The ratio of W/C thus takes the following very simple form

$$W/C = [(b/d) - 1]/[(b/d) - (a/c)]. \tag{3.5}$$

This ratio is a dual for each producer, the *producer's* deal criterion, to the theta deal criterion of equation (2.3) imposed by the aggregate buyer.

The deal as seen from the producer side of the market can alternatively be assessed by the ratio

$$(W - C)/C.$$

The formula is, for $k = 0$,

$$(W - C)/C = [1 - (a/c)]/[(a/c) - (b/d)].$$

This other producer deal criterion is also called the cash-flow rate or operating profit margin.

The most generally familiar rate is profit; denote it by the Greek letter pi, π. Its definition is

$$\pi = (W - C)/W. \tag{3.6}$$

One can compute for $k = 0$:

$$\pi = [1 - (a/c)]/[1 - (b/d)]. \tag{3.7}$$

This says that the return on sales of the representative firm does not depend on its level of quality n. So profitability is constant across all firms. It follows that neither profit nor operating profit rate, $(W - C)/C$, varies with the absolute size of the firm for $k = 0$.

The differences that remain for $k = 0$ between firms in a market are in aggregate performances, such as in gross revenue and net cash flow $W - C$, and thence also in market share. These will be taken up in chapter 7.

Let's turn to the market plane to guide interpretation of these equations. Reexamine figure 3.1: With $k = 0$, and thus the same profitability for distinct firms, their common rate of profit will tend to be extremely high along any ray near the diagonal through the origin to the anchor point. Figure 3.2, which repeats the framework of figure 3.1, reports three curves in the state space along each of which, for $k = 0$, the value of W/C is a constant.

Each curve is, in fact, a straight line, as follows from the formula. This is a line that runs through all, and only, the two main regions in which $k = 0$ is viable. It can be seen that industry profitability varies sharply from one line to another, and thus as one shifts location on an arc within a given region. The ratios for the lines drawn in figure 3.2 are between zero and unity.

Consider markets represented by points closer and closer to the diagonal ray: One expects to find higher and higher profit rates, and, as it will turn out, lower and lower absolute size and differences in size. Along the vertical ray, $a/c = 1$, the outcomes are reversed: Profitability sinks to zero and aggregate size grows with quality such that the largest firm becomes the only representative.

It is time to locate some actual examples of industrial markets. Let's examine some qualitative fits developed from case studies concerning the 1970s (White 1981a). Approximate locations in that decade are shown for a score of industries in figure 3.3.

One can go on to suggest likely tracks of change of a given market mechanism (see chapter 13), and possible disruptions of it by other sorts of social organization (see end of chapter 11).

Values for absolute amounts, such as volumes from firms or total payments in a market, can only be computed using specific locations of the whole set of firms on the quality index n. These are reported, from numerical computations, in the appendix tables for particular markets, placed just before the glossary. These are for some particular points in the market space, and they give absolute volumes and revenues for particular sets of quality index n. They also report Gini indexes of inequality for those particular sets of firms.

The Gini index, which varies from zero to unity for maximum inequality, is a cumulative index constructed to reflect the degree of inequality in a given variable distributed across a population. Ginis for persons range from as low as 0.2 for pay in some hierarchical organizations through 0.4 for

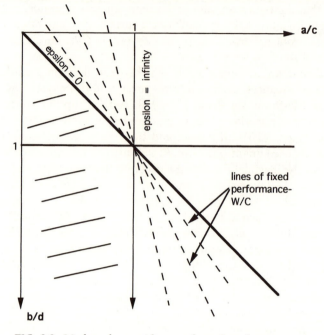

FIG. 3.2. Market plane, with rays of equal performance

income across Western populations to 0.7 for wealth. Now, however, the population becomes the set of firms in that market, although equations (3.18–3.19) below will approximate it as a population continuum.

REVENUES AND VOLUMES BY QUALITY

Relative assessments of firms' performance is important to participants, entrepreneurial or not. They are much more likely to calibrate valuations for firms in a market with respect to one of their members as an anchor than to apply some absolute formula with a calibration constant such as r or q. The analyst can similarly calibrate using a quality index. Through such a calibration the analyst, too, can bypass the messy formulas and issues of units that arise around r and q.

First, consider revenues, W. Seek exact formulas, even though they are only obtainable for $k = 0$. Designate the base firm's quality by n_o, and its volume by y_o. This could be the largest, the smallest, or the median firm, but in practice one would choose the firm with the best data available. Define $S(y_o, n_o)$ as R and $C(y_o, n_o)$ as Q, in effect treating the quality and volume for the base firm each as unity. Thus, for each other firm,

$$S (y, n) = R(y/y_o)^a(n/n_o)^b; \tag{3.8}$$

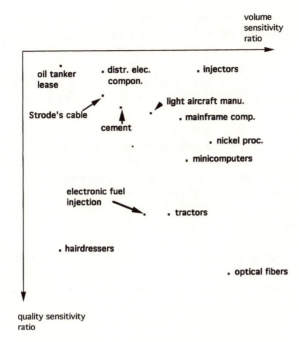

FIG. 3.3. American industrial market locations in the plane

$$C(y, n) = Q(y/y_o)^c (n/n_o)^d. \tag{3.9}$$

But y is determined by the value of n through the formula for the market profile, $W(y)$. And by hypothesis, $S (y, n)$ stands for every n in the same ratio, theta, to $W(y)$ at its $y[n]$. So, with $k = 0$, each valuation can be expressed as a power of n times the appropriate base. Straightforward but tedious calculation yields

$$W(y[n]) = R(n_o/n)^{d\varepsilon}, \tag{3.10}$$

where

$$\varepsilon = [(a/c) - (b/d)]/[1 - (a/c)]. \tag{3.11}$$

Designate this epsilon as the *discount rate of revenue with quality*. (Note that ε is just the reciprocal of equation (3.5) for operating profit rate defined as $(W - C)/C$.) The cost is discounted with quality just like W:

$$C (y(n), n) = Q(n_o/n)^{d\varepsilon}. \tag{3.12}$$

Let's examine how these formulas apply within the *abcd* space by returning to figure 3.2. In particular, along the diagonal through (0, 0) and (1, 1), the exponent of (n_o/n) goes to zero; so along this ray, every firm in a market has the same revenue and the same cost, with market aggregates simply being R and Q times the number of firms. By contrast, along the vertical ray with $a = c$, all but one firm in the market is vanishingly small: for $b > d$, this is the firm with the highest quality n, whereas for $b < d$, it is the firm of lowest quality. Throughout the ORDINARY region, volume increases as the quality of the firm decreases.

Such mechanistic calibration disregards entrepreneurship, maneuvering, and contingency, all of which will appear in the next chapter. Yet this calibration does provide a baseline comparison of how a firm scales with respect to another firm in revenue when everyone follows its own script in that market. These scripts are for optimizing choices by all, when taken from rivalry profiles not displaced by nonzero k. Quality thereby becomes the focus as the underlying framing of cause and effect.

No longer is the central vision one in which individual executives think deeply and strike out boldly on their own. One way to explain how the approach through $W(y)$ models is different is to point out that it denies the separations among structure-conduct-performance of firms that underlie much of both institutionalist accounts of firms in networks and industrial organization approaches (Chandler 1977; Scherer and Ross 1990). This is developed further in chapters 7, 12, and 14.

Second, turn to volume of production flow y. Now, we will seek answers for any viable schedule so that k is no longer restricted to zero. That means the answers must be computed numerically. They cannot be shown as formulas, such as equations (3.11–3.12), and they are easiest to show as curves on a graph. Each curve will be a transformation of the volumes y from a market profile into a function of the underlying quality index n. Again we are treating the representative firm rather than any particular set of firms in that market: Designate the function as $y[n]$.

The general nature of these curves, $y[n]$, will differ according to the region of the market plane where that context is found. And of course the curves will shift as k is changed for the given market. For the point in the ORDINARY region designated as (i), both in figure 3.1 and following equation (2.11), curves $y[n]$ for three different values of k are laid out in figure 3.4

Two of the corresponding market profiles are viable, though, as can be seen, they translate into substantially different variation of volume with quality.

*Asymptotics and Limits

The third kind of guidance comes from the application of asymptotic methods (Bellman 1972; deBruijn 1961). Three distinct applications are made, the last two being for Gini indexes and for boundary lines and points in market space.

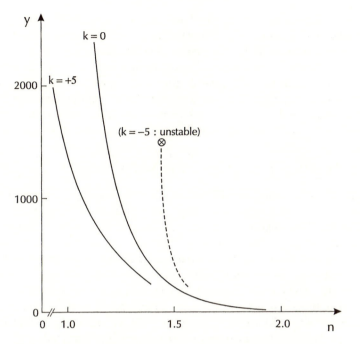

FIG. 3.4. Production volumes y as a function of quality n, for various k, for a market in ORDINARY region

Explicit formulas have just been derived for $k = 0$, but prudence suggests examining how robust these formulas are to at least small deviations of k from zero. Even extensive numerical calculations cannot provide complete assurance, so we turn for guidance to general if approximate formulas about changes in outcome variables when k departs from zero. We derive, in short, asymptotic results with respect to k.

Apply these perturbation techniques to general equations for revenue and volume. The main question is whether the change in the given outcome variable is positive or negative for a given departure of k from zero. Consider $W(n)$. Let $W_o(n)$ be the known (explicit but intricate) formula when $k = 0$ (reported for a more general setting later, equation (7.8) or (7.13)). To a first approximation, for k of small size, asymptotic analysis of the general equation yields

$$W(n) = W_o(n) \, [1 - k(bc - ad)/\{(c - a)(b - d)W_o(n)^{(b-d)/b}\}]. \quad (3.13)$$

Note that k and the power of W are in the same units, so the bracketed multiplier of W_o is a pure number, as required.

Take the ORDINARY region as our first example. In this region, any positive k yields a viable rivalry profile; so assume k is positive and small. The sign of the product of coefficients in the second term of (3.13) is positive, so

$W_o(n)$ is multiplied by a factor less than unity. Thus, in ORDINARY the W for the representative firm always decreases as k increases from zero, and thus the aggregate revenue W for the market also decreases.

In the ADVANCED region, the departure of k from zero can be either an increase or a decrease. All three of the parentheses of parameters in the second term of equation (3.13) change sign. So in the proportionate change of $W(n)$, $[W(n) - W_o(n)]/W_o(n)$, the linear slope factor rises with the deviation of k above zero and falls with the negative deviation of k from zero:

$$[W(n) - W_o(n)]/W_o(n) =$$
$$-k\{(bc - ad)/\{(c - a)(b - d)\}W_o(n)^{(b-d)/b}\}. \qquad (3.14)$$

This linear slope factor will go to zero along the diagonal ray and when, instead, $c = a$ will become very large. This also holds true for the ORDINARY range. Note that $b = d$ is not possible in either of these regions.

In both regions, when well away from the ray with $a = c$, the $k = 0$ special case should be quite an accurate guide for outcomes. These hints from asymptotic approximations for small k will be elaborated and generalized in the course of discussing tracks in state space in chapter 13.

The search for asymptotic formulas for outcome variables encompasses only contexts that admit $k = 0$. In regions TRUST and UNRAVELING, there are no asymptotics because there is no allowed boundary value of k to be approached. Since $k = 0$ is disallowed in these contexts, the approximation in (3.13) does not apply.

One can still exploit the exact solutions for some guidance. As an example, consider the formula for $W(y)$ at some context in the TRUST region with $d > b$, $a > c$. One cannot solve explicitly for $y(n)$, but one knows there is a viable solution $W(y)$ only if $k > 0$. It follows that

$$W(y) = 1/\{k + [K/gf]y^{-|g|})]\}^{|f|}, \qquad (3.15)$$

where, again, | | denotes taking the absolute value and we simplify by using again the K, g, and f defined in equation (2.11). The convolution of signs of powers is such that $W(y)$ is a monotonically increasing function of y. Now, the maximum value of $W(y)$ will clearly come as y grows infinite, and it will be just

$$\text{maximum } W = 1/k^{|f|}. \qquad (3.16)$$

Whereas the minimum value of $W(y)$ will come when y gets as small as it can, the smallest value that still yields net profit, $W < C$, namely y_{pos} (see table 3.2). Factoring the result yields

$$\text{minimum } W = 1/k^{|f|} [1 + (1 - (b/d))/((a/c) - 1)]^{|f|}. \qquad (3.17)$$

Note that for reasonable values of the powers—say $a = 1.5c$ and $d = 1.5b$, the minimum W is three-sevenths of the size of the maximum W; or for

$a = 2c$ and $d = 2b$ the max/min ratio for W is three to two. Realizing the maximum and minimum values in (3.15–3.17) requires, of course, that the corresponding values of n (which could only be found by numerical calculation) would have to be present among the market producers.

The point to be made by this example in equations (3.15–3.17) is that a closed form solution just for $W(y)$, such as was obtained in chapter 2, can yield valuable guidance, even for an arbitrary k and/or even in regions where asymptotics on k do not work. This point can be exploited in applications from chapters 12 and 13. Observe that this ratio of max to min does not depend on k at all. The maximum possible range of revenues across producers in a market, in other regions as well as this one, can be assessed approximately without knowing the particular path of evolution of that market, the particular k.

In the special case of $k = 0$, the Gini indexes for inequality, cited earlier in the chapter for numerical calculations reported in appendix tables A.1–A.5, can be expressed in explicit algebraic formulas in the parameters. One does not need to cumulate numerical outcomes for members of a particular market, which makes it much easier to assess variation of inequality across the market space. This does require using some pro forma distribution across quality; so this use of Gini indexes will be a form of asymptotics.

The uniform distribution was taken because it suits the representative-firm perspective. Firms, of whatever number, are distributed with equal spacings along a range of quality index n extending from zero to infinity. The inequality index for revenue W of firms within the market whose context is specified by $abcd$ is

$$\text{Gini} = 1/[1 + \{2(c - a)/(bc + ad)\}]. \qquad (3.18)$$

Since products are differentiated by firm, the meaning of aggregate physical volume, sum of y's, is not as well defined as aggregate revenue, but one can derive a formula:

$$\text{Gini} = 1/[1 + \{2(c - a)/(b + a)\}]. \qquad (3.19)$$

The nearer the point for market context is to the diagonal shown in figures 3.1 or 3.2, the nearer the Gini indexes, for either profitability or market share, approach zero, complete equality. So one expects more and more equality in market shares despite fixed differences in quality. But the profit rates expected by the firms are increasing. In short, there is less and less spread to sustain the $W(y)$ market mechanism at the same time as there is the enticement of growing profitability of footings in such market schedules. Such schedules may not be viable substantively, tending to fall apart despite meeting all the formal criteria. Chapter 4 takes this discussion further. Implications can and should be drawn for policies for participants and observers and for likely or desirable strategies for participants. These can be taken up in chapters 12 and 13 after extension and generalization of the $W(y)$ model.

Let us turn, next, to asymptotics at boundary lines and points in market space. Asymptotic methods also are applied to the exact equations derived for market profiles. But now the small deviations are in parameter ratios of the market space. One derives formulas for market outcomes that are valid in the limit of approach of parameter ratios to those defining boundary lines and points.

The two principal rays here are the diagonal defined earlier and that for $a/c = 1$. For these, as well as other boundary lines and points, table 3.3 gives formulas for one important outcome variable, revenue. (Again, some distinctions from later chapters are folded in.)

These asymptotic analyses of aggregate sizes for extreme varieties of market give some insight into sensitivity to quality. (More extensive discussion, especially of the mathematics, is given in the "Numerical Computations" section of chapter 7.)

How likely are equal shares in a market, which imply firms with the same quality rating? Nearly equal shares in market revenue imply an unstable market mechanism and thus are rare, but they offer high profitability to producers. But mutual searches will continue for viable market schedules with possible quality increments and reorderings. Either such a quality ordering will reestablish itself, or else some new configuration into industries will be precipitated.

RATIOS OF AGGREGATE SIZES

In the special boundary case, $k = 0$, relative performance of different firms is the same. Formulas for ratios in costs and revenues of the representative firm also apply for the ratios of market aggregates. One can bypass the explicit sums over particular quality indexes to be reported in chapter 7.

Designate by $\mathbf{W}$ the aggregate payment made to all producers in an industry from the buyers collectively. This aggregate requires a summation over the points on the market profile chosen by each producer, the universal formula

$$\mathbf{W} = \text{sum over } W(y[n]). \tag{3.20}$$

The sum is over the quality index values n for all the producers in that market. This aggregate revenue $\mathbf{W}$ is the prime measure of market size and will be used throughout subsequent chapters. Not only is $\mathbf{W}$ an observable, it is the market characteristic that is most familiar and most widely cited both by actors within that market and by others observing from the larger economy.

The volumes chosen by each producer, the $y[n]$, call for separate calcula-

TABLE 3.3
Asymptotes for Market Revenue[a]

Variety	Conditions	Asymptote
Pure competition	$b \to 0,\ a < c$	$\{(r/q^{a/c})(a/c)^{a/c} \cdot \#^{1-(a/c)}\}^{1/[(1/\gamma)-(a/c)]}$
Pure taste	$d = 0$, and with $k = 0$	$\{(r/q^{a/c}) \cdot \#^{1-(a/c)}\}^{1/[(1/\gamma)-(a/c)]}$
No leverage for trade-off	$(a/c) \to (b/d)$	$\mathbf{W} \to 0$, and furthermore $k \to 0$
Equal variability with volume	$a \to c$, and $d > 0$	$\{(1 - k)r/q\}^{\gamma/(1-\gamma)}$, and $k \to 0$
Equal variability with quality	$b \to d$	$\{(1 - k)\,[1 - (a/c)]\,r^{c/a}/\{[1 - (d/b)]\,q\,\#^{(c/a)-1}\}\}^{(a/c)/[(1/\gamma)-(a/c)]}$, and $k \to 1$
A runaway market	$c \to a\gamma,\ c < a$, and $b \to d$	$\exp\{(k - 1)/(b/d) - 1]\}/\exp\{q\,\gamma\,\#^{1-\gamma}/r^{1/\gamma}(1 - \gamma)\}$
Equal variability and no leverage	$(b/d) \to (a/c) \to 1$	$\{(1 - k)\,r/q\}^{\gamma/(1-\gamma)}$

[a]**W** for varieties lying along boundaries in downstream state space (fig. 5.2), with $\tau = \mathbf{V}/\mathbf{W} = 1$ (breakeven for aggregate buyer).

tion, whose complexity depends on the historical path that led to that $W(y)$. Derivation of an explicit formula for $y(n)$ will lead to an explicit equation for **W**. These hold, however, only in the special case of $k = 0$. Following a less direct approach, the second section of chapter 5 estimates that if two markets with much the same parameters are collapsed together, the resulting aggregate size will tend to be less than the sum of the previous two separate markets. Such an approach can be taken also for predictions, as in part 4, from removal rather than addition of firms.

A parallel aggregation of the producer side is required. Let **C** designate aggregate of costs to all firms included in the terms of trade for a given market, formula **C**.

$$C = \text{sum of } C(y[n], n). \tag{3.21}$$

W must be greater than **C**, since each producer separately insists on its revenue exceeding its cost, and thus

$$\mathbf{W} > \mathbf{C} \tag{3.22}$$

for aggregates also. The operating profit rate for the firm is defined by $(W - C)/C$, and this too can be extended to the aggregates.

There is a formal parallel for the buyer side. Aggregate across all the producers the valuations $S(y, n)$ by the aggregate buyer to define

$$S = \text{sum of } S(y(n), n), \tag{3.23}$$

where the sum is over each quality of product in that market, so that again the summation requires knowing the $y(n)$ for all firms. Buyers will enforce equally good buys, equations (1.1) or (2.3), so that

$$S = \theta W. \tag{3.24}$$

(This formal equality will not prove useful, as is, because the dimensions are awry—see chapters 6 and 7.)

The ratio of W/C takes the same simple form as earlier in equations (3.4–3.6):

$$W/C = [(b/d) - 1]/[(b/d) - (a/c)]. \tag{3.25}$$

The ratio $(W - C)/C$ also assesses the deal as seen from the *producer* side of the market taken as an aggregate. The formula is, for $k = 0$,

$$(W - C)/C = [1 - (a/c)]/[(a/c) - (b/d)]. \tag{3.26}$$

This producer deal criterion, also called the cash flow rate or operating margin, thus is the industry-wide "markup" of revenues over costs.

The more familiar profit rate, called pi as in equation (3.6), is defined as

$$\pi = (W - C)/W = [1 - (a/c)]/[1 - (b/d)]. \tag{3.27}$$

All these results so far hold only for profiles with $k = 0$ and even then are only for the ratios of aggregates. To go beyond these ratios, we must deal with substitutabilities and feedback.

Filling Out an Economy

A larger field of other markets has so far been taken for granted as the overall context in which the particular market being modeled works out its fate. All the parameters introduced in modeling the market mechanism presuppose— and in principle they are to be inferred from—flows and responses into and from such larger setting of other industries, some sector or economy. The development thus far of the $W(y)$ model already permits imposing a requirement of self-consistency in cumulations of flows, of inputs and outputs reckoned among industries (to be elaborated further in chapter 7). At this section's end, a contrast will be drawn briefly with an alternate aggregation by an economic theorist.

The issue is the appropriateness of boundaries. Cumulate all the flows through some set of markets described by $W(y)$ models: When will they sum consistently with the records kept concerning some particular sector or economy?

Throw aggregated costs from the markets into one pot and all the aggregate revenues into another pot. But previous sections have shown costs for each industry being accrued as revenues by industries upstream from it.

And this continues to hold at remove after remove from any starting industry. This suggests some equality between the two pots, of overall costs and revenues.

On the other hand, the aim (normally accomplished) of each producer who continues in a market is to make a profit, and the $W(y)$ model indeed predicts continuing profitability. This confrontation leads to criteria for a first test of self-consistency in the choice of boundaries for an economy whose markets fit with the $W(y)$ model. The accounting identities involved are easy enough to write down.

Sum the aggregated costs borne by all the producers in all the industries included in a market field and designate the result as COSTS. Then repeat with a parallel sum for all the revenues received by all the producers in all the industries; designate the result as REVENUES. Viewing costs and revenues as aggregates, one would be surprised to find these equal, for many reasons.

The underlying point of a production economy is, after all, to provide goods and services for ultimate consumption, which consists in disappearance from the economy into the maws of the consumers. Second, some markets are at edges: K-Mart and Sears are unlike other producers in that they are not selling to yet other layers of actors who are themselves producers. And further, the underlying basis of a production economy is to draw on resources such as raw materials whose acquirers do not play the same role as other producers because they are not acquiring from still other producers.

Thus, there should be a disparity between aggregate costs for and aggregate revenues to the producers who figure in the given market field. This disparity results from, and thus is found in, the differences in transaction flows with actors outside the market field. Various macroeconomic accounting frameworks elaborate on this, but a simple formula will suffice here:

$$\text{COSTS} + \text{consumer expenditure} + \text{exports} = \text{REVENUES} + \text{raw materials} + \text{imports.} \qquad (3.28)$$

As a next step, group consumer expenditure together with exports since both are flows from inside the market field that terminate outside it. And similarly with raw materials and imports. Regroup the simplified terms:

$$\text{REVENUES} - \text{COSTS} = \text{exports} - \text{imports.} \qquad (3.29)$$

Note that the role of buyers has been elided in the derivation of these equations. Every producer-as-buyer has already been included as suffering the corresponding costs tallied in that accounting aggregate. And the revenues are tallied from the market profile, which gives the perspective of the producers as producers, not as buyers.

Extensive tabulations are available, from government and banking sources, for the terms on the right-hand side of equation (3.29), for a number of different choices of which sectors of industries to include. The task is to derive predictions for the left-hand side of the equation by making some sort of summation into aggregates from the $W(y)$ model as applied to individual industries of that market sector. This can yield tests of the consistency of the model.

The problems in doing so are formidable, and not just as to practicalities of measurements and of model predictions on such a scale. There may be dependence of the $W(y)$ parameters that have been fit to one market upon the parameters fit to other markets that are somehow connected, and there may be other interaction effects that complicate the cumulation of aggregates from distinct markets.

But an instructive beginning can be made using a representative-market approach. Survey the regions in the state space of figures 3.2–3.3 in search of candidates to approximate a "representative" market. Derive results for the difference between aggregate costs and revenues for just one market, taken to be representative. Multiply this by a count of the number of markets in the field, and use that as an estimate in the above equation.

Figure 3.2 not only supplies candidates for a representative market for cumulation, it supplies whole lines of such candidates in the state space. Along each such straight line, the ratio of **W/C** is the same for the representative firm and hence for the market in aggregate. The cumulation equation becomes

$$\text{(number of markets)} \cdot [1 - (a/c)]/[1 - (b/d)] \\ \cdot \text{(average } \mathbf{W}) = \text{exports} - \text{imports.} \tag{3.30}$$

Consider just the middle line in figure 3.2, where the ratio **W/C** is 2. This equation of balance should hold so long as the typical market, within the boundaries of the economy, can be approximated by any one of the varieties of market that lie along that line. Indeed, it should hold if the field of markets is thought to be approximated by any distribution whatever of market varieties located along that line.

Now invert the perspective. Use this equation to predict some average set of parameters across all $W(y)$ models. For each of an array of plausible estimates of this excess for, say, the present American industrial economy, compute what the parameter combination on the left side of the equation would have to be. In that way one could at least work out that certain regions in market space are unlikely to figure largely among the markets of that economy. Note that there will be a trade-off between the value from the combination of parameters and the number of markets multiplied by the average size of markets. Both the latter figures can be estimated from censuses.

Return to the prediction in equation (3.30) of the excess of export over imports. Now compare it to the approach of the economic theorist Paul

Krugman (1980) in a classic article relating international trade to aggregation of productions exactly by firms with differentiated products, citing an article on "Chamberlinian monopolistic competition" (Dixit 1982). This, like the Flaherty (1980) article on size distributions to be discussed early in chapter 11, requires that returns to scale be constant—in present terms, that $c = 1$. Moreover, each firm in effect constitutes a market by itself, with unique products equally attractive to all buyers (or, equivalently, all products are variants of one other)—so $b = 0$ in present terms, and furthermore firms have the same cost structures—$d = 0$. This is a highly specialized case of the $W(y)$ models, which requires the limiting asymptotic solutions of the section before last (see table 3.3).

Krugman is working toward a different goal. He is estimating aggregate size for this whole economy under three macroeconomic assumptions: (1) full employment; (2) a closed labor market, in which all production costs, as wages, are equated to all purchases by those same persons; and (3) free entry of new producer firms, which drives to zero the net profit of each of the firms present in equilibrium. The goal he pursues, with this whole array of assumptions that he admits are extreme, is to assess foreign trade with another such economy. His conclusion is that indeed there would be trade despite the two countries having comparable industries (just as most international trade is between the largest economies and exactly in those industrial sectors where each is large).

PRINCIPAL FEATURES OF THE MARKET MECHANISM

The previous chapter derived an explicit formula for $W(y)$, the profile that can reproduce itself. Let's bring out the elegant simplicity of this formula (2.9) for a representative firm by simplifying the notation still further beyond that in formula (2.10) to yield

$$W(y) = (Ay^g + k)^f. \tag{3.31}$$

The only descriptors of this representative firm included are y, its volume of product, and W, its revenue and hence market share. None of the participants measure quality explicitly, and so it properly remains out of sight.

We analysts do stipulate quality as explicit values of the index n; these are held to be consistent both with ordering of producers via the cost structure each perceives *and* with the relative satisfactoriness to buyers of a given amount of one distinctive product vis-à-vis another producer's distinctive product. Business analysts themselves also (see chapter 12) make judgments of quality, and most crucially of proper boundaries for markets. Zuckerman (2000) provides convincing evidence that firms are thereby pressured into sticking with this market-as-molecule frame from which $W(y)$ models derive.

So, in actual observation the profile is a few points in the W and y plane, one for each of the firms, rather than the continuous curve shown in previous figures for the representative firm. Also, there is a representative history involved, which is itself indexed doubly within the formula, once by the shift constant k and once by the deal criterion theta. Each value of k specifies a different one of the family of similar profiles of formula (2.10), and similarly for theta. Each is an index of the history or path of interactive jockeying by firms and buyers from which emerged the profile.

The deal criterion, theta, although depending on the particular path or history, will tend to be set by mores that have emerged across markets in that sector of the economy as to how good a deal buyers expect to settle for. That requires attending to influences from whole other markets around the given one. That will be modeled in chapter 6. For some, and possibly also for any, values of shift constant k, a market profile is subject to unraveling by competitive pressures within the market, the topic that leads off the next chapter, 4.

The purpose of the present chapter was to identify the context of a market together with corresponding outcomes. Performances of firms in the market depend on context, context in addition to particular quality levels of member firms. So too, of course, for the viability of the profile, and both these dependencies interact with history or path dependency as summarized in theta and k. The shift constant k is held to be more labile than quality locations and theta, and these, in turn, are held less stable than the main features of context for the whole market represented by the other parameters.

Only because the description of this market context itself is kept so simple does the $W(y)$ model emphasize, through the market plane, this context as the crux of market survival and outcomes, which are the dependent variables. The particular niche a firm achieves on quality does, of course, seem crucial to it. But to understand and predict outcomes for the market as a whole, only the existence of some appreciable range in quality matters, rather than the particular values of n. Chapter 8 does show in detail how one can work back from observed outcomes for all firms in a market to the set of n values, but they can be put on the shelf for present purposes.

The real crux is the trade-off in valuations as seen by the two sides. But this is twofold. One trade-off is with respect to how valuation of sheer volume grows for one side, as compared with the other.

Our modeling strategy insists on estimating each of these growths in valuation by a *single* number, in fact the exponent of a power function. That is what greatly simplifies the portrayal and hence yields solution as an explicit formula, and it can be justified as an approximation on those pragmatic grounds. But this is also the assumption natural in an account of what these businesspersons are themselves jointly constructing out of their own ongoing perceptions and assessments

A market profile $W(y)$ is not the work of some mathematician or some bunch of engineers; it is more like the discipline observable in conversations

(Sachs 1995; Gibson 1999), or in greetings among kinfolk (White 1963), or in vacancy chains (White 1970; Stewman and Konda 1983), or in residential segregation (Schelling 1978). These interactions are intricate and involve subtleties, but commitments can issue only on the basis of approximations that are workable off the cuff, in the field. In the same spirit, the trade-off of the two sides' valuations is taken to be just the ratio of these two numbers, exponent a for the growth in buyer satisfaction with volume, to exponent c for the growth in the cost the producer anticipates with volume growth.

A number that stably characterizes some situation, process, or entity deserves special recognition. If such a number is not just an idiosyncrasy but rather a representative of such measurements across some determinate family, it is called a *parameter*. For the family of production markets and their members, a and c are parameters. The same emphasis on seeking and using parameters characterizes some orthodox econometrics, as we shall see in chapter 11.

If that were enough, varieties of markets could be mapped into just points along a line measuring context by size of a/c. Indeed, that (plus allowing for theta, but not k) is close to the claim orthodox theorists make for their dreamworld of pure competition (see chap. 11). Instead, turn to the second trade-off.

The $W(y)$ model does argue that the distinctiveness of the various firms and their products within a market can be captured in their order by quality portrayed by n. But those actual values of n have been put on the shelf as secondary. What really counts for market survival and performance is not these values in themselves, but rather the trade-off between how the buyer side valuates quality growth and how the producers' side valuates quality growth (in their cost). Again, a single parameter, an exponent, is used for each valuation, b and d respectively. And again the trade-off is equated with the ratio, with b/d.

Hence figure 3.5. The plane of figure 3.5 is descriptive of all varieties of market mechanism. One dimension is a/c, the other is b/d. The valuation schedule of neither side is at issue for market stability and performance, but rather only trade-offs, one with respect to volume and one on quality.

If we return to the formula (2.9) for market profile $W(y)$, inspection will show that, indeed, these two ratios are prominent there. But not only they; so why is the plane a sufficient description? Two of the many symbols in the formula, r and q, are merely scale factors, for which location on the quality index n can be substituted, as was shown two sections ago. The historical constant k, which is a chief concern throughout chapters 3–10, was itself shown in an earlier section to depend crucially on location in the market plane. The impact of the other historical constant, theta, will be shown in chapters 6 and 7 to require introduction of a third dimension described by a parameter, converting the plane to a cube.

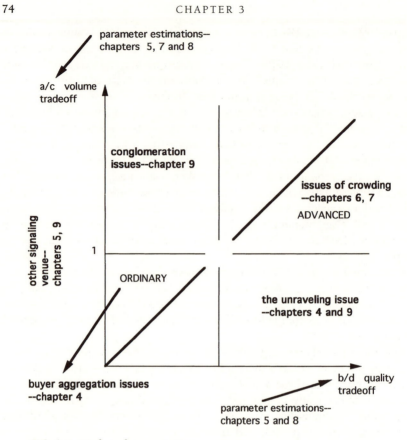

FIG. 3.5. Market plane, overview

But here, the core is still the plane. What makes the whole model work is this state space. Markets are seen to operate quite differently depending upon where they are located by the intersection of the parameters of relative buyer demand and product supply-cost for both volume and quality. This follows from the market's construction through niche seeking, through searchings for identity by firms, in terms of signalings. The plane assigns a niche to a market as a whole according to these two trade-off ratios governing the balancing of its firms' niches into a viable profile.

Viability and performances of markets are distinguished according to a split into four quadrants around the point $(1, 1)$ shown at the center. These are constructed by crossing the two regions in which a/c is less than 1 or greater than 1 with the two regions in which b/d is less than 1 or greater than 1. In words, $a/c < 1$ is where for any growth in volume, demand goes up more slowly than producers' cost; whereas $a/c > 1$ is the region where demand goes up more rapidly with volume than does producers' cost. On the other dimension, similarly, $b/d < 1$ is where for any increase in quality, demand goes up more slowly than does producers' cost; whereas $b/d > 1$ is the region where demand goes up more rapidly with quality than does producers' cost.

Quite different histories are characteristic of the markets of these four quadrants, and also different tendencies to turn into nonmarket forms of one sort or another, as chapters 4 and 11 will elaborate. And primarily, of course, there are differences in patterns of profit and pricing expected, along with market size and the relative shares of firms in it. Thus, price variations can be predicted from the four ratios of the four basic quality/volume and demand/producer-cost parameters.

Two of these quadrants tend toward symmetry: In the lower left, the upper hand is held by buyers as to both volume and quality increases. Here producers vie for buyers who are relatively limited in their demand for volume and quality relative to what they cost producers. High-volume production is lower in quality, lower in cost. Here it seems hard for producers to grow, and there may tend to be more of them in a market, in conditions similar to those in population ecology theories of organization (see chapters 11 and 13). And this is closest to pure competition, the idealized model convenient for orthodox economic theory in which buyers see no differences in quality (see chapter 11).

These two lines splitting the plane at unity ratio will, of course, cross at the center point, $(1, 1)$. But this crossing is left blank in figure 3.5. Performances predicted for a market are extreme for either ratio being unity, but in opposite ways, so that the predictions break down when they intersect. Just around the central point is a black hole of contexts that will not support a $W(y)$ market. This is just as we should expect, since the market interface equilibrates itself by trading off variation in volume valuation with variation in quality valuation, which becomes difficult as sensitivities on the two sides tend toward equality.

This suggests why the performance of markets, measured in percentage or relative terms, tends to be the same along rays through the central point. The most significant ray is not either of these two splitting lines at unity values that are parallel to the axes. Shown in figure 3.5 is the diagonal ray running from the origin through the center point $(1, 1)$. The profit rate will tend toward equality among firms, at a very high value in a market along this diagonal, while at the same time the absolute volumes and revenues of the firms are shrunken. By contrast, along the splitting line at $a/c = 1$, the market will tend to be swallowed up into one large firm, which, however, will not be profitable at all.

On one side of unity, the triangle between these two rays is labeled ORDINARY, and on the other side, the comparable triangle is labeled ADVANCED. The mathematical solutions above, which will be filled out further in chapter

7, enable one to see just how markets in ORDINARY straddle the two extreme performance packages just described, according to the intermediate
ray along which they lie. Equilibrating the market profile depends here on
the volume valuation trade-off ratio *a/c* between the two sides being *larger*
than the quality valuation trade-off ratio *b/d*. Exactly the opposite statement
holds with respect to the triangle ADVANCED.

This is where intuition gets exercise and at the same time concedes how
essential is guidance from the explicit $W(y)$ model. In the dull contexts
where valuations by buyers both of volume increases and of quality increases
are below costings of these by producers, the two sides will not come to
agreement on a profile of compensating payments W to producers *unless* the
volume valuation sensitivity ratio is more nearly even than that for quality. In
those dull, ordinary contexts, quality difference can't play as much role as
relative sensitivity to volume shipped if a market is to sustain itself as a
viable profile.

The real test of intuition is then to argue out why the opposite balance
between volume and quality sensitivity ratios applies when both instead are
high—in hot markets, so to speak, where buyers pressure harder. This is left
to the reader as an exercise with this warning: This quadrant of contexts is
more vulnerable to location among other markets and will thereby be shown
in chapters 6 and 7 to splinter into subregions of different viability and
performance.

As important, the other triangle making up the quadrant with ORDINARY
is made up of contexts that *cannot* sustain a market, contexts that fail the
viability test for any value of *k*.

Numerical, and thus messier, solutions of the $W(y)$ model are needed to
guide interpretation of the other two quadrants. But in neither is there a
sharp break by subregions. The one labeled TRUST tends, as perhaps intuition will suggest, toward a conglomeration among producer firms; chapter 9
will offer a fresh perspective on that, and also on the other quadrant. This
latter, labeled UNRAVELING, is the initial topic of the next chapter.

Let's recapitulate the $W(y)$ story thus far, seen as a replacement for the pure
competition story (chap. 11) about markets involved in production:

> As firms continue to make product X in an evolving economy, they form a
> new type of tie with peers, not with suppliers or buyers, on the basis of
> structural equivalence within these existing networks of procurement
> and sales. Such a set becomes known jointly as a package, as each firm
> jockeys for distinctive quality. The resulting market as an array of niches
> on quality becomes established as the place to go for X, as the market
> for X. Thereby, that market or industry converges on recognizable levels
> of curvature and displacement in valuations for its production flows.

The individual niches that result become ratified from outside. Thus eventuates a definite location in a state space for the market as a whole. This location in market space, in turn, both leads these firms to sustain their level of quality n—at which they have chosen volume y to optimize profits—and obliges any new entrant to try to choose an n consistent with overall a/c and b/d constraints.[1] Few try, as chapters 11 and 12 will argue.

A $W(y)$ market is, of course, simultaneously a construct (analogous to a grammar), a tangible system of discourse, and an actor with ties to other markets. We turn to these aspects in subsequent chapters.

~~~~~~~~~~~~~~~~~~~~~~~~

CHAPTER 4

Quality and Unraveling

In everyday life, to see well enough even to walk about safely often requires lenses. Walking and working also presuppose, but overlook, the social lenses from custom and talk that frame the realities we see. Everyone, including businesspeople, visualizes our economy and polity through lenses thicker yet, folk theories. Effective analysis requires uncovering these social lenses that underlie the social construction of markets. Here we continue this exploration, particularly around the construction of quality, which was begun in chapters 1–3 and will continue in most of the remaining chapters.

This chapter probes beneath the determinism of the market model. Just as the model centers around an ordering by quality, so too do perceptions guiding and maneuvers to be expected from participants. Quality standings in a market are joint social constructions, so it is natural for them to be a principal focus and lever of participants. These standings bear the marks of their history. They are not intrinsic individual qualities.

Participants can find their profile footings in the interface without explicit estimates of quality, but not observers. The first section dissects how these quality standings get established. It takes up the varied indications of producers' qualities that participants and observers may make use of. Then comes discussion of a whole quadrant of the market plane in which market profiles are typically vulnerable to unraveling by some participating producers. Likely riposte and counterorganization by producers is sketched next, followed by puzzles of aggregating the buyers. The chapter ends with a broader look at entrepreneurship and how it may evoke different kinds of signaling than production volumes.

QUALITY DISCRIMINATION

The obvious approach to quality measurement is consultation with market participants as the experts. Quality in a market comes to be perceived through and across particular situations and vantage points. Only occasionally will a quality index n have become reified during the evolution of an industry. This might be done by a trade association. Such an index can become taken for granted so that it functions, like the IQ index, as a particular numerical scale that is widely accepted, by participants and observers alike.

Benjamin and Podolny (1999) have put together such a scale for producers largely from an industry's own constructions: It is a special industry,

California wine producers. But this scale addresses quality in the eyes of the buyers. The reference of quality, like "intelligence," should embrace perspectives from both sides—in this case, both producers and buyers.

The quality ratings of production firms reflect the evolution until then of that market as an interactive and joint set of footings, which may be affected by some larger set of markets, as shown in this and the next chapters. An account is desirable of how quality spreads evolve through some history that becomes marked in a local culture (see chapter 15). This is the approach taken in the Porac field study of the Scot knitwear industry (see chapter 6). Sets within some population of actors producing and buying may, over time, sort themselves out as able to sustain a market profile in terms of trade with some downstream buyers. Historical contingencies will combine with constraints from the presence of markets already established.

While academic game theorists in economics discuss high-powered manipulations, and microeconomists aggregate hypothetical response curves on blackboards, most practicing entrepreneurs and managers, like most purchasers, are busy seeking and supporting a concrete social grounding to guide them. Each maneuvers to become sufficiently akin to other actors to become recognizable as their peer. In the course of such diverse and multiple maneuvering, all the actors end up constructing a quality array jointly with the other side of the market.

Each position or footing allows for individuality but also commits incumbents to following a general direction sanctioned in common and thus to supporting the legitimacy toward which marketing theorist Laufer (1990) points (see section below). This evolution includes the producers' investments in their footings, including improvements not only through equipment but also through operational and marketing technique. A guiding light will be fleeing situations where few or no differences in quality are perceived among members of that set.

Differences in quality are induced as the necessary basis of a market discipline. Even just from the buyers' side, quality does not refer to some single, well-circumscribed process or property or attribute. The "product" whose quality is appraised normally is, in fact, a differentiated set of products—one for each producer in the market. Such a set has come to be seen in a convention of that market as constituting the normal line of business of producers in that market, which has, however, numerous facets.

When in a given market the items are tangible physical products, then variants by size, color, shape, material, and so on are likely to be grouped as what those producers offer. If the market is in men's shoes, for example, an array of sizes and colors may be taken together as that line of business. Quality from the buyers' side is an index that asserts, like IQ, an underlying commonality of relative worth across a variety of particular skills—here, aspects of the product. Or one can speak instead of a variety of concrete embodiments, of specific models of cars or of shoes within that producer's brand, rather than distinguishing abstract dimensions of difference.

Some producers or some buyers might undertake to construct an independent index of quality from observations for an industry. These assessments could derive either from buyers' reports of taste (see Griliches and Ohta 1976 on hedonic prices for automobile brands) or from producers' accountings on cost. The former correspond to n raised to the power b, whereas the latter correspond to n raised to the power d. Thus, estimates from neither source would be approximations of n. Instead, n could be estimated as some geometric mean of the indexes estimated both from the buyer side and from the producer side.

Usually, only an ordering by quality becomes explicit in activities of a market, rather than comparisons of quality levels being offered as ratios or differences, much less index values. Ordinarily, then, in order to make specific cardinal predictions from the $W(y)$ model for an industry, the observer or interviewer somehow has to convert qualitative judgments into a set of quality indexes for the industry's firms. The logic is the same as used in adjusting cost-of-living indexes and in estimating consumer demand for particular brands: see the compendium edited by Terleckyj (1976, 399–451). And understanding such judgments by other participants can inform and fuel maneuvers for advantage. (Bothner 2000b pursues this through simulation studies; see also Bothner and White 1999, 2000).

The empirical fitting task is to seek an imputed quality array such that predictions yield a good fit with data on revenues and flows across a set of firms being examined as a production market. The formulas from the $W(y)$ model are simplest to interpret across a set of the n when k can be set to zero. But Leifer (1985, appendix B) early laid out a clear and simple procedure for numerical computation in general. Illustrative calculations for various nonzero k will be found in appendix tables A1–A5, below, but only for arbitrarily stipulated sets of quality values. Chapter 8 derives the set of n from an observed profile.

As an example of how insight can be gained on the basis of even an ex post, formalist interpretation of n, consider the entry of new firms, one by one. Entry of an additional producer can precipitate changes in the quality array recognized for firms already in that market. Perhaps some firm that had been left out previously may be able to break back into a given market profile, with repositioning of other firms as a consequence. The entry of a new firm may even unravel some existing profile. Although many suppliers and buyers may continue their habitual ties for a while, prices and volumes of flow in some of those earlier ties may nonetheless become problematic.

If locations on the quality index are stable, market shares should be stable. Empirical studies give mixed judgments (see Han 1991, 1992 on "churning" of individual firms' shares even within markets that appear stable in overall size and other characteristics). In any given concrete context for a market, a host of forces, some deriving from larger technological and ecological changes, can shift or overturn existing perceptions of quality ordering. Vulnerability of a quality array to disruption over time is thus an aspect of measurement.

Trial-and-error searches are induced. Entry of an additional firm into a given market brings influences from its ties within its prior industrial setting as well as requiring it to form new ties in the new market setting. So one outcome could be incorporation of producers by vertical integration either upstream or downstream (see Eccles 1985; Perry 1989). This could preempt governance by any market mechanism, as will be discussed again in chapter 11. But instead, search could yield again a niche in a reestablished market profile with an enlarged set of footings in its market profile—now in accord with repetitions of habitual transactions in an enlarged set of ties. Full modeling of such trial-and-error search calls for extended treatment of network and identity evolutions in terms of blockmodels (Pattison 1993; Wasserman and Faust 1995), as suggested by Waechter (1999).

VIABILITY AND UNRAVELING

To examine maneuver and perception, one needs to include the other members of a market. The issue is not one level but a whole set of values on quality. The representative-firm device will no longer suffice, nor will market aggregates.

Let us begin extending the model to capture not just one but a whole set of firms. The first gaps to plug are in testing market profiles for viability, testing that was begun in chapter 2. The empirical issue is what range of quality n is represented among firms actually contesting for positions in the given market. If none of the values of n are present that would induce choice of a range of y where one of the two tests from chapter 2 is violated, then that inequality restriction is inoperative. Profiles for further values of k may then be able to establish themselves, profiles rejected by the across-the-board tests. That is, hitherto prohibited values of k may become viable given some restriction on quality spread. That is the positive angle for viability of market.

There is a negative angle, too, and that supplies the main themes of this section. There is a third general test of profile viability to add to maximization and profitability by individual producers. Those were the two tests of chapter 2, which are duals to the equal trade-off enforced by the aggregate buyer. This third test is for an additional sort of market failure of the signaling equilibrium. Designate it as unraveling, since a profile may unravel for some configurations of quality among would-be producers. Designate corresponding market ranges as being subject to unraveling.

Unraveling can result from "freeloading" onto an otherwise viable market profile on the part of producer firms with quality too low to sustain a proper individual footing. In their review of economic thinking in sociology, Baron and Hannan (1994, 1141) assert: "Insights into the social efficiency or inefficiency of alternative equilibria is one place where sociologists can make an enormous potential contribution and where fruitful integrations of economics and sociology are possible." The analysis of unraveling is such a place.

Table 3.2 thus must invoke, besides the two inequalities (2.15) and (2.16), also this third test, a probe of unraveling that is more subtle:

> The range of values for $y[n]$ allowed by the first test must include the range allowed by the second test.

Each producer observes the volumes and revenues of its peers. This third test states that throughout the range in which each producer can earn positive profits, it also must be able to locate its own optimum volume, distinct from the volumes of its competitors. Otherwise, in technical jargon, a "corner solution" obtains.

Substantively, the possibility of unraveling arises insofar as the scope of producer qualities is sufficiently broad that, rather than each locating a unique optimum volume on the market profile, some subset of firms can turn profits by converging on a single "corner" value. So in this subset, each firm does find a (common) best choice even though it is an edge value rather than the usual individual optimum niche from along the profile. The buyers of course will reject this collective choice, and so the model's prediction is that the signaling mechanism will fall apart. The buyers, of course, simply choose not to pay the corner subset and so veto their inclusion. This is an instance of a subset of producers being out of line with the trend in trade-offs of value against cost across the other firms: Their shadow positions on quality index cannot be realized.

Figure 3.1 grouped together, as one of the four regions, in the lower left, a triangle and adjacent rectangle under the common label UNRAVELING. Indeed, here is where the third test is *not* met for *any* value of k, even though positive k does satisfy both the first two conditions for viability. These are the *only* two subregions where the $W(y)$ schedule is *always* at risk of unraveling, subject to the range of quality across firms either already included or seeking to be. As an indication, cross-hatching is used, as well as the label UNRAVELING.

This third test elsewhere also can restrict the range of k. In the triangle designated ORDINARY in figure 3.1, k being negative would also be allowed except for this third test. Although only for $k > 0$ are viable profiles guaranteed, for k negative the profile is viable if y is simultaneously less than the boundary values of y from max and from pos constraints (table 3.2). But from the formula for y_{max} one sees it is less than y_{pos}. This means that with $k < 0$ in ORDINARY region there can be a range of firms that can garner positive cash flow but not with individually distinct optima as their footings.

Manhattan Grocers

Let's turn for a homely illustration to grocery markets in and around Manhattan. Volume dependence must be specified in order to locate these examples. In Manhattan, luxury apartments house small families who eat out often, so their satisfaction valuations S are likely to crest out for larger volumes. And the grocers quickly run up against limits when they try to squeeze more volume through their stores, so parameter a will tend to be small along with c tending to be large. Thus Upper East Side grocery markets are likely to be in the rectangle on the left with $a/c \ll 1$.

As to quality, picky East Siders will value an increase in attractiveness— whether by a larger array of goods, or more alert service, or the like—but probably not as much as the correlative increase in the grocery store's cost structure given the prohibitive cost of rental space in this neighborhood. So $1 > b/d > a/c$ seems likely. This is the odd triangle below and left of the region labeled ORDINARY in figure 3.1, the triangle that is part of UNRAVELING region. Unraveling will be a problem as larger-volume grocers running operations less than premium try to encroach on this market (probably at the edges, of Spanish Harlem, Lower East Side, and so on); see that panel in table 3.2.

(However, with a car one could escape from Manhattan to the big suburban groceries across the river in strip malls. Here, conditions are nearly the inverse: In New Jersey suburbia, the market profile of groceries will lie way down and to the right in the region of figure 3.1 marked ADVANCED. Or one could drive upriver to towns with a more normal range in cost schedules, and buyer needs, where a garden-variety competitive structure would lead to contexts in the ORDINARY region.)

So the vulnerability of a market profile to unraveling varies by location in the market plane, and by other aspects of context, as can be seen from table 3.2. There are too many parameters for comfortable scanning even by computations. But we are also showing that vulnerability depends especially on the qualities that come to be imputed to the firms seeking footings.

Suppose the calculus test reports no optimum for a producer because the first derivative is not zero for its quality location, but yet the producer is able to earn positive net income at many choices of volume. So one of those points will indeed be the unique optimum in the eyes of that producer even though the point does not satisfy the second derivative requirement from calculus for proper optima on smooth curves. The standard solution, equation (2.9), misses that these "corner" optima are vulnerable to rejection by buyers.

The substantive implications are clear. Which firms, in terms of quality level n, are trying to participate in a given market is a chief issue in unraveling. With more than a handful of producers being potentially suitable for an industry, unraveling can prove disastrous. A whole cluster of producers, each distinct in quality, may find themselves picking the same volume, and anticipating earning net revenue even though at most one of them can also be satisfying the aggregate buyer.

Signaling breaks down in such a situation. Unraveling comes in a history of firms each choosing the same extreme value of volume, which thus signals not a unique but a whole range of quality n. All do expect to gain positive incomes, but they cannot be delivering the same payoff of value over payment; so the buyers no longer accept any shipment from producers issuing that signal. But then this process repeats itself at the new lowest acceptable signal—and so on.

Let's explicate unraveling one last time, with different mathematical presentation, and applied to an example from an ORDINARY context, where for *some* historical path settings k there are viable schedules that indeed satisfy all three tests for viability. Consider for this point the whole array of possible profiles $W(y)$ corresponding to each possible value of k. But, to clarify the unraveling danger, convert each profile into the corresponding graph of the quality level n that corresponds to each volume y. That is, each market profile $W(y)$, for various k, is translated into a smooth curve of locations in this y, n plane. The result was figure 3.4, which shows market profiles for each of three different numerical values of k for a context in ORDINARY.

Observe that the curve for a negative value of k is unstable. The problem, of course, is that buyers, who will not accept the offerings from this bunch of lower-quality producers, in this process of rejection will also reject the bottom-most quality that does fit on the curve. And so on, for the next try: After a few former niche-holders have been booted, the ones with quality just above them will now be at risk. It is in this sense that the market profile will unravel. Still another example of unraveling profiles will be laid out at the end of the first section of the next chapter (see fig. 5.3).

GUILD COUNTERACTION

The possibility of unraveling suggests joint strategic countermoves and a resulting multiplicity of equilibria. How great is the possibility? Exposure to unraveling can always be assessed as follows. Compute the allowed ranges of y both for the maximization and for the net income inequalities. If the former range includes all of the latter range, that $W(y)$ is viable. But if there is a range of volumes y where a producer can earn positive net revenue but yet not satisfy the inequality test for optimization, that schedule can be unraveled. So it all depends on the range of quality levels n already present among the producers with that market schedule. If there is one choosing a y at the edge of the range allowed by optimality inequality, its footing is at risk. Other producers of lower but nearby quality will wish to opt for that same volume of production. But the buyer side will not find that the resulting average quality yields as good a deal; so they will veto it, and thereby also veto the initially legitimate producer and that whole lower range of quality in a revenue schedule they can accept.

Say it yet again. The shape of the market profile for some k values can encourage producers of low quality to enter the market, yet not lead them to develop a distinctive quality niche of their own, despite offering positive profits to a range of them.[1] The unraveling comes because the heretofore legitimate, although lowest-ranked, producer is likely to find that the volume niche of the next producer up in quality offers it a positive net revenue, but now as a "corner" solution. After subsequent veto of this, the unraveling process can go a next step and erase acceptability of more and more of the volume range across which initially the producers were spread out in distinct quality niches each acceptable to the buyer side. In short, more and more of the initial set of footings for firms in that market can get eroded.

It is reasonable to consider what counteractions might be taken among firms confronted with this possibility of unraveling by others of lower quality. The guild is one such opt-out from a $W(y)$ mechanism undergoing unraveling. Speaking formally, the guild option replaces the historical constant k with a control variable, which may be designated by h. Speaking substantively, the guild option is for allowed producers to combine such that each and every one insists upon the same minimum markup, a ratio in revenue received over cost incurred. This ratio is the control variable h.

Consider one particular scenario for opt-out. The urge toward guild organization is an enormous motivation on the part of lower-quality producers who yet do retain niches to organize against the lowest-quality ones. The latter likely will be seen pejoratively as freeloaders. There may be enough motivation for the overall "betters" to also collaborate to set in motion dynamics of mobilization that can produce some form of guild control.

Many sorts of historical, strategic, and cultural considerations can affect the exact level of markup that a guild, whatever its genesis, will attempt to enforce. One plausible possibility is choice so as to maximize cash flow, revenue less cost. It is easy to compute that this maximum will result from

$$h_{\max} = (c - a)/a. \qquad (4.1)$$

But, of course, both higher and lower markups might become established.

The guild opt-out at first seems just the same paradigm of action as was assumed earlier for the buyer side in deriving the market mechanism, with the guild markup h being equivalent to theta. But only one markup ratio h can be enforced, whereas any particular numerical value for the ratio theta can be and is enforced: This is just a matter of the buyers in aggregate accepting, not declining, the offered pair of (revenue, volume) from each of the producers, who each period have to choose the volume to produce. There is no such passive mode available to the producers. To sufficiently overcome the $W(y)$ discipline resulting from buyer pressure in order to establish a uniform markup of h requires explicit social organization outside of and in addition to the market mechanism—exactly a guild discipline (e.g., Kramer 1927).

The guild opt-out dispenses with the historical constant k that indexes path-dependent shape for a market profile. Instead there is a uniform markup profile. Such a profile cuts across the assignments of volume to quality in $W(y)$ profiles. Turn to the examples previously shown in figure 3.4. The k in such figures is bypassed as an index of profile location. It is supplanted by the markup norm, h, and the resulting shape of $y(n)$ is parallel to the bordering curves and to the $k = 0$ profile (if any).

The important point for the theory is that the outcome profiles obtained by producers in this guild mode for the market do cover exactly the same subspace of possible individual outcomes as for the $W(y)$ model. In fact, for one particular value of h (less than h_{max}), the profile of outcomes is exactly the same as a profile for a particular value of k, namely for $k = 0$. But all the other guild outcomes (curves from constant markup) cross-cut the set of market profiles from the $W(y)$ mechanism, for all values of k except $k = 0$.

At the other extreme, some ruthless counterassociation across the aggregate buyers might somehow coerce the guild into enforcing a markup of just zero. Thus, the outside envelopes around all outcomes from the opt-out option, the guild, are the same as those around the whole array of regular $W(y)$ profiles, as figure 5.3 will illustrate for a context in still another region. What is different is the relative profile of fates to various producers.[2] The important point for theory is that all the associations of volumes with qualities obtainable by explicit organization also turn up on one or another of the profiles whose path dependence is indexed by k.

This exemplifies how, within the mechanism, constraint from enactment of roles within some discipline such as a profile by quality can coexist with the possibility and the actuality of innovation, counteraction, and entrepreneurship.

An important substantive point is that the aggregate buyer side can be better off from the $W(y)$ mechanism's being used. The guild mechanism, in fact, proves to mimic the outcome when, instead of fitting into the $W(y)$ profile mechanism, the producer side and the buyer side (which perhaps may be a single organization) agree upon terms that reward producers exactly proportional to the valuations in their substitutability schedules S.

Turn again to the producers' view. The producers can seek more control and better outcomes than they are getting from some established $W(y)$ market, *whatever* its region or its vulnerability to unraveling. Guilds, with their peer control by concertation, come into existence most readily exactly for producers in favorable, strong situations that are *not* subject to threats of unraveling. Then later such a guild format can be learned about and borrowed by producers in less favorable circumstances.[3]

A complicated set of cultural and organizational arrangements seems to be needed to support a guild discipline, oriented against erosion by defection. On professions as analogues to guilds see Abbott 1988, and on artisan guilds see Baxandall 1980. Each of these authors offers astute analysis—the former more sociological, the latter more economic.[4] The accounts offered by both, working with very different institutional contexts, suggest a strong tendency for a guild to reduce any initial spread of actors on perceived quality into a set more nearly homogeneous.

Underlying the market profile mechanism is quality discrimination, but production will get accomplished even where this production market mechanism is not viable. But the unraveling/guild examples illustrate that even a replacement for the market profile may still focus around quality. The guild reduces and controls quality spread rather than building around it. (For other alternatives see chapters 7 and 11.)

PROBING THE BUYER SIDE

In the social construction of a market profile, a producer's signal is being picked up and interpreted not only by its peers but also by a composite buyer in comparison with like signals from the other producers. Bounded, indeed modest, rationality, together with attentiveness to recent market happenings, suffices for estimating just the market profile $W(y)$ as a schedule guiding choices. Producers could go on to conjecture how various particular buyers do, and would, react to prices and quantities that might be offered by the various producers that some set of buyers sees as competing peers in that industry. This implies that each producer might also be conjecturing as to how the other producers may speculate and act. But producers typically avoid the vertigo of estimating such double contingency under uncertainty as they come instead to refer to a market profile as a pragmatic guide.

The aggregation of buyers is the crucial step for modeling this $W(y)$ market mechanism. This is an issue for the representative firm, since buyers are aggregated for each producer and not just for the market as a whole. This aggregation reflects that producers are turning away from buyers to look at each other in the market as a one-way mirror. So this aggregation is the antipodes of conventional marketing, which concerns breaking down buyers into sets that can be predicted and catered to (compare the survey of price discrimination in Varian 1989).

A professional marketer would focus on individuals as choosers, rather than, as here, aggregating a diverse population of buyers for a market as a social formation that is laced together through all sorts of social networks and cultural influencings that have evolved together over time. The marketer may be skeptical about the $W(y)$ model. Mr. Skeptic may say: "I have an acute sense of the quality of each of the items that I myself possess, but none whatsoever about the volume sold. The new shoes I bought were sold to me by a reputable store that I've patronized in the past. My computer was highly regarded by computer magazines when I bought it years ago. My watch is a Timex and everyone knows that they last forever, and so on. So I cannot be anything but skeptical about any suggestion that there is a causal connection between this quality and the volume of production."

Buyer aggregation need not be at issue even so, however, since many individual buyers will be directly influenced in their evaluations by how common a variety is and hence by its volume of production. What is at issue is the claim that the same index can be used both in C and in S. This does not impute a strong or homogeneous relation between volume of production and the quality that becomes attributed to it by buyers. The claim insists on a monotonic relation, and such is hard to deny.

Computer magazines gave space to evaluating Mr. Skeptic's computer years ago because the volume was big enough to justify it (and perhaps to influence the judgment). Likewise for Timex. His shoe store having a good reputation is all wound up with the volume of customers attracted because of its stocking well-known—and high-volume—shoes. The model passes over the ideas with which a particular buyer justifies his buying in order to summarize effects through diffusion and circulation of endless such ideas and concrete experiences and perceptions around and around through social networks, as in other diffusion processes (Burt 1992).

A scholar of French marketing has proposed a legitimacy theory of marketing that supports the assumptions underlying the approach to quality assessment in the first section (Laufer 1990; Laufer and Paradeise 1990). In contrast to the stance hypothesized for the skeptic, Laufer argues that marketing of products is fundamentally concerned with establishing legitimacy, which comes in the wrapping of an identity. Such legitimacies can best be established for a set, within a field of comparability—in short, in a market of the sort envisaged by the $W(y)$ model.

Related to legitimacy is regulation. The state in various ways can impose product standards that set floors for quality and thus change the mean and range of quality in a changed mix of brands. Oster (1981) analyzes the welfare impacts of such regulation and applies her results to three diverse types of goods and services (mobile homes, auto repair, and credit). There is no consensus among economists, however, on normative approach to quality (see the overview in Terleckyj 1976, 529–75).

Buyers need not concern themselves with the whole schedule of possibilities, with the continuous market profile from which producers chose.

Instead, buyers are concerned with just the set of actual offers from the particular producers. Volume of production y becomes perceived by buyers as how commonly they encounter that producer's variety with its distinctive quality. The outcome will be a nesting of satisfaction schedules in the same order as the cost schedules are nested by perceived quality. Such nesting is consistent with some analyses of cases (see figure 3.3 and specific cases reported in the next section and later).

Theta in equation (2.3) is a satisfaction-per-dollar ratio for the buyers collectively, which is the same across all the producers. The aggregate buyer is accepting the observed commitments as a set of equivalent deals. All buyers get the same deal across different exchanges (Leifer 1985). The practical consequence is that buyers do *not* converge on a single producer, but instead the market reproduces itself across time in this set of differentiated products, with variance across transactions sustaining variance across producers.

Each actor on the producers' side has been assumed to choose a commitment so as to maximize profits. An aggregate yet unorganized buyer side might find it hard to "choose" any particular level of theta, much less to choose theta so as to maximize their net return. But they can certainly boycott buying if theta is such that their net returns are negative. Whether by maneuver or luck, the buyer side may end up exploiting the producers, as they stick to some given $W(y)$. Theta could be renamed the exploitation constant, analogous to k as the historical constant. We return to this in chapters 5 and 12.

Entrepreneurship and Alternative Signals

Entrepreneurs search for advantages from shifts in the underlying footings. These need not be defensive maneuverings as in a guild. They may come from additional investment, weighed in terms of estimated increases in producers' profits over against outlays to improve footing. See Thornton (1999) for a broad survey of literatures on entrepreneurship. Figure 3.3 indicated some predictions of performance according to location in state space that derive from $W(y)$ models, and some such predictions are surely in entrepreneurs' minds.

Options for the actions a producer may take in efforts to change and improve position can be summed up as, or are at least reflected in, change of n. Typically, a program of additional investment in equipment is expected to succeed in shifting the firm to higher perceived quality. So, of course, may increases in advertising, which Chamberlin put in the center of his theory of monopolistic competition—a theme still under active development (see, for example, LeBlanc 1998). The list of particular options worth considering in addition to facilities upgrades is endless: charitable contribution (Mizruchi 1992), prize-winning headquarters design (Larson 1993), and so on.

Shifts on quality indexes are no routinized matter, however, since the root of quality is mutual comparison, in which interpretive moves are perceived relatively and also can be countered. A move to change quality by even one producer will, according to the $W(y)$ model, tend to shift the whole terms of trade for all actors in the market. The task of the analyst thus becomes formidable, as will be explored in later chapters, especially chapter 12.

Light Aircraft Manufacture

We turn now to work out an application with some detail in history and circumstances. We take as a concrete example the manufacture of light aircraft, one of the industries located in the market plane of figure 3.3. In the era before World War II, all sorts of aircraft were being developed, but consistent production initially was confined to the military and airlines. Frank Beech in 1932 created the Staggerwing biplane with an enclosed cabin for use by professionals and business executives, of which the Kansas firm he created was eventually to sell nearly a thousand. The Cessna company was developing smaller planes more for recreational use, to sell in much larger numbers through a larger network of dealers. One could analogize these two to Cadillac and Ford, but it was only after World War II that demarcation lines of an industry came to guide perceptions and choices by producers so that one could hope to code quality indexes and valuation schedules for niches in a market that kept churning out streams of production.

As years pass, technological and social contexts change so that valuation schedules may shift, and new firms enter and old ones perish, all with impacts on individual quality indexes of continuing firms. Piper became important, and by the mid-1960s there were two more producers with market shares of at least a few percent, plus a penumbra of ten others that were included in the light aircraft industry, which was now recognized in the aviation sector by government agency and trade association alike. The four-firm concentration ratio was about 75 percent, not low but by no means extreme.

Applicability of the $W(y)$ model had become plausible, but as a moving target. The airline industry itself was evolving, and its producers had dropped smaller planes, opening up new possibilities for light aircraft to supply planes to air taxi and third-tier airline operations. Beech concentrated more than the others, especially Piper, on two-engine planes. Yet it was the peripheral fringe alone (some producers in Europe) who sought a market in planes for twenty or more passengers; none ever made a profit despite subventions from governments and the like.

The crux is what producers in a market come to cue on, how they choose, not what some journalist or government agency says. Yes, the five or so principal producers sought guidance by watching each other as competitors both on volume in number of units and in price. Yes, cost variability was key to their decisions. Yes, also, there was considerable overlap among their customers, who in any case were obscured by an intervening layer or two of dealers.[5]

So far, so good, but there are difficulties to be discounted. Piper may not neatly fit an intermediate—say, Chrysler—slot; it is hard to know, because the industry believes that Piper extensively discounts its planes "off the books."[6] Although Beech historically concentrated in a high-end segment, it, like the others, had a strong motive to compete across the board of plane types, as the $W(y)$ model requires so that volume flows are comparable across producers.[7] The quarterly production interval assumed for most applications of the model to industry is not appropriate, in particular because Cessna, the largest producer, chooses to produce all of a given model type for the year in a month or so, whereas Beech and others spread production out evenly to reduce inventory cost despite losing some sales through delay in delivery. Each cost schedule can be approximated by a power law, but the underlying bases are distinct, since Beech and others are job shop, customized producers, whereas Cessna and others attempt standardized, mass production.

Some aspects of strategic interaction are clearly being obscured in the model, notably the frequent introduction of variations in product model. Not all owners and managers of firms in any industry will be content to continue operations on the basis of just maintaining their existing position, their quality niche. Some attend also to a longer horizon, to refurbishment and upgrading, as is traced further in chapter 12.

What the model does do is sort out and make approximate predictions for the large array of industries interacting in networks across a production economy. The location assigned to light aircraft (circa 1970) in figure 3.3 derives from approximating available data with the postulated power law schedules. Comparison to figures 3.1 and 3.2 puts this point near an anomalous region, in between TRUST discussed briefly in the previous chapter and a region CROWDED, which is the focus for chapter 7. Subsequent analysis in chapter 9 will suggest some likelihood for an entirely different construal of the industry as being oriented back upstream, perhaps to sources of finance or of technological innovation.

Alternate Signals

Thus far in modeling the production market mechanism, the volume offered by a producer has been taken as itself the signal. But business observation suggests that the signal around which a market profile builds may not be volume per se. Perhaps volume level becomes standardized across firms on bases that are arbitrary and uncorrelated with perceived quality. Some entrepreneur may spot this and seek advantage. Entrepreneurs can lead a switch to another decision variable that comes to be taken seriously also on the other side of the market. In some industrial contexts, research and development may become so predominant as to be taken as a primary signal. In other contexts, such as consumer goods, it might be advertising budget that comes to play this signaling role vis-à-vis large buyers on the other side (see the analysis by LeBlanc 1998). Estimation of saturation parameters, a, b, c, d, would have a different basis, but the same abstract framework of solutions will continue to apply (see summary in figure 2.5).

With signals other than volume the phenomenology is, of course, somewhat different. The perception of volume indeed is ordinarily linked in economic life with perceived quality. Greater volumes do reliably index changes in costs, which makes volume plausible as a signal, just as different quality levels reliably imply distinct costs. But that need not exclude volume's becoming habitualized, in either absolute or market share terms (for example, for the United States see Buzzell and Wiersma 1981; and for the United Kingdom see Hay and Liu 1998). So other ordinary observables can become read as signals of quality that can frame possible terms of trade, a menu of footings for producers. Perhaps even the level of some sort of bribing could come to function as such a market signal, depending on institutional context and on volume commitment having become conventionalized.

It becomes even clearer that the buyer side is evaluating the quality of a given producer from what is seen as an integral commitment, rather than as separate signals for items in some package of varieties accepted as standard for that industrial line of products, such as shoe sizes and colors from last producers. The signal y remains an amount, whose indicator may now be some dollar amount, such as the advertising budget committed for next period. Then the different producers have settled into identities, into different footings by perceived quality. Take the example of advertising as a signal. These footings must be such that, first, their costs are different for achieving the same level of effective publicity for their product commitment. And, second, the downstream public will be valuing the commitment differently corresponding both to that producer's quality and to the exposure level to which the producer commits.

$W(y)$ continues to mean the total revenue received by a producer signaling commitment of strength y. But here, even more clearly than for volume as signal, price (payment per item or unit of volume) is a by-product of, rather than the source of, market equilibration. This is contrary to the rhetoric of neoclassical economics texts. It still is not a matter of clearing the market in terms of average signal but rather an issue of market viability that is settled in terms of signal variability.

Glass Manufacturing

Now let's examine alternate signals from the context of a second specific case. We return to the glass industry, to Corning Glass in particular. Corning has always been at the high-quality end, emphasizing advanced technology for new products and yet highly attentive to judgments of ultimate consumers. The Fiberglas corporation was created as a joint subsidiary with Owens Illinois to sidestep lacks by each in order to establish a niche combining innovative technology with very large volume.

The crux of market signaling is what senders think in terms of, and thence what are available for, viewers. Sheer volume may be most common as signal, but in a world such as Corning's, where as much as 80 percent of the products sold this year may be new (by some criterion, at least technologically distinctive) since five years before, no one product carries enough flow, like the Staggerwing did for the Beechcraft corporation early on, to be an acceptable signal of niche choice. Chamberlin's advertising does not give enough leverage with immediate purchasers to serve. Research and development outlay (R&D) may be the best bet.

What options have Corning people examined as to criteria of strategic choice and thence signal? Turn to a 23-page booklet of May 14, 1981, *Research and Development in Large Manufacturing Corporations*, authored by William H. Armistead, the long-serving executive vice president for research and a contender for chief executive officer. His bottom line—reiterated in talks to industrial associations over the next years

> R&D spending must increase in order to
>> develop superior products
>> improve productivity
>> make our products worldwide competitive again
>> help reduce inflation
> and
>> MAKE MORE PROFIT while doing it

Armistead, a Ph.D. chemist, backed this up with six pages of graphs of company performance in various sectors, accompanied by eight pages of analysis in regression and table. The message is that proportionate expenditure on R&D is extremely highly correlated (rhos of .72 to .99) to sales growth rate in high-technology industries, but not within other industries. And he shows that industries taken as wholes also show high correlation (0.60) with sales growth rate—which suggests self-similarity such that the correlation should also extrapolate back down to the scope of individual product markets within high-tech sectors.

Armistead also shows that conventional measures of innovation such as sheer count of new patents do not correlate as well to sales growth, *except* in sectors of lower technology. This suggests that he sees R&D expenditure itself as the best signal, one he expects and for which he would watch. This is a single officer of a single competitor, but he clearly expects his brief argument to be accessible and convincing to others like himself.

Such examples are treated more systematically in chapters 12 and 13.

Let's turn to a general discussion of entrepreneurship in quality changes. The distinction in investment between outlays for upgrading and for maintenance is itself somewhat fuzzy. One could fold outlays for routine refurbishment into the cost function of a producer, the $C(y, n)$ introduced in chapter 2. But subsequent additional refurbishment may be viewed by producers and customers alike as innovation, which contributes to a shift in the perceived quality index. It is not just detached observers who make this distinction. All this can shift perceptions of a firm's quality, its index value n. Here, this quality is a generic idea applicable to characterize niches for producers whatever the signal used.

One can explore this with the $W(y)$ model. The place to begin is differentials in motivations. Higher motivation comes from more improvement, in volume or earnings, for the same investment. In the $W(y)$ model, where are derivatives of volume or earnings with change in n the highest? This is where to look for the highest investment. The market context—the location in state space—is important, but, depending on that context, derivatives may be high only for some ranges of n. This suggests looking for correlations between close clustering of firms at the top of a market, implying closely packed quality indexes, and particular regions or rays in the state space. Cross-sectional correlations can thus be implied by evolutionary tracks. These themes are developed further in chapters 12 and 13.

~~~~~~~~~~~~~~~~~~~~~~

CHAPTER 5

Signaling and PARADOX

T he original modeling of signaling by Spence and others is shown both to construe market mechanism quite differently and also to induce an additional market half-plane for the present mechanism. That, labeled PARADOX, is hereafter adjoined to the plane of chapter 3 (fig. 5.1). Spence's signaling model for matching pay with personal qualifications treats quality as an inherent attribute, a separate individual ability, rather than one aspect from the interactive construction of a market. We explore this monopsonist formulation of Spence's and then we introduce an alternative form of market molecule for the present mechanism.

The subsequent discussion of other models for the economy suggests still wider applicability for the present mechanism.

THE PARADOX REGION

In some contexts for a market, a negative value of d, the exponent for growth in cost with quality, can be appropriate. Perception of better quality normally is triggered by better processing that also is more expensive processing. So valuation of some industrial product shipment by buyers can be expected to correlate positively with its cost of production, and so d is positive. But that need not be so. Negative d can refer to sorts of goods markets that are *paradoxical* as regards quality.

Such context likely involves some intrinsic feature rather than just attributes of equipment and procedure subject to upgrade. One example would be copper mining, where those with an early, rich strike have not only lower costs for given volume mined but also find their product appraised as purer and more valuable by buyers. So in mining one would expect that the first big strikes for some metal ore will be both richer and less costly to mine than subsequent strikes. Could a $W(y)$ market be sustained nonetheless? If we return to the procedures in chapters 2 and 3, the answer proves to be yes *and* no.

Enlarge the market plane of figure 3.1 to include negative d values, as shown in figure 5.1 Hereafter, label by PARADOX the region of production contexts with $d < 0$.

Examine the right half (to this PARADOX quarter of a whole plane): that is, set $a > c$. So the unit costs of production rise less rapidly with volume

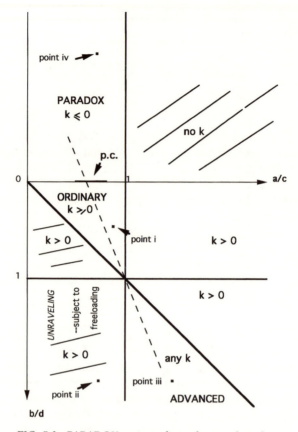

FIG. 5.1. PARADOX region adjoined to market plane

than value perceived by the buyer. In these contexts will the $W(y)$ mechanism yield viable markets?

The tests for viability from chapters 2 and 3 can be adapted here. The
configuration taken, for example, by inequality (2.15) whenever d is negative
is

$$Ky^g[(a/c) - 1]/[(b/d) + (a/c)] < (ad/bc)(-k),\qquad(5.1)$$

where the abbreviations used are those defined in equation (2.11) to yield
the simple expression in equation (2.10). Table 3.2 already includes a panel
for PARADOX. It shows that if $d < 0$, when also $a/c > 1$, one or the other
constraint forbids for any value of k, positive or negative, all values of y. No
market is viable in such contexts. So the right side of the upper half of figure
5.1, with $a/c > 1$, is cross-hatched to indicate that no market profiles can be
viable there: The range of k that satisfies one of the two inequalities (2.15)

and (2.16) does not overlap with the range of k needed to satisfy the other inequality. The first answer is no.

No such blanket exclusion had to hold anywhere in the previous array of contexts, the quarter plane in figures 3.1–3.3, in which, instead, d is positive. But remember from chapter 3 that by no means all these contexts in which d is positive yield viable market profiles. Indeed, formulas for viable profiles, such as the ones illustrated earlier, profiles (i–iii) following equations (2.9–2.12), prove to be *more* varied in the bottom half of the state space, and their layout in state space is more intricate where d is positive. The bottom half of the plane, with d positive, as in figures 3.1–3.3, was split between four other regions, whereas the top half is split only in half.[1]

Now return to PARADOX region, but its left half. Intuitively, it is harder to locate a $W(y)$ signaling curve to accommodate a range of different quality producers, the more nearly their own costs go up right along with the kudos they earn from the buyers. So paradoxical contexts seem to be where mediation by market profile should be *easiest* to achieve.

Take up this left half, $a/c < 1$, still with $d < 0$. Anywhere here, for k less than or equal to zero, the only restraint on y comes from the second inequality (positive profit), and it is that y be greater than a cutoff value

$$y_{\text{pos}} = \{k'\}^{1/g}.$$

By contrast, when you take $k > 0$, still for $a/c < 1$, while all y values do survive the positive constraint, equation (2.16), by the other constraint, inequality (2.15), y must be greater than y_{max}. But this latter inequality implies exposure to unraveling, for firms make money whatever y they choose in this region. Thus, within PARADOX in the market plane of figure 5.1, k is shown as having to be nonpositive to support a viable profile. The formulas in table 3.2 for this left half of PARADOX region are inversions with respect to the formulas already given earlier for ORDINARY region.

Figure 5.2 supplies examples of estimated locations of American industries and thus extends figure 3.3 for the plane half with $d > 0$.

The rays of chapter 3 that indicate lines along which performance in profit stays constant (for $k = 0$) extend across into PARADOX, as was shown in figure 5.1 for one of the illustrative rays in figure 3.2.

Let us explicate how the label *unraveling* from chapter 4 can apply to an example from a PARADOX context where for some historical path settings k there are schedules that satisfy both the positive and the maximal income tests. Market profiles from one of these paradoxical contexts, designated as point iv here and in figure 5.1, are exhibited as figure 5.3. Here each $W(y)$ profile is converted, as before in figure 3.4, to a solution for y versus n. Curves for three values of k are given for this context in PARADOX. These are parallel to figure 3.4, but note that the portions activated in viable profiles no longer correspond to the complete range of output y from zero to infinity as they did in figure 3.4.

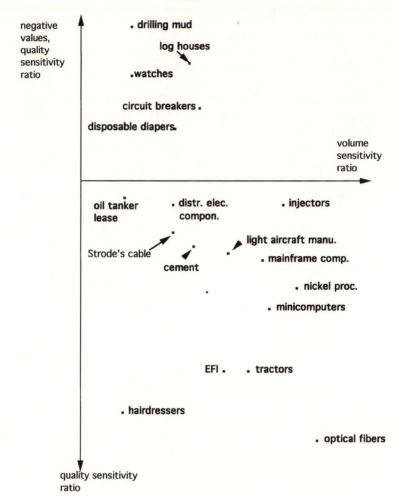

FIG. 5.2. Extension of fig. 3.3 to PARADOX

The upper cross-hatching in figure 5.3 marks the potential solutions $y[n]$ that would yield a negative cash flow, $C > W$. The lower area of cross-hatching marks the region where no proper optimum would be found by the producer with that n and the corresponding $y[n]$. The curve for $k = 0$ lies along a diagonal away from either forbidden region, confirming that zero k is an allowed value in the PARADOX region. Furthermore, one can see from the one curve shown with a negative value of k that any such profile will be viable. At first the one curve shown for a positive value of k seems to imply a viable schedule also.

But it need not be viable. There will be a problem of unraveling, for the

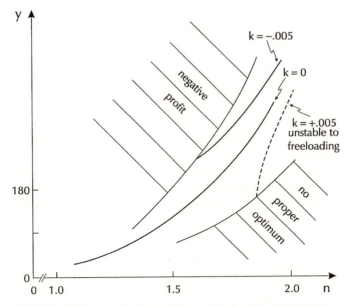

FIG. 5.3. Variation of volume with quality, by k, in PARADOX

circumstances in figure 5.3, when there are producers active whose quality index n values are, in this example, below about 1.8. It can be seen that there are no places for them, no footings along a market profile described with positive value of k, shown by the dotted line. Yet they are way away from circumstances of negative profit. Although net income is not plotted, it turns out to be highest, for all these candidates with quality n below 1.8, at the bottom point on the dotted line, where volume y is about 170. Rather than each finding a distinctive volume-revenue position, a separate footing, and thereby being spread out, they all instead choose the same one extreme solution for the lowest n on that dotted curve.[2] But that same context does support viable schedules when the sign of k is the opposite.

Turning Spence to Social Construction

In the books and articles in which he formulated the signaling mechanism being adapted in the present book, A. Michael Spence (1973, 1974a, 1974b) took labor markets as his central application. Their phenomenology differs from that for production markets, especially as regards signals and their basis in quality and timing. Pursuing the differences will clarify the mechanism for production markets generally and in particular the preceding section on PARADOX as well as the preceding chapter on unraveling and the quality index. My reformulation of Spence's mechanism to apply to the social construction of production markets will be shown to supply also a whole additional half-world of varieties for Spence's application of signaling.

Spence insists that the cost to the producer of emitting a given level of signal *decreases* as quality increases. His "producer" is a potential employee selling his services to an employer who corresponds to our "aggregate buyer" in chapters 2 and 3. Spence takes education as the signal, and he thought it normal for the cost of acquiring a level of education to be lower the higher the (unobservable) quality of the signaler.

The flow being purchased by this employer is productivity of the producer, which will come from some mix between effort and intrinsic attributes (IQ, social facility, whatever). Spence emphasizes the unimportance of whether education achieved does in any real causal sense swell the productivity delivered. Instead of the level of signal, the y measure itself, being a tangible flow, it is, as education, at most an influence on the flow. Education is important in that it is both visible and irrevocable while also correlated with the employer's valuation of that employee.

Expansion of the analysis will be laid out twice. The first is more from my perspective and the second more from Spence's. Following upon that, some roots in theory are traced.[3]

Spence is not distinguishing, as the present model does, between a volume y and its associated quality n such as together shape the valuation placed on the flow in a producer market. Those instead he wraps together into the putative productivity that the employee is expected to deliver, to which the education serving as signal need contribute nothing in fact. That is what frees y in Spence's original version of the model to be the level of education publicly displayed and irrevocably associated with that producer, whereas in Spence's formulation n just by itself becomes the implicit productivity intensity supposedly correlated to y. And correspondingly, of course, Spence's views of time horizon and succession are different, as will be dissected later.

The deeper difference, however, is that Spence treats a market by itself rather than treating it as embedded in a network. Correspondingly, he conceives a very large number of producers spread out along wide swaths of both his education signal y and his productivity index n. Larger sorts of understandings and extrapolation that he thereby misses cannot be made clear until chapters 6–10. Look now just at how it shapes his actual modeling of the market.

Spence is content, given this vision, to prove existence theorems, directions of variation, and the like. He conveys little sense of setting up for fitting to an actual situation. He seeks considerable generality in his description of market context so that these results will have bite despite being rather general and abstract. So Spence does not parameterize, as he would have to in order to cope, as in the present book, with modeling a large number of markets, each small in membership and in continuing network of interaction (see further discussion at the beginning of chapter 8).

The Cobb-Douglas descriptive framing of context chosen in previous chapters is in common use (see the section on econometrics in chapter 11). This framing does fit within the more general stipulations that Spence offers, so that his setting and results can be specialized to Cobb-Douglas. And, conversely, Spence's account of results can be read as a generalization for the PARADOX region of the preceding section, for production markets as well as for his labor market setting. This PARADOX region is adjoined to the market plane henceforth in the present account of production markets. A later section of the chapter will show that signaling models formulated by other microeconomists, that fit within the Spence framing but not the Cobb-Douglas one, obtain solutions resembling those of preceding chapters.

Here comes an irony with two facets. Spence's signaling mechanism works fine, also, for his labor market as well as production market contexts, when the correlation of productivity with signal is positive! Again one finds the whole set of regions of figure 3.5, those for $d > 0$.[4] Spence thus missed the bigger and more varied set of contexts consistent with his model mechanism.

The technical apparatus that is relevant is developed in Spence (1974a, appendix A). Proposition 6 states, "The signaling system is destroyed" if the cross-derivative of cost with y and n is negative, which is in Cobb-Douglas framing to say that $d > 0$. This is wrong, as is obvious from the previous chapters taken as a counterexample.[5] Proposition 6 (Spence 1974a, 124) invokes proposition 1 of the same appendix, but that itself *stipulates* a generalization of $d < 0$. The second facet of the irony is that the error would have been more apparent if Spence were working with explicit parameterization such as is offered by Cobb-Douglas fittings. In the main text of his book, as in the articles, Spence relies on specific numerical or graphical examples. One can see that Spence works below as well as above the level of parameterization such as found in Cobb-Douglas.

And, as stated earlier, pressure for parameterization comes from dealing with a network population of markets. Spence's interest lay in a different direction, as indicated by his subtitle: *Informational Transfer in Hiring and Related Screening Processes*. To a sociologist, this seems like focusing on the spin-off or by-product instead of the causal core. "Information" is nebulous as a concept when extended beyond the technical transmission coding introduced by Claude Shannon. Spence presupposes independent minds as originators rather than by-products from, and brokers for, the interactive social constructions that are seen here as the proper focus (White 1992a). Spence is especially concerned with racial and other group discrimination, and yet Schelling (1978), who was one advisor for the Spence doctoral thesis from which *Market Signaling* derives, modeled (residential) segregation very effectively, around that same time, without hypostatizing information.

Screening is certainly an interesting and important social process. Can that focus by itself explain why Spence was not exercised to override his error and look at positive d? In his chosen region of $d < 0$, the market profile indeed does remain viable even for small values of a, signals of little intrinsic merit, and thus of a/c. The preceding chapter established, however, that in the analogous part of the region with $d > 0$,[6] the market would unravel. But, oddly enough, and perhaps again because of not parameterizing, Spence never notices the possibility of unraveling. Yet table 3.2 shows that unraveling can occur also in PARADOX, the Cobb-Douglas specialization of Spence's chosen domain.

What Spence saw as a cognitive construction has here been refashioned into a social construction of more diversity and wider application, the production market. Like many social constructions it also is smaller in extension and yet also more varied than models such as Spence's posited for a person's thinking. It is a tribute to Spence's own insight in modeling mechanisms that his could be adapted also to contexts so remote from those he envisaged.

The account above derives from the stance of the present book. It is well to go over much the same ground again, but now more from Spence's own perspective. Various labelings could be changed, for a start. It is only for my application to production markets, after all, that Spence's own preferred context seems paradoxical. Conversely, the present formulation shows Spence's mechanism to apply for a whole additional half-world of varieties for d positive, which perhaps deserves a label.

Spence supposes a central intelligence, a monopsonist buyer of labor contemplating a whole spectrum of talent, rather than consumers confronting product differentiation. Spence conceives not of market molecules but rather of market worlds. He focused on big pools of applicants that his model embraced by integrating over a population, for which he hypothesized a continuous distribution over talent, his index n of quality.

Observation and observability of signals in Spence's talent market do resemble those here for production markets, but they are less widely exercised, since not producers, but some hypothetical employer, is doing the observing.

Now consider some particular large market for labor from Spence's perspective. An employer in hiring wishes to assess productivity of candidates. Productivity depends heavily upon talent, but talent is not observable directly or immediately at the time of hire. Such uncertainty will elicit the construction of some sort of institution. This could be a market guided by signaling.

Such a market depends on perception in common by applicants of a schedule of wages that could be expected in response to various signals of talent discerned. Spence focused on managerial labor, and one thinks of a single massive employer as the other side of such a labor market. It might be AT&T developing a schedule of monthly wage offers for new white-collar employees. Its goal is for the productivity of a hire over time to parallel the wages paid. It looks for some reliable signal of productivity.

Spence singled out education, measured, say, in hundreds of months, from among several plausible signals for talent and thence productivity (or in previous notation, n and S). The employer need not believe in some underlying talent n, whether or not indexed as by an IQ measure. To Spence, all that matters is that the signal correlate closely with productivity. Spence's key point is that even though education may contribute little or nothing directly to productivity (as later observed among those actually hired), it still can function effectively as a signal. Previous chapters accept this argument but treat such cases as minor in substantive significance.

The gap between career income being offered and self-expenditure on education is the analogue of profit in the mechanism applied to production markets. Such signals by candidates must be commitments upon which the employer can rely, best when they are already sunk costs. The employer cannot create or shape, but can either veto or accept the candidate. Veto power ensures that each hire offers as good a ratio of signal (and thence productivity) to wage as any other hire. Spence argues that such a signaling market will indeed work when the more talented candidate finds a given level of signal less costly to acquire.

Spence was interested not only in negative correlation between quality and cost but also in signals that have little intrinsic merit. The signal for Spence is not also the measure of production volume and so itself need contribute but little to buyer appreciation. These interests do dovetail, since, according to the previous chapters, model profiles are unstable for pure signals when $d > 0$.[7] Spence also missed the possibility of unraveling, even though this can be shown to occur also in the PARADOX region. Perhaps unraveling takes so long to play out that it seemed inconsequential, given a large pool of candidates. (These various misperceptions' roots in orthodoxy are taken up at this section's end.)

What height and shape of the offer curve (wage versus education) is required such that the feedback is consistent? A person of each productivity must, because of employer pressure, have picked that education level such that the offer curve translates into a wage that is no smaller a ratio to productivity than for any other person. But the candidate will so choose only if at that level of education the general offer curve of wage for education lies highest above the candidate's own curve of costs rising with education level.

Once equilibrium is reached, the employer is confirmed in its reading of each education level chosen as being a reliable index of the productivity level of those who have chosen it, and hence of ability level, which is not directly observed. Each hire, which has signaled with its own education level, proves to have the productivity to justify the publicly known wage offer going for that education. Note that the employer need not and probably does not know the education cost schedules experienced by different candidates, any

more than it has access to some index of true talent. That completes the
basic argument.

Take an example. Suppose that the cost of education for any candidate just
rises proportionate to its length. That cost schedule is just a straight line
(through the origin), and so too is the cost schedule of a more talented
candidate—but with a lower slope. A set of such cost schedules is easily
drawn, with above each an offer curve of wage versus education that will
motivate each of these candidates to choose the education level that will
validate that wage offer by the productivity reflected in its talent. Not only is
the talent unobservable directly but also no one else need know where a
candidate's own cost schedule for education lies.

In what tangible circumstances will such a pool distribute themselves, by
their own self-interested choices, across much or all of the range of education, with the employer getting its same money's worth out of each? Of
course, not every candidate would work out as predicted even when such an
offer schedule confirms itself, nor could any employer validate productivity
for every last employee. Spence's argument was never that AT&T, or any
other employer side, figured out this feedback loop. Nor is skepticism required concerning the intrinsic contribution made by education. One instead
thinks of any observed offer curve as having reached stability through confir-
mation over an extended period of trial and error of all sorts.

The same signaling model might work for some consortium of employers
with different perspectives and motivation. Will their side go beyond insisting on equal payoffs, productivity equaling wages for all employees, to seek
some sort of aggregate optimality? Or conversely, may not the employees
band together as a guild and thus invoke authority to recast their market
position?

One assumes that the answers depend partly on the robustness of the
signaling equilibrium across variations in context. Chapter 4, in turning to
how quality is discriminated in production markets, and chapter 6, in turning to interactions across distinct markets, develop further the social construction implicit in the signaling mechanism invented by Spence, as will the
monopsony section later.

Misperceptions in orthodox economics will be discussed in more detail
below, in chapters 11–14. Here the focus is tracing some distortions in
Spence's work that are linked to orthodox custom as much as to orthodox
doctrine. All five pieces by Spence that I cite from this era (1973, 1974a,
1974b, 1975, and 1981) present models either much more or much less
general than the parametric specification adopted in this book, and thus
more remote both from empirical application and from detailed checks of
consistency.

Any claim of generality becomes nebulous because of lack of grounding in
parameters. Where Spence does adopt the exponential specification (Spence

1974a, 309), he considers only $b = c = 1$, $d = -1$, and then lets a go to zero. In the widely cited first article (Spence 1973), the entire argument is carried with particular graphs and numerical coefficients. And the same is true of the main text of his book.

The philosopher-king syndrome is the complement to the use of general equations. One is encouraged to spend, as Spence does, much effort in assessing putative overall effects on welfare from a set of alternative general mechanisms. Yet there is no attempt to specify the larger setting of other particular markets, as will be done in the following chapters. When Spence seeks closure of his economic system, he resorts to a world consisting of two industries, education or labor and a consumption good produced by labor (1974b, appendix D) or a general equilibrium theory (1974a, appendix F— and see chapters 11 and 15 below). The central difficulty is that orthodoxy leads Spence away from specifying and surveying social constructions.

The derivation of self-confirming shapes for the market profile $W(y)$ in chapter 2 solves the riddle of the mechanism for the production market, which has baffled microeconomics for a century (see last section of chapter 2). Yet the inventor it traces to, the economist Spence, focuses instead on solving riddles of signaling by individuals. Preceding paragraphs reprised several sources of this distortion that are rooted in economic orthodoxy, but unorthodoxy also claimed a toll.

Both orthodox and unorthodox theory leads Spence toward hypothetical and primarily cognitive assessments, and this despite his intended focus on interaction and path-dependence. The wonderful technical power and diverse insights exhibited throughout these five publications are thereby hobbled. Phenomenology is left vague and nebulous, as in Spence's discriminations between "index" and "signal," whose definitions he borrows from a political scientist concerned with a totally different institutional context (Jervis 1970). Spence's discriminations make sense as logic but not as phenomenology in Edmund Husserl's sense.

In the era of civil rights, arbitrary discrimination claimed attention. Spence's applications to discrimination are, however, ad hoc in comparison to his main exposition, wherein the fascination with deceptive manipulation derived from Robert Jervis (1970) and thence Erving Goffman (1969) as well as Thomas Schelling (1978, 1963). Yet, other economists (e.g., Riley 1975) were to point to the strategic interaction being slighted in Spence's book.

I argue here that markets are matters of ecology across populations rather than of threat and bluster among actors. This is not to say some of Spence's diverse and ingenious formulations could not be adapted to, say, coalition formations in Jervis's bailiwick of international relations. Diane Vaughn (1998) investigated the sources and spread of Spence's theory. She verified that the many co-citations of works reflected personal ties (through the Harvard Center for International Affairs and mediated by Thomas Schelling) among Jervis, the sociologist Goffman, and Spence.

Vaughn also makes good use of the unorthodox strands in Spence for her own project in sociological theory. Orthodox economic theory leaves many imprints on Spence's work, but its central impetus is unorthodox. Microeconomics and Industrial Organization theory both suppose that increased quality goes generally with higher cost structure, whereas Spence makes the opposite assumption explicitly, and I am showing how Spence's mechanism can be applied in both cases. In a sense, I rescue Spence's work on markets for economic orthodoxy—even though I replace its view of interaction across a field of markets in subsequent chapters by a social constructionist view based in social role and network theories. *Market Signaling* has many facets not mentioned above and is chock full of interesting ideas, as well as formalisms in the numerous appendices, that call for further application— such as in the next section.

QUALITY BY STREET NUMBER

Formulas and graphs so far have conceived the market as a molecule of a set of member firms that play off each other's positions. The analysis so far has been carried out in terms of a single firm as representative of its members. This device of a floating index permits the researcher to survey individual firm variation within any given market while exploring the market's overall tendencies.

Even the analysis of unraveling in the previous chapter bridges to this floating index, since, although that process involves a whole set of putative producers, it rolls through one additional producer at a time. Firms themselves rely on observations of particular firms that they regard as benchmarks of possible adjustments. Rather than always scanning across all firms in the market, a firm will tend to focus on some one or two firms as representative for possible adjustments of rivalry profile across that market.

Now we turn to entertain additional models of the market that extend those lines further. Consider markets that do not exhibit membership as a partition. This stands quite apart from how many firms there are, and how far spread on some index of quality they lie. Let's turn to a different visualization of markets, one that no longer conceives them as discrete molecules made up of a few firms as atoms. Such a visualization obviously fits also with Spence's view on markets, just treated. Yet the model of the previous chapters remains relevant.

Take a relativized view of the market from the perspective of successive firms in the role of ego. This is by no means a new idea: Chamberlin discussed it in terms of "chain linking" and overlapping market areas (1962, 103–4); and see chapter 7 of the *Handbook* cited earlier (Schmalensee and

Willig 1989). The point is that the $W(y)$ model can be adapted to this view and also fit with quality regimes as envisaged in the economics-of-convention paradigm treated at the end of chapter 7. Indeed, fuzzing the boundaries of markets may fit the presuppositions of the latter paradigm better.

Geographic dispersion is one major basis of such nonmolecular markets. (For an economic survey of such dispersion see Eaton and Lipsey 1989. For recent sociological case studies see Haveman and Nonnemaker 1996 and Baum and Mezias 1992).

Marina and Gambling Industries

A colorful exemplar is the development of the Las Vegas Strip of enormous casinos in the Nevada desert.[8] An initial cluster of casinos from the 1940s along Las Vegas Boulevard was followed by successive foundings of additional casinos reaching further and further along this boulevard, decade by decade, but now outside the older center of town. These casinos also then fill in holes along the arc of the Strip, which in width reaches out only as far as the adjacent boulevards paralleling Las Vegas Boulevard. The Strip, thus, is a literal, physical model for an array of producers by quality n in a service industry. (This exemplar is developed further at the end of the next chapter.)

Let us next discuss in some detail the market in services provided by marinas to boat-users. Whether along an ocean coastline or along a river, marinas are bound to be arrayed along a geographical curve of distance. Much the same would be true of fast-food stops along a highway, or of stores of a given sort along a city road, as long ago emphasized by Hotelling (1927) in a seminal article.

The basic issue goes beyond interpretation of some quality index to assessment of the kind of entity the production market must be—whether it derives from boundaries rather than throwing up boundaries (cf. Abbott 1995). Competition continues as a driving force, as in interpretations from both orthodox and institutionalist economics. But this is so only as competition embeds into some larger context that is confusing and frightening enough to induce exactly the protective yet still competitive huddling among peers that is parsed as the crucial dynamics in the production market.

Perhaps much the same $W(y)$ model can continue to apply, even to markets that are not discrete molecules. So let us reconceive the model. Let the value of n for ego be unity and apply it to the marina example. All other marinas then have smaller values of n. As they stretch away in both directions from the ego marina, they are perceived as having higher cost structures because of their greater distance from ego's customers, greater both in travel costs and in the shift of prevailing conditions, tide, littoral, and the like. Yet, at the same time, these more remote marinas are less attractive to the customers calibrated around ego marina. Only a $W(y)$ market model taken from the PARADOX region could apply. The ego firm is always the top-quality firm, and yet its costs for a given service offered are lower: $d < 0$.

Construe the buying side as also being arrayed in location parallel to the marina processor side, such that customers in Maine would have no impact on marinas in New Jersey, and vice versa, but Connecticut marinas compete with Rhode Island ones in the affections of sailors around that corner of New England. A fixed number of nearby marinas can be included in the $W(y)$ calculations, but it is a sliding bracket around the ego marina. The $W(y)$ model no longer concerns a separate molecule of atoms, but rather a neighborhood in a very long linear molecule—exactly the definition of a polymer molecule (de Gennes 1979). The notion of boundary fuzzes over, however, so that there are no clear analogues to the market aggregates defined as in equations (3.21–3.23) and elaborated in chapter 7.

OTHER NEW MICROECONOMICS

The second section of this chapter traced the $W(y)$ mechanism back to Spence's work, and chapter 2 grounded it in work by a number of earlier economists. Chapter 2 explained how $W(y)$ profiles can supplant the price-quantity planes portrayed in microeconomic textbooks (e.g. Mansfield 1975; Henderson and Quandt 1980). The market space replaces their cumbersome, and hypothetical, sets of schedules of supply and demand. Other work by microeconomists besides Spence also challenges textbook microeconomics, and the 1980 contribution by Krugman discussed in chapter 3 joins the Spence book in showing the interpenetration of macroeconomics and microeconomics.

The important commonality between $W(y)$ and many other newer economic models is that there is a tangible mechanism in procedures of observation and inference, operational for the market. For example, Winter and Phelps (1970) conceive firms as individual observers, scientists really, who for guidance examine changes in sales achieved by various changes in their own prices over time.

Often missing in even the new microeconomic work, however, is recognition of distinct levels of actor such as to constitute nested network populations and any attempt at modeling of interaction across them. But more than half a century ago, Edwin Chamberlin, in his theory of monopolistic competition, was recognizing distinct levels of actor in complex fields of interaction, cultural as much as economic. His work primarily focused on the buyer interface, while at the same time Joan Robinson developed a differentiated product view of the producer side. Microeconomic theory has been unable effectively to pursue their lead to new economics; so the impetus has passed to business economists, who call more and more insistently for a theoretical framing that can support their investigations (see the discussion, in chapter

14, of work by Michael Porter, who is a coauthor of several studies with Spence).

New microeconomic modeling can contribute to extending the present $W(y)$ model in regard to its particular Cobb-Douglas functional forms for cost and evaluation schedules. Akerlof's version of signaling (1976) was contemporaneous with the Spence job-market model described earlier in this chapter. Difficulty of working conditions replaces education as the signal y. Akerlof uses additive rather than multiplicative functional forms (see his section 3). Convert to $W(y)$ notation:

$$C(y, n) = y + q_1(y - n)^2; \qquad (5.2)$$

$$S(y, n) = r_1 y + r_2 n, \qquad (5.3)$$

with r_1, r_2, and q being positive constants. Note that neither C nor S goes to zero when y does. And note that, as in the $W(y)$ model, the relative levels of y and n interact in effect on C. The employer derives value both from the ability of the employee and from the employee's working in difficult circumstances. The employee's pain or cost goes up with difficulty, of course, but increases by extra amounts according to how much that difficulty deviates from the level comfortable at that quality.

An equilibrium schedule must be of the form

$$W(y) = k \exp\{-(2q_1/r_2)y\} + (r_1 + r_2)y - r_2(r_1 + r_2 - 1)/2q_1, (5.4)$$

where k is the constant of integration, so that

$$n = y_W[n] - (r_1 + r_2 - 1)/2 q_1 + (k/r_2) \exp\{-(2q_1/r_2)y_W[n]\}. \quad (5.5)$$

This solution by Akerlof can be shown to parallel that in earlier chapters.

The Corner Constraint (against unraveling) excludes positive values for k. Figure 5.4 reports my solution for the particular context with $r_1 = 1$, $r_2 = 2$, and $q_1 = 3/8$. One can see by inspection that this solution closely parallels that I reported in figure 5.3 for a point in the PARADOX region (although, of course, the numerical values of k are, except for $k = 0$, very different from those identifying parallel profiles in figure 5.3). PARADOX is what one must expect, since work with a given level of difficulty is less costly to a higher-ability employee, who is closer to his or her comfortable level.

Rothschild and Stiglitz (1976) proposed, also in that era, a theory of insurance markets that is akin to Spence's signaling theory: "What is required is that individuals with different risk properties differ in some characteristic that can be linked with the purchase of insurance and that, somehow, insurance firms discover this link. . . . The argument hinges on one crucial assumption . . . customers purchase but a single insurance contract" (640–41). Again let's set up an analogy to the $W(y)$ model: Persons are the "producers." The face amounts of the policies people are seeking to instate are the $W(y)$,

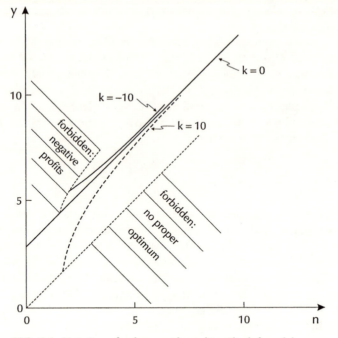

FIG. 5.4. Variation of volume with quality, Akerlof model

with y measuring the reciprocal stream of premiums from persons who form that set of given quality.

A particular value on the quality index n is a given degree of avoidance of causes of the event being insured against. The $C(y, n)$ dollarizes the level of anxiety/cost for that set of persons. $C(y, n)$ will, of course, go up as y goes up, and by a factor that will tend to decrease (on social class grounds) as avoidance level goes up. The buyers, here insurance companies en masse, will naturally evaluate a contract as more desirable when the avoidance level goes up, by a factor that will increase as the premium level goes up. So it is worth exploring such insurance markets with a $W(y)$ model, expected to be of the PARADOX variety. The main point here is that these authors, like Akerlof, get results parallel to $W(y)$ from quite different functional forms.

These two contributions, along with Spence's and others such as Rosen's (1974), remain scattered islands, however, which do not reshape micro-economics as coherent theory. The embedding space for $W(y)$ markets is, to be sure, less general, formally, than the families of functions that are presupposed in microeconomics theory. But it is also terser in practice, closer to business viewpoints, and yet has a generalizability absent from special cases such as Akerlof's above. The $W(y)$ model seeks the middle ground between formal generality and illustrative anecdote.

Another new development in economics has been a turn toward biological evolutionary models as guide, often coupled with simulation analyses to handle nonlinear and dynamic aspects, sometimes of microeconomic problems. This turn reappears in chapter 11 (see discussion of Flaherty 1980), and in chapter 12 around multidivisional firms, and then is pursued in some detail in chapters 13 and 14.

Niche Plane for Monopsonist Subcontracting

A producer market is not static, it is a social construction rather than some component in a mechanical system or electronic gear. The model should accommodate various sorts of realignments in profile and setting, including reversion to putting-out or other contractual nexus, whether these result from deliberate intervention or as happenstance. This section explores alternatives to producer markets in controlling network flows of production. It turns to one generalization beyond the market profile mechanism, along lines suggested by the preceding account of Spence's labor market signaling, which shows that mechanisms other than market profile can mediate the processes of valuation and flow. Subcontractor and monopsonist will be the roles invoked. Monopsony can be seen as an opt-out from market profile that inverts the guild opt-outs surveyed in chapter 4.

One can think of the market plane as a niche plane, in which each niche for a market is specified on two dimensions: the ratios of dispersions in valuation on the two sides of the interface, one for volume y (or other signal), a/c, and the other for quality n (in a rank order), b/d. But more is needed to describe where niches come from. Reciprocal chains of flows, of valuation in return for service, reach through market interfaces in production networks. So these parameters a, b, c, d must somehow be characterizing the upstream and downstream network context of the market and its firms, right along with characterizing the behavioral profiles and cost functions that are affected by the insides of the firms.

The parameters are going beyond describing the insides of a market as free-standing structure, to incorporate influences of geography, technology, and the like. Thus, networks of ties among firms and markets must be important mediators of these parameters, and we will later, in chapter 8, even be able to derive some estimates of parameters from such influences. So, indeed, niche is label for a complex nexus of constructs.

But much the same network statements can be made regarding putting-out and various other brokering arrangements in production flows. Williamson (1975) has emphasized this from the beginning of his markets and hierarchies work. So we seek a way to construe an environment for contracting, and in particular monopsony. We will seek to do so in terms of a niche plane that can characterize monopsonies, a monopsony plane. To make it comparable to the market plane, we will need, even though values on n do not appear directly in the market plane, somehow to compare contracting arrangements with the market interface according to the quality of the product.

It is well to build up this search slowly, a step at a time, and without attempting proofs. The aim is a comparison of different institutions, but only a limited range is included here. (For further detail consult White 1978, 1979 and see the section on exploitation in chapter 12).

At any given time, some lines of business will operate along networks of habitual transactions in a contracting mode, as suggested already in chapter 1. Consider some entrepreneur who is contracting out production to an accustomed set of suppliers upstream and then selling to accustomed buyers downstream. He may construct a table of the costs he expects to pay according to volume delivered from that given supplier. This he can match to some table of revenue that he would count on receiving downstream, corresponding to various volumes produced using shipments from his suppliers.

Let's simplify further to derive from such homely tables explicit formulas that are simple enough to permit tracing complex chains of action and feedback. Assume the following simple power laws:

Let cost be proportional to volume y raised to a power, c.

And let the sales revenue S expected be proportional to y when now raised to the power a.

If the exponent c is unity, direct costs are constant across all volumes of production that could be chosen. But this is unlikely, given effects of fatigue and since the equipment must have capacity limits. Similarly, having $a = 1$—that is, constant price received at whatever the volume shipped— seems unlikely. Possible placements of the goods by the downstream purchasers may well saturate ($a < 1$), but also sometimes, if these goods "catch on" with buyers at large, a given volume will just whet appetite for still more, and thus willingness to up prices ($a > 1$). Even with such simple approximations, the array of possible outcomes is complex.

To a first approximation, the entrepreneur will encourage the volume of production from the supplier that maximizes the revenue received net of paying the cost for those supplies, borne by that supplier directly or in contributions by the entrepreneur. Thus, the choice will tend to be of the volume y that maximizes the gap between sales revenue S and cost C. This occurs only when their slopes are equal, when

$$aS/y = cC/y, \tag{5.6}$$

if such volume y can be found. At this optimum, the ratio of revenue to cost will be

$$S/C = c/a, \tag{5.7}$$

so that operating profit

$$(S - C)/C = (c - a)/a. \tag{5.8}$$

One seeks to interpret such a ratio as specifying a niche for that supplier in transactions mediated by the entrepreneur. This ratio on the right side of equation (5.7) is just the inverse of the ratio discovered to be the horizontal dimension of the market plane of figures 3.1 or figure 5.1. So far, so good. But unlike in figure 3.1 the ratio a/c in this contractor application must be capped at unity.

For c less than a, equation (5.7) does not locate maximum but instead minimum profit. Only when the buyers' saturability, a, for this supplier's goods is less than the proportionate rate c at which its cost grows with volume, only then will this equation identify an optimum volume. Small c and large a, by contrast, mean booming demand coupled with economies of scale in production. The rub is that the entrepreneur would lose his role in such a situation. The intermediary would be knocked aside, there being no need for his guidance in judicious choice of volume to which to commit, since the more volume, the more profit.

But the entrepreneur does find a role. She is locating not one but rather a number of producers each of whose volumes she is handling for distribution across her whole set of accustomed buyers. Monopsony is one formulation of this entrepreneur's subcontracting.

In some actual case, historical or current, this may be as far as the analysis can go. The entrepreneur may rock along with whatever set of suppliers is at hand so long as he or she does not lose money on transactions for a given supplier. One can hardly speak of a niche being supplied to a given supplier by the entrepreneur's tying it into sales downstream by some arbitrary agreement.

But, being the sole customer, the monopsonist is more concerned than customers generally with the continuance, the future of its suppliers. The monopsonist, not just the producers, is in a role of commitments. The parties will seek out some way to continue in what thereby becomes a recognized line of business.

The central issue facing the entrepreneur is establishing some sort of comparability among these suppliers from his role as stand-in for the subsequent buyers. It is likely that these suppliers will be similar in scale and scope, as well as in geographic locale. Quality gets evoked in such a situation as a key social construction.

The entrepreneur's different suppliers will experience different cost tables, and these differences are likely to become coordinated over time to differences in buyers' attraction to their goods. Quality perceived will, naturally, show up in valuations by these buyers, which have been reflected in this entrepreneur's tables of S, a table for each supplier. Undoubtedly, quality will also be reflected in the various cost tables.

Let us reify quality as an index variable denoted by n, which will index the proportionality in S. It will also index the proportionality in cost C, but not in the same way. Suppose that, analogous to the formulas in y, the impact of quality on valuations is the index n raised to some exponent. So let

$$S = ry^a n^b \tag{5.9}$$

and

$$C = qy^c n^d, \tag{5.10}$$

where r and q just calibrate the curves.

We are brought back to equations (3.2) and (3.1), but now without any such figures as 1.2 and 2.6, as yet, and without any reference to a $W(y)$ profile or market! Instead, the mechanism is an entrepreneur as monopsonist who orchestrates the set of producer firms. But the setting does correspond to that for a production market: Just take the "aggregate buyer" as being literally a single massive buyer, as supposed by Spence in his job-signaling model. In short, equate this entrepreneur to a monopsonist.

Given this context as further specified in equations (5.9, 5.10), what terms of trade will be established? Will they be determinate enough, as $W(y)$ is, so that one can discriminate between and thus identify niches? These are the questions. The monopsonist may, after estimating a demand profile S for each producer, seek to maximize its own net revenue across them. Perhaps there is a solution of some determinacy. Let's work on this by means of a tangible illustration.

General Motors

The example will be General Motors in its heyday. Consider its procurement of a specialized good from a set of completely dedicated suppliers, subcontractors. Let it be specialty fabrics for interiors that are suitable only for GM cars. A comparable example would be a construction firm such as Brown and Root for a massive project, a turnkey project built on some greenfield, that draws on all subcontractors in some isolated region.

The situation is complex (it will be pursued with further tools in the exploitation section of chapter 12), and one need not expect a unique, determinate answer.

1. GM perhaps could adapt a passive, disaggregated stance. It could simulate outcomes from the $W(y)$ mechanism by insisting only on equally good deals. The solution in previous chapters would then apply, corresponding to the market plane. But this is not plausible, in particular as to interpretation of the historical constant k, and as to whether GM would ever concede even implicitly that its schedule S was such that $a > c$.

2. Or GM could explain to each producer its estimate of that producer's S schedule and then say it would pay some large, fixed percentage of that, and leave it to each producer to choose the volume it thought optimal for itself.
3. More likely, GM could choose to announce an explicit offer schedule, replacing the trial-and-error $W(y)$ of the previous sections. It can be to the advantage of GM to offer a $W(y)$ schedule, whether or not it has the information and administrative capacity to instead negotiate pay on the basis of valuations $S(y, n)$ for each individual producer. The administrative task is lighter, and the value it receives can be as least as high a ratio to expenditure.

In its prime era, GM could successfully ordain such a schedule. The producers—small, specialized subcontractors—would continue to choose volumes of production to optimize their net incomes. They would know neither GM's assessment of their quality nor GM's own valuation functions, although some observer could, and perhaps GM itself would, construe them in terms such as the $S(y, n)$.

4. This combines (1) with (3). The market profile offered, $W(y)$, is at the discretion of GM. There is no role for a historical constant k dependent on path. But GM could (if it read this book!) choose to simulate any such $W(y)$. So k can now be seen as a control parameter (Bryson and Ho 1969) that is available to GM. The task is to see what GM might choose as a value for k, and with what impact on GM and on its suppliers. This solution will be useful at least to calibrate other strategies GM considers.

GM might choose any of several criteria to guide strategy. Suppose the criterion it chooses is to maximize net income to itself. The net income to GM is simply $S - W$. Equations (3.20) and (3.23) apply here. Since the ratio S/W is defined as theta, net income can be rewritten as $(theta - 1)W$. So now θ can be interpreted as a profitability ratio. Straightforward calculation will show that this ratio is maximized for GM when it chooses the value

$$\theta_{\max} = (c - a)/a. \tag{5.11}$$

However, the maximum is on a rather flat curve, so net income to GM is rather insensitive to the exact value of theta in this neighborhood.

Now use option 4 to calibrate the result. This is best done for an explicit example, because it requires considering the array of qualities over the producers involved. Turn to the situation just discussed and portrayed in figure 5.3, from the PARADOX region favored by Spence. There was shown to be a problem of unraveling for that context, and negative values of k, if low-quality firms were present. Here, the monopsonist is in control, so that is no problem.

The issue is what offer schedule will be optimal, and for whom. The offer schedule is expressed without reference to the unobservable quality n, of course, but it can be transposed into a corresponding curve on the plane of y versus n. Straightforward, albeit tedious, calculations will show that the curve corresponding to $k = 0$ has desirable properties for the monopsonist.

Let us sum up. It can be shown to be advantageous for the monopsonist as well as each subcontractor to let each of these producers choose its y so as to maximize its own benefit given the S schedule revealed to it. This was GM's approach 2. The other approaches can yield solutions close to, but dominated by, this one.

The monopsony arrangement, grown out of contracting-out, thus yields well-defined outcomes. The varieties of monopsonist arrangement can be portrayed on a plane parallel to the market plane. Subcontracting can ape the market.

Its niche space is shown in figure 5.5. The dimensions are the ratios used in the market plane. The phenomenologies are different, of course, but the parameters specify contexts in similar fashion. The monopsony can reproduce itself for every position in niche space with $c > a$, but for no other position.

In contrast, viabilities of $W(y)$ markets are as shown in figures 3.1 and 5.1.

The niche space thus is more general than any particular mechanism. It can be called an interaction context space. But outcomes will differ between mechanisms. Even where monopsony and $W(y)$ mechanisms both are viable in the same location, their dependent outcomes may be different. The *monopsony operating profit* (see equation (3.22)) is the ratio

$$(W - C)/C = (c - a)/a. \tag{5.12}$$

It should be contrasted with the corresponding ratio given earlier for the $W(y)$ model by equation (3.26), which reduces to (5.12) only when b is zero. This latter ratio not only holds for any particular member firm, but also, in the special case corresponding to historical constant k being zero, it holds for the ratio of market aggregates.

Let us now turn from ratios to the size of revenue. For the subcontracting situation, revenue is S, which in effect has become the market schedule W. Follow the calibration procedure introduced in chapter 3, where each revenue is referred to that of a base firm in the market, at the given location in *abcd* plane. The striking fact is that these equations (3.8–3.9) continue to hold. Thus, the *same quality discount factor* from equations (3.10, 3.11), n^{de}, as well as the same niche space are applicable. This is true even though the $W(y)$ mechanism is being replaced by another. (Many other alternatives besides this monopsonist-subcontracting mechanism also yield such parallelism.)

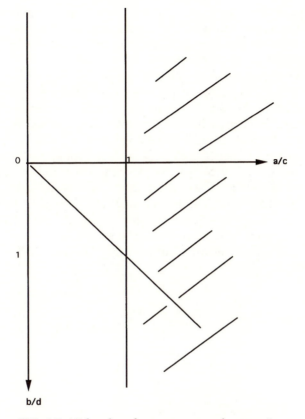

FIG. 5.5. Niche plane for monopsony subcontracting

What *does* change is the meaning of the discount exponent, $d\varepsilon$, which for the market is seen by inspection to be just the reciprocal of the operating profit, equation (3.26). This operating profit rate for subcontracting, however, formula (5.12), is quite unlike the reciprocal of the discount factor ε, which it equals only in the special case where $(b/d) = 0$.

The impact of the $W(y)$ mechanism can now be seen in the contrast between *abcd* planes, figure 5.1 versus figure 5.5. For monopsony subcontracting, the whole band of points with $a < c$, and *only* those, yield viable situations, whereas for the $W(y)$ mechanism, the trapezoid below the diagonal through $(0, 0)$ and $(1, 1)$ yields markets vulnerable to unraveling. On the other hand, the $W(y)$ mechanism can offer (see chapter 7) viable markets in the whole region with

$$a > c \text{ (and } d > 0). \tag{5.13}$$

Increasing returns to scale are not a barrier to a viable market. One sees that the point $(1, 1)$ indeed does serve as the key pivot point for changes in a market form of $W(y)$. Yet there is an underlying core of similarity between these two mechanisms, market and contracting, which accounts for their parallelism in niche space and in discounting revenue by quality index. Both pump production along networks of social relations.

The principal parameters are those specifying the niche space. Specifications of these parameters for context thus derive from networks of business relationships for market profiles as much as they do for monopsony contractors. But there are other parameters. The calibration parameters of valuation scale, q and r, may be common across a whole sector of markets, however, and need not derive directly from local network configurations and perceptions, and they should be comparable between market and monopsony.

The historical constant k and the trade-off measure theta are contingent measures that reflect maneuvers and manipulations in ongoing processes that have no direct analogue in this monopsony-subcontracting mechanism. They may well be affected by network context, but they are not fixed by it. The number of producers, similarly, is an outcome of historical origin subject to path of maneuvers.

PART

Markets Compete, Too

The first two chapters of this part situate the market cross-stream. Chapter 6 studies interactive substitution between markets in parallel positions within the network system of generalized exchange, each market offering niches to the differentiated producers within it who transact upstream and downstream. In chapter 7, the plane map from chapter 3 is seen to be just one of a sheaf of parallel maps that can be laid out along a third dimension of substitutability. Together these two chapters establish the molecular nature of the market as an actor distinct in level from its differentiated set of constituent firms.

Chapter 7 both extends and fills out the findings of previous chapters. It goes on to trace the close correspondence between present findings and those of the French economics of convention. Then in chapter 8 formulas are developed that guide fittings of index values and parameters from observed outcomes in particular markets. Chapter 8 also derives predictions for values of two key parameters from their network contexts.

~~~~~~~~~~~~~~~~~

CHAPTER 6

Substitutability Extended

T he end of chapter 3 summed up the basic market model and pointed to chapter 4 on quality discrimination and vulnerability to unraveling. Chapter 5 then noticed paradoxical extensions of quality orderings. Now we look at competitive rather than complementary relations with other markets, cross-stream rather than along the streams.

The first section presents a case study of the evolution of a set of industrial markets in perceptions of the participants. It reminds us that real markets usually come with parallels to others within a sector of their own, and it examines the subtleties of boundaries for markets. It returns to the use of "folk lenses."

The chapter then examines spread and density in quality locations, which may affect efforts to shift them. This leads into a more general notion of substitutability. This is a substitutability that has obverse facets, within a market and vis-à-vis other markets. The bulk of the chapter models this substitutability with some care, tracing out the feedback loop from firm to market sizes. It ends in Las Vegas.

BOUNDARIES: PORAC'S CASE STUDY OF THE SCOTTISH KNITWEAR INDUSTRY

Our underlying claim is that each industry is a set of producers that have come to treat each other and to be treated by the outside world as structurally equivalent through the evolution of input and output networks of ties. This hypothesis should be tested directly. Models for such evolutions of multiple networks are becoming available in anthropology and sociology. The ways that particular sets of producers coalesced into distinct markets can be inferred from data on previous flows among all producers by the use of network algorithms that output possible partitions, each into sets of structural equivalence and of role equivalence.[1] In addition, one can scan histories and quiz present participants as to how they perceive and conceive their markets.

Attention should be paid to the intersubjective basis of the boundaries of these socially constructed markets. Knowing oneself, and being known, to be in a given market is the single most important aspect of getting established in business. Porac and Rosa (1996), psychologists in a business school, give a theoretical overview of how cognition and perception figure in the embedding of firms into production markets, and Porac with coauthors presents convincing empirical studies (e.g. Porac and Thomas 1994).

They thus extend the social construction approach adopted in $W(y)$ modeling. A whole tradition in economic sociology, clustering around work of Granovetter (1985) and Lindenberg (1995, 1996), centers on issues of framing in perception and cognition from the perspective of social interaction and thus touches both $W(y)$ and Porac approaches. All these authors are examining construction of cultural patterns, while also aiming at making explicit predictions and testing their hypotheses.

Regardless of intersubjective basis, these boundaries of socially constructed markets become hegemonic social facts. Private as well as public collections of data tend to respect these boundaries. Maneuvers and strategy bear them in mind.

It should be no surprise that the finer levels of census coding are regarded as confidential. Just a few firms are included in a production market, and this comes close to industries defined at the fifth and finer level of the SIC code. Thus, one can infer performance measures for particular firms from public data at that level. Firms are sensitive to relative performance figures that industry participants exhibit, even aside from the data's effect on stock prices. These firms are rival siblings within a molecular family.

Porac and his colleagues (1995) conducted an extensive field, questionnaire, and archival study of the Scottish knitwear industry, which produces about a quarter of the total British output. They brought a $W(y)$ perspective to bear on this material and discriminated a considerable number of separate markets within this regional textile sector as well as describing some representative firms. The sector's sense of identity had led it to commission a monograph (Gulvin 1984) that traces the sector through three centuries and offers reliable, detailed data covering the last hundred years.[2]

Porac's team noticed several sorts of signal, but its main focus was membership, not operations: the question is who rather than how. They probed managerial perceptions and argued persuasively that, whatever the social realization of markets, cognitive categorization processes must be involved. Their analysis provides a way to heed Paul DiMaggio's calls (1992, 1997) for again folding node attributes into network analyses and for extending relational analyses to encompass cognitive mechanisms. Porac and his colleagues find quality to be central.

Until 1850 high-quality woolen stockings were the main product of the Scottish sector, but then there was a switch to high-quality woolen underwear, products that are long-lived and fashion-conscious. By 1900, millions of items were being produced by firms with multiple products, including shirts, vests, pants, dresses, body belts, underwear, and hose—altogether 58 distinct. Just one of these clusters, hose for women, boasted 27 different sizes, each in 13 gauges of cloth. Soon after 1900 came in outerwear, which today is the primary signification of knitwear—as jerseys, sweaters, shawls, cardigans, made mostly on so-called hand-knitting machines.

What markets in Scottish knitwear gain recognition and become institutionalized at different eras? Certainly, there was a high degree of competition among manufacturers as well as fierce tussles with retailers, solo and chain, over control of product differentiation through brand names and the like. Firms developed particular footings, just as the Scottish industry as a whole developed a distinctive place within U.K. textile industries. Mass production had come in during the 1800s with power equipment imported from France and Belgium, especially the circular needle frame. But mass production settled in England, leaving what was called the "fully fashioned" wear to the Scottish industry. After 1914, William Cotten's frame machine increased production by a factor of twenty. There continued an inflow of small new firms using hand frame techniques, but these increasingly were operated along factory lines.

Such is the complex and confusing maze in which participants typically must settle on market identities. Porac and his colleagues provide one path:

> Market boundaries are socially constructed around a collective cognitive model that summarizes typical organization forms within an industry. This model is produced when firms observe each other's actions and define unique product positions in relation to each other. . . . At this microscopic level, ecological and transactional definitions of competition fail because they disregard the constitutive role of the managerial mind in making markets. . . . The boundaries of markets are thus ambiguous and must be inferred. . . . At the collective level, shared definitions of rivals stabilize the boundaries of a market and allow firms and customers to coordinate decision (Porac et al. 1995, 203–5).

The Scottish knitwear evidence could also be construed with more attention to very small firms and how they can be fit, fuzzily, into an industry construct. This latter is the approach of Lazerson (summary in Swedberg 1994) to the knitwear industry in Modena, Italy, which has fewer large firms than the Scottish industry does. The knitwear findings remind us that history is woven in actions, many of which not only do not conform to but instead attempt to break or revise preset patterns. Entrepreneurship and agency influence arrays on quality.

The $W(y)$ approach emphasizes discrete molecules of a few relatively large producers, although the previous chapter briefly discusses long linear molecules with a floating ego. The Porac team goes on to argue for a model that is a cross between molecular and floating ego. From twenty-odd preliminary interviews with managing directors, they constructed a detailed questionnaire answered by managers of nearly 100 of the total population of 262 firms with which they started. On average, managers cited 3.3 rivals among the other firms in their sample.

Managers in their answers were especially concerned with the kind of production and related organizational form. The Porac team combined these answers with data on firm sizes and the like to infer from a combination of data analyses who was in what markets and how these were connected in the perceptions of managers. Six production markets were discriminated.

These six were validated by a blockmodel analysis (Wasserman and Faust 1995) that examined the density and the symmetry of perceived competitive relations. These are ties of attention rather than the usual sociometric ties of affect. The Porac team found evidence for hierarchization in cognitive schemes and for some hierarchization in attention given between the six markets (see fig. 6.1). Only one of the six markets identified lacked a heavy concentration of attention ties among its own members: This one, presumably, would not operate through a market profile.

The Porac approach can be viewed as expanding the definition of social network tie to include cognitive perceptions. Focusings of attention establish which firms cluster together as competitive molecules. This can be accompanied with a further partial ordering in ties of attention between markets, which correlate with degree of similarity in production methods and, possibly, customer profile.

Fully modeling the operations of these Scottish knitwear markets undoubtedly will require a sophisticated approach, with special emphasis on interactions among historical measures k and theta. It also requires focus on substitutability among markets, which leads to the introduction of a new parameter, gamma, in this chapter; see also the PIMS section of chapter 12. But each market in the Porac study is less sharply bounded than is supposed by the $W(y)$ mechanism, and so its substitutabilities with other such markets may be difficult to approximate with a single parameter such as this gamma.

Quality Spread within a Market

There is a tension in the $W(y)$ model between the array—the linear order of quality—among members of a market and the seemingly arbitrary bounds on exactly who is a member in that market. This bounding has been referred to the accidents of participation in the formation of that market Substitutability within a market shades into substitutability between markets. We begin, in the present section, with further examination of the former.

No profile could get established if too many firms were jockeying for position or if the firms were too far apart in quality. This has just been illustrated in the historically based modeling by Porac et al. (1995). The numerical examples in the appendix tables already presuppose a small number of firms. They are not spread out much on quality index. Each ranges between an arbitrary upper bound of $n = 2$ and an arbitrary minimum quality bound of $n = 1$, as discussed in the first section of chapter 8. But no evidence has

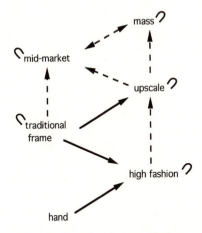

Code: dotted arrow for weak, solid for strong tie;
arrow from originator; loop for self-choice;
6 labels of markets from Porac et. al. 1995

FIG. 6.1. Partial ordering of knitwear
production markets (Based on data
analysis in Porac et al. 1995, table 4
and appendix)

been given as to what the maximum spreads of volume and revenue would
be that could be managed effectively by the perceptual apparatus guiding the
various firms' decisions on offers.

What are the feasible spreads of n? How might these depend on values of
other parameters, and the reverse? Let's begin with how far away from its two
neighbors on quality a producer must be to sustain a distinct footing. This
will depend in part on issues of sensory perception and cognition. But it
depends in part on the cultural regime that has grown up in that industry
around quality and its distinctions. (Four specific regimes will be discussed
under the economics of convention at the end of the next chapter, and then
estimation formulas are derived in chapter 8.)

Spread in quality must relate to the total number of member firms. But the
distribution need not be uniform in spacings. Subgroupings of product
might get institutionalized, such as high-line, middling, and low-line. (There
is a related literature on strategic groups within industry; see Oster 1982).

Let's explore an extreme case of coincidence of quality locations. Consider
some market with a given set of producer firms and estimate the valuation
by buyers in aggregate of the product flow from each firm by valuation
schedules keyed to their distinct quality indexes. As an example take the
market for earthmoving equipment of one type produced by an American

industry with several firms, all large. Now suppose that these valuations by the aggregated buyer side in the United States would not change even when new producers entered the scene. This could be when an equal number of Japanese manufacturers enter this market.

Assume that all these new entries introduced just this same one type of earthmover. Suppose the Japanese firms are ranked with respect to each other in quality much as the American ones are. Further assume that the buyers in aggregate do not discriminate Japanese from American on the quality index n for that type of product. A little thought will show that the effects of such an enlargement can be captured with exactly the same $W(y)$ model as before, except for recalibration of the scale constant q.

Even if new firms are able essentially to duplicate an existing variety of the product, heretofore obtained from an established producer, it is true that the buyer may still care about auxiliary aspects—familiarity and service—so the valuation function would not apply to a new producer. But suppose the given valuation functions $S(y, n)$ for an industry do *not* change upon the intrusion of new individual producing firms. For simplicity, assume an extreme case in which each firm that offers a given quality level n is duplicated, or otherwise multiplied in number (or even halved), without any change in the aggregate buyer valuation $S(y, n)$ for that quality good as a function of the total volume of it on offer to the aggregate buyer. Let the number of producers, then, be multiplied by copycats of each existing firm entering the market to duplicate the capabilities, both in quality and in cost structure, of each existing firm. Suppose the new number of firms with each given value of the index n is z.

Then each firm will face the same situation as the original firm of that n, except for having to split up the revenue $W(y[n])$ between all z of them. Suppose the revenue is split equally among the z. Each firm's choice of volume will continue to be for maximizing excess of revenue over cost. The cost function $C(y, n)$ is unchanged, by hypothesis; the perceived revenue is obtained by dividing $W(y)$ by z.

From the aggregate buyers' point of view, however, the whole $W(y)$ is still being paid to producers of that quality n, so in equation (3.4) the $W(y[n])$ is unchanged. Thus, the trick to an easy solution is to multiply the equation for producer's optimum through by z, and then incorporate this z into a new *substitution*

$$q \to q', \tag{6.1}$$

where $q' = (q \cdot z)$. The mathematical convenience is great: $W(y[n])$ can continue to designate the total revenue paid out to all z firms with that quality n. Thus the solutions from earlier carry through, but with q replaced by its multiple q'. The tests of profile viability stated in chapters 2 and 3 are unaffected, as is the test for unraveling in chapter 4: In equation (2.9), just replace q with q'. In many cases, imports entered on a domestic market by foreign firms may bring with them little additional buyer interest, so the effects of their introduction can be modeled as above (compare with analyses in Bhagwati 1965; Krugman 1989).

THE TWO FACES OF SUBSTITUTABILITY

To compute aggregate production, one must take up the whole set of firms at once and allow for substitutability. Substitutability among the differentiated products was already implicit in equation (2.2), the formula for buyer-side satisfaction as a valuation that is dependent on both the volume and the quality of that product. It is because of this substitutability—its inner face within the market—that the sizes of outputs of the various producers (under the guise of representative producer) are constrained to follow one of the derived market profiles. So, even on this first level, volumes of different firms do influence one another across their whole array on quality within that production market. Each firm's choices depends on those made by the other firms.

Chapter 4 discussed the whole array of qualities, but that had been bypassed in chapters 2 and 3 through the use of the device of a representative firm. In those early chapters, only the relative shape of the market profile was predicted. Establishing an absolute scale for the market profile predicted by the model does, however, require explicit computation across the whole set of particular quality indexes for the firms of a given market.

These computations across a discrete set can be even more complex than integrations over continuous distributions (such as for the Gini indexes in chapter 3). The path dependence indexed by the historical constant k for the profile is one reason for this computational complexity, as will become evident in later sections. This constant can take any of a range of values without disturbing the equivalence of offers by producers as assessed by buyers' satisfaction. Although chapter 3 did develop explicit formulas for calibrating sizes across all firms in a market, in terms just of their qualities relative to some one base firm's, those formulas only hold for one path, $k = 0$.

The main reason for the complexity, of course, is that we have to allow for substitutability of one firm's product for another's when assessing the aggregate production that will be placed with buyers. In the model as developed thus far, commitments by individual producers optimize their respective profits within the frame of the particular $W(y)$ offer curve accepted downstream. The set of commitments along such a curve is veto-proof vis-à-vis the buyer side. But surely in fact the resulting total package of products from that market was only accepted according to assessments by buyers that were affected by the sheer number and sizes of the producers in that market.

The $W(y)$ model has each producer's output determined from the aggre-

gate output together with the array of spacings on quality, so there is a
feedback loop between firms' outputs and market aggregate. Thus emerges a
first specific difficulty of allowing for feedback in dealing with the complexities from substitutabilities. Since these latter are reflections from the satisfaction of the buyer side, feedback also shifts the formula for the ratio of satisfaction to payment. So breaking into the feedback loop also involves a
second specific difficulty from having to gauge buyer power vis-à-vis producers' interests, within the given market.

There is a second level of substitutability, an outer face. Surely the total
package of products from that market was in fact accepted by the buyer side
only over against commitments offered in other markets, notably those in the
same industrial sector. All these distinct markets did coagulate out with some
degree of substitutability in use between the set of outputs from one market
and those from other markets. We must broaden our attention to embrace
substitution among some set of industries that are parallel with respect to
upstream suppliers and to downstream purchasers (chapter 9 will develop
this further).

Buyers certainly do view transactions with one firm as substitutable to
some degree with transactions with other producers in that industry. One
builder may buy a great deal of unseasoned lumber instead of a lesser
amount of lumber from a higher-quality supplier. Yet substitutability extends
also between distinct markets, as when a builder refrains from purchase of
any (or some) lumber and instead substitutes procurements from manufacturers of canvas or concrete or plastic.

Substitutability is, in short, an issue not only within a market but also
between markets, especially those that share similar, structurally equivalent
locations in the networks of a production economy. This chapter thus looks
beyond the single market, even when taken together with its upstream and
downstream setting, toward influences among markets that are in similar
locations within the flow networks. Substitutability will be seen to be a root
also of buyer power not only over differentiation of products within a market, but also over relative sizes of nearby markets.

To recap, spread in quality frames substitutabilities between producers in a
market and thereby affects the revenue each achieves, calibrated by the locations of all firms on the quality index within that market. Goods from one
market also are exposed to substitutions from products of other markets so
that there is feedback between market aggregate and individual firm sizes
additional to that among firm sizes that has already been modeled through
the market profile. This chapter extends the $W(y)$ model accordingly.

Substitutability Parameter and Buyer Power

This section will specify indirect interactions among markets that are cousins
within a sector, neither buyers nor suppliers to each other, but instead paral-

lel. The focus in previous chapters has been on differentiation between producers as supported by buyers' actions when taken in aggregate. Even then, there was a major omission. The formula for the valuation by composite buyer of the volume committed by a given producer, equation (2.2), treats each producer as entirely separate.

This was inadequate for the two reasons laid out in the previous section. First, surely buyer valuation of one producer's package should be contingent on the packages being committed by the other producers in the market. And second, surely the overall valuation of these various commitments taken from that market as a whole must be influenced by what is available from other markets.

A simple device can deal, approximately, with both inadequacies. Let us introduce a single substitutability parameter for industry and designate this parameter as gamma.

A single parameter makes intuitive sense. Think about possible entry of a new firm into a market. That will bring a measure of crowding to the existing market as a new partial substitute to existing products or services is added. But now suppose that same firm instead becomes a new entrant to an industry making cognate products in the same sector. Surely there will be some commonality between the substitutability effects.

On one level, an estimate is needed for how much some product from one firm gets substituted for product from another. This substitution must be at some discount implied by how far apart their market footings are spaced. But on a second level that market as a whole is to some degree substitutable for another. Each industry is just a social construction, whose membership is just one alternative among many others that were possible. Thus, each market was constrained by concurrent emergence of other industries. It follows that there must be some interaction, some degree of substitutability between output from the given industry and other industries in similar locations across various production streams. This is a second level of substitutability, across a sector whose boundaries become recognized from where substitutability is falling off.

The simplest possible representation of these two levels in substitutability is used in the $W(y)$ models. Specifically, the buyer side's valuation of each producer's output is nested within an overall valuation of these separate valuations, a superaggregate for that market as a whole. The constituent valuations continue to be designated by the $S(y, n)$ from formula (S) at the beginning of chapter 2. The *superaggregation* will be designated by V, which will replace the simple sum in equation (3.24). That equation is transformed:

$$V = [\Sigma(\text{over each } n)S(y, n)]^{\gamma}. \qquad (6.2)$$

This reduces, when the exponent gamma, γ, is unity, to the previous simple sum in (3.23) over the substitutability schedules given by equation (2.2).

The substitutability parameter was implicit in earlier chapters at its baseline level of unity. No additional parameter will be introduced in portraying the second level, external substitutability. Our claim is that substitutabilities between distinct markets can be approximated as the obverse of the intra-market substitutability, but note that markets are *not* arrayed along any index of quality.

The more similar the product ranges of two industries, the greater the substitutability of one for the other. This translates into gamma being further below the value of unity that implies minimal substitutability with products from other industries. But notice, further, that the value of gamma affects the valuation of each separate producer's commitment. Gamma approaches unity as substitutability becomes complete. This is where the market is no longer distinctive as a whole, no longer has identity in contrast with other markets. So the $W(y)$ modeling results thus far may overestimate how attractive buyers in aggregate found any given producer's commitment to be.

Surely most of this aggregate substitutability will be with respect to markets in the same sector, with similar products or services. This is substitutability with other markets that are cousins within the same sector to which a given market is subject. There will be little or no substitutability with industries that are downstream or upstream from the given one. Thus substitutability can be seen as evoking and covering only a genre of products for other parallel industries. Such a common genre is ceded to all producers in a sector as an aspect of their membership in markets within that sector.

So gamma, γ, is the exponent power—normally less than unity—by which is discounted the sum of the evaluations of individual producers by the buyers. Thus, γ designates the parameter that approximates overall substitutability in the evaluation (aggregated from downstream) of one market's products against those from all other markets. Gamma can be seen as a cruder approximation for market level of the picture of interactive substitutability of firms obtained from a given market's profile. Gamma is analogous in part to the parameter a. But gamma folds in a second facet, being also analogous to n^b except that the distinct actors (now markets) are being taken as being equal rather than ordered by quality. This is discussed again around pure competition in chapter 11, which will reexamine economists' notion of "pure competition" as an extreme of substitutability, in order to yield a new perspective on pure competition as an ideal type. Mainly, though, gamma is sui generis as a statement of the degree of irreplaceability of a given market taken as a whole.

*Feedback between Profile and Aggregate Production

Feedback can be seen from earlier chapters to depend on a trade-off level between buyers' satisfaction and what they pay, designated as theta. It was specified already in equation (2.3). Only profiles with theta greater than unity were viable. With gamma introducing flexibility in the degree of substitutability (internal and external), theta must be generalized.

This section introduces an aggregate trade-off level, labeled *tau*, which becomes equal to theta when the substitutability parameter gamma is set to unity as in chapters 1–3. Profiles are viable only for this tau above a cutoff. (Chapter 8 will assess the consistency among this growing array of parameters.) Like gamma, tau should be regarded as a historical constant.

Exactly how market aggregates in revenue and volume will be affected by substitutability through feedback is not obvious. It will be affected by opposing pressures from buying and selling sides. Each $W(y)$ rivalry profile is shaped by the constraints exerted by buyers upon optimizations by the market's constituent producers. The resulting individual footings for firms will prove to depend upon the aggregate size of market revenue from that profile, which reflects buyer pressure.

Being constrained within the trade-offs implied by that rivalry profile, optimizations by individual producers leave them subject to some potential of exploitation as a group by the downstream buyer side. The buyers accept or reject the producers' commitments, rather than determining them, so the buyers do not exert control over the respective profits of individual producers, but they can, by veto, exert pressure on the overall balance.

The buyers are treated in aggregate, and a measure of balance for them is the ratio of total aggregate valuation V received by all buyers (see equation (6.2)) divided by the sum of all their payments to producers, which is aggregate market revenue W. *Designate this ratio as tau.* The defining equation is

$$\tau = V/W. \tag{6.3}$$

A larger ratio correlates with greater exploitation by buyer side, and tau must be greater than unity for buyers not to balk:

$$\tau > 1.$$

Designate tau equaling unity as the *break-even value* for buyers.

The aggregate revenue that buyers collectively are paying out can be seen, alternatively, as the aggregate costs of these same actors when seen, from further downstream, as producers. This aggregate cost C, defined in equation (3.21), is not computed or even known by any one producer, unlike its own cost. Yet the firms in an industry may develop some sense of its level and use that as a baseline for guildlike protective efforts: They may try in concert to drive down the margins of those upstream from whom they are buying. Indeed, that is one scenario for a possible switch in market orientation, which is introduced in chapter 9 and examined further in chapters 12 and 13.

The degree of balance is influenced by feedback through substitution, such as was traced in the preceding section, and therefore depends on the value of γ. For example, gamma greater than unity would suggest demand so explosive as to preclude effective substitution from other markets' producers. Large gamma thus should militate against high tau, against any exploitation of the given market's producers by their buyers in aggregate. There can be dynamics in the reverse direction for high substitutability (low gamma) where buyer counterpressure, when somehow aggregated effectively, will increase tau.

Buyer pressure was initially expressed in equation (2.3) in terms of a different parameter, theta, called there the deal ratio. In chapter 2 theta equaled the ratio of V to W, since with gamma unity these aggregations (6.2) and (3.24) are both linear so that one can just sum the equations (2.3) for different n to obtain the equivalent of equation (6.3). This changes once substitutability (of degree other than unity) is introduced. Then one derives from equation (6.3)

$$V^{1/\gamma} = \theta W. \tag{6.4}$$

It follows that the mapping between tau and theta is

$$\tau = \theta^{\gamma}/W^{(1-\gamma)/\gamma}, \tag{6.5}$$

and reciprocally,

$$\theta = (\tau W^{1-\gamma})^{/\gamma}. \tag{6.6}$$

This last equation makes aggregation problematic. The aggregate revenue W is just the sum of the revenues for firms, to be computed for each firm from equation (2.9) for the rivalry profile. But this equation, as well as equation (3.2) for the $y[n]$ of that firm, depends on θ. And now equation (6.6) shows that θ itself depends on W, which depends on θ—thus a feedback loop is set up in the calculation.

Market aggregate revenue W is the sum of the contribution from each firm, equation (3.20). To compute each $W(y[n])$ requires a specification of the y yielded by each n. But, in general, one cannot solve equation (3.2) to obtain an explicit formula for $y[n]$ to substitute into equation (2.9). Thus, resolving the feedback loop generally requires extensive numerical calculation, for which, as laid out in subsequent sections, computer programs (described in the appendix) are essential.

Again the special case of $k = 0$ permits explicit solution and so offers guidance. With $k = 0$, equation (3.4) becomes, after substitution from equation (3.3),

$$W = [r/q^{a/c}(W^{(1-\gamma)/\gamma})\tau^{1/\gamma}]^{c/(c-a)}$$
$$\{(1 - [ad/cb])/[1 - (d/b)]\}^{a/(c-a)} \cdot [\Sigma n^{(bc-ad)/(c-a)}]. \tag{6.7}$$

One derives an equation between W, on the left-hand side and, on the right, an expression involving the constant **tau**, but also a function of W itself; namely,

$$W^{(1-\gamma)/\gamma}.$$

Feedback appears as nonlinearity, but one can now disentangle it.

All the terms in W can be gathered by themselves on the left side of the equation. Then, by taking the root, one finds:

$$W_0 = \{(r/\tau^{1/\gamma}q^{a/c}) \cdot \left[\frac{(b/d) - (a/c)}{(b/d) - 1}\right]^{a/c}\}^{\gamma/(1-(a\gamma/c))}$$

$$\cdot \{[\Sigma \; n^{(bc-ad)/(c-a)}]^{1-(a/c)}\}^{\gamma/(1-(a\gamma/c))}. \tag{6.8}$$

This equation will be a key guide to subsequent analyses. To repeat, W is subscripted with 0 as reminder that the formula applies only when $k = 0$. In the special case of breakeven for the aggregate buyer, then this **tau**, τ, the industry deal criterion for buyer side, is unity and therefore can be ignored.

The feedback conundrum, thus, is mixed up with a substantive issue, namely, the power of the buyer side of the market. Let **tau** be fixed according to pressures and opportunities for the aggregate buyer in the larger surrounding context of industries. Then, by inversion, theta becomes a known function of W together with this constant **tau**. This function is expressed purely in terms of gamma (see equation (6.6)), so the latter, a parameter for aggregates, is joined with an aggregate to supply a criterion for application *within* the market. Thus, gamma supplies the missing link in a feedback loop that reaches from market aggregates back to their insides, that is, to the profile as the micromechanism of the market.

Interpreting Feedback Formulas

Deriving these formulas that relate tau and gamma and market aggregates just begins the explanation of feedback. The measure theta was defined in terms of individual producers (see equation (2.3)), but it is now seen to have some bearing on the overall balance between the two aggregate sides of that market. Feedback interaction surely must be specified between theta and the total revenue size reached by all producers in the market taken together.

The definitions of **tau** and theta can be shown to be mutually consistent in substantive terms as follows. Derive the valuation by the aggregate buyer of a *particular* producer's flow $y[n]$ in terms of the *change* in total valuation V when that producer is removed. Calculation yields for this change the following approximation:

$$\{change \; in \; V\} = \gamma S(y[n]; \; n)/V^{(1-\gamma)/\gamma}. \tag{6.9}$$

But then requiring the ratio of this {change in V} to $W(y[n])$ to be the same for every n just yields exactly equation (2.3) for theta all over again, since the multiplier drops out as being the same for each constituent flow:

$$\text{multiplier} = \gamma/V^{(1-\gamma)/\gamma}. \qquad (6.10)$$

What these last two equations are saying is that when a firm leaves the market, the loss of market size is just from its S if gamma is unity, but if gamma is less than unity, the market will not shrink by that much. Turn back to the two equations (6.5, 6.6) resulting from feedback reciprocity between tau and theta. Examine from equation (6.10) what happens when *tau is set to the break-even point*, $\tau = 1$. The value of theta for this borderline of break-even for the buyers slides along with the aggregate size of market W. Only when gamma is also unity will break-even theta take the value unity. The point is that theta, though useful and interpretable, should not be seen as a parameter.

This also says that theta is not an independent measure, such as the historical path measure k. But tau is indeed to be regarded as an independent measure. It may not be under the control of either side. It is a second historical constant.

Only in the special (and important) case when gamma is unity does tau reduce to equality with the deal criterion theta. Theta is consistent with tau, but only as a dependent outcome. The measures of the buyers' perspective that have been substituted for theta, namely gamma and **tau**, are both more transparent than theta and closer to recognized market measures.

The deal criterion for the aggregated buyer, tau, plays a role for the aggregated buying side of the market of a given industry that parallels, in part, the role of cash flow, $W - C$, for individual producers. As an illustration, consider the experience of a typical consumer who, in a concrete transaction, lays out dollars and receives value in return. The consumer feels fully satisfied insofar as tau is high, but as tau sinks toward unity he might feel that capitalism needs a shot in the arm and/or that competition sooner or later will force producers to deliver more value for the money. The intensity of these feelings in a typical consumer would shift according to the average degree of substitutability reflected in the value of gamma.

The feedback difficulty was not just a technical one. Substantively, it reflects the passivity of the buyer role within the model for the market mechanism. Within an industry, the market profile has the producers shaping choices by choosing volumes, with the buyers being confined to a yea-or-nay role. In the model as developed thus far, buyers appear to have been given short shrift, but this reflects that commitments are required in production and these are in the hands of producer firms.

As seen in a longer time frame and larger context, the buyer side seeks effects on terms of trade and aggregate sizes beyond mere acceptance or rejection of an individual deal. Acceptance by the buyer side of a given production market, and thus the deal criterion, should reflect perspectives that include whole other industries, those from which possible substitute products could be bought. So the overall levels reached in the terms of trade that result from a market profile will reflect tuggings back and forth across industries in their trial-and-error searches that establish the aggregate size of the market for each given industry. This is to say that aggregation of terms of trade from profile in one market interacts with aggregations in other markets. That is what the gamma parameter is concerned with, together with the reciprocal buyer pressure summarized as tau.

Further scrutiny of aggregation for the buyer side will also deepen understanding of the feedback loop. The aggregate valuation **V** must reflect some combination of the various satisfaction schedules $S(y, n)$ for that industry, but these evaluations of separate flows from various producers in a market should interact in forming the overall evaluation **V**. (Indeed the nonlinearity of any one $S(y, n)$ in the size of flow volume is an analogue on a smaller scale.)

In general, this valuation by the buyer side collectively of a set of flows from some given producers will be altered, even lowered, when an additional set of flows from yet other producers come to get accommodated into terms of trade for the market of that industry. Although interactions through substitution may be very complex in detail, a main effect can be approximated by treating the separate flows homogeneously, by transforming them to valuations, magnitudes that are interchangeable and hence can sum directly.

For $\gamma < 1$, valuation **V** per unit will decrease as further product flows from the given industry (as weighted in S) are added in. In this context, the valuation **V** of all the flows together, by the ensemble of buyers, which is calibrated in monetary units, increases *less* than proportionately when each of the uncalibrated valuations S for separate producers is increased by the same multiple. The approximation lies in having this substitutability not vary with respect to various particular products within the industry, and also not vary according to which other industries afford substitutes. (And, indeed, one assumes that gamma will be much the same when one of these other parallel industries of the same sector is taken as the focus.)

Evaluations concerning other industries thus play into this determination of **V**. The size of gamma reflects the substitutability of products from other industries for products of the given industry. As gamma rises, the composite buyer becomes increasingly dependent on the goods of the focal production market, whereas for gamma falling, the buyer side sees the output of comparable markets as increasingly viable substitutes. These cross-influences are made fungible by monetarization. An industry ignores this at its peril, as, for example, the U.S. steel industry discovered repeatedly with respect to substitutions of plastics and other metals for steel in products at times of steel price hikes (Scherer 1970, chap. 8).

LAS VEGAS PARADIGM

An extended, yet figurative, example will be a vehicle for an updated review of $W(y)$ modeling. We may reframe and summarize the mechanism using a gambling industry as illustrar. Such a different context can highlight assumptions made in modeling that are as yet implicit, and it can illustrate variation in modes of signaling as well. It also, of course, suggests possibilities for wider application of the $W(y)$ model.

The Las Vegas gambling industry was introduced in the middle section of chapter 5. The original hard-core gambling casinos for males were followed by an explosion into glittering casinos featuring top-line show-business acts. These attracted huge middle-class clientele, which in earlier decades were adults only but then increasingly included whole families. In the 1990s boom, the Strip spun again far out into the desert with new, elite casinos combined with education programs for executives and the like.

Let gamblers be the producer firms. Endless rivalries among pairs of them are transformed into a duel of each with the gambling house in some games requiring skill. The individual house is now taken as the market, rather than being a producer firm as in the previous chapter's section on the Las Vegas Strip.

The muscle for the house, its dealers, corresponds to the aggregate buyer in the $W(y)$ model. The y is the level of gambling presence chosen by the gambler, his or her number of hours at the tables coupled with his or her level of bets. Each gambler sees the house as offering a profile of trade-offs— the $W(y)$—observed across the presences adopted by fellow gamblers. $W(y)$ becomes the money winnings paid by the house through dealers to the gambler committing to y. $W(y)$ and the various y's both are observed and discussed by other gamblers.

A cost schedule $C(y)$ reports a gambler's monetarized perception of the negative impact from gambling with volume y. And each viability inequality (chap. 2) states a restriction from the self-interest of a representative producer-gambler in its search for an optimal result from his impersonal duel over a period with the house. The house values these gambling commitments differently according to commitment size y, estimated as a schedule $S(y)$. Only a certain shape of profile can validate itself in the criteria both of gamblers and of the house.

The house dealers have varying predilections for and success with different gamblers, so that the house overall values differently a given gambling volume for different gamblers. Skill, corresponding to quality n, varies across gamblers and is the major correlate to dealer success with them and hence to the house valuation, now marked as $S(y, n)$. The house cannot force commitment levels on gamblers, but it will insist on getting as good a trade-off of S for V from gamblers of all skills. But the skill of a gambler is unknown and unlikely to be easily measurable by anyone; so reliance has to be on inference from signaling by the gambler identifying him- or herself by choice of y.

How good a deal is acceptable to one house can differ from the level of deal imposed by another house: This corresponds to variation in payoff ratio tau held to by the aggregate buyer in the $W(y)$ model. One house can differ from another not only in tau but more generally. Differences between industrial markets in producer firms and products correspond to differences between houses in the sort of gamblers they attract with their sort of gambling.

What can one expect for parameter values? Both C and S go up as gambler exposure y goes up, of course, so that c and a are both positive. If wagers are, on average, higher per hour at a table for higher y, then a may be well over unity, but if, on the contrary, tapped-out gamblers in the regime of this house bet less and less intensely the more of their time they spend at the table, then exponent a may be less than unity. But the house is concerned both with aura and with filling the house, which are aspects of receiving more than it pays out in winnings W, and these concerns also would be reflected in and shift the size of the exponent a. It might seem that the cost to each gambler will just go up linearly with length of exposure, $c = 1$, but, as just argued from the house's perspective, the average size of bets need not be linear in the y measure.

And cost schedule C for Las Vegas includes, besides money bet, costs of stay—and, possibly, depending on the perspective of the given gamblers, the opportunity cost of alternative business use of that time. After adding these in, one would expect $c > 1$. But then there is also the Las Vegas institution of courtesy suites (not to mention meals and drinks) being allocated preferentially according to gambling presence y. That suggests the possibility of c instead being below unity, but it need not affect house perception of payoff ratio theta from that gambler, since the house considers its set of suites a fixed cost of doing business. As always, parameter estimation must be keyed to particular context as well as to history.

What about effects of skill, reflected in parameters b and d for S and C, respectively? The (unobservable) parameter b is less than zero, since skilled gamblers lose less to the house for a given exposure level, whereas in industry the higher-quality producer delivers more value to the aggregate buyer. The personal cost to the gambler of exposure level y would seem to show just the converse effect: increasing skill lowers cost, as reflected in a negative value for d: This would translate into positive ratio b/d and thus exclude the PARADOX region.[3] And yet PARADOX is not excluded, for one could suppose that inept gamblers bet more impulsively and foolishly relative to ept gamblers the longer is the exposure y committed to, which could shift d from negative to positive.

As to gamma, the substitutability parameter, Las Vegas stands out. Let's now shift point of view back to the casino, not the gambler, as the producer. Las Vegas gambling as a whole has had enormous success in multiplying the size of its markets, both in persons and in cash flow, by orders of magnitude. This counteracted any tendency for the interpolation of new firms (casinos) at much the same quality level to decrease aggregate revenues when the customer base was unchanged. Such a decrease would ordinarily be expected, according to equation (6.8), failing an increase in customer base to go with the growth in the number of producers; the next chapter will examine this again.

Finally, according to the $W(y)$ mechanism the market profile is path dependent: At a given season or year, play at a house has evolved to generate any one of a package of viable trade-off profiles, whose size corresponds to the range in the $W(y)$ model of k, the measure of local history. One can think of k as a marker for the tacit rules of poker that vary across house and time, for example. If the parameters put a house in the UNRAVELING region, or if the particular profile for a k value is subject to unraveling, gamblers could have a motivation, as can the house, to restrict the skill level of players allowed in, so as to avoid unraveling. If the context fits a CROWDED niche such as introduced in the next chapter, general discouraging of new gamblers could ensue.

Conversely, the gambling context can suggest extensions and variants to the general model, just as different specifications of the C and S schedules were offered in the sections of the previous chapter on new economics (e.g., in equations (5.4, 5.5)). It can also suggest new ways of viewing phenomenology of signaling and of quality. Zelizer (1989, 1993, 1998) develops a general idea of multiple moneys, of which gambling furnishes an illustration. Zelizer emphasizes distinctions between the economy and other institutional contexts where moneys are used, such as for charity or for life insurance, but her arguments, with some adaptations, apply within business as well. Money flows have different significations and effectiveness in the steel industry, say, than in the movie or gambling industries.

CHAPTER 7

~~~~~~~~~~~~~~~

Market Space:
CROWDED and EXPLOSIVE Regions

Analysis of feedback has led to formulas for aggregate size both of firms and of the market. These are to be interpreted in terms of all the relevant parameters. The substitutability parameter, gamma, γ, requires generalizing the market plane of chapter 3 for market contexts to a market space.

A CROWDED region of each market plane will be identified where the aggregate market size is shown to *decrease* with addition of further producers (and with $k = 0$). This region is defined by certain combinations of substitutability degree, measured by the parameter gamma, with volume saturations, that is, with levels of a/c.

Market concentrations and also aggregate sizes are to be assessed. Numerical computations are usually required.

A section will then recap predictions developed from the market mechanisms as social constructions. Chapter 7 concludes by bringing together the results of chapters 2–7 in order to trace the close correspondence between the present findings and those of the French economics-of-convention school.

GAMMA AS A DIMENSION

Gamma approaches unity as substitutability becomes complete. This is where the market is no longer distinctive as a whole, no longer has an identity in contrast with other markets. Gamma other than unity for a $W(y)$ market does not imply any internal discounting within that market of the attractiveness of one producer's shipment flow vis-à-vis those of its peers. Instead, there is some disciplining of aggregate supply by overall demand applied across all firms. But this must somehow find expression within the microdiscipline of producers filling footings in a tangible $W(y)$ schedule of revenue versus volumes shipped (these latter being taken as stand-ins for quality).

The key approximation is thus twofold: Subsumed within gamma is the substitutability of the given industry vis-à-vis all other (even distant) industries, taken overall; and each of its firms' valuations S is equally subject to this external substitutability. The previous chapters, in disregarding this second level, this external substitutability, must be seen as having assigned to gamma the value of unity.

Although as a parameter gamma refers to larger scale, it combines mathematically in schedules and outcome formulas with the microsaturation parameters: a, b, c, d.

Thus, gamma provides a third, independent dimension for a market space: the market plane generalized by specifying external substitutability. For each given value of gamma, there is a whole plane like figure 3.1 or 5.1. The market space as previously shown in these figures can now be visualized as but one sheet in a sheaf, one sheet for each value of gamma. On each sheet *only* this one new independent parameter gamma, which identifies the larger context, need be specified in order to check the viability of markets with those combinations of parameters. (No constraints on viability depend on values of r and q.)

This sheaf of state planes can be treated as a cube. Turn to figure 7.1, which defines another genre of state space, a plane section taken through the cube at some fixed value of b/d. This is a plane with a/c as one axis, but with 1/gamma as the other axis.

Figure 7.1 is thus a cross section taken through a sheaf of the market planes of figures 3.1 or 3.5 as extended in figure 5.1 to include PARADOX, $d < 0$. Now turn to figure 7.2, which repeats the original plane state space from figure 5.1, but now with figure 7.1 projected onto it by specifying a break on the a/c axis.

CROWDED AND EXPLOSIVE REGIONS

The experience of being crowded goes together with being substitutable, as when one refers to the fast crowd or the techie crowd. Crowding can apply both across producers within a given market and across distinct markets that are in structurally equivalent positions, which is to say, within a layer.

One region in the substitutability plane of figure 7.1 is designated CROWDED; it was included in the overall region labeled ADVANCED in figure 5.1 and has also been labeled in figure 7.2. Of this region, with parameter boundary

$$1 < a/c < b/d,$$

CROWDED is seen to be the part subject also to the constraint

$$a/c < 1/\gamma. \tag{7.1}$$

For the varieties of markets that have this combination, aggregate market size decreases as more firms are added. This is true even though each new firm is construed as bringing along its own additional demand $S(y, n)$. It is an outcome of the feedback loop from chapter 6 in operation.

One of the principal goals of applying the $W(y)$ model is to explore how the advantage of the buyers varies across industries. This is particularly key

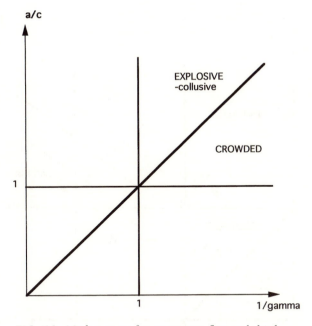

FIG. 7.1. Market space for aggregates, first and third dimensions

for the CROWDED region. Figure 7.3 supplies an example of the effect of new entrants on aggregate revenue flow **W** in a market, as the number of firms, with otherwise fixed context, grows from three to nine.

Being in the CROWDED region also has major implications for outcomes that firms experience and for possible entry by new firms to a market. Economists have long proposed models for such situations (see the survey in Scherer 1970, 225–30).

Table A.3 in the appendix reports outcomes for markets at three contexts in the CROWDED region of figures 7.1 and 7.2. The emphasis for this region on the number of firms suggests holding the state space parameters the same across all three examples in order to focus on the effects of number of firms. This number (designated by #) is taken much larger than the minimal three used in the other four appendix tables, so it is inconvenient to report a separate row of results for each firm, as is done in appendix tables A.1, A.2, A.4, and A.5. Instead, we rely on averages and Gini indexes.

First, note that the value of theta provides only treacherous guidance to the size of **tau** and to comparison across contexts. In the first panel of table A.3 for nine firms, there are two cases, each with all other parameters the same, except for a sharp decrease of 20 percent in theta—which leads to a modest *rise* of 4 percent in **tau**. (And this larger **tau** is a closer approxima-

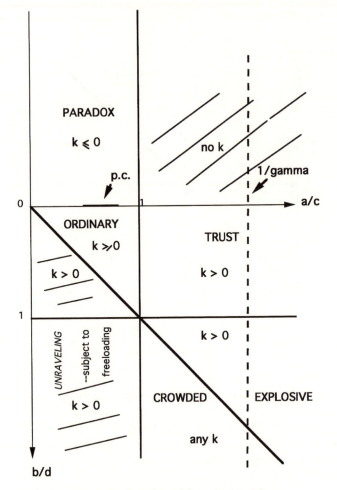

FIG. 7.2. Projecting the value of the substitutability
parameter, gamma (the third dimension), onto fig. 5.1

tion to the **tau** in the next, middle panel, even though that has the same
theta value of 6 as the first case.)

This next, middle panel in appendix table A.3 has essentially the same
array of parameters, excluding **tau**, as the first case in the first panel, but two
of the nine quality locations are omitted, so the set of nine firms has dropped
to seven firms. As expected, the aggregate size of the market actually is substantially *higher* with the *smaller* set of firms, and in physical volume (.607
versus .403) as well as in revenue (9.76 versus 7.28). And, since it is a
general result that the aggregate size of a market decreases as the buyers

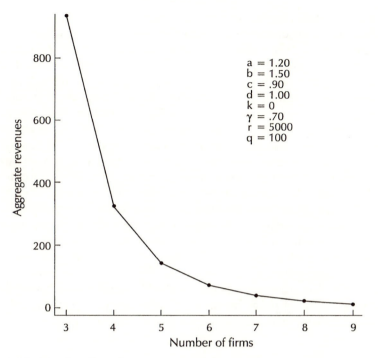

FIG. 7.3. The effect of new entrants on aggregate flows: CROWDED region

payoff ratio **tau** increases, the contrast is underestimated because a slightly larger value of **tau** comes with the middle panel. So the predictions from exact formulas for the special case of $k = 0$ are supported by the numerical solutions here for $k = 0.2$.

It is worth pointing out that the profit rates for producers are a good deal lower here than in examples from other regions, whereas the buyers are a good deal better off. Different regions look very different in comparisons of the two sides of the production market. One limitation of these examples, however, for all the regions, is that the inequality in quality among the producers has been kept quite restricted, as can be seen from the values of Gini indexes of inequality.

Turn back to the cross section for constant gamma shown in figure 7.1. The region abutting CROWDED is designated EXPLOSIVE. The region previously labeled ADVANCED, in the plane state space before gamma was introduced, figure 5.1, is thus being split, as shown in both figure 7.2 and figure 7.1.

For market varieties in EXPLOSIVE, the aggregate market size just keeps growing if more producers—accompanied by buyer valuations $S(y, n)$—enter the market. And even with **tau** (the industry deal-criterion) fixed, the absolute size of buyer surplus also keeps growing. But the main point, as we see in the next section, is that there are viable profiles for any given context.

An interesting characteristic of market models with contexts from this EX-PLOSIVE region is the dependence of aggregate sizes **W** upon r and q as well as **tau**. Here, in complete contrast with earlier results, the aggregate size actually *increases* as q/r increases! This striking prediction follows from the feedback loop as its most extreme manifestation. It is perfectly sensible that aggregate size grows as more producers (each accompanied by its own demand term) are incorporated in the market. What the model is pointing to is that as **tau** is increased, in these contexts with high a/c, each producer firm is lured to a higher volume on the $W(y)$ market profile as being its footing for maximum of revenue over cost. Whereas, conversely, if aggregate buyer valuation level is increased—as r increases—then such slippage along a market profile is inhibited. This explains the hyphenation of EXPLOSIVE with Collusive as joint label in figure 7.1, since there is at least some joint reward for the two opposing sides of the market colluding to raise the market profile. One thinks of examples such as novel industries coming on line with greenfield construction of plants by the initial members: perhaps the initial wave of integrated steel rolling mills.

*Market Performance

It is instructive to calibrate producers' versus buyers' perspectives on how good the terms of trade are as an overall deal, even though, according to the model, neither side has any operational way to seek or establish a particular level of overall deal-criterion for the buyers. The producers' deal criterion, **W/C**, can be contrasted with this complementary overall deal criterion for buyers, **tau**. This is the ratio of buyers' aggregate valuation **V** to their aggregate payment **W**, the **tau** of equation (6.3).

In particular, when will the two sides be equally pleased? One criterion is when

$$W/C = \tau. \tag{7.2}$$

Buyers then do as well for themselves as producers. This equality can be projected back into figure 3.2. So isoclines of profitability, the straight lines of figure 3.2, computed for $k = 0$, can also be imputed for buyers. All of these results on relative performance are, when $k = 0$, independent of the number of firms, their distribution over the quality index, and also independent of the buyer deal criteria, **tau** and theta, and of r and q.

Participants will attend to differences in performance levels of markets in recognizing and discriminating among sorts of market. Figure 3.2 is suggestive here. How lush producers find a market, assessed by margin of revenue over cost aggregated over the market, tends to be much the same along a given ray in the state space through the point (1, 1) in the state space. (And parallel statements hold for the aggregate buyer side, as just noted.) The same gross margin is found for very different absolute levels of a given parameter, depending on ratios to others. The prediction is that knowledgeable participants in an industrial sector will tend to give common accounts of quite different particular industries nearby in niche space. A further and more striking prediction is that even if one ratio takes a range of different sizes, the aggregate performance margin, and thus the likely reputation of a market, will stay much the same, if . . . If, that is, another ratio of parameters diverges from unity in an exactly complementary way. This reflects some sort of comparison by participants, the descriptions corresponding to two push/pull ratios diverging to the same extent from equality. These perceptions, and the resulting stories, are sensitive neither to volume considerations in valuation nor to quality considerations per se, but rather to whether both were equally skewed.

Take two sorts of examples that can be placed along the ray shown in figure 3.2 (and extended into PARADOX by figure 5.1) for gross margin 1.25. First comes a homely example from my neighborhood. On 125th Street in Harlem, the 99-cent store market is for most items higher on a/c than on b/d, perhaps about right to lie on that ray, well into the ORDINARY region. On 33rd Street in mid-Manhattan, the analogous Woolworth-type market will have parameters translating into a point on the same ray but much closer to (1, 1). Despite their absolute differences, the two markets carry much the same aura, the same sort of business identity stories among the knowledgeable. But, further, the prediction (actually, postdiction) is that the Woolworth type, being closer to (1, 1), will be less stable.

For a second sort of example, look at two of the industrial markets shown in figures 3.3 and 5.2.[1] The oil tanker and the tractor markets fall almost exactly along the same ray. Suppose that at some period no incidents have shifted their paths of evolution, so the market profile of each has $k = 0$. Then, despite their difference in position along the ray, they should have the same profitabilities, so proportionately they should be equally attractive to investors (see chapter 12).

Examine the enlarged market state space further. How do different regions in this cube of contexts appear to the producers (putting aside the buyers)? The plane cross sections given in figures 7.1 and 7.2 are at right angles to each other within the cube. As in previous chapters, neither the scaling factors r and q, nor the set of quality indexes for firms directly affect market viability. And the only constraint on market viability from the deal criterion **tau** (which supplants the earlier criterion theta) is a universal one, the same throughout the sheaf of state spaces, namely that **tau** be at least unity. So viability depends on k for given a, b, c, and d parameters. Therefore, we set $k = 0$ until the next section on numerical computation.

Return to aggregate sizes, mapped into the enlarged state space. For some locations and regions, conclusions will resemble those obtainable from the existing microeconomics of monopolistic competition. But some predictions are quite different. Not only aggregate revenues but also volumes and prices are of interest.

The first aspect is concentration across the firms in a market. We may factor that into two effects. One is the impact of the actual spread of firms on quality index. The other is how the impact of a given quality spread changes with location in state space. The latter is captured by the Gini index formulas in equations (3.18, 3.19), which stipulate a fixed distribution of firms on quality. The former is best treated for particular examples, aided by the discussion in chapter 4.

If locations on the quality index are stable, market shares should be stable. Empirical studies give mixed judgments: see Han 1991, 1992 on churning of individual firms' shares even within markets that appear stable in overall size and other characteristics. In any given concrete context for a market, a host of forces, some deriving from larger technological and ecological changes, can shift or overturn existing perceptions of quality ordering. Vulnerability of a quality array to disruption over time is thus an aspect of measurement.

The second aspect is how actual revenue in market varies, both by various regions of the market space, now taken as three-dimensional, and with detailed location within a region (as fleshed out later by numerical computations for k not equal to zero). Turn back to figure 7.2. It parallels, within the market space cube, the original plane of figure 5.1, but the plane of figure 7.2 has gamma less than unity: The dotted line is set for $a/c = 1/\text{gamma}$. The diagonal, along with other rays running through anchor point $(1, 1)$, is where the output performance *ratios* such as profit rate π are constant, along each of the rays illustrated in figures 3.2, 5.1, and 7.2.

But now there is an additional anchor point, *call it the gamma point*, at the intersection of the diagonal with the dotted line for $(1/\gamma) > 1$. It is indicated in figure 7.4. Along straight lines through this gamma point, along these *displaced* rays, the *absolute size* of market revenue tends to remain the same, given $k = 0$ (and for given spread on quality). Examine equation (6.8). The sum over n in equation (6.8) can be converted to the number of firms in that market times a suitable average of the quality values.

Designate this average of quality, for revenue across firms, with boldface as **n**. Return to the equations (3.8–3.11) for calibrating revenues of all firms as a ratio to a base firm in that market. Revenue size is discounted in the ratio of the base n_0 divided by n, as raised to a power $(d\varepsilon)$. This scaling exponent ε

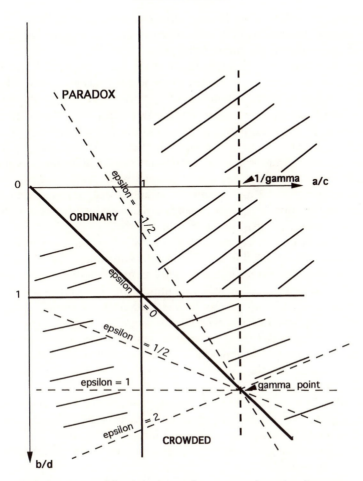

FIG. 7.4. Lines of fixed discount of revenue with quality for given gamma

from equation (3.11), the discount rate epsilon, can be generalized with insertion of gamma to be epsilon prime:

$$\varepsilon' = [(a/c) - (b/d)]/[(1/\gamma) - (a/c)]. \tag{7.3}$$

Figure 7.4 illustrates the variation of epsilon prime. It plots, for the market regions that admit $k = 0$, these lines of constant discount.

Inspection confirms that the exponent ε' remains the same along each straight line through the point designated gamma in figure 7.4, which has coordinates $(1/\gamma, 1)$. These lines are still called rays, by analogy to the rays of figure 3.2, which, however, had $(1, 1)$ as hub point. The fixed value of epsilon prime, ε', will be unity for the horizontal ray, and range from above 1, when sloping down to the left, back down through zero along the diagonal ray and to -1 on the ray through the point $(1, 0)$.

Note the difference in focus between figure 3.2 or figure 7.2 and figure 7.4. Rays in the former two figures examine performance ratios only, and these, with $k = 0$, are independent of aggregate size of market revenue. Hence theta need not be invoked, much less feedback and tau. Figure 7.4, by contrast, looks at aggregate size, which invokes theta and thence, by equations (6.5, 6.6), the feedback loop that recalibrates theta into tau. Along a (displaced) ray in figure 7.4 one encounters the set of locations in market space that yield the *same discount of revenue* with quality index, whereas along a ray in figure 3.2 one encounters locations that may have very different revenue discounts by quality index but yet, whatever the set of qualities, the *same performance ratios*, profit and the like.

In the summation of equation (6.8) for **W**, this average **n** will appear raised to the power $d\varepsilon'$, for the ε' given in equation (7.3). Much as the formula $W(y)$ took different forms by range in market space, as illustrated in the profiles in figure 2.6, so will the summation. The entries in table 7.1 report three key features of these distinct qualitative forms by region: Each entry shows in a product just whether the aggregate size is proportional to some positive or instead to some negative power of tau, and similarly of **#** (the number of firms), and similarly of average quality, **n**. (This latter average index over quality has the sign of the product of d [negative for PARADOX] with ε'.)

This table thus supplies overall guidance on how revenue is affected by major aspects of market mechanism as these are affected by location in market space; see PIMS section of chapter 12 for an application.

Table 7.1 for aggregates derives from equation (6.8), which converts into

$$\mathbf{W}_o = \{(r/\boldsymbol{\tau}^{1/\gamma}q^{a/c}) \cdot \left[\frac{(b/d) - (a/c)}{(b/d) - 1}\right]^{a/c}\}^{1/[(1/\gamma) - (a/c)]} [1/\mathbf{\#} \cdot \mathbf{n}]^{d\varepsilon'} \qquad (7.4)$$

with **n** the suitably averaged index n of quality, with ε' from equation (7.3), and as before with the subscript 0 indicating $k = 0$. The market concentration, on the other hand, requires that we return to equation (6.8) to compute an inequality index over whatever the particular set of quality index values in that market. These results are built upon in later chapters.

Parallel derivation of formulas for volume y can be combined with the above results on variation for revenue to estimate the variation of price. In particular, price can be shown to decrease (as expected) with quality increase for $d > 0$ when

$$b/d > (a - 1)/(c - 1). \qquad (7.5)$$

TABLE 7.1

Parameter Dependence of Market Revenue by Region (**W** as direct versus indirect power of each key parameter)

Region		
	For k = 0, and Downstream	
ORDINARY	$(1/\gamma) > 1 > a/c > b/d > 0$	$\mathbf{W} \sim \#/\mathbf{n}^d \tau$
ADVANCED-CROWDED	$b/d > a/c > 1; (1/\gamma) > a/c$	$\mathbf{W} \sim \mathbf{n}^d/\# \; \tau$
ADVANCED-EXPLOSIVE	$b/d > a/c > (1/\gamma) > 1$	$\mathbf{W} \sim \# \; \tau/\mathbf{n}^d$
PARADOX	$d < 0, (1/\gamma) > 1 > a/c$	$\mathbf{W} \sim \# \; \mathbf{n}^d/\tau$
	For k → 0	
TRUST	$(1/\gamma) > a/c > 1 > b/d > 0$	$\mathbf{W} \sim 1/\# \; \mathbf{n}^d \tau$
UNRAVEL	$a/c < b/d; a/c < 1 < (1/\gamma)$	$\mathbf{W} \sim \# \; \mathbf{n}^d/\tau$

Note: ∼ represents dependence; **n** stands for average quality over firms in the market; # is the number of firms; and τ is the buyers' deal criterion, the ratio **V/W**. See text, chapters 6–7, for equations and further detail on γ.

Beyond this level of parsing, it is more effective, even with $k = 0$, to resort to explicit numerical computation. There are a number of regions in figures 7.1 and 7.2 that are distinctive as to computed behavior of aggregate revenue. Seven distinctive major regions are discriminable (keeping gamma less than unity), after distinguishing the CROWDED and EXPLOSIVE regions (see fig. 7.1 and table 7.1) as distinct parts of ADVANCED. On the CROWDED region, see the previous section.

To sum up, first, market outcomes with $k = 0$ were reported across the market space. Performance ratios such as profit depend only, and linearly, on coordinates in the state space (figs. 3.2 and 7.4). Many sorts of examples were cited in illustration. Market aggregates such as revenue and cost, by contrast, depend on averaging over the quality index values, as well as on scale factors r and q, and on buyer pressure tau. The state coordinates—the ratios of valuation exponents, a/c and b/d plus gamma—have an impact mainly as contributions to exponents to which the quality index and tau are raised in equation (6.8) rather than in numerical factors: Table 7.1 highlighted that fact in the turnovers between regions in dependence on size of quality index and the like. With this general guidance, one can turn to explicit numerical computation for general values of k, as in the appendix tables.

NUMERICAL COMPUTATIONS

The task is to provide guidance on how performance, including but not limited to aggregate sizes, varies with position in state space. This interacts with path dependence. Consider, for example, how the degree of substitutability, the gamma parameter, affects the impact of path dependency as measured by the range in the historical constant k. There is an underlying tendency for higher substitutability to increase the expected or average rate of profit of firms in that market, but there is also a dependence of the profit rate on which particular one of the market profiles is established, that is, on size of k.[2] And yet only when $k = 0$ can the equation (3.2) for n in terms of y be inverted to yield an explicit formula for y in terms of n.

When k is not zero, some guidance can, however, be gained just along the edges in state space from formulas derived by asymptotic methods for small k applied just near boundary points and lines in this market space. Table 3.3 gave such formulas for one important outcome variable, aggregate revenue. (For a general discussion of asymptotic mathematics see deBruijn 1970, and for applications in dynamic systems see Hirsch and Smale 1974 and Hoffbauer and Sigmund 1988.)

For example, along the diagonal where the two ratios are equal, dependence of W on y appears from equations (2.11) to vanish, since the exponent g of y goes to zero, but for any given n from equation (3.2), y itself can be shown to tend to zero. The overall result is that revenue $W(y)$ becomes small, even though, as pointed out earlier, the profit rate will tend to be high. Derivations of entries are intricate and we pass over details, but asymptotics for the perfect competition case are given extended substantive treatment in later chapters.

Numerical computations are necessary for most analyses. They yield, for each particular value of k and the context parameters, a numerical value for volume chosen by firm of quality n, $y[n]$. (The computer software required for these computations is discussed in the appendix.) This $y[n]$, however obtained, yields one term in the sum (6.8) for aggregate market revenue, the revenue of that firm.

For points in each of several regions of the state space of figures 7.1 and 7.2, examples are reported in tables A.1–A.5 of the appendix. Specification of a context requires, in addition to eight parameters and constants (a, b, c, d, r, q, k, γ, τ), also the distribution of the producers on quality index n. Some of the contexts are those specified in figure 3.3 for some American industries. The number of firms, designated by $\#$, varies from three to nine. Dependent variables include both market aggregates and distributional indexes for several outcomes (Gini indexes from chapter 3).

The outcomes in most of these example begin with terms of trade for each constituent producer. The value assumed for k in some examples is not in the range, shown in figure 3.1, sufficient to ensure market viability for that region. This is because the set of quality stipulated for firms did not extend to the range where firms would be motivated to freeload on the schedule. The concentration ratios that obsess industrial organization theory (see Carlton 1989: introduced in chapter 11 and discussed in chapter 14) are included here as dependent variables rather than viewed as causal inputs.

Rather than n or d separately, it is melding them as a power that is important, as seen in earlier equations. On phenomenological grounds it will be rare for firms to be sustained together in the same market when this joint power varies as widely as does the volume sensitivity, y^c, which can vary by as much as a factor of 5 or 10. It is convenient to calibrate lowest quality as $n = 1$ (and thus also $n^d = 1$), which also calibrates the cost parameter q as per unit physical volume of production flow. Then the upper limit of n can be set for convenience: In tables A.1–A.5 the largest n is 2 and the smallest 1. Then one expects that d will be no larger than 3 in any observable case. And similarly for b.

Consider just one table here as an illustration. Appendix table A.2 illustrates outcomes of markets with just three firms evenly spaced on quality, for particular contexts in the ORDINARY region. The first panel reports the terms of trade and aggregates from the viable profile found for a positive historical constant k. It reports no viable profile, as predicted from figure 3.1, when the sign of k is reversed for that context—but there is a viable profile when, with all else the same, the value of product differentiation, b/d, is tripled (still within ORDINARY). In all of these particular varieties, the profits of producers outshine the benefit ratio, tau, for the aggregate buyer.

The important point is to notice how complex it is to assess the results presented in one of these tables, whatever the computations needed to produce them. Since they are intended for interpretive guidance and illustration, not as actual applications to particular case studies, it would seem that a better method of scanning is needed. It can be supplied with higher-level computer programming to search particular regions on particular criteria.

CLAIMS AND IMPLICATIONS

This completes the derivation of the basic $W(y)$ model for a market. The next chapter develops estimation formulas, and then chapter 9 models a dual format for a market. Succeeding chapters analyze in greater depth how both firms and markets fit into larger strings and sectors of markets, and on that basis develop extensions and applications. Let's pause here to assess the results derived so far.

Each observed market is the outcome of a particular historical path, so any one of a number of market profiles could have established itself as viable in a given context, as seen in cross section. Predictions must be fuzzy. Let us take that as the very first claim from the model and ask what the evidence is. The most persuasive studies of particular industrial markets are ones developed from insider information. These include the nearly 10,000 available from case-writers of the Harvard Business School as well as individual studies cited for figure 3.3. These studies, and in particular those related to the PIMS series to be surveyed at the end of chapter 12, suggest time after time that markets do get shaken up and settle into different configurations without significant changes in the underlying context (parameter values).

One striking implication of the $W(y)$ model is that profits do not tend toward zero, as required by standard economic theory. Nor do profits or market share tend toward equality among firms within a market. These predictions derive from the mechanism itself and therefore hold for essentially all contexts. Yet another implication is that increasing returns to scale can be compatible with viable market profiles.

Another striking implication is that "supply equals demand" sinks to the level of bromide. It becomes recognized as an inert tautology. This is because both supply and demand are being determined as by-products of a local algorithm by which dispersions in valuations are equilibrated between the two sides of that market and with respect both to volume and to quality. Chapter 3 began near its end the discussion of how determinations so localized become reconciled across broader sectors of an economy, a discussion that will be continued in chapters 8 and 10.

Markets work through and by dispersions: This is the key claim, from which the others derive. Variances rather than means are the key measures. It is matchings across these variabilities through which markets establish themselves as profiles and embed themselves across social networks into industrial sectors. Observed spreads among a market's constituent producers—on other characteristics as well as profitability—build up from these variabilities.

Claims may be faulted when they derive from the standpoint of an observer rather than of participating actors. Yet the actors may engage in practices that they cannot expound. Abstract questioning may elicit only folk theory unrelated to practice. The decision theorist Baruch Fischhof (1993) lays out this conundrum in all its intricacy, and so from a very different perspective do psychoanthropologists K. Gergen and R. Harré. Intensive field studies can be just the right antidote as well as providing detailed data to support numerical predictions.

From quantitative estimates of at least some parts of schedules for some producers, one is often able to distinguish which industries can be assigned to the PARADOX, CROWDED, and ORDINARY regions, as was done in figure 3.3. Producer markets that appear subject to instability may correspond to UNRAVELING regions. (Better diagnoses of other regions as yet unlabeled will be developed in chapter 9: see figures 9.2, 9.3, and 9.6.) Previous equations, tables, and figures have shown the corresponding predictions. Some predictions derived from the $W(y)$ model hold for most examples of a variety of market and so are sweeping enough to be appraised even in largely qualitative field studies and surveys.

Prediction is a somewhat misleading term here. Usually no explicit index of quality is observable. Thus, the first step is to work backward from an observed set of revenues, volumes, and the like for a given market to some set of parameters and quality indexes from which some approximation of the observed set can be predicted. Formulas for this are derived in the next chapter. Then only with data from a different period could one test predictions. This issue was illustrated by the discussion of the light aircraft industry in chapter 4, and it is pursued further in chapters 12 and 13.

Predictions from the $W(y)$ model of outcomes for various producers and their market as a whole are contingent in at least two senses beyond this backward induction and the historical lability discussed earlier. That lability, expressed in terms of the model, derives from the range of feasible offer curves $W(y)$, and the k measure flags this range of indeterminacy. The third contingency that attends predictions from the $W(y)$ model is that the market mechanism may get supplanted by some other form of social organization, as was taken up at the end of chapter 5. One can hope to find studies of market failure that point to particular sorts of alternative organization suggested by the $W(y)$ model for certain regions of state space.

There is a dual aspect to this third contingency, an activist aspect. Direct assaults on the market mechanism itself do occur. Entrepreneurs outside the given market, along with those already participating in the market, may attempt to disrupt a schedule and gain cooperation from many or all producers, depending on context. This third contingency is explored further in subsequent chapters.

Fourth, outcomes for any one producer will depend, in ways that also are hard to estimate, on just which other producers are in the market. This becomes especially apparent in the PIMS studies surveyed at the end of chapter 12. The ratio between saturation parameters b and d may seem sufficient to characterize how a shift in underlying quality index n would translate into net shift of footing, of market position, mediated by competing valuation impacts (cost and taste). But such a claim overlooks impacts on the remaining producers. This chapter has shown how interaction among particular locations of different firms on quality is what fixes their overall sizes and thus market aggregates.

Deriving predictions and indeed interpretations from the $W(y)$ model is not a mechanical process. The model has been kept simple, so the endless special circumstances and variations encountered in case studies cannot be mapped directly into the model, say with parameters of their own. Subsequent chapters explore possible reinterpretations and resitings of parameters, especially of gamma, k, and tau, that can accommodate some of these variations.

THE ECONOMICS OF CONVENTION

The $W(y)$ models address puzzles for orthodox microeconomics—such as the continuing differences in profitability between industries, as well as between firms. They also supply practical tools to evolutionary economics. Yet these models also should address the ambiences, the phenomenological atmospheres of different industrial sectors. For an example we may turn to an unorthodox theory of markets that is emerging in works from a group of French economists and sociologists. These combine neoclassical and institutionalist features, economics, and sociology.

This new economics of convention distinguishes different regimes that govern markets. There is some commonality in the sense that all regimes are social constructions. But they are constructions by very different sorts of actors operating in and inducing very different sorts of interactive contexts, milieus.

This new theory shares with $W(y)$ models a focus on quality, but it remains surprising that these distinct regimes, which were derived entirely independent of the $W(y)$ scheme, appear to correspond well with the discrimination of distinct regions for markets in the market space shown in figures 3.1–3.5 and 5.1. So the hypothesis is that a single general mechanism supports all regimes, however different their actualizations in particular cultural practices may be. Four regimes are proposed in this paradigm: Favereau 1989 is an early overview; Orlean 1994b is a subsequent compendium; and for the most recent statements in English on their findings see various chapters in Lazega and Favereau (2001).

This group's *régime industriel* may correspond to the ADVANCED region as described in early chapters. But more particularly, the characteristics of *industriel* appear to correspond to predictions for the CROWDED region. This distinctive subregion in three-dimensional market space is bounded by the value of the substitutability parameter, gamma. Joint research can clarify and test the correspondence of substitutability with features of the *industriel* regime.

Their *régime domestique* appears to correspond to PARADOX. Eymard-Duvernay (1989) has presented a coherent, overall phenomenology for a substantive class of industries—*Domestique*—in which *rising* production cost does indeed accompany *declining* quality as perceived by buyers. Note the convergence also with the Spence model in chapter 5.

Eymard-Duvernay's essential point (1994) is that this can only come about through a culture held in common that shapes and is shaped by particular sorts of social relations. They run on networks of trust and of dedication among producers. The flavor is of kinship, as in Aristotle on household economy.

The descriptive account does correspond to part of the top region in the state plane (fig. 5.1), where b/d is less than zero. With d negative, if a/c is greater than unity (which is the right half of the upper region in figure 3.1), no market profile can be viable, since, for positive k, only minima, not maxima, are identified by the profile curve, whereas with k negative, no value of *y* leads to profit. Thus, given $d < 0$, only with $a/c < 1$, the left part marked PARADOX on figure 5.1, will there be viable market profiles.

One variety of PARADOX market was the subject of figure 5.3. Rather than reporting the market profile $W(y)$ itself, this graph transcribed from such a profile how *y* will rise as quality *n* rises (exactly the supposed paradox). In figure 5.3, three such transcriptions were illustrated, two from allowed profiles with *k* at a negative value and at zero. The dotted line is the analogous trace from a profile that could unravel from freeloading (a positive value of the historical constant *k*).

Is the PARADOX label justified? This $W(y)$ model is a cross-sectional one that is ill-equipped to accommodate over-time cumulations. But suppose we are looking at a long-established industry in which some of the larger firms are dinosaurs that have high cost structures and that also are turning out dated or tacky products. That supplies one scenario for negative correlation of quality with cost that could accompany a persisting market. And other such scenarios can be brought to mind.

Table A.1 in the appendix illustrates market outcomes for three particular contexts in the PARADOX region. For simplicity, the smallest plausible number of firms, $\# = 3$, is used, and they are spaced evenly over a range between $n = 1$ and $n = 2$. As expected, the volume of production *rises* quite sharply with quality level *n*. Profitabilities of the three firms are nearly the same or at least stay within a narrow band. In the first two contexts, the profit rate proves to be comparable to the overall benefit to the buyer side, but in the third context, where buyer taste for higher volume is very limited ($a/c = 0.1$), the buyer benefit criterion is set lowest, whereas the profit rate is highest, more than 50 percent.

According to the example in figure 5.3, in PARADOX region the market profile can come unraveled only for a positive value of *k*. The main point of appendix table A.1 is to illustrate that whatever the particular threat to viability of that market profile from unraveling, market failure for "disallowed" values of *k* remains a possibility whose realization depends on the exact range of quality *n* present. French observers would not necessarily be able to distinguish positive from negative *k*. All six contexts were picked with *positive* values of the historical constant *k*, but with the range of *n* set too high to occasion unraveling.

Prices are not shown explicitly in these appendix tables, but they can be calculated as the ratio of revenues over volumes. One computes that prices actually *decrease* as one moves to a higher index of quality *n* in this PARADOX context. Yet for a given volume, the buyer valuations are higher for higher *n*. This is not an anomaly. The higher-quality producers' cost structures are so low (in this PARADOX region) that they are led to produce very large quantities in order to maximize their gross profit (rather than their price per unit). Take a simple example. In New England there is a local soft drink (nasty to outsiders' taste) called Moxie that is never discounted and thus sells for a premium price per unit, higher than the products that are in fact much preferred, unit for unit.

Next turn to the *régime marchant* in this economics of convention. It appears to correspond to ORDINARY. Their label suggests a regime that is businesslike in a more conventional sense. In particular, merchandising becomes important to support sales of products not perceived as greatly differentiated. The account of *marchant* in various working papers (e.g., Eymard-Duvernay and Favereau 1990) appears to fit the definition of ORDINARY region.

For one context in ORDINARY, figure 3.4 illustrated market profiles as curves, one for each of three values of the historical constant k. Table A.2 in the appendix illustrates market outcomes for six additional contexts in the ORDINARY region. The issue of market failure arises here. The first context shown in table A.2 has a positive value of k known to yield a viable profile, which here yields a modest decline in production volume with quality, a buyer surplus[3] of only about 19 percent, but producer profit rates high—and indeed highest just for low-quality producers. If the sign of k is reversed, however, but with no other changes, the profile is no longer necessarily viable (see figure 3.1 and table 3.2). In particular, the footings on this second putative profile turn out to be minimizers yielding negative profit.

However, the same negative value of k does yield a viable profile in the next context, where there is one change in parameters, a tripling of the b/d ratio. Failure because of unraveling in particular would come for this context only from producers whose quality indexes were less than 0.178. These low values of n would yield high values of volume y, above 5.42, which is far above the range reported for the firms in the example. Profit rates are about as high as before, but they no longer vary with quality, and the buyer surplus is down to 16 percent. In later illustrative contexts, the k value remains negative, though sharply reduced, and along with the reductions shown in other parameters, again yields a profile that is viable. The buyer surplus, 64 percent, is now higher than the producer profit rates, which are almost the same for the three firms.

An example of a convention more likely to be found in ORDINARY than other regions is formula pricing, which is compatible with the French group's account of *marchant*. In the American economy, this was, for example, the practice for considerable periods in as much as half of the meat-packing industry: "A number of packers turned to a contractual arrangement known as formula pricing to stabilize transactions. . . . Formula pricing involved a contract for product delivery at a future date and at a price based on market prices reported, on the specified date. . . . [F]ormula pricing is trading on someone else's price" (Campbell, Hollingsworth, and Lindberg 1991, 288–

89). Such a formula derives easily from market profiles as proposed in the $W(y)$ model.

The UNRAVELING region, finally, appears to contain parameter combinations that do fit the context of certain French industries in which markets have in fact been unraveling: in particular, regional road hauling markets designated as *routier* (Biencourt 1995; Biencourt and Urrutiaguer 2001). But to work on this match, first, the network context for a $W(y)$ model needs further specification so that it can handle geographic and other overlaps, a development begun in the previous chapters. Second, the model should be enlarged to encompass the special importance of perishability and delays for trucking (De Vany and Saving 1977). And, third, a dual orientation of markets to be introduced in chapter 9 may be important.

~~~~~~~~~~~~~~~~~

CHAPTER 8

Estimating Qualities and Parameters

This chapter derives, at its end, two key parameters in the $W(y)$ model from the network context of markets. This will articulate part 1 on the basic model with part 3 as well as the present part 2. The chapter also articulates the estimation of parameters, and thus also their meaning, in terms of a construct from the discipline of physics, the self-consistent field, known also as the mean field approximation.

The chapter begins, however, with more straightforward problems of identifying parameters and searching for equations to estimate the quality index. Three sets of estimates have to be developed together: quality indexes of particular members, but only as complemented, first, by parameters of the market space (which refer to the market as a whole) and, second, by measures of performance and outcome for firms and markets.

PARAMETERS

W and y are the commitment or choice variables that continue only as they reproduce a market profile $W(y)$. Five sorts of parameters are needed to report embeddings of such market profiles. Characterizing them helps derive key interrelations among individual parameters. Only certain clusters of parameter values characterize viable embeddings of profiles.

Locations in market space are specified in the parameters a, b, c, d, as well as gamma for the third dimension. While gamma refers a market to markets that are parallel in the flow stream, the ratios a/c and b/d each correlate a market with both its downstream and its upstream. That is, a and b refer downstream, c and d upstream, and gamma cross-stream.

All five of this first sort of parameter are dimensionless exponents, unlike the calibration parameters r and q, which relate valuation to volume dimensions. Each of these latter two measures melds aspects of local context, such as the industry technology and work rules, together with macro aspects, such as the size of the economy and level of prices. Such calibration can also be stated (chap. 3) as ratios to revenue and cost observed for some firm as anchor.

An intermediate sort of parameter is the position of producers on the quality index n. Producers' positions derive as the pecking order of competition within the market, but only as confirmed externally, in buyers' appreciation as well as in costs from upstream. These quality positions also can be stated as the number (#) of firms together with a distribution over n with upper and lower bounds. In the computer programs of the appendix, these bounds are chosen for convenience to be 1 and 2.

The remaining two sorts of parameters are situational and thus are reported ex post as constants. Path of evolution over time becomes summarized as a single number, the historical constant k. Strategic situation is characterized, ex post, by the fifth sort of parameter, theta and tau.

Theta is operational for the individual firm, as the aggregate buyers' Occam's razor for equally satisfying purchases from all producers. Whereas tau characterizes the degree of exploitation, by buyers taken all together, of producers taken as a set. Only tau is operational for market aggregates and actual revenues. What this says is that no market is a self-contained unit within the production economy. Chapter 7 related sizes of both firms and their market to this measure of exploitation, tau—wound up with gamma, for substitution across stream—but that as yet only implies without explicitly mapping interdependencies among markets along stream.

*Estimation Equations for Qualities and Parameters

Each illustration in figures 2.6, 3.4, and 5.3 was derived by working backward from a stipulated structure, and similarly for the appendix tables. Figures 3.3 and 5.2 emerged from working backward from observed structure and performance reported in case studies. They thereby assigned particular points in market space to a score of American industries, as observed in the mid-1970s. Each industry is put together from estimates for a particular set of firms with particular spacings on the quality index.

Let's work backward from an observed set of performances of firms in a market to what set of locations on n would yield such outcomes. That has to precede predictions. The practical research task is to seek an imputed quality array such that predictions yield good fit with data on revenues and flows across a set of firms examined as a production market. Leifer (1985, appendix B) laid out one clear and simple procedure, which simulation work by Bothner (2000b) has carried further.

There are three quite different clusters of quantities to be estimated from observations as framed by this $W(y)$ model, whose mechanism evolved to tame Knightian uncertainty. One cluster is the quality indices. A second is parameters not dependent on historical path. The third is a residual category including r, q, and theta.

I lay out an estimation procedure in five phases. The second, third, and fourth phases are brief.

First Phase

The first phase is to set up estimation equations from available observations, which will be designated in boldface.

First, the revenues for the firms in the market: to simplify notation, again use the integer index i for firms, from the second section of chapter 2. It ranges from 1 to **#**, and thus we may label these revenues $\mathbf{W}_i$. Next, the physical volume y associated with each of these firms: label these $\mathbf{y}_i$.

The earlier equations (2.2, 2.3) combine to yield a set of equations, one for each of the **#** firms. They are expressed in terms of these 2**#** numerical observations, $\mathbf{W}_i$ and $\mathbf{y}_i$, together with the parameter a, along with the quality indexes and the scale constant r. In order to economize on the number of distinct parameters to be estimated, we may meld the exponent b in with n to define m for buyers' perception of producer quality,

$$m = n^b. \tag{8.1}$$

Given the frequent exponentiation, it is convenient to convert all observations into logarithmic form. *Adopt the convention that the logarithm is designated by the opposite case:* thus w_i for ln $\mathbf{W}_i$, and Y_i for ln $\mathbf{y}_i$. By the previous convention, M_i designates ln m_i (which is just b ln n_i).

So the estimation equations derived from equations (2.2, 2.3) for the buyer's side are

$$w_i - a\,Y_i = M_i + \ln\,(r/\theta). \tag{8.2}$$

But there are **#** values M_i to be estimated from these **#** equations, so further observations appear necessary in order to also estimate a and the r/θ, not to mention the cost side parameters.

Equation (8.2) expresses only the buyer side's insisting on equally good deal-ratios θ from each of the **#** firms. But observations must also be consistent with each producer's insistence on maximizing its profit. This optimization translates to equality, at the point y_i, between the slope of its cost schedule C and the slope of the revenue schedule it perceives, which for *every* producer, regardless of its underlying quality standing, is just the market profile $W(y)$. The slope of the cost schedule was derived earlier as the right-hand side of equation (2.6).

The first key point is that an observer can estimate the slope of $W(y)$ at each of these points y_i. This is the additional set of observations that are needed to complete estimations. Define this observed slope (the left-hand side of equation (2.6)) as Z_i; and again assign the lowercase letter z_i for logs.

The second key point is that a single additional parameter suffices to define quality indices from the cost side for the **#** producers. This is the parameter $\underline{d}$, which in terms of the earlier notation is

$$\underline{d} = d/b. \tag{8.3}$$

Use of this exponent d rescales the m_i for each firm to yield just the n^d factor that is required on the right side of equation (2.6). The rescaling just restates the earlier postulate: Qualities perceived by buyers are not only in the same order for firms as the quality levels firms perceive from their own costs, but in fact one set is just an exponential rescale (by parameter d) of the other set of quality indices.

So the new equations involve a further set of **#** observables, the z_i, that convert equation (2.6) from being a mathematical to an observational statement. These estimation equations become, in logarithmic form,

$$z_i = (c - 1)Y_i + \ln cq + dM_i. \tag{8.4}$$

Now multiply equation (8.2) by d. Then from the resulting equation subtract equation (8.4). M_i is thereby eliminated, so one obtains equations for estimating just the parameters referring to the market as a whole:

$$d \, w_i - z_i - (ad - c + 1) \, Y_i = d \ln r/\theta - \ln cq. \tag{8.5}$$

The *good news* is that there can be a lot of these equations, as many as the number of firms in the market, **#**, whereas there are just a few market parameters. The *bad news* is that this set of **#** equations is no longer in the unknowns, because of multiples such as the term (ad). So the standard easy solutions (e.g., Aitken 1951) for a set of linear equations is not available.

We may proceed by subtracting off the equation for the bottom firm, 1, from each of the other equations (8.5). To simplify notation, set

$$(w_i - w_1) = w_i, \tag{8.6}$$

and similarly for the other observables.

The result is

$$z_i = dw_i - daY_i - (c - 1)Y_i \tag{8.7}$$

for $i = 2, 3, \ldots, $ **#**. A $W(y)$ market can only sustain itself if there are at least three firms, which means there are at least two of the equations (8.7), and so on. There are three market parameters to be estimated, namely a, c, and d.

Use two equations, say for integers k and i, to find the parameter d. Begin by rearranging the equation for i to

$$c - 1 = -(1/Y_i)(ad \, Y_i - d \, w_i + z_i). \tag{8.8}$$

Thence

$$z_k = d \, w_k - daY_k + (Y_k/Y_i)(ad \, Y_i - d \, w_i + z_i), \tag{8.9}$$

which, since the terms in a cancel, can be solved for d in terms of observables only:

$$\underline{d} = [\underline{z_k} - (\underline{Y_k}/\underline{Y_i})\underline{z_i}]/[\underline{w_k} - (\underline{Y_k}/\underline{Y_i})\underline{w_i}]. \tag{8.10}$$

Introduce a final new and neatly symmetric notation, *designating with brackets* { }:

$$\{\underline{Y_i}, \underline{z_k}\} = [\underline{Y_i}\underline{z_k} - \underline{Y_k}\,\underline{z_i}] = -\{\underline{Y_k}, \underline{z_i}\} \tag{8.11}$$

and similarly for any other distinct pair of observables. Equation (8.10) becomes

$$\underline{d} = \{\underline{Y_i}, \underline{z_k}\}/\{\underline{Y_i}, \underline{w_k}\}. \tag{8.12}$$

This new notation simplifies deriving estimates for c and a. Return to equations (8.2, 8.4). Note that the absolute size of the index value of quality for the lowest firm, m_1, can be set arbitrarily (with r, q, b, and d available to take up the slack). Choose unity for m_1:

$$m_1 = 1, \text{ so that } M_1 = 0. \tag{8.13}$$

So, then, for i not unity:

$$\underline{w_i} - a\underline{Y_i} = M_i \tag{8.14}$$

and

$$\underline{z_i} = (c - 1)\underline{Y_i} + \underline{d}M_i. \tag{8.15}$$

This amounts to *calibrating each observable as a difference from that observable for the bottom firm*, thus eliminating for the moment the sizing constants r and q. We may combine the last two equations to obtain one for $\underline{d}$:

$$\underline{d} = [\underline{w_i} - (c - 1)\, Y_i]/[\underline{w_i} - a\underline{Y_i}]. \tag{8.16}$$

The right sides of equations (8.10) and (8.12) then can be equated with one another, and the result expanded and the terms gathered, yielding in terms of the notation from equation (8.11),

$$\{\underline{z_i}, \underline{w_k}\} = (c - 1)\{\underline{Y_i}, \underline{w_k}\} - a\{\underline{Y_i}, \underline{z_k}\}. \tag{8.17}$$

These equations for various integers i, k, are, finally, equations for a and c expressed in terms of observables only. But note that a minimum of four firms are needed to yield the two distinct equations required to estimate both a and c. These four firms consist of the bottom firm, 1, which is the calibrator, and plus the firms j, i, and firm k.

Cycle back now to the firm indexes m_i introduced in equation (8.1), where, by equation (8.13), m_1 for the bottom firm has been set to one and so M_1 to zero. Thus, the sizing constants q and r (actually r/θ) are determined at once from equations (8.4) and (8.2) with i set equal to 1. The other quality indexes M_i can then be computed from either equation (8.14) or equation (8.15). This appears to complete the estimation protocol![1]

How is it that the historical constant k did not figure in this estimation? This procedure avoids explicit use of the $W(y)$ formula, equation (2.9), and thereby avoids any need to estimate k. This measure k accompanies the use of the device of the representative firm.

The key is the use of observed slopes of $W(y)$ at the observed outputs $y[n]$ for the various firms. Taking the derivative of the formula yields an expression in a power of W times a power of y but without any appearance of k.[2] The deal ratio θ does figure, however, and so it becomes the measure specifying the particular profile obtaining in the estimations (this is explained more fully in the fifth phase).

Second Phase

The second phase is to carry out detailed application for a small number of firms. The fewer there are, the greater the possibility of degeneracy among apparently distinct equations in observables that are being used to formulate estimates. Even for just three firms, there are nine observations (for y, W, and the slope of W), and there are only five independent parameters (a, c, $\underline{d}$, m_2, and m_3), plus cost scale q and the scaling size r/θ for buyer valuation, that need to be estimated.

But note also that such bare counts of ostensible degrees of freedom need not be sufficient to guarantee being able to estimate all parameters. The analysis in the first phase depended on using slopes of $W(y)$, and those might appear to be dependent on the W and y observations and thus not to add new information; see the illustrations in the preceding note. Such is not the case because each location $y[n]$ depends on what the locations of the other firms are, through a feedback loop to aggregate market size. The fifth phase will be devoted to explaining this.

Third Phase

The third phase is assessing degrees and kinds of deviation from the perfect fit to the $W(y)$ model that has been assumed thus far. This is a matter of pragmatics. If the fit is good enough for the use at hand, no more need be done. Otherwise, one can assess deviations in terms of inconsistencies among multiple estimates of one or more parameters, since more observations are available than have been used in the above procedure to estimate all the parameters.

Thus, we recompute parameters with previously unused combinations of observations. The range in the estimates of a given parameter is a measure of goodness of fit. This procedure can be converted into a systematic search for estimates that minimize some overall measure of goodness of fit across all the parameters. Statistics, and more specifically econometrics (on which see chapter 11), offer a range of effective procedures.

If the fit is poor, it is sensible to explore allowing the set of quality indexes for n more flexibility than just being an exponentiation of the values m_i. Only for the case of three firms does that introduce no more flexibility; and the more numerous the firms, the greater the additional flexibility. However, introducing this additional flexibility can introduce inconsistencies in other aspects of the fit. Guidance can come from substituting the best estimates of parameters into the general formula for $W(y)$ in order to also estimate k. All the results formulated above in terms of k then become available.

A final brief discussion will lead into the next phase. Crocodile tears mark the present style of statistical fittings in social science. Ostensibly, the investigator is sad about poorness of fit. In practice, however, assuming various kinds and degrees of badness of fit often becomes where the investigator puts energy and attempts to make a contribution. This pretense encourages the investigator to stop thinking about and exploring intensively for a really good theoretical interpretation and model. A litmus test for this pretense is whether parameters are being sought—quantities thought to be of some stability and bearing on theory—or instead just a set of fitting constants. The importance of the latter is in any case overridden in current practice by attention to so-called significance levels estimated with virtually no attention to the maze of highly restrictive and theoretically empty regularities often being assumed, all in order to achieve legitimation by formal derivation from principles of statistics that are not grounded in the specific theory at issue.

Fourth Phase

The fourth phase goes to the substantive core of modeling markets. It is dealing with the issue of whose constructs are being estimated. The $W(y)$ model, like Knight's vision (1971), has the business manager making the key choice, that of volume to optimize profit given the observed market profile as menu.

This means that the cost schedule being estimated, the $C(y, n)$, is the observer's mathematical representation of the assessment frame thought to be guiding the manager in his choices. The apparently naive and overly simple exponential form used in the model so far is better suited as such representation than is some elaborate estimation formula that an econometrician would use if he envisaged, contrary to reality, making the choice. This discussion will be continued in chapter 11 around work on production markets by the econometrician Mark Nerlove. He does *not* engage in the practices parodied at the end of the phase 3 account. What he is up to is making a careful investigation of the wrong target.

Fifth Phase

The fifth phase is estimating a parameter for substitutability that has been left implicit so far. That requires complementary adjustment of the coefficient r/θ for the buyer side. The earlier phases developed formulas for separately estimating each of the parameters then considered, both quality indexes and profile parameters. These previous phases established that there was no need to establish a value for k or even deal with it as part of the estimation process for parameters and qualities. However, the deal ratio theta has been included, in a needed scale coefficient, and so it served to specify the particular profile. Now we seek a formula for estimating the substitutability parameter gamma, γ.

Chapter 6 has shown how the feedback loop between theta and aggregate market size works, mediated by the vector of quality indexes. On the one hand, the ratio r/θ is an important measure in estimating observables. Exactly for that reason, it has, on the other hand, no bearing beyond a particular market realization. By contrast, tau itself can be seen as setting a ratio of aggregates that need not depend on aggregate size on a particular occasion.

To the extent that it is transposable, tau functions as a parameter. And gamma is construed as a parameter. The meanings of tau and theta have been shown to be interrelated, and one cannot be estimated without knowledge of the other. For a market whose producers are aggressively pushing their products, one may expect that tau is held close to the value unity, below which the buyers would evaporate. In a context favorable to aggressive buyers, tau might tend toward the value that optimizes the gap between $\mathbf{V}$ and $\mathbf{W}$: this is easily seen to be $c/a\gamma$ (cf. equation 12.2). In either case, one could at once compute the value of gamma by substitution into equation (6.4) or (6.5). But either value is a mere supposition.

In practice, to derive an estimate of gamma, then, one has to use observations of *changes* in the given production market from a changed context. One waits to observe a change in the market context and thus in revenues and outputs from individual firms, known to be in a feedback loop with the market aggregate. The change may be an improvement of production technology common across the firms or of quality of the materials being procured by those firms such that the returns-to-scale exponent c changes. Compare the new with the old.

Observation will provide before-and-after values for market aggregate $\mathbf{W}$. Likewise, phase 1 estimations can provide before-and-after values for theta. Now suppose that both gamma and tau can be regarded as staying the same, before and after a change such as in the parameter c. Then equation (6.5) yields an estimate of gamma: equate the right-hand side for before with the right-hand side for after. Substituting the result back into the equation then yields an estimate of tau also.

*PREDICTING GAMMA FROM OVERLAP AMONG BUYERS

The substitutability parameter gamma asserts some homogeneous tendency toward substitution, for flows with the given market, of flows in ties with structurally equivalent markets. This is an idealization. Each industrial market is a historical construction whose networks of relational ties ground particular comparabilities that both presuppose and provide the basis for invidious ranking of producers by quality. But the networks also reflect and shape overlaps in the use of flows from different markets, and thus comparability and thence substitutability with other markets' sets of product varieties. Gamma is to reflect both faces of substitutability.

A heuristic model can be devised to explain and estimate processes that determine the size of gamma. These are processes of substitution within the competitive flows of an economy. Let's take an ecological perspective.

The model is not one of growth over time in the number of firms in a population, for the $W(y)$ model seeks to estimate cross section equilibrium. Equilibrium can, however, be arrived at by competing processes of growth when accompanied by removal processes. In population ecology, the removal is death; here, the removal is transfer of valuated product to the next layer of markets in production networks. In population ecology, the births are of firms, whereas here, markets are necessary homes for firms and thus are the limiting factor.

Within this view, think of the focal market as competing with a single representative market, from among those markets with enough structural similarity to offer some degree of substitutability in products to the focal market. We may adapt the familiar Lotka-Volterra equations[3] to yield a heuristic model, designating the aggregate revenues of the focal market, 1, and the representative other, 2, by W_1 and W_2. Think of them as counts of the numbers of units in production flows.

There is overlap in who buys from markets 1 and 2. We may represent this by a simple Venn diagram and designate w as the fraction of overlap: the proportion of all buyers of the focal market's goods who also buy from market 2. The equilibrium sizes reflect a balance achieved in competitive growth to levels of shipment.

The Lotka-Volterra equations are themselves already heuristic rather than exact, as the survey already cited by the biomathematicians Hofbauer and Sigmund (1988) makes clear. Let

$$dW_1/dt = R_1 \, W_1\{[V_1 - \rho_1 W_1 - \rho_2 \omega_{12} W_2]/V_1\} \qquad (8.18)$$

and

$$dW_2/dt = R_2 \, W_2\{[V_2 - \rho_2 W_2 - \rho_1 \omega_{21} W_1]/V_2\}. \qquad (8.19)$$

The basic step is to take the aggregate buyer valuation V defined in equation (6.2) as being a measure of the carrying capacity of the environment for production flow **W** from that market. The two differential equations (designate them L-V 1 and 2) govern the interacting growths of the two markets with overlapping customer environment. The basic rationale is straightforward. The rate of growth is proportional to its existing size as multiplied by a restraining factor {in brackets} that reflects the gap between carrying capacity and present size.

Here the real point is the interaction term, the third term in brackets in L-V 1 or 2, which inserts the additional constraint from intrusion of some of the other market flow into this one's carrying capacity. Let's make the simplest assumption. Let both the interaction coefficients, the omegas, be the same: assert a symmetry between the focal market and the other. Suppress the subscripts, so this common interaction coefficient is just ω.

One key step is to equate this coefficient ω with the Venn overlap coefficient w between customer bases that was defined in preparing equation L-V 1. And in the $W(y)$ model, from equation (6.3), carrying capacity **V** is a specified multiple of current size **W**: $V = \tau W$. The goal is to derive conditions for reaching equilibrium sizes, rather than trying to solve for (very complex) time paths. So the R coefficients can be disregarded.

The other keys are the coefficients ρ_1 and ρ_2, which calibrate by how much an existing population size **W** eats into the carrying capacity. But this translates into what change in **V** goes with what change in **W**. Chapter 6 suggests an answer (see equations (6.9–6.10)):

$$\rho = \tau_1\gamma_1. \tag{8.20}$$

and similarly for market 2. The equilibrium solutions of L-V 1 and 2 are well known (Hofbauer and Sigmund 1988, 56–58 and 149–52).

These equilibrium equations become

$$\omega_{12}\tau_2\gamma_2/\tau_1(1 - \gamma_1) = \tau_2(1 - \gamma_2)/\omega_{12}\tau_1\gamma_1. \tag{8.21}$$

For simplicity, set $\gamma_1 = \gamma_2$. Setting coefficients for one market equal to those for the other can weaken the stability of the equilibrium, but it is a substantive assumption of the $W(y)$ model that gamma should be approximately the same across the set of markets structurally equivalent to the focal one. The solution of equation (8.21) follows at once:

$$\omega^2 = (1 - \gamma)^2/\gamma^2. \tag{8.22}$$

From this follows an important identity to use as heuristic guide to the size of gamma:

$$\gamma = 1/(1 + \omega). \tag{8.23}$$

It cannot be more than a heuristic: Note that the maximum substitutability (minimum gamma) it allows is ½, which occurs when all the customers of 1 are also customers of 2. But it does give insight into the etiology of gamma.[4] It is a view consistent with that adopted in the next section in analyzing reciprocities between layers.

Parameters from Valuations along Stream

Commitments by firms must become embedded in a distinctive way into the networks of social relations along which production flows evolved. This must be traceable in terms of the market space parameters of volume flow valuations, a and c. Commitments by producers reflexively signal their own internal scale of operations in a period, as well as signaling quality to receivers. Tracing the commitments to volume made by producers in successive markets identifies dependencies along production streams. This is where parameters a and c, exponents that assess valuations of flow volumes, establish themselves as primary.

Tracing flows through commitments thus will give us insight into relations between the parameters a and c. These cannot be seen just as attributes of each given industry referred to some residual environment. Instead, these two parameters reflect the characters of analogous market interfaces that are neighbors to the focal one along the flow of production.

A large collection of input flows, many small and perhaps from several different firms in a given industry, are pulled into firms in a given industry. Think of a shoe factory, buying various leathers, treated to several degrees and colors as well as other materials like cords and metals. The output of each firm is seen as a package, sized by the volume commitment for next period's production, even though, in practice, an array of variants in sizes, colors, styles, and so on can be discriminated within the package of volume y with revenue $W(y)$.

These flows, in turn, become available to firms downstream of the given industry as *their* upstream procurements. Now shift the focus to what these producers are seeing as their own individual cost situations. Optimizing is getting the largest net return, the greatest gap between revenue, from the market profile, and cost. The rub is that cost still lies, at the time of commitment, in the future of that firm's subsequent organization of actual production from out of its procurements. But there is a saving grace: The producers have come to see, back on this upstream side of theirs, the uncertainties as being actuarial and accountable.

So the producers are comfortable with relying on estimates of likely costs according to the scales of production to which they consider committing. This can be portrayed in a simple graph showing how cost is thought to rise with volume produced in a period. Examples of such cost curves were included in figure 2.3. The cost curve refers to estimates by the producer, which justifies using the simple power function as shape. The analyst cannot second-guess firms' expectations and still come up with an account of what transpires in markets. Cost schedules indeed can be more individual and private in operation compared to rivalry profiles, but all the more they require and derive from cultural forms engrained in the discourse registers.

But what comes to determine the size of the power, the parameter c? Reaction tendencies of actors of several sorts are what are being cumulated and approximated by valuation schedules, $C(y, n)$ and $S(y, n)$ in the $W(y)$ market model. But these tendencies are forming and in turn being influenced by relations, relations in which actors are reaching through intermediaries. Thus the network setting of a market is crucial to parameters of the model.

Each reach-through can be seen as a linearization, and this will permit assessment of dependencies among values of the a, b, c, and d parameters across markets. At minimum, three positions along a flow are involved in each of the decisions about commitments to production volume, which thus are formed in a context unlike those for other species of economic market. The analysis will work toward suggesting how values of parameters at one point along a stream of transfers may relate to parameter values for market commitments in a subsequent layer.

Some set of firms comes to see itself and be seen by others as a production market when, and only when, products from each firm come to be seen by buyers downstream as comparable enough to constitute a product line distinct from the product lines characterizing other industries. These producers draw on upstream suppliers as they jockey as peers for quality niches in a profile of distinctive flow volumes that are being sold downstream. Figure 2.5 laid this out in words, and figure 1.1 in a concrete diagram that now we abstract from and elaborate on in figure 8.1.

This diagram emphasizes the transformations during production. There are two separate interfaces in actions between three layers from upstream, through ego, to downstream. A nonlinear transformation is, in general, effected across each of these interfaces.

There is no common metric between volumes of the input goods and of the output goods across an interface. This is where valuations in monetary terms become key. We shift now from the aggregate revenue measure W we used up to this point to the more familiar notions of price per unit in order to make the discussion easier to follow.

Array each market in the layer with the ego market as an oval with a vertical slice indicated for each producer. Then proceed similarly with the layer of markets procuring from one or more firms of the ego layer, and similarly for the upstream layer, which is supplying the ego layer. This is the layout in figure 8.1.

Let i, j, and k index the firms across all market molecules in a given layer. The layers are hereafter designated u for upstream (index i), e for ego (index j), and d for downstream (index k). Summation over i, j, or k will be understood as over firms separately or over their whole markets, as appropriate, to spare excessive detail in notation.

The essential point is that two very different kinds of transformations are being concatenated through these layers. A set of inputs to ego from the

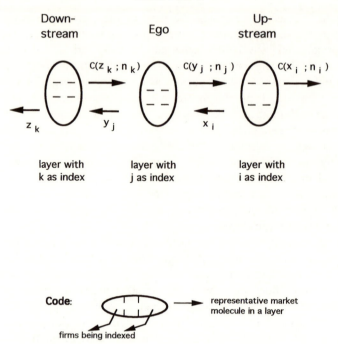

FIG. 8.1. Markets as molecules along production stream

upstream layer, measured in values paid for volumes, is gathered for non-linear transformation across the firm in the ego layer into an output volume and value for it. The second transformation is linear: exactly the weighted combination of these outputs of ego layer into the various sets of inputs to the downstream layer.

This second transformation is linear because all procurements are effected at the same unit price, off the shelf, so one has the value of inputs as a weighted sum of prices times volumes. *Designate* these weights as $f_{j,k}$, and designate prices by p. Different firms within a given ego market will have different quality products, and since these may be used by downstream producers in different proportions, the i, j, and k indexes run separately over all the individual firms. So the cost to producer firm k downstream is

$$C(z, n_k) = \Sigma(j) f_{k,\ j} p_j\ y_j. \tag{8.24}$$

Again to avoid cumbersome subscripting, designate volumes downstream by z's instead of y's (and, similarly, use x's for volumes upstream). The next step is to note that the cost schedules of downstream buyers are expressed in z's: for firm with quality n,

$$C(z, n_k) = q_k\ z^c, \tag{8.25}$$

where the quality multiplier n_k for k has been folded into q_k. But this expression must equal that in the previous equation (8.24): What is paid out is received.

Given estimates of parameter values, this transformation of y's into z's is straightforward to compute by determinant methods (see Aitken 1951). It is the solution of a set of inhomogeneous linear equations, with the y's being linear terms and the z's the (nonlinear) inhomogeneities. The z's can be thought of as given amounts on order. Any such calculations would in practice be difficult. The solution for the y's is subject to degeneracies unless coefficients are sufficiently distinct. Also, of course, these three layers should be seen as possibly in the middle of a stack of others. But one gains qualitative guidance from just this partial analysis.

The key move comes now. Observe that $S(y, n_j)$ derives substantively from the values those buyers in the k layer expect to obtain from sale of their own products, the z's. The function $S(y, n_j)$ is, of course, not known to the producer j, by hypothesis of the $W(y)$ model. But the observer notes that it ultimately derives from the valuation a representative z receives for her own product, which is $p_k z_k$, as one of the many contributions from the downstream layer to the ego layer. *The key move is this finding that the S function for an ego firm is proportional to some downstream producer volume, some representative z_k.*

But this volume of the downstream firm's product is found from equating (8.24) with (8.25). These sets of equations in combination become too intricate to solve, but a qualitative guide can be discerned: In the S function for firm j, the power y^a will behave like a z raised to the power of $1/c$, using the c value appropriate to that k layer of markets.

The suggestion is that, so long as one layer along a stream generally resembles another, the parameter a for a market may approximate the *reciprocal* of the c parameter of markets in the next layer downstream. It was worth some effort to reach this guide. It is the first pointer to possible dependencies among parameters for different markets. The degrees of dependence, and thus of stability, of the a, b, c, and d parameters clearly is central to the usefulness of the $W(y)$ model.

SELF-CONSISTENT FIELD

How does a market fit with others into networks of flows through a production economy? One hopes to develop tests of consistency between the relational structure among a population of markets and their distribution in the market space. A broader view thus is required that includes but goes beyond network topology.

Return to the larger network setting to consider issues of self-consistency about parameters. Assignment of a particular value to a parameter for some market may not be valid unless the parameter values for various other markets lie within certain bounds. And parameters across all markets may fall into some distribution of values that is not consistent with the overall character of the market sector presupposed in setting the parameters.

Historical evolution of the production economy was previewed in chapter 1 (and chapter 13 will offer projections to the future). The discussion of microeconomics in chapter 2 focused on Chamberlin's (1962) seminal theory of monopolistic competition, and the spread and substitutability analyses of chapters 3–7 are an explicit realization as a model. But Chamberlin's theoretical vision extended to evolution of a sector or a whole production economy, and this calls also for spatial structuring,

Spatial constructs have remained problematic in the social sciences.[5] Chapter 1 suggested structural equivalence within social networks as the key theoretical infrastructure for modeling production economy,[6] and this can assimilate geographical location, partially and indirectly. Both the preceding sections suggest carryover from structural equivalence to propinquity.

Structural equivalence is also manifest in the metric spaces postulated in the natural sciences and related fields in mathematics. In most natural science contexts, space is the prime focus, so we can hope for guidance from their models in handling structural equivalence as well as parameterizations. Claims of structural equivalence as the basis for market formation, here in the guise of substitutability, raise issues of consistency as well as of dependencies between markets along production streams. The self-consistent field (SCF) has for a long time proved a powerful approach to approximate modeling of complex physical systems (de Gennes 1979; Van Vleck 1932; Ziman 1979). The nub of the SCF approach is identifying those values for one or more parameters locating a representative atom such that the overall field that results across all atoms is consistent with the field and atom attributes assumed initially.

In earlier chapters, something like this approach has already been applied to firms within a market. Chapters 2 and 3 established consistency among the fits of firms into a profile for a given market, as atoms into a molecule. This SCF is now also to be applied across a set of such markets as molecules. For each molecule there is some set of molecules whose products are to some degree substitutable. Each molecule is also involved in transfers of products upstream and down. What sets of parameter values can ensure consistency?

A large number of parameters have been introduced. One must verify that these parameters fit together consistently, as preliminary to seeing how the parameters characterize embedding of markets into networks. So this first challenge of articulating consistency leads to the challenge of coming to understand more deeply the parameters that were differentiated in this chapter's opening pages.

Chapter 7 dissected how size and performance of a market interact with size and performance of its firms *and* of other parallel markets. Two of the key trio of parameters, gamma and tau, reflect the buyers' perspective, while the third key parameter, path dependence k, reflects interaction across the interface over time. The parameter tau, defined in equation (6.3), correlates positively with the power of the buyer side. Even the most passive collection of buyers would walk away if the ratio dropped below unity. Buyer counterpressure to producers, if somehow aggregated effectively, can increase tau; so tau reflects some degree of exploitation of the producers as a set constrained by the offer schedule. This is the important notion of countervailing power introduced long ago by John Kenneth Galbraith and others, who give leads as to the social processes by which such exploitation comes about. The tau observed will depend on historical path, the range of whose outcomes is indexed by k, but it also will depend on gamma.

Adding the other parameters a, b, c, d for market space dimensions permits, together with k and the scale factors r and q, full characterization of which rivalry profiles are feasible across a whole market. This remains true whatever the particular n values represented. But these quality index values n, which shape attempts at entrepreneurial interventions (see chapters 4 and 12), themselves respond to network context. And so must the other parameters, as was partially developed in the preceding two sections. The next chapters show how interventions also can lead to shifts from or to organizational alternatives to markets.

Just as the actors face path dependencies, so the analyst confronts many sorts of feedback loops within market processes in networks. The self-consistent field approach is designed to sidestep endless particular feedback loops. Feedback can confound attempts to infer underlying structure and parameters from surface performance. Take as an illustration the presumed opposition between the two sides of a profile. The motivation attributed to producers as a set is maximization of the producer's deal criterion, defined in equation (3.5), individual niche maximizations being taken as given. This deal criterion, like its spin-off in profitability, is the same across firms when $k = 0$. The formula in equations (3.5) and (3.25) is both extremely simple and somewhat paradoxical. Consider just the impact of changes in a/c.

The *smaller* is the responsiveness of buyer valuation to volume produced, as a ratio to responsiveness of producer cost to that volume, that is, the smaller a/c is, the *larger* the producers' deal criterion. This again results from a feedback loop! What's going on here is that, as value per unit drops across volume faster for buyers, the terms of trade, the market profile shifts and producers in turn optimize at volumes that raise the ratio of revenue to cost. This illustrates the impact that establishing self-consistency can have on tangible outcomes, but also that it differs between ORDINARY and ADVANCED.

Chapter 3 showed how, by use of Gini indexes, the set of numerical values on the quality index could be relegated to secondary status, being supplanted by exponents b and d and some information on bounds and distributions. Chapter 3 similarly relegated the value-scaling constants q and r to secondary status. Chapter 6 showed that the deal criterion theta also is secondary. And combinations of these various parameters into other parameters, such as epsilon in equation (3.11) or pi in equation (3.27) and the K', e', and f of equations (2.10–11), or the h in equation (4.1), are palpably secondary, mere conveniences.[7]

A nonsecondary parameter should relate different aspects of the causal mechanism being examined, as do gamma and tau. The parameter's usefulness depends on considerable constancy, but that is not sufficient—witness quality indexes and value scales. The path constant k is in a class by itself; it is an index of the particular perceptual framing that gets established with equilibrium in a market. Left implicit is what might in analogy be termed the "boundary constant," the choice of extent and content of populations to be modeled.[8]

The outcomes thus depend on feedback across a market's interface as well as with other markets. Outcomes of this complex interaction have been modeled, but no attempt is made to trace these disequilibrium processes. Instead, the SCF logic of verifying consistency across a set of outcomes in equilibrium is followed. Waechter (1999) is more ambitious. He sketches how earlier works on network and identity formation in relation to control (White 1992a, 1995a; White, Boorman, and Breiger 1976) can be interwoven to further specify the maneuverings that bridge between successive dynamic equilibria being portrayed here.

The general claim of this book is that business is socially constructed within networks of relations that shape institutions, relations that can be observed, specified, and interpreted in fieldwork by social scientists (see Romo and Schwartz 1993; McGuire, Granovetter, and Schwartz 1993). Underlying a production market system are the networks of continuing relations of various types from which it evolved. The goal has been to set computable models for production markets within a self-consistent field of interactions among firms across markets. The outcome is a three-dimensional array of models such that one can be mapped, albeit approximately, onto any particular market at a particular time.

Markets along Networks

Chapter 9 recognizes and models an opposite polarization of the market to face upstream. Edge markets, along with decoupling and embedding, thereby come into focus, and chapter 10 wrestles with the conundrums of theory that ensue. These are models that combine determinism with room for agency, since embeddings into distinct new levels of actor induce decoupling along the way.

Orthodox economic theorists, by contrast, strip markets from network context to yield a limit form, pure competition. Chapter 11 probes such suppression of real market competition.

~~~~~~~~~~~~~~~~~~~~~~

Chapter 9

Facing Upstream or Down

In previous chapters the $W(y)$ market has been viewed in only one of two possible orientations. That was the one with interface toward downstream, with the downstream being portrayed as an aggregated buyer. The upstream side of the producers was taken for granted as the source of needed procurements, at prices taken for granted by the producer. One accordingly may well affix the label of "pump" to this market mechanism of the previous chapters. The present chapter introduces and specifies a "pull" mechanism that also can sustain a production market, still with its environment split between a downstream and an upstream.

Figure 1.1 already diagrammed a pattern of production flows and market profile around a focal industry, and the firms making it up, within an overall patterning of generalized exchange in the economy. We now point out that this shows the context only for a market whose interface is oriented downstream. An entirely different market with interface can be constructed from among the same three distinct layers of actors that contribute to production flows of this industry in figure 1.1 that is oriented downstream. Figure 9.1 portrays in context such a dual interface with market oriented back upstream. One can call it polarized upstream.

In this upstream orientation, the $W(y)$ mechanism depends not on comparative satisfactions but on comparative reluctances. Examination of this dual mechanism will begin to clarify how decoupling and embedding both are at work in both push and pull markets. This will be developed more fully in chapter 10.

In either of these two modes of orientation, the production species of market establishes itself as an actor only when and as the relational ties and associated choices of its producer members become asymmetrized, downstream from upstream. These terms *upstream* and *downstream* have been taken for granted so far, as is common in writings by economists.[1] But this chapter must be more explicit as it goes on to position an array of markets, whether push or pull, along streams in procurement and supply.

The vision thus far is of firms gathering in and combining procurements from upstream, which each firm is transforming into subsequent flow of its own distinctive product for disposition downstream through a common frame, the market rivalry profile. But this overlooks a key substantive point: The producers constituting a production market are exposed to possible risk on *both* fronts, and ameliorating risk is what engenders formation of *any*

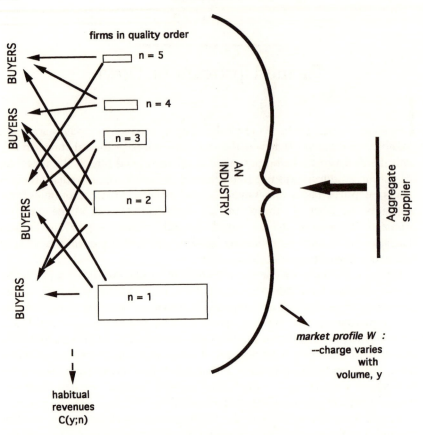

FIG. 9.1. Configuration of upstream flows dual to fig. 1.1

market interface. Rather than focusing around pushing product downstream, a market interface may instead orient to pulling key procurements from upstream, with the terms for downstream delivery treated as unproblematic in comparison.

So it is that footings for producers of a market may be sought in either of two orientations. One is directed back to upstream. The other is the one so far assumed, which is orientation downstream. Simultaneous orientation in both directions is unmanageable.

Let us pause to examine an irony. Let one side of a market interface be engrossed into a single actor. If that side is buyers, the market is called a monopsony; whereas if it is the producers who are combined, the market is called a monopoly. Monopsony is analogous to a production market with a downstream orientation, whereas the production market oriented upstream is the analogue to the monopoly. Presumably it is because of their obsession with pure competition as guide (see chapter 11) that economic theorists take so little note of orientation for production markets in general while yet separately labeling and analyzing the special cases of monopoly and monopsony.

In the next section we spend time clarifying phenomenology. Subsequent sections of this chapter will specify the upstream model and its solution, followed by contrast with downstream solutions and further discussion of market niche spaces.

Upstream Orientation and Market Roles

The discussion of Las Vegas gambling at the end of chapter 6 can be extrapolated to furnish a first, vivid example of upstream orientation of a market. Some of the initial examples in our research on upstream orientation from manufacturing sectors seemed labored or dependent on inflationary era, and in this chapter I often turn to service industry examples like Las Vegas casinos.

One can argue that in recent decades the issue for the gambling entrepreneurs was not how to accommodate needs (some would say, fleece customers) in the casinos. There was complete confidence in the almost mechanical generation of revenue from people once they had arrived in the casinos. So the problematic side, the challenge to which the market profile responds, is *upstream*, that is, in *getting* people to the casinos. Indeed, a better way to see these people is as the intermediate good being processed.

The puzzling part of the processing, the competitive part for the casinos, is getting the people in the door. Once they are there, the "sales" of gambling losses are predictably under the control of that casino. The casinos, in fact, were spending lavishly and competitively to attract lambs for fleecing. Las Vegas hotel rooms have been bargains, cheap by big-city standards. Lavish food is provided inexpensively, and alcohol is virtually free. The most expensive entertainers were lured by casino prestige and their paying higher fees than elsewhere. How can this sort of inverse producer market be modeled?

To develop a general analysis, one must recognize and resolve the seeming paradox discussed in the first section of chapter 2 as being latent in the account given of the downstream model: This is the paradox of asymmetry in perception from the two ends of a given relation. Such resolution clarifies upstream orientation.

The duality between upstream models and downstream models of the $W(y)$ market reflects a general asymmetry between ways of acting on the two sides of a market profile according to whether this profile governs the interface on the upstream side of an industry or on its downstream side. In the upstream orientation the producing firms are defined by their role as buyers. In upstream mode emphasis is on the buyers "pulling" from their suppliers, whereas the producers in a downstream orientation are "pushing" their chosen volumes. So, with the focus kept on producers as the center of any given market, the upstream and downstream models are also designated as the "pull" and "push" markets, respectively. Recognition of decoupling comes from examining the asymmetry between pull and push markets.

The market profile as a whole is on a different level from the particular niches taken along it by individual processors in view of their own operating characteristics. Each $W(y)$ market is a role structure. It is constituted as an identity, a distinct level of actor that is embedded into, while also decoupled from, its settings upstream or conversely downstream. These identities come into existence through embedding just because and as they are enabled to act by decoupling.[2] But what does this mean on the ground in observable behavior?

The push designation captures the focus on pushing the product into buyers' hands, with procurement and assembly being routine. The upstream mode, by contrast, is a pull mode since the problematic is acquiring indispensable input: Surplus over payment for input is what is problematized, and thence maximized, with the push downstream of the results being taken as routine. For example, perhaps the German metalworking industries, following their spring 1999 settlement with their major union, started seeing the choice and provision of total labor as the key bottleneck on which to focus attention as a joint interface.

How can one distinguish the two orientations through local inspection? What does the polarization consist in? Commitment is directional and is also the orienter. This means, for example, that a cost schedule is seen differently from downstream than from up, in either orientation: Seen from one side, a cost schedule derives from routine computation, whereas from the other side it becomes the construction of market profile (as will be elaborated later).

The directionality of commitment and of stream also implies that there must be edges, sources, and sinks for the flows. Locations near edges may affect polarization of markets. Markets in raw materials are a setting where the critical decisions in committing to production volume may well appear to be on the upstream side. And, as in the example just above, the same may hold with labor markets, which, like raw materials markets, often are conceived in aggregation across production markets and then called factor markets. The dual upstream form of the $W(y)$ model will then be appropriate, and it also may be appropriate at the other edge to production streams, the edge in distribution of products to final users.

In the upstream orientation, producing firms jointly focus on terms of trade concerning suppliers back upstream. Now at issue, therefore, are the *comparative reluctances* to ship to these various producer firms on the part of suppliers taken in aggregate. These may be suppliers of raw materials, labor, and other services, as well as of previously processed and finished parts and goods, depending on the particular market emerging. It is the same population of characters as previously introduced for downstream markets, but now the casting of these characters into market roles is different.

The *upstream polarization is dual, not duplicate*, for there is a difference in timings. Each producer is still fixing on the signal level optimal for it, now taken from along the profile for an upstream market. But now the signals are more anticipations than commitments, since the time order is reversed from the downstream case. The suppliers, who now are the actors aggregated by the valuation schedule, are simply responding to the diverse offers of the producers, which become equally attractive to the suppliers in aggregate to the extent that they fall on the market profile for that upstream situation.

On the profile of a given upstream market, the aggregate supplier holds affirmative veto power over each (volume, price) niche perceived as being offered by a producer. Detailed commitments in their ties downstream can be made by the producer firms, but realization depends on suppliers first conforming to their presumed sizes of deliveries. In downstream orientation, by contrast, the producer can commit to production with orders from upstream suppliers, with subsequent exposure to veto power from downstream buyers in aggregate.

The specifics are that there has to be a flow of revenue from each producer to its suppliers, as recompense for their reluctance. The producers are ensconced in a puzzling environment. There may have been recent contentions, as in labor strikes or in raw material crises or in changes in legal terms for supplier contracts, and the like, such that habitual prices for supplies have been washed away. The attention of all parties then will tend to be focused on these upstream transactions, rather than on the downstream ones that now will conform to customary or taken-for-granted prices. The producers will seek guidance as to terms of trade with suppliers upstream, terms that are sustainable but not overgenerous compensation for the latter's reluctances.

Differences in reluctance can, of course, depend on all sorts of historical and local factors, as well as on more abstract attributes that have come to be prominent in the culture of that production economy. The central assertion is much the same here as for the downstream market. An upstream market can and likely will emerge only if and as the different suppliers' reluctance comes to be ordered with respect to a penumbra of quality, a quality ordering compatible with that reflected in later routine sales downstream by the producers.

This could be quality as reflected, for example, in the experience of labor working in a Ford as opposed to a Chrysler or Toyota plant, or it could be the experience of labor in, or suppliers to, a Benetton as contrasted with a Textron firm (on garment trades see, for example, Lazerson 1993, 1995; Waldinger 1986). Experience, as well as reputation, of reliability in payment and also as to continued letting of business would loom large both for labor and for other suppliers (see, for example, Uzzi 1996). Location as to region, particularly in border and free-trade zones (Salzinger 1998), would factor in.

Let's turn from conventional manufacturing, and from distinguishing deflationary from inflationary eras, to consider firms that are basically selling talent in some special service. This could be a booking agency for selling musical performances. It could be a mid-Manhattan law firm. It could be a heart clinic for bypass and transplant surgery. The prime decision-concern and thus commitment for each such firm is the scope of talent it can retain and offer. This is a matter of negotiating payment terms with the upstream supply, a pool of relevant talents. Different law firms—or clinics or agencies—will come to be seen in an array by quality n. Given that, the law firm—or clinic or agency—will have no trouble allocating the talent at habitual prices across a set of clients. Its problem is continuing to obtain from upstream the level y of talent scope to which it commits. So that talent industry's signaling interface, the one-way mirror the peer firms look into, is oriented back upstream.

This class of service examples suggests an edge market, that is, a market at the edge of the production streams of an economy, the upstream edge, a sort of labor market. Of course, as an economy develops, there will be a tendency for this "talent" to no longer be thought of as springing out of the ground but rather as itself the product of antecedent productive efforts (of hairstylers, voice coaches, wardrobe consultants, etc.). Similarly, there can be edge markets at the downstream edge that are themselves oriented upstream: wholesaling markets provide an example, just as the earlier class of examples was introduced first by humdrum shoe manufacture. And such a downstream edge may recede as (in Lancaster 1970 spirit) consumers make a production out of their consumption.

Orientation is, however, not a question that is restricted to or by location on edge. The real issue in upstream versus downstream is where *within* the compass of a focal industry the key transformation is accomplished, and thus where in this compass the commitment-makers focus. In the previous chapters on downstream mode, the focus came with the accomplished transformation, when distinctive product was ready for sale. In an elite law firm or talent agency, by contrast, the focus is usually on the input side, on choosing and locking in the needed level of the key talent. The transformation is not at or before but after that point, as the endless minutiae of scheduling performances across the firm's range of topics and customers is accomplished.

Mechanism for Upstream Orientation

The market in upstream polarization will prove easy to model. Properties of the upstream market do differ from those of the downstream market in important ways, but the mathematical derivation is similar. Instead of six chapters parallel to chapters 2–7, this and the next section of the present chapter will suffice for setting up and solving the upstream model. Phenomenology then becomes the focus again in the final section, phenomenology of contexts favoring varieties of market mechanism associated with upstream.

Given an ordering by imputed quality, whatever the sector of industry, the terms of trade can sort out such as to support a *market profile* for upstream that is analogous to the downstream one portrayed in figures 1.2 and 2.2. Again, then, the volume of production is serving as a signal of differential quality, which is implicit or imputed rather than coded through public and explicit measurement. As before, the other side from the producers—now suppliers rather than buyers—cannot prescribe scales of production but can rigorously enforce equal desirability as between the (volume, revenue) offers from the various producers. Again there will appear some range of historical, accidental variability in what profile gets established. But then again the profile, once established, is a social fact leaving little play at that time as to sustainable terms of trade to the given producer.

Intuitively it should be clear that the upstream mode, although parallel in some respects to the downstream mode, will have rather different dynamics. In this upstream or pull mode, the commitment-makers come later in the flow after their problematic counterparts providing inputs, whereas in downstream mode the commitment-makers come earlier in the flow than their problematic counterparts downstream, the buyers. Even the cross-sectional equilibrium solution for $W(y)$ models will show marks of this difference in temporal placement.

The mathematical solution for the upstream orientation consists in turning the solution for downstream orientation "inside out." As in all the previous chapters, the environmental responses to which a market is subject are approximated in functional forms so simple that a few key parameters—notably a/c, b/d, and gamma—are sufficient to assign a market's variety and its location in state space, together with aspects of performance of firms within the market. *No additional parameters* are required, just alternative interpretations of existing parameters. There will be distinctive varieties of upstream market as there were of downstream.

Each firm knows its *revenue* structure $C(y, n)$ and chooses its commitment y from along a $W(y)$ payment curve of offers to talent so as to maximize net revenue $C - W$. This payment profile $W(y)$ will survive and be validated if and only if the talent pool upstream judges the trade-off offered by each firm as equivalent to that of the others. Each trade-off is a ratio of recompense level $W(y[n])$ they receive from firm n over their felt discomfort, monetarized as $S(y, n)$ in combination with their level of effort in performing for that particular firm n.

There is thus *both* a formal parallelism in the solution to that for the downstream production market and also a crucial duality, both of which mainly consist in *substituting minimization for maximization*. It turns out that most of the framing and calculations of the downstream model can be carried over, with some crucial transpositions, so that *relabeling is the key*:

The volume made and shipped by a producer remains as y.

$W(y)$ is now the *cost* to the producer of making that amount y. This is now a cost that is problematic, rather than formulaic, because of the unknown (de)valuations by suppliers of the firm's process of production. One interpretation would be for a labor market in which (homogeneous) laborers had differential distastes for working for the different producers.

The index for niceness or quality remains n, as before, but now this is quality of difficulty perceived by suppliers for themselves, for example as laborers, as regards that firm's process of production. This is of products that then are shipped off downstream for routine sale at habitual price and so yielding calculable revenue.

The producer thus is able to compute from its own records and experience $C(y, n)$, which now is the *revenue curve* that the various volumes would bring from dispersed buyers downstream. As before, n is a label we apply as observers. Producers have little hope of estimating quality index values for their peers. Even its own quality need not be known to the producer, it being a matter of tangible immediate judgments (of distaste) aggregated across the suppliers.

This industry's suppliers, taken in aggregate (whose own *revenue* is $W(y)$) are influenced in two ways in their reluctances, which are their (de)valuations seen in the form of costliness to them, in supplying a given firm. First, both the volume and the quality of the flow influence them, according to a function $S(y, n)$. And second, they are influenced by what they are also supplying to all firms in the industry taken together, according to an overall valuation function, namely, the V defined in equation (6.2).

All the formulas from chapters 2–7 continue *unchanged in form, subject to the above relabelings* according to which the senses of monetary flows are reversed: Our claim now is that each producer knows the *revenue* it will receive from producing various levels of volume y. The cognate claim is that it is now the *suppliers* in aggregate who perceive the aggregate valuation reported in formula (6.2).

Before turning to the few changes in the mathematical equations, consider the changed substantive meanings of some key parameters: Having parameter a be less than 1 could be the result of heavy start-up costs to supplying any given producer (e.g., a hiring hall). The value of a could, on the other hand, be greater than 1 if there was some saturation effect, either per unit (such as laborer) or from some common bottleneck that caused crowded unpleasantness as supply y to a given producer goes up. The parameter b reflects how different producers are distinguished overall, with a high value of b/d reflecting even greater difficulties in providing supplies to a higher-quality product as seen downstream than is gained by the producer in price.

There are analogous substantive parallels. It should be clear, for example, that there is an *upstream dual* to the guild option, sketched in chapter 4, for bypassing a downstream market profile. The dual to guild control resembles in its substantive features early trusts, such as the Havemeyer Sugar Trust, which around 1900 came to engross all the raw material production from whole regions. Vulnerability of an existing profile to unraveling, or just possibilities for enormous profits, could engender cabals to attempt enforcement of an administered price structure. This could be a markup on minimum cost, which would bypass the path dependence of the profile. Of course any such trust for exploiting raw material producers could also be seeking exploitation on its downstream side as well.

The mathematical derivations go through exactly as before *except* that *maximization is replaced by minimization*, for each producer in choosing its volume; and *except* that the producer insists on

$$W(y[n]) < C(y[n], n), \tag{9.1}$$

rather than the reverse shown earlier in (2.13); and *except* that the aggregate supplier insists that

$$\mathbf{V} < \mathbf{W} \tag{9.2}$$

rather than the reverse shown earlier following equation (6.3). These *three reversals* follow because the relabelings interchange incomes with payments.

All equations continue in force, and in particular those for locating an extremum. The only changes are reversals in the inequalities. Hence the same expression, equation (2.9), continues to hold for market profile $W(y)$. Profiles can be computed for particular examples of markets in upstream orientation, in exact analogue to computations for figures 1.2 and 2.6. However, interpretations of these profiles are very different, as will become apparent.

The niche space will be split by boundary lines into the same pattern of regions as in figure 5.1, *but* the interpretation of each will differ entirely. So also will the ranges of k, the historical constant, which yield viable schedules differ, because of the reversals of inequalities.

There is no change in the complex of conditions (concerning maximization and positive income) that obviate the danger of unraveling. Again, the range of y allowed by positive cash flow to the producer must be contained

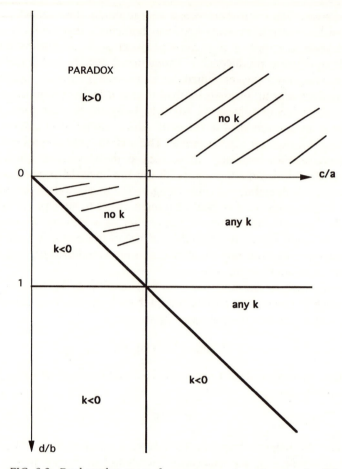

FIG. 9.2. Dual market space, for upstream orientation; see fig. 5.1

within the range in which a distinctive extremum (now the minimum) is found. But now the cash flow is $C - W$, rather than $W - C$.

Figure 9.2 is the dual state space, of niches in a market facing upstream. In order to make it comparable to figure 5.1 as to substantive meaning, each ratio defining an axis has been inverted. For example, c/a now has the substantive meaning that a/c had before; namely, of volume sensitivity of revenue (here to producers) relative to volume sensitivity of cost (here to suppliers).

Derivation of the viability ranges for y and thence k, by region, can be left as an exercise for the reader. Table 3.2 can be paralleled. Let's work out just one key example, the triangle in the ORDINARY region of figure 3.1 or 5.1:

$1 > c/a > d/b$, and so $e > 0$ (note the inversion of ratios). The first two viability criteria take the forms (for abbreviations, see equations (2.10, 2.15–2.16), or the note to table 3.2):

$$y^{ce} < - [1/(c/a)]ke/K \qquad (9.3)$$

and

$$y^{ce} < - (1/(d/b))ke/K. \qquad (9.4)$$

But then it is clear that for k positive no y values are allowed. And for k negative, one derives

$$y < y_{max} = [|k|a/cK]^{1/ce}; \qquad (9.5)$$

$$y < y_{pos} = [|k|b/dK]^{1/ce}. \qquad (9.6)$$

So for $k < 0$ the market profile is subject to unraveling, because manifestly

$$y_{pos} > y_{max}, \qquad (9.7)$$

whereas parallel derivation for the former UNRAVELING region has all y allowed for any negative k (though for positive k there is exposure to unraveling just as above).

The equations for aggregates **W**, **V**, and **C** carry through from earlier chapters. Also carrying through is the resolution there of the feedback conundrum. This resolution, which was developed in detail only for the special case $k = 0$, continues to apply.

Turn now to pressure from the aggregated side on the deal criterion theta: See equation (2.3). Since these dual markets face upstream toward problematic *procurement*, the aggregate side is now the suppliers, who will prefer *lower* values of the deal criterion, that is lower level of disdain S for given revenue received W. Now consider the *industry* deal criterion tau. Again, one will expect tendencies (now stimulated from the supplier, upstream side) toward equalizing this tau criterion across the overall deal. But now the pressure is toward lower values of tau: *the inequality between* **W** *and* **V** *is reversed*. Note that the results will have

$$C > W > V. \qquad (9.8)$$

And what had been the ratio of aggregate revenue/cost for the downstream market satisfies the same equations, but now it refers substantively to the cost/revenue ratio in the special case of $k = 0$ (see figure 9.2 for allowed regions).

Return to the previous substantive interpretation of parameters: gamma becomes the interaction effect, overall across these distinct reluctances vis-à-vis different producers on the part of the aggregate supplier. Gamma can reflect wholly distinct opportunities to supply other industries, and/or

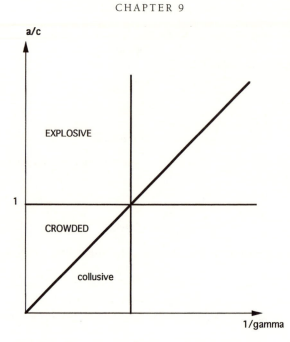

FIG. 9.3. Upstream market space for aggregates dual
to fig. 7.1

gamma can be a capacity constraint, which would imply a certain closure as
a fixed population of suppliers (e.g., Columbian coffee growers).

Gamma less than one means that some of the worst mismatch of supplier
to producer can be palmed off onto other industries "nearby." An alternative
to *substitution* as label is "dis/economies of scale." Gamma greater than unity
signifies an explosion, possibly a crowding or bottleneck effect that worsens
the unpleasantness of supplying when they are all going on together across
the distinct *n* producers. See figure 9.3, which is dual to figure 7.1.

There is no need for extended discussion of figure 9.3, since how aggregates and profiles vary with size of gamma is the same, formally, in the dual
market models. Thus, much of the discussion concerning figure 7.1 carries
over.

Substantively, however, the incidence of gamma is different. No longer
does the observed value of gamma indicate substitution (as gamma < 1 did
in the case of downstream market), but instead it indicates the tendency
toward involution. In an upstream market, one expects gamma to be *greater*
than unity. An interaction effect multiplies disdains for supply to individual
producers in assessing overall disdain from aggregate supplier to that industry. Thus, the disdain aggregate for one industry is larger (rather than being
smaller) because of substitution effects.

*Downstream versus Upstream

Figures 1.1 and 9.1 suggested tangible configurations of profile accompanying ties to firms for markets with each of the two opposite polarizations. Figure 9.4 gives two schematic renderings of how markets polarized one way or the other may stack into a flow stream. A whole sector may, during a period, seek and follow a consensus as to which direction to face, which direction is the more problematic, but polarization may differ, industry by industry.

In the left column of figure 9.4 is shown a downstream mode for the Charlies, while the right column shows them all in upstream market orientation.[3]

Understanding when one orientation is invoked, and when instead the other, is challenging. An answer suggested earlier in this chapter was *factor markets* for upstream. This term designates an abstract aggregation into upstream orientation for a dispersed context. Examples are the labor market, for occupations as distinct from professions, and the wheat market cited earlier.

More specific illustrations are helpful. Return to the lower-left region of the downstream state space. This region was labeled UNRAVELING, since a market there is subject to unraveling *regardless* of k, depending on the quality spread found among would-be entrants. Chapter 7 identified candidate markets for this region in the road-haulage or *routier* industry (not included in the U.S. industries of figures 3.3 or 5.2). One scenario to stability might be the introduction of explicit regulation of working conditions in these road-haulage industries, or equivalently of some sort of guild control of terms of trade and employment. Another scenario, possibly made more likely by regulation, could be a switch of attention of haulage firms back upstream, to focus on obtaining drivers and to take customers more for granted.

The truckers might detest overtime, but be relatively insensitive to which particular firm they drove for. The firms would find good service expensive to provide but necessary to continued custom. Then again in the upstream state space the *routier* would be in the same lower-left region. But now this market would no longer necessarily be subject to unraveling. On the contrary, in upstream orientation this is one of the two regions most profitable and accessible for market formation. (Switching will be analyzed further in chapter 13).

Now turn back to the discussion in chapter 5 of Spence's signaling market for labor. His key assumption was that a (and hence a/c) tended toward zero because y for him was primarily signal and only secondarily a tangible contribution to valuation. That is, Spence confined his model to the left panel, and only the PARADOX region offers a viable market profile there, from the present model with enlarged state space.

two examples of production flow strings

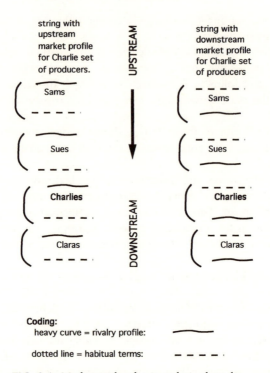

FIG. 9.4. Market molecules in polarized stacks

Spence's special empirical referent was the market in hiring of managerial labor. Figure 9.2 suggests that an upstream version of such a market could function not only in PARADOX but also in the region below it, which is now no longer subject to unraveling. This upstream market would have a rivalry among managers striving for recognition as the market mechanism. It brings in open competition to replace Spence's monopsonist market-maker. Yet such a market mechanism could still also operate in PARADOX.

Take one other example. Return to the downstream niche space, to the region called TRUST in figure 3.1 just below the abscissa. This goes with the dual just discussed to the UNRAVELING region as one of the two most profitable and accessible for market formation in upstream polarization. Here one may find upstream markets of wholesalers, or other brokers to consumers that exhibited Galbraith's countervailing power. Organizations such as Wal-Mart or People's Drug can be thought of as having rationalized distribution through their numerous branches to the point that sales volume and terms are predictable; so their focus is upstream, dealing with various manu-

facturing industries. In some instances, one would model the ultimate consumers as the buyers; in other instances, one should model the operator/
owners of subsidiary small retail outlets as the buying side from the perspective of the wholesalers. Retailers might be rather insensitive to quality, at least
over some cutoff, but very desirous of stocking brands that will generate
large quantities in sales. The manufacturers upstream might prefer dealing
with smaller- than with larger-volume wholesalers and yet might also be very
sensitive to the quality of service provided. This configuration would indeed
suggest a location in the region labeled TRUST in the downstream dual space
first shown in figure 3.1. Work by Porter (1976b, discussed at greater length
in chapter 14) suggests such an interpretation.

One can also refer market polarization to environment more broadly. During a business downturn, producers are unlikely to have troubles with supplies from upstream but instead will experience uncertainty as to purchases
by actors downstream, where they shift their attention. But then, conversely,
in inflationary periods, producers expect and turn to face difficulties with
raw materials and labor and others of their upstream suppliers, without any
trouble in placing continued flows with their downstream purchasers. So in
inflationary eras the ground is prepared for common orientation upstream by
nearly all markets. Abrupt external disruptions such as war might be the
occasion to induce wholesale switching to upstream orientation (see the discussion of U.S. mobilization in World War I in Cuff 1973).

Explicit contrasts between the models for downstream and upstream orientation need to be worked through. Since by construction each is a mechanism in equilibrium, incidents or cumulative pressures are required to impel
a switch in either direction (see chapter 13), but viability of the end-state
would still be at issue and is the concern in this chapter. Contexts in some
regions of the state space may be inhospitable for one orientation, and various other regions may be inhospitable for the other. The first step is to
specify the comparison, which aims at the aggregate profitability of producers as a set.

Contexts encourage downstream or upstream orientation of a given market mechanism according to which orientation offers the larger advantage to
the producers as a whole. Downstream, let us measure this advantage as the
ratio **W/C**, which is the operating margin plus unity. The analogous criterion
for upstream derives from the same algebraic equation with appropriate inversions of ratios.

Figure 3.2 traced, *for the downstream model of chapters 2–8*, rays in the
state space of figures 3.1 and 5.1 along which the criterion ratio **W/C** was
fixed, each for the central case of $k = 0$. Figure 9.5 is the exact analogue of
figure 3.1, again for market profiles with $k = 0$, but now for *upstream* orientation. Note the entirely different form and location of the lines. How can
this be?

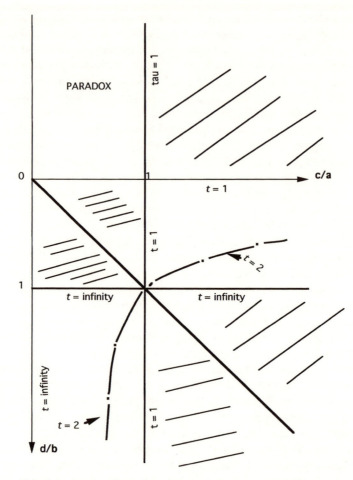

FIG. 9.5. Curves of equal performance, upstream market space

The *key point* in figure 9.4 was that exactly the same neighbors, Sues and Claras, abut the Charlies in both orientations. Thus, the **V** in the downstream mode is valuations that concern transactions with Sues by the Charlies, whereas it is the **C** in the upstream model that concerns valuations of transaction to the Sues by the Charlies. And on the other side, the transactions with Claras by Charlies are being valuated for the upstream model around **V**, whereas for the downstream model it is **C**.

This elucidates just why, in order to compare how the Charlies do in upstream mode with how they do in downstream mode, one must invert each of the valuation sensitivity ratios. That was already done to yield as figure 9.2 a niche space for the upstream market model that was directly comparable substantively with figure 5.1 for downstream state space.

The results shown for market in upstream mode in figure 9.5 are straight-forward to derive. Just repeat earlier equations, such as equations (3.25, 3.26), but with two sorts of changes. Now on the left side the ratio is inverted: **W/C**, as compared to **C/W**. And on the right-hand side, each ratio of parameters is inverted in each appearance, as in the transformation from figure 3.1 to figure 9.2.

Let t represent the size of the fixed ratio **C/W** whose locus is to be shown as a line in state space for upstream orientation. This is the analogue, the dual to equation (3.25) for downstream from chapter 3, with t here corresponding to **W/C** there. The equation becomes

$$t = [(d/b) - (c/a)]/[(d/b) - 1]. \qquad (9.9)$$

One sees that, since numerator and denominator must both have the same sign (or t would be negative), the locus for t can only cross two regions of the state space. These are exactly the only two regions that allow profiles with $k = 0$ in the upstream niche space already given, figure 9.2. Except that in the PARADOX region the d is negative, which flips the negative signs in the equation to positive. So altogether a given numerical value of t can take loci (line segments) in each of three regions of the state space.

In order to further clarify the structure of equation (9.9), displace the origin: Let the volume sensitivity ratio *minus unity* be defined as Y; let the quality sensitivity ratio *minus unity* be defined as X. So these shifted coordinates have as origin the point where both ratios are unity, just the same point in the downstream mode through which went every line of points in the state space for markets that had the same operating ratio, as shown in figure 3.2. A little algebra yields

$$Y/X = -(t - 1) - t \cdot Y. \qquad (9.10)$$

The particular case of $t = 2$ yields $Y/X = -1 - 2Y$, which translates into the curved line in figure 9.5 that is labeled $t = 2$.

The contrast is clear. For example, along the diagonal, given by $(c/a) = (d/b)$, where in figure 3.2 the downstream mode receives unlimited profitability, here t is zero, so it is the least desirable location of all contexts to producers in upstream mode, since they earn no revenues at all. But there is also some limited similarity. For *both* upstream and downstream modes, all those cases where $a = c$ yield just a break-even operation ($t = 1$ here).

The line of contexts most advantageous to producers in upstream mode is $b = d$, together with the line at right angles that represents the case of production of extreme luxury goods, where volume sensitivity ratio, (c/a) in the upstream mode, approaches zero. Note too that in addition to $(c/a) = 1$ being break-even for upstream, so are all the contexts with zero sensitivity ratio for quality and with volume sensitivity ratio greater than 1. So one can understand why the lines of constant t must bend like parabolas passing through the point $(1, 1)$: They spread out thus through the two rectangles

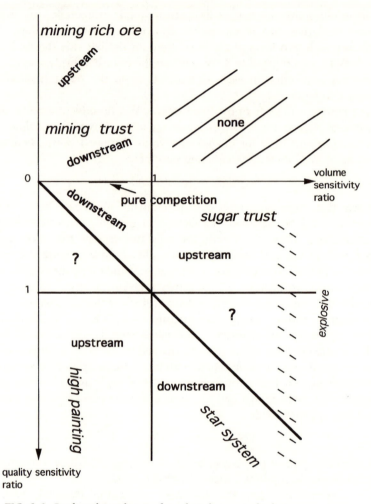

FIG. 9.6. Predicted incidence of markets between dual spaces

outlined (in heavy solid and dotted lines in figure 9.6) by the limiting cases
of breakeven and of huge payoffs for producers

Although all these formulas are where market profiles have $k = 0$, the
general picture seems clear and can be confirmed in detail for regions of
special interest by numerical solution such as those in appendix tables A.1–
A.5 for the downstream model. The two rectangular areas labeled in the
downstream state space, table 3.2 and figure 3.2, as TRUST and RAVELING
are much more likely to find sets of producers who orient as a market to the
upstream mode, whereas in the three regions through which positive profit
lines pass in figure 3.2, CROWDED, ORDINARY, and one other, one would

expect to see orientation to the downstream mode. Figure 9.6, which integrates figure 9.2 with figure 5.1, lays this out.

To reduce confusion in this and subsequent figures for upstream models, the two axes are just labeled blandly in words, as volume sensitivity ratio and quality sensitivity ratio, for respective valuations of cost and of satisfactions.

The ADVANCED region and especially its subset, the CROWDED region, where more producers yield a smaller market aggregate, appear also in the upstream polarization. The aggregate size of markets in CROWDED still decreases as more producers are added, even though each brings equivalent buyer valuations in along with it. When one allows for buyers' desire to maintain if not improve their industry deal ratio tau, there is pressure toward a decrease in the number of distinct producers.

A peculiar divergence seems to appear, however, in the contrast between these upstream markets and the analogous downstream markets from the CROWDED region of figure 7.4. Turn to figure 7.1 and correlate it now with figure 9.3. The central distinction results not from the formulas but from the likely size of gamma. It is in the upstream market that gamma is likely to exceed unity: the left region of figure 7.1, which has not been discussed hitherto.

In these circumstances, one has, for upstream markets, the CROWDED effect of pressure toward fewer producers. But, second, this feature is combined with the feature already noted for the EXPLOSIVE region, earlier, that aggregate size increases as q goes up, and inversely decreases as r goes up. But, once converted to substantive terms from formal terms, the peculiarity evaporates, since now in this *upstream* market, q has the overtones of consumer demand and r the overtones of cost.

So in the upstream models, what seems peculiar *substantively* is instead the proportionality of aggregate size to r/q for *small* ratio a/c. That is, the substantive analogue for upstream markets to the peculiar interactive feedback effects uncovered for EXPLOSIVE downstream markets occurs in the hitherto unmarked lower triangle in figure 7.1. The labelings appropriate for the upstream markets have been inserted in figure 9.3, which is exactly parallel to figure 7.1. This discussion also further explains and justifies why the conventions for the ordinate and abscissa ratios have been inverted in figures 9.2 and 9.3, which show the dual upstream models.

Of course, the unmarked triangle that appears in figure 3.1 could be relevant for some downstream markets too, but these would tend to be short-lived and peculiar. They would be markets for fad products or perfumes, where no other sort of good, no good from another industry, can substitute at all but where nonetheless one does not much *like* the particular actual producers and products: a dream industry (or, perhaps better, a "nightmare" industry).

Analogously, for upstream models the weird cases substantively are for gamma less than unity. Here, the aggregate laborers' distaste for working in a noisy Fordist plant would, when combined with their disdain for working in a slipshod Fiat plant, and so on, all add together less than linearly in their aggregate assessment of their employment overall across that industry. It would require that they be unready to consider other industries as alternatives for employment: Miners could be an example where there is insularity of culture, as evidenced by developments in the 1990s in Britain, the Continent, and Russia.

In chapter 3, the summings of aggregate flows to boundaries of a market system were computed for markets all in downstream orientation, equation 3.30. Parallel results hold with all markets in upstream orientation, and an exactly parallel equation can be derived. Now, of course, the set of markets of which the economy is supposed to be composed are varieties that lie on the parabolic lines illustrated in figure 9.5. But actual economies may be patchy mixtures of the two orientations in whole sectors or individual markets.

DUAL MODES AND SPLIT REGIONS

The upstream orientation, also referred to as mode or polarization of the market, is not a simple inverse or reverse of the downstream mechanism of chapters 2–7. There is a subtle slippage between the meanings of a, b, c, and d for downstream and upstream, resulting from a shift of dimensional units. Return to figure 9.5 and envisage the dual diagram for downstream mode. Note that more is required than just the switchings of C with W, of V with W, and thus of minimization for maximization. The variable committed to, the variable output designated by y, changes also.

Think of the market interface as a house with both a front porch and a back porch. In downstream mode, the disparate ingredients are delivered to the back porch. The singular volume y committed to, of product made from those ingredients, is assessed and shipped from the front porch to aggregate customer on terms read off that market rivalry profile.

In upstream mode, much the same physical flow and money counterflow are passing through the house via the porches, but the polarity is reversed as to valuations and their labelings. On the front porch there accumulate the predictable packets of money $C(y[n])$ being received from diverse customers of firm n in return for its shipments to them along customary ties. *The key is that all shipments come from the total committed to by that producer firm as measured in* units of the factor $y[n]$ being purchased, at terms set by upstream market profile $W(y)$, from the suppliers of producer factor, treated as an aggregate.[4]

It is substantively appropriate to substitute c in upstream orientation for a in downstream orientation. Each exponent is measuring curvature of valuation by customers of physical flow received. However, the physical flow is measured in different units, which could make a considerable difference. For now, assume this is not so and proceed to compare performances of upstream with downstream mode for comparable niches. (The next chapter will return to this issue.)

To gain clarity, let's work out the duality comparisons for some particular region of niches. The PARADOX region warrants special attention. It is true that the downstream mode yields positive profitability of all degrees at contexts in PARADOX. But this is also the case in the upstream mode, because d now has a negative value. Here then is the most interesting region of all for comparing downstream versus upstream.

A set of producers in every context from the PARADOX region, at all points there, can sustain a market profile with $k = 0$ both in upstream and downstream orientation, and moreover there will be at least some profitability in either mode. The obvious question is to ask, point by point in the region, which mode does better. We seek the boundary line between subregions where the upstream does better and regions where the downstream does. In fact, PARADOX is split into just two parts. Equality occurs when the t defined by equation (9.9) is equated with the corresponding ratio from equation (3.25), $\mathbf{W/C}$.

Routine manipulation of the resulting equation yields as the borderline curve between upstream and downstream modes in PARADOX

$$\text{(volume sensitivity ratio)} = \text{(quality sensitivity ratio)}^2. \qquad (9.11)$$

This equation defines a parabola, beginning at the origin and crossing over into the forbidden region where both sensitivity ratios are unity. Figure 9.7 shows this parabola overlaid on figure 9.6. This unique single boundary parabola divides the regions of state space in which one or the other mode is preferred, by the criterion of profitability for the set of producers. The inner points, approaching pure competition, are where the downstream mode is favored.

On the other, bottom half of the plane, where d is positive, exactly the same equation (9.11) results from equating profitability ratios. So that bottom half-parabola is also shown in figure 9.7. Many of the points in the bottom half do not support profiles with $k = 0$, for one or the other of the orientation modes, up and down, as has been reported in figures 3.1 and 9.2. And, in fact, there prove to be several disjunct regions where a given mode is favored, rather than the one contiguous, compact region as for the PARADOX region. Figure 9.7 reports these results too.

Only performance ratios yield manageable comparisons between upstream and downstream markets, even with $k = 0$. Aggregate sizes are, however, vital to realistic appraisal of differences between the two polarizations. They can be compared via numerical solutions, for which qualitative guidance is invaluable.

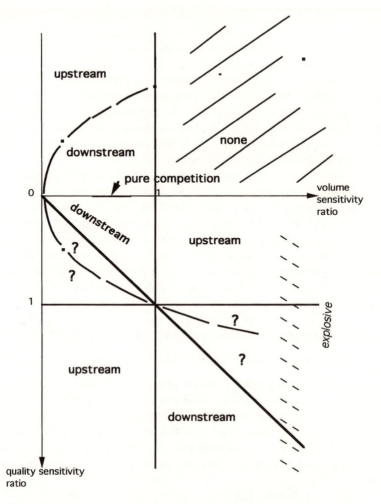

FIG. 9.7. Boundary curve for locations with downstream market profit rate higher

Hereafter, we may use x for d/b in upstream (and for b/d in downstream), and similarly abbreviate c/a by v. In this notation, the formula for upstream W_o that parallels equation (7.4) for downstream (itself derived from equation (6.8)) is

$$W_o = \{(r/\tau^{1/\gamma})^v (q/v) \cdot [(x - v)/(x - 1)]_{\#}^{v-1} \, n^{e(v-x)}\}^{\gamma/(v-\gamma)}. \quad (9.12)$$

When, for qualitative guidance, one computes from equation (9.12) the equivalent of table 7.1 from equation (7.4), the result is striking: Table 7.1 still applies, with the one exception that tau is replaced everywhere by its inverse. There is no need for a separate table. The inversion of tau is, in substantive terms, instead a parallelism. Tau is counterpressure on the producers as commitment makers on y. The pressure in upstream is from suppliers, and it consists in their favoring *minimizing* the (substitutability valuation in) discomfort S, which they exchange for payment W. So lowering gamma upstream is substantively parallel to raising the downstream gamma.

So, just as the other two dimensions are inverted, under the common labels of x and v, the third dimension of state space is inverted, with gamma functioning as 1/gamma. But further, on substantive grounds also, it is not $\mathbf{W}$ that should be compared from upstream to the downstream W of equation (7.4). Instead it is $\mathbf{C}$, with $k = 0$ still. But guidance breaks down for this comparison. The $k = 0$ profile is applicable in both upstream and downstream markets only for PARADOX regions. For the two regions, former TRUST and UNRAVELING, where the $k = 0$ solution is viable upstream, it is not (see figure 3.1) viable for downstream aggregates and so cannot furnish a comparison. And conversely, for the two regions where the $k = 0$ solution is viable downstream, ADVANCED and ORDINARY, it is not viable in upstream mode (see fig. 9.2).

~~~~~~~~~~~~~~~~~~~

CHAPTER 10

Embed and Decouple

Every market must embed into, but also decouple from, networks of relations across the broader context of the production economy. This chapter probes the implications of this necessity. Decoupling of relations is needehd to lubricate the choices and bargainings that make up a market. But a pervasive polarity of upstream or downstream survives this decoupling as to exactly which particular firms and markets transact with each other in a given period. And so does the embedding of producers into their rivalry profile.

The modeling of the individual market molecule, in chapters 2–5, was completed in chapters 6–8 by setting it among markets similar enough to be substitutable, instead of lying upstream or downstream of it. Then chapter 9 noticed that an opposite orientation is possible for this market molecule and went on to propose and develop a dual form of the $W(y)$ model. The resulting vision, implicit already in figures 1.1 and 9.1, is complex. The present chapter attempts to articulate this vision within a theory of social construction (and thus is one specification of White 1992a, chaps. 2–5).

The next section, on embeddings, leads on through a section on pragmatics of the market as molecule and then a section on decoupling. That sets up a sketch in the final section of how overall dynamics depend on patterns of connectivity in a network of markets. It speculates that "small world" connectivity among these market networks can tame disruption in dynamics of flows through the field of market molecules.

TWO EMBEDDINGS INTO NETWORKS

The basic point of $W(y)$ theory is that operation of markets can be modeled only with reference to embedding and decoupling in network context. The siting of a production market into flows of intermediate products is what most distinguishes it. This market only takes on a life of its own as a distinct actor, a separate identity, in gaining general recognition of its siting into flows among firms. This remains true even for markets at the edges of flows. A network relational view is thus called for across both firms and markets to express their embeddings.

This production market is rather newly recognized as a species, and accordingly it is not yet well understood in social science. In the $W(y)$ perspective developed in this book, such a market builds an identity that is quite as binding upon its constituent firms as is authority within a clan or bureau-cracy. The market profile is shaped by trade-offs between local variabilities that sustain the market interface. An ordering within a market by quality of firms along with their products becomes imputed during the course of establishing such trade-off.

And this market thereby comes into existence embedded into network. Footings for firms were introduced in chapters 1–3 as positions in some market considered by itself. The meaning was quite evident: location along a rivalry profile. Each representative firm seeks a footing for itself from a location along the $W(y)$ profile of this market.

Such a location can be designated as a niche. Breadth of a representative firm's niche translates, within the $W(y)$ model, into some spread in quality around its index value n and perhaps also some spread in time horizon. This was discussed in chapter 4 and again in chapter 6, although boundaries were defined only fuzzily, either as to dimensions or as to the range on any particular dimension.

A further level of embedding, and thus of identity, is essential in the constitution of markets. The notion of the representative firm and its niche suggests the further notion of niche for market as such. The shape of the rivalry profile does, after all, adapt to the context of the market as a whole, context that is being specified by a, b, c, d, and gamma parameters. Thus, locations in these *abcd* planes of previous chapters can also be seen as niches for some allowed band of the rivalry profiles taken as wholes, as distinct from the niches of particular firms along one such profile. The derivations in chapter 8 relate these context parameters explicitly to the setting in networks. So market is embedded in network.

Firms caught up in a given market are also thereby decoupled from having to be bound to habitual ties downstream. This is because the firms' rivalry in and as a market in part insulates their commitments to particular deliveries of production flows. All this has to find expression in a common idiom among them. Embedding is elaborated in this section, and decoupling is the focus later in the chapter.

Formulas for embedding of firms in a market define niches in a first sense. Let's pause to elaborate on this first sense of niche before proceeding with the larger argument on embedding.

Myriad requests and searches, each perhaps minor to its originator, cumulate in an overall pressure on some market of producers who are each baffled as to the overall responses from across that profile to their particular product. Self-consistency emerges with respect to substitutability and other parameters in the social field (Bourdieu 1995) thus generated. The producers jointly substitute a perceived market profile as their binding discipline. Of little interest to them is that each other market that is home to some one of these

myriad transactors of theirs is cushioning that transactor in a like cocoon for
transactions still further along.

There is a varied basis in detailed phenomenology, in perceptions of actors, for modeling such a niche embedded in network. Parameters a and c
especially concern "pull" and "push" of flows of intermediate goods, with,
respectively $a \to$ infinity for strong pull, and $c \to 0$ for strong push. These
issues of depth are pursued in the next sections. How many paths of access
downstream and upstream are afforded by the observed networks around the
given market? This can be assessed and predicted not just from the density
of connections but also from their involution. Standard computer software
packages are available for making such estimations (e.g., UCINET and
STRUCTURE). The greater difficulty is devising fieldwork techniques for efficient specification or estimation of a network, which will require astute de-
visings of sampling frames for networks (Wasserman and Faust 1995).

The parameters b and d, on the other hand, map comparative assessments
of different firms as to monetary valuations resulting from perceived quality.
An inquiry toward network bases for formation of economic valuations will
be pursued in chapter 15 on business cultures. Estimates of all these four
parameters will derive not only from the involution or inbreeding of ties in a
network but also from overlaps in the incidence of different types of ties
representing distinct bases of relation.

Now return to the general argument on embedding, with niches in this
first sense combining into embedding-1. How do markets in turn fit among
other such markets? In its first sense, niche is one of a set, as niche for one
producer within the rivalry profile established in some market. Niche also
can be used in a second sense for the market as a whole when taken as an
actor on a second level. Call this niche-2.

This is niche within a context intercalating markets in networks of ties and
flows of product. This book correspondingly has two phases, the first primarily concerned with the market as molecule, chapters 2–5, and then chapters 6–9, concerned especially with how markets fit into broader network
context; designate this as embedding-2. The whole set of parameters for the
$W(y)$ model reflects the perceived and interpreted impacts of context, including network ties. Both the insides and outsides of the given market contribute to such parameter values. But if gamma approaches the value of unity,
there is less degree of binding of firms into the market as a distinctive identity, and when it approaches infinity, there is little of separate identity formation for the firm apart from its identity through the market. In these special
cases, the reach of the market field is slight.

These are the special cases of the $W(y)$ genre of models in which one
would expect to find network-oriented models of Leontief's input-output
genre to be most applicable. Guidelines could be sought for this.[1] Burt
(1992), for example, derives terms of trade (or more exactly divergence of

terms of trade from their median value) from the topology of the network in that locale, under the rubric of structural holes. And see also several other analogous approaches (e.g., Baker and Faulkner 1991; Breiger 1991).

Ties are always the raw material. Firms can be constituted independent of markets, but they always emerge with continuing ties to other firms. The crux is that any social tie is as much a projection as a record. To participate in a tie is to be enmeshed, to know of further warranties and entailments, which justify and require further ties to some of those tied to your alter. When, for example, a person strikes up pleasant chat with a stranger at a bus stop, this does not constitute a network tie. What counts is that each actor (person or not) is, and knows it is, committed to some entailment to still other ties. Expectations are set up as to sorts of references and to sorts of realizations in action that will be encountered, according to agreed type of tie. In short, a social tie presupposes this network it comes from and tends to generate further ties in that and/or other networks. Even in present society, although you may not like or seek out your cousin, this person remains known socially as your cousin. Although you don't perceive a tie to this cousin, that person is embraced by cousinhood in social reference.[2]

Our modes of discourse take the parallelism between firms and persons for granted, personalizing firms as actors; so can network analysis. The present analysis traces back to views of Bott (1955) and other anthropologists on traditional sorts of personal embeddings in networks of affective ties. So none of this is peculiar to specifically economic organization. Strong and intense ties yield clusterings in cliques and other highly interconnected formations, whether for persons or for corporate actors. Weak ties (Granovetter 1974) serve as bridges between such clusters, leading to "small world" phenomena (Watts 1999a, 1999b), such as are taken up at chapter's end. Burt (1992) has showed us that they also guide strategic maneuvering around "structural holes."

The nodes, the actors in most previous network analyses, are all of a piece, treated as on the same level, whether it be that of persons or of firms or other corporate actors. MultiDimensional Scaling (MDS) is typically applied to generate what can be seen as an ecological space for the network actors. This network-relational view is being extended in the present book to supply a common context to both firms and markets within the broader social organization of the economy. The market space of figures 5.1, 5.2, 7.1, and 7.2 defines an ecological space for the markets, but it remains to fit this ecology more clearly with the networks. The siting of markets amid networks of firms is this new form of embedding, embedding-2, which is, of course, coordinate with the second sense for niche.

Production markets are constituted only through embedding into networks, but this embedding is more general than the standard current definition, which was provided by Granovetter (1985) and corresponds to embedding-1. His explication, which is meticulous and of general applicability, is confined to actors on some one common level. Embedding for him especially concerns how affective relations of trust both derive from and contribute to objective assessments of business actions. Brian Uzzi has carefully traced variable implications of such embeddings in his study of network relations among diverse business firms within the New York garment manufacturing industry (Uzzi 1997) and between firms and banks (Uzzi and Gillespie 1999).

It is not that persons are not involved. The point is that the patterns of action can, in some contexts, come to be interpretable as, and taken as, emanating from actors on a second level. The acts of such market are imputed and inferred from observed joint behavior patterns constituting the market interface of chapters 1–3. This is observably so for participants in production market settings, acting across levels. See Pedersen and Dobbin 1997 for a parallel account of the firm and other organizations as distinct actors. Their treatment melds ideology with culture, whereas levels are here argued to emerge in a more involuntary sociocultural process (and cf. White 1992a). A more remote analogy also can give insight here. Let us turn back to kinship.

The puzzle of generalized exchange has motivated much of the present line of inquiry, which traces to Emile Durkheim but is more specifically rooted in the theories of Claude Lévi-Strauss. Notable studies (Rose 1960; Hart and Pilling 1960) inquiring into aboriginal kinship as economic organization reached a culmination in Bearman (1997). Recognizing this analogy supplies insight into possible emergence of a distinct new level of actors. Markets in this book are analogous to sections in classificatory kinship systems (White 1963), but need not have analogies in other kinship systems.

To sum up, embedding, either -1 or -2 sorts, can result from each actor's not only knowing entailments and warranties but also being known to so know. Thus the firm may become subject to, and be known to be subject to, the hegemonic pressure exerted by the others engaged in the continuing reproduction of a distinct identity as market. Such a market is itself embedded within networks in ways that at the same time constrain, as embedding-1, the actions of firms. Such a market is an actor on a distinct level.

Embedding-2 can build a public subculture across actors at both levels within a particular sector of markets, even though commitments and decisions remain tied into catenations and compoundings of particular ties. The subculture recognizes, and personalizes, actors of different levels while providing customs of switching from calculus for one to calculus for another.[3] Participants in the various markets act as if embedded in a curious web of cocoons (see Tilly 1996 for an analogous term) among markets that also come to constitute a self-consistent field, such as discussed in the final section of chapter 8.

Parameter sizes in the model must reflect tangible perceptions by participants and the common story-lines for networks into which they are woven.

They are, in that sense, a cultural articulation of the situation. The set of values on index n, in particular (see chapter 4), peg firms by quality and so identify firms at a given period. This pegging sets off joint mulling over identities by some or all firms.

Yet the quality ordering is a property of the mechanism of the market as a whole, core to its identity. The market space can be seen as a network-2, a more abstract sort of social space, which is a by-product of greater freedom of connection together with less freedom of valuation. Yet parameters a, c, and gamma are also affected by the small-world connectivity property of network-1 (see the last section below). Both modes of network do share in a continuing elision of ordinary geographical space.

How does it come about that habitual ties are decoupled from the setting of the next period's production commitments made with guidance from the market profile? Common membership in a market by firms does derive from similarities in what ties they have had with all the other sets (markets) in the evolving partition into markets and not upon their being connected with specific other firms as such. Embedding-1 also is a decoupling for firms from the original underlying networks. No longer do warranties and entailments approve or embargo particular further ties across the downstream market interface. The social discipline over member firms by market profile, itself built from networks, is strong enough to substitute for these habits and particularistic injunctions.

There is a transmutation of hitherto entailed ties into market parameters. The market is, in effect, projecting a new, more abstract sort of tie. This tie-2 is the asymmetric envelope that is recognized as market profile. Warranty and entailment on the level below are thereby abrogated, as to addressee if not interpretive content.

The three-layer depth of production markets (see figure 8.1) translates in the model into each of the a, b, c, and d parameters having an impact only in the appropriate ratio. Each ratio expresses that the size of parameter for upstream is important only in contrast with that for downstream (and conversely):

The ratio b/d as a parameter is a warranty-2. It runs from the individual pecking order of dominance as quality order, whether informal or imposed by contractor monopsonist.

The ratio a/c as parameter now measures entailment in relation to the other side of the market interface.

None of these translations is a matter for a particular market; instead, each presupposes, and only emerged with, a new subculture of business relations (see chapter 15) that went beyond patronage and agency. Indeed, there had to be a prior enactment of analogous translation. This was the transition from barter to monetary transactions, which was a necessary precursor to production markets in networks. (Introduced in chapter 1, it will be taken up again in chapters 12 and 15.)

Topology of such bi-level networks is not a matter just of connectivity and inbreeding and popularity distributions across a population of nodes. Rather, it concerns deriving structural equivalence between markets as a new sort of actor from out of their perceived locations in flow networks. This view derives from the basic sociology of roles in positions (White 1963; White, Boorman, and Breiger 1976; Boyd 1970; Pattison 1993), which expresses how a construction out of multiple networks can come to constitute an integral actor filling a role in a new level in social interaction among other such actors (White 1992a). Here the $W(y)$ market is such an actor along with firms, but on a level distinct from theirs. The substitutability parameter gamma is a translation of degree of structural equivalence.

MARKETS AS ORIENTED ACTORS

We may turn from this rather abstract account of embedding to view action in more tangible terms and elucidate further much the same issues. According to the $W(y)$ model laid out in chapters 2–7, patterns of relations between markets are not fixed as in a highway or train network, or in the "input-output" array devised for an economy by Wassily Leontief (1966). All that needs to carry over from a Leontief vision is the distinction drawn between upstream and downstream for each given industry.

Different possibilities of arraying markets ensue from such flexibility, and so there must be decoupling of markets. Decoupling is signaled by the seeming paradox in the asymmetry between the view from downstream up along a tie in contrast with the view from upstream down along such tie. Recapitulation is in order.

In figure 1.1, an industry is shown as a set of producer firms that has transaction ties to specific other economic actors upstream, but with guidance from a joint market profile that overrides specific ties downstream. This is a profile sustained vis-à-vis some generalized "other," consisting in a cumulation of unspecified counterpart actors downstream. It emerges as the envelope from struggles by those becoming members of just this profile, rather than of such profiles for other industries. The struggles are governed by a perceived schedule, a market profile from which derives a set of terms of trade across the specific processors that proves sustainable in the given context.

On the habitual side, by hypothesis, individual producers are ordinarily dealing with, and focus on, their ties to diverse other individual firms rather than paying attention to whole industries. There will be some tension from their alters, the other ends of the ties, being oriented toward rivalry with producers parallel in their own market rather than toward particular transactions with particular alters in that downstream market. Exactly the same account applies for a market in the upstream mode, figure 9.1, the difference being that the habitual side is identified with the downstream rather than the upstream.

How can ties decoupled when viewed from upstream be habitual when viewed from downstream, and vice versa? Some broader cultural framing that encompasses both polarities must be manifested. The continuing joint reproduction of a market profile binds producers such that their ensemble becomes treated by themselves and others as a player. This player is a molecule in which constituent firms are bound as atoms.

Yet also this is a player with an identity, a player that participants and observers alike speak of as taking action, and that guides interpretations. Embedding is defined in and by this process. Each production market is thus also a folk theory that reproduces itself out of the continuing perceptions and actions of all participants in a market. The market is an actor with an ontology different from firms, whose actions are clearly on a different level.

Embedding and *level* thus refer to configurations in which there emerge identities from networks of continuing business relations.[4] These identities have become marked by their orientation in production stream. Identity and folk theory both continue rooted in and shaped by patterns in these underlying networks of business relations of various types. That constitutes embedding.[5]

The larger issue (to which we return in the final section) is how a whole set of these embedded markets array. Return to figure 8.1, in which each industry is drawn as a polarized molecule with its firms inside as atoms. Each industry activates one rivalry profile, with transactions across its other side being habitual. In figures 1.1 and 9.1 the profile is symbolized by a heavy bracket. This convention is adopted also in figure 9.4 with a dotted line standing for the other side. Each column in this latter diagram is one example of how flows transmit through a succession of the industries into which producers are partitioned, but there can be a great many further examples.

A narrative answer is suggested by previous chapters. Much of the time, producer firms can be running on automatic pilot, filling and placing a variety of customary orders with other firms again and again. These orders will be at some habitual terms of volume, price, and service, which no doubt got established in some earlier market context. However, some firms may court or force changes, or new actors may appear, perhaps from abroad, or technology may twitch, or the environment may shift. A nightmare of conjectural variations can emerge in which a producer imagines what some set of others, and self, may do in response to various changes in the responses conjectured for some given actors.

This is fertile soil for the social construction, or reactivation, of some joint profile offering common guidance. Such a profile presupposes positioning with respect to other markets. It may be a new positioning.

Look in the left column of figure 9.4 at a molecule of producers labeled Charlies. Below them are the producers, labeled Sues, in one of the industries whose firms buy from Charlies—firms that lie downstream with respect to Charlies. Above the Charlies are a set of producers, labeled Claras, from one of the industries that supply Charlies, from whom Charlies procure. And similarly for the right column, in which Charlies are now downstream of these Sues and upstream of the Claras, the whole column having reverse polarity.

But Charlies, Claras, and so on can choose independently. The choices of each set of producers lying within a series such as shown in a particular column of figure 9.4, the choices between upstream and downstream orientation can be made independent of that of each other set. So the columns shown in figure 9.4 are just two of a huge number of variants. If, say in the right column, the Charlies change polarization to return to a downstream orientation with respect to the Sues, that does not have to affect the polarization either of the Claras or of the Sues as production market molecules.

Equally basic, any one column attempts to trace through just one particular chain of purchases. A myriad of such chains can be observed. This removes any need for assumptions about the relative scales of the successive sets of producers in any particular column in figure 9.4. The whole set of counterpart industries to the Charlies can be a totally diverse array in scale, through whatever profile obtains, on either the downstream or the upstream side. For example, in building airplanes, you need to buy office supplies as well as engines and struts.

Pressure on the robustness of any relation being coded as a tie may come when the other end also perceives itself as in a rivalry profile of its own that subsumes the origin end of the tie. That is, what might appear symmetric cannot be symmetric because of the differences in the concrete embeddings. Neither end of the tie focuses on it as relation; both ends are concerned instead with their places in their own rivalry profile. The strain is greater than with just one end of the ties anchored in a market rivalry profile.

Thus, the likelihood of disruption is predicted to be greater for a tie whose two ends face one another from distinct profiles. Consider, for example, production streams in the computer sector. The likelihood of disruption is higher when component manufacturers orient downstream toward PC vendors while these same vendors are orienting upstream toward their suppliers as the problematic, the profile side.[6]

In contrast, disruption is less likely when a tie, and then connecting ties in a chain, are passing through a sequence of profiles of the same orientation: either all upstream or else all downstream. This suggests friction in juxtaposing upstream vis-à-vis downstream mode (perhaps even more than in switching between the two modes—for which see chapter 13). By this argument, either of the two pure extremes shown as the two columns of figure 9.4 may be much more likely than any one of the endless other variant stackings possible. Overall, as mentioned before, the pure downstream stacking would be more likely in a deflationary period and the pure upstream stacking in an inflationary period.

The key issue of the dynamics from which can emerge a $W(y)$ interface is when and where the representative firm's flows come to be perceived together as an overall commitment y rather than as merely some collection of rivulets. In the downstream orientation, it is delivery rivulets that get chunked together as a commitment. In the upstream orientation it is the rivulets of procurements that somehow must come to be perceived together as overall commitments by the peer producers as they eye one another. In either case, asymmetry is seen to be basic to relations.

The Back Side

From chapter 1 on, attention has been focused on the profile of a market, the profile that as an interface in that direction protects the producers from Knightian uncertainty. It is time to give more sustained and explicit attention to the other side of the market. Whether the orientation of the given market is upstream or downstream, there is a back side.

On the one hand, transactions in this unproblematic direction are construed as taking place in continuing ties according to habitual terms of trade. In a habitual tie, say to an upstream supplier firm, prices paid to the supplier will tend to stay the same no matter what the volume: There is some attention to deviation, so that sanctions could come into play against deviation from habitual. This defines the processor as a price-taker.

Even these terms, which are unproblematic, may, of course, require computation, computation perhaps even more complex arithmetically than for the problematic direction; but they are routine computations when not merely repetition as habit. One might say that producers within the given industry do not pay enough attention along this unproblematic direction. But this back side of the industry reflects the whole network evolution—and not just particular habitual transactions—through which that processor market came into place along with other markets.

Producers are assumed to be price-takers in that direction because bounded rationality, in the form of habitual decision rules, ensures reluctance to try to focus in both directions. Transactions of these producers with firms in some particular other industry may well be seen not only as habitual but also too small in comparison with their totals in that direction to seem worth strategizing, worth fussing over. These producers may not perceive possibilities to exploit variation in pricing between producers of quite similar product varieties in that other industry. In the problematic direction, on the other hand, especially when faced with some disruptions in habitual sales or procurement transactions, processors are impelled to look away from those particular ties and instead derive guidance from perceptions arrived at jointly.

A Note on Embedding

Embeddings surround us. They indeed overwhelm us and thereby become hard to discern in explicit analyses. Much recent discussion would have you think embedding necessarily implies fuzziness and perhaps mushiness accompanying emotional warmth. This is not so.

One reason for this note is that existing overtones of the term *embed* in ordinary discourse incline us to miss the very induction of a new level of actor that is central to this whole book. I return to ordinary discourse framings below but first place embedding within recent social science discourses. Embedding has been used, too narrowly I argue, in and for the critique of rational choice approaches, especially within economics.

In his influential article, Mark Granovetter (1985) presents a convincing account of social extension and involvements as the gist of embedding. Yet this is, as it were, a two-dimensional portrayal, one that neglects any emergence of new levels of actor from embedding. By contrast, linguists are clear about the emergence of levels but neglect much of his social extension because of their focus on the dyad. The contributions here of Michael Silverstein are taken up in detail in chapter 15; here, I focus on the views of linguist M. A. K. Halliday.

"Embedding is a mechanism whereby a clause or phrase comes to function as a constituent *within* the structure of a group, which itself is a constituent of a clause. Hence there is no direct relationship of an embedded clause and the clause within which it is embedded; the relationship of an embedded clause to the 'outer' clause is an indirect one, with a group as intermediary. The embedded clause functions in the structure of the group, and the group functions in the structure of the clause" (Halliday 1994, 242). Exactly so are we characterizing the relations among levels of firm, market, and sector or economy. But there is nothing esoteric about embedding across levels.

Consider two very crisp and yet general examples of the embeddings in which our social lives are enmeshed. The first has to do with geographical space. Consider the last envelope you addressed. The second line was, say, "Apartment 243," and the third line, say, "Redwood Street." This address you wrote was exactly an embedding. By itself, "Apartment 243" means nothing, and so too "Redwood Street," until each is embedded into the address. The first line may, of course, be an identity taken as being independently fixed, no doubt a person, and the last line similarly will have some fixed identity from geography—if we except the castaway's message set afloat in a bottle.

Now turn to time. How was your weekend? What is your day like on Wednesday? Again here, your life is completely shaped around an embedding, now into levels of time. Here the social construction is of days as defined through, *embedded* into, a seven-day *week*. Only in an intensive care unit, a submarine, or some other of Goffman's total institutions can you even partially escape from embedding into the week—which is hegemonic in that it is utterly taken for granted.

There need be little warmth or fuzziness about either of these two commonplace examples of embedding in social constructions. And each also induces us to recognize a necessary complement ot embedding, namely, decoupling. Those who moan about the "problem of social order" are all too likely to forget they should moan too about strangulation by social habit—on which see Udy 1970.

Production markets indeed constitute an ingenious social invention that gets results by playing off this trade-off, through mechanisms that decouple as they embed actions by firms into markets sited within larger networks in flows of production. A paradox is confronted and overcome. Markets emerge from networks of firms exactly insofar as they suppress networks through their embeddings.

We turn back now to discussion of market modeling, moving on to decoupling in production networks. But still more aspects of embedding will be developed. One will be around formation of identities in chapter 15 and another around rationality and networks in chapter 14.

DECOUPLING AND EDGE MARKETS

The $W(y)$ mechanism decouples each market from, even while also embedding it as a distinct identity into, production streams. This claim deserves further elaboration, which will offer another angle on much the same issues as the preceding sections. This angle opens up further discussion of boundaries, edge markets, and auxiliary markets.

Is there a contradiction between the inward-turned markets portrayed in chapters 2–4, on the one hand, and, on the other hand, the sitings of both markets and firms into production streams of an economy in this chapter and in part 2? No. At the next level underneath market, the distinct acting entities are firms, which become recognized in roles of carrying out transactions that often are habitual and mostly are with other firms. But this system can reproduce itself within the contingencies, the Knightian uncertainty, to which commercial life is subject only if a new emergent level of markets decouples the firms from many of these very ties with other firms from and in which they draw recognition.

Decoupling concerns dependencies. Dependencies express themselves in ties. The expectations from which any market profile is constructed can be seen alternatively as resulting from ties and at the same time as recasting ties. Decoupling is the process aspect of establishing and thus embedding a new sort of identity, compounded from firms but raised to a distinct level with ties newly configured. Among previous analysts of embedding, Granovetter (1985) slights the decoupling aspect, but not Burt (1992) or Evans (1995).

Market members orient to each other's parallel commitments and thus tie to their peers. This is instead of seeking (given downstream orientation) to cultivate particular network ties with the array of buyers downstream. These counterparts downstream, however, perceive those producers as just a few within a myriad of procurements from firms in some large set of industries back upstream of them. The price/volume profile offered downstream— which constitutes a set of terms of trade for niches by quality—remains decoupled from its backside, the enactment of habitual ties of procurement from disparate firms upstream. Thus decoupling is a subtle process in which a given market distances itself from any particular ties with particular other markets. Even if the previous ties of a producer to particular firms are retained, those habitual partners and thus their industries are decoupled from the market interface.

It is because of these decoupling phenomena that analysis with the $W(y)$ model can accommodate auxiliary forms such as professional service markets along with mainline production industries, and also industries on the fringe, such as mining and merchandising. The variety in the latter is endless (see Lindenberg 2000; Porter 1976b; and Uzzi 1996, 1997 for analysis). At this fringe, "A market is often identified as a city, or a sector of a city in which a number of showrooms of related product categories are located" (Donnellan 1996, 205). Donnellan reminds us that High Point, North Carolina, largely consists in 150 showroom buildings displaying wares of thirty-one hundred home furniture manufacturers, whereas misses apparel centers on a major showroom building at 1411 Broadway, Manhattan. Ingram Merchandising Services is the nation's largest distributor for books, records, and so on, as a "rack-jobber": it does inventory management and promotion for diverse product lines within a variety of outlets such as food supermarkets and the like. And the "edge" is encroaching: some manufacturers just assemble parts; others are design companies that contract other manufacturers to produce to specifications (cf. Bothner 2000a on the computer sector).

Much the same internal mechanism does function whether transactions for a particular $W(y)$ market occur near middles or near ends in some tangible chains of procurements and supply among firms. According to the socio-logic of decoupling brought out here, each production market operates as a role structure of firms that is embedded among other such markets, but with room enough also for agency. Decoupling leaves room for exercising options jointly, as reflected in the historical constant k. It also leaves room for options exercised severally on firms through investment. (This will be sketched in chapter 12.) This uncovers patterns of financial binding between firms across markets, patterns that may affect the trajectories of change studied in chapter 13.

Sites near boundaries between markets and surrounding social context are the ultimate sinks and sources for a given economy, as reported, say, in an input-output network (e.g., Carter 1976). The consumer edge, where it is devolution of downstream market, is taken up in the literature on distribution chains for all sorts of products. Such devolution processes are very little treated in microeconomic theory proper (but see Porter 1976b; Katz 1989; Perry 1989). The guild opt-out is a homely example. The guild has been analyzed in chapter 4 as an organizational variant derived from the market. A guild can be seen as another species of corporate organization, a monopoly form specially adapted to contexts at the edges of the economy.

It is devolution at the other (supplier) edge that has been the focus of most research in recent decades, if one counts only research that gives some attention to implications for theory. This research is particularly concerned with subcontracting in various guises.[7]

With decoupling, the context need not extend either upstream or downstream beyond the core tripartite distinction of roles as procurement, transformation, and sale. That is why one is justified in using the more general label of processor market. A processor market does not just transfer ownership, as does an exchange market. It is steward to a line of business through the agency of its member processors.

Consider enactment of decoupling for a processor market. For example, department stores stock shoes, but so do independent shoe stores carrying wide arrays of brands as well as tied shoe-stores, and television and Web shopper services tied to warehousing if not to the Wal-Marts of big-time retailing. Each producer instead eyes its peers, fellow members of that market in construing the terms of trade.

None of the nodes or arrows in figures 1.1 and 9.1 have been identified with such auxiliary markets of production. Yet some of these services are performed in separate firms, which come to be perceived as making up "industries" of their own, markets that site in with production flows among industries (Baker 1984, 1990; Han 1995; Faulkner and Baker 1996). These auxiliary services thus contribute to the network settings of industrial markets, such as are parameterized in the niche spaces of figures 3.1, 5.2, and 7.2. Some of the professional services, such as accounting and law, are older, and some, such as advertising and head-hunting, are newer. (Nonprofit operations within a capitalist economy are excluded from purview, however, unless they are explicitly tied with production markets.)

The $W(y)$ model is applicable to homely examples as well as to Fortune 500 markets. Consider, say, a market of barbershops on the Upper West Side of Manhattan. Other patrons and I who enter a shop (together with a towel supply and steam heat) are also, once shorn, the products (along with bottles of hair oil) debouching from that producer. On other occasions, we may patronize different barbers, as well as other sorts of services, but there need not be any dependencies across the various flows. Whereas the motors and sheet metal being procured from diverse fabricators by a supplier to some refrigerator-freezer producer are also being supplied by him to washer-dryer producers—and also are being procured by other suppliers who are the procurement sources for still other industries. Yet where there is market pricing, there is recognition of a market as a player in its own right.

A further distinction comes to attention with this broadening: To use the term *industry* is to assume that the actors whom the industry faces upstream are nearly disjunct from the actors whom it faces downstream, as was illustrated in figures 1.1 and 9.1. By contrast, a processor such as a dry cleaner may recruit customers from a largely local population that has come to see this and other establishments as offering comparable service (perhaps varying as to such options as drop-off Laundromat service), where the same population is also the destination of the cleaned clothes. What is universal, however, is that the peer members of any processor market almost never trade with one another.

Within a field of $W(y)$ markets, of whatever kind, the markets need be arranged neither in particular vicinities or mutual locales nor in particular chains of production flows. Thus, decoupling supports inclusion of the street number or polymer market arrays introduced in chapter 5.[8] Effective scopes may, however, reach beyond single markets and ties. Markets grouped in a sector by business convention will tend to be in nearby positions in networks of flows. Network locations may, like similarities in technology, be what, through a distinctive history of production and routing, transmute mere sets of markets into market sectors. A further level may emerge, beyond the scope of the present model.

Allegiances of firms to their respective markets reflect the degree of structural equivalence within existing networks of procurement and supply relations. This structural equivalence guarantees some similarity in situations encountered over time. Nesting and overlap of perceptions may accord with some distribution of attributes correlated with region as well as technology, but in any case they are from their evolution in accord with structural equivalence in the networks of the production economy. Nesting and overlap are important, since a particular sector may well have a recognizable subculture yet share various key, generalizable aspects with various other sectors.

The basic point is so obvious that it is easy to overlook: In any $W(y)$ market, whether of processors only or of industrial producer firms, the transaction flow with upstream, procuring, is distinct from, but coordinated with, that directed downstream, selling, so that market process invokes not only the peer producers but two other layers of actors. And so, as much for local processor market as for industrial producer markets, there emerges a collective identity, associated with, rather than opposed, to decoupling.

It is the phenomenon of decoupling that argues against believing in a planar and singular network among industries such as suggested by the imagery of the input-output school (Leontief 1966; Carter 1976). There is no need to reify a production economy in terms of a singular input-output network. Such relaxing of perspective better accommodates the diversity of observed markets, which obtains notwithstanding the fact that these have been devised and evolved in interpretive cultures with considerable overlaps and borrowings that reach beyond immediate siting.

Instead of a population of parallel actors such as firms, the focus in $W(y)$ is a nesting of distinct levels of actors. The integral identity of a market should not be seen as strange. It, like the identity of a firm, is modeled on identity of the individual person, and that too is the envelope projected by dynamics among parts (White 1992a). (The latter claim is tested against findings from personality psychology in White 1995a, which is developed further in Waechter 1999.)

Burt (1992) focuses on the autonomy that is made possible by decoupling. He looks separately at two levels, market and individual, rather than relating market to the intermediate level of firm. Nonetheless, in his insightful chapter 4, much of the $W(y)$ interpretation is mounted and contrasted with a parallel analogy to population ecology models. Burt reads autonomy directly from network context and does not specify the price mechanism that enables autonomous ingenuity to do better. If the parameters a, b, c, d, and gamma can be inferred from network topology, the $W(y)$ model might supply the mechanism, but in tension with using the same network ties again to assess autonomy of firms, as of markets. And the earlier sketches for a, c, and gamma suggest how difficult the inference would be. Burt instead proposes spread on a quality index to assess autonomy for a population ecology interpretation. Another approach could be inferring niche spread not from n, but from n raised to the power implied by the $W(y)$ model; see equations (7.3–7.4). Considerable exploration is needed.

Processes of decoupling and embedding supplant birth and death of particular actors as the focus. Demography is not the point. Decoupling is essential to the paradoxical duality of markets and firms as being embedded in tangible networks among concrete actors while also being actors with scripts for relations that are transposable and interpretable.

W-K COUPLING ACROSS A SMALL WORLD

Decoupling signifies considerable flexibility in connections of markets through firms. Within a firm, hierarchical organization is a traditional control over timing of activities and flows. Flows between firms are outside such organization, and so, accordingly, is regulation of their timings. Instead, such flows are implicated in the market mechanism. Flows through and from markets thus are exposed to disjunctions in timings.

None of the previous chapters has paid attention to timings in flows. Decoupling means that there can be considerable variability. Will serious mismatches develop in timings along the flows from suppliers, through producer processings, on to deliveries to purchasers at terms set by the market interfaces? The implicit assumption has been that mutual signaling will pace commitments and actions concerning any given market so that such mismatches are not problematic. The comparative statics of the market mechanism may capture the essential residue of local dynamics at a market interface, but that does not speak to timings on a larger scale across whole skeins of markets and networks.

The goal here is to develop approximate insight into how the possibility of such turmoil relates to the pattern of network connectivity among markets. Assume that firms as to timings are fairly well locked in to peers in a market by signaling. Supplier ties to individual firms can be assigned to that firm's production market, and so on. So take the markets as the actors, say with months or quarters as the period of time. The market is a molecule only in one direction, but that subtlety will be suppressed. Impose symmetry on the ties, since each has monetary flows indexed to product flows in the other direction along that tie. Timings may depend on whether the orientations of the markets are upstream or downstream, but in the interest of simplicity disregard that as well.

This exploration will lead apparently far afield, to models of flows in networks not set in any particular context. Conjecture and supposition derived from these abstractions will substitute for explicit modeling and for evidence from observation. But the conclusions derived will be surprising and counterintuitive, and the framing is plausible.

Think of your last experience driving on big, crowded roads in a complex metropolitan network. Your immediate locality is unproblematic as to timing (except perhaps in Boston and Buenos Aires!), as rational drivers with long practice allow for each other's spacings and lane changes within quite stable cocoons of cars that pass down the highway. The formula works at that scope. But surely you remember those times when for no apparent reason the traffic choked up and you spent a half-hour going a few miles—and likely without even encountering a car wreck or repair shunt as you moved down the road.

Similar sorts of turbulence surely can be problems, of course on a much coarser time scale, across a production economy of markets in network flows. Turbulence appearing in flows of goods and revenues may be preceded and/or followed by turbulence in signalings and other coordination attempts by actors in and for markets. Extensive data and analyses were required to attain understanding of the incidence of disjunction and turmoil in traffic networks and have been developed along with stochastic models of queuing. But the links in networks with characteristics akin to those in the human social world, of which the production economy is a special case, are not as permanent as in auto traffic. The links are stochastic as well as the flows. So a closer analogue than traffic would be the dynamics of personnel flows among or within organizations (e.g., Stewman and Konda 1983; White 1970), but comparability is still not high since there can be hierarchical organizational controls over timings there.

These market networks are large, which in practice means well over 1,000 nodes. Intuitive insight is totally inadequate to assess the dynamic behavior in such large networks; instead, abstraction, modeling, and extensive simulation is required. An explicit model of coupling along networks is needed, and it needs to be kept simple. So we may turn to results from abstract modeling of systems of oscillators in order to gain guidance on flow dynamics in economic networks.

Arthur Winfree (1967) pioneered the approach now widely used in abstract modeling. Winfree's framing can be shown to be consistent with more tangible modeling for markets, either the model here or parallel work such as by the evolutionary economist Alan Kirman (1997, 492–93). The suggestion here is that markets be taken as the oscillators, say over the period of a quarter, and that the coupling with any particular other market be measured by the flow between.

What represents the coupling of one market with other markets as nodes? There are two plausible answers. First, let the flow of revenue from one to another particular market reflect the coupling. This choice stresses the flows of physical production in the input-output networks of a production economy as envisaged by Leontief. One can impose symmetry on these ties, since each has monetary flows indexed to product flows in the other direction along that tie.

The other choice is to focus instead on coupling through overlap in shared customers or other audience between markets that lie parallel to one another in structurally equivalent locations. It is plausible that firms and their market attend to communication from such cousin markets as intently as they obviously must attend to signaling from markets lying upstream and downstream from them in relations of procurement and supply. Again with this second choice, it is plausible to assume that the ties are symmetric.

The first choice corresponds to the parameter ratio a/c in the $W(y)$ model of markets, and the second choice corresponds to the parameter gamma that reflects overlap in buyers (see chapter 8 above). Given the simplification of mapping onto the highly abstract model of Winfree, the two choices of coupling measure both are plausible when it comes to interpreting model results. The subsequent argument applies to each.

A system of coupled oscillators can form self-sustaining equilibrium configurations that are, moreover, stable with respect to external perturbations. Visualize this in terms of runners on a track, whether these be persons or racing cars. Watts (1999b) points out that runners in a race tend to cluster as they go round and round the track, even though each has a different maximum speed. One can locate each runner by the angle she has reached in running around the circle: call it the phase. See figure 10.1.

Winfree described a system of phase oscillators by an equation relating each phase to a sum of its intrinsic frequency (runner's speed) and a sum of influences, given the sensitivity of the given runner, from the phases attained by the other runners. Winfree showed that in a considerable range of circumstances a dramatic transition would take place to a globally entrained state in which all the runners settled into a steady bunch circling the track.

Further simplifications ease computation of results from these abstract models. Kuramoto (1975) simplified Winfree's equations by assuming the same coupling coefficient (sensitivity) for each, so that ties of each oscillator had the same form of dependence on the phases (in fact, the sine of the differences in phases). Kuramoto modeled the resulting system as a self-consistent field (see chapter 8, last section) with all oscillators locked in when the coupling coefficient is above a critical value, confirming the Winfree results with more detailed solutions. This would correspond to a smoothly running production economy not beset by gluts and jams or panics in decision circles. And a host of other reports in the literature can be used to expand on these conclusions (e.g., Lumer and Huberman 1991).

All of these results, however, apply only where every oscillator is coupled to every other one, a fully connected network. This contradicts the fact that market networks are sparse. Once in a blue moon, an industrial market may procure from the perfume market, but the bulk of relations being coded as links are to a restricted sector of markets. Similarly, decision makers in an industrial market are unlikely to read *Variety* or go to restaurants frequented by agriculture magnates in assessing commitments to make; so decision coupling ties between markets are also not numerous.

The number of ties from a market node thus are an order of magnitude less than the total number of markets in a production economy. And there is a second key fact. The ties between markets tend toward local clustering, corresponding to cliques in human terms. Thus, market networks are akin to human acquaintance networks rather than the fully connected networks specified to obtain explicit mathematical solutions for abstract oscillators, as for orthodox economics.

Watts (1999b) has surveyed a range of examples in engineering systems, neural networks, and human societies where populations are large and networks are not only large and sparse but also locally clustered. Watts keeps his models of connectivity simple: only one type of node, and only one type

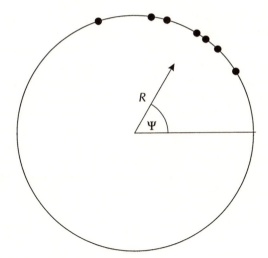

FIG. 10.1. Race-track dynamics

of tie, which also is taken to be symmetric (all consistent with our approximation to a market network). Even so, the results are rich.

Watts's key question about these large and sparse, yet clustered, networks is what *sort* of bridging across local clusterings is sufficient to convert them to a "small world" in their degree of connectivity. Operationally, this translates into the surprisingly small "six degrees of separation" sufficient to span the human world via chains of acquaintanceship. Whatever degree of intuitive insight one might have is totally inadequate to assess even the connectivity properties, much less the dynamic behavior in such large, sparse networks. Watts turned to computer simulation disciplined by mathematical models and subject to qualitative guidance from a variety of field examples. The results are surprising: Watts (1999a, sec. 9.2) adapted his powerful simulation approach to establish that a small proportion of *random* connections is both necessary and sufficient to yield small-world graphs. And a host of other reports in the literature can be used to expand on these conclusions about connectivity among the abstract oscillators (e.g., Lumer and Huberman 1991; Niebur et al. 1991).

The principal result of the analysis appears indeed paradoxical when applied to the market system. To achieve coherence in timings, absence of disruptions in flows in a production economy, there should be some small proportion of ties that couple markets at random across the whole field. Stability requires disorder; coupling requires decoupling. This is only possible with a social construction that although embedded is also decoupled. Such are the production markets of previous sections.

This result emerges from analysis that interweaves cross-sectional complexity of connectivity together with a complexity of dynamic feedbacks. One could say that identity as a production economy requires a degree of disjunction and disorder in processes and structure linking constituents. That suggests and feeds back into the basis argued in chapter 1 for emergence of production markets as distinct identities, actors on a level apart from constituent firms. That basis was exactly the search by firms for shelter from the winds of Knightian uncertainty. An empirical study focused on much these same issues is Padgett's (1981) on the emergence of a federal budget out of erratic disjunctures in collating claims from a network of organizations negotiating claims with the OMB in the Lyndon Johnson presidency. It would also be interesting to adapt Watts's approach to a later study (Padgett and Ansell 1993).

~~~~~~~~~~~~~~~~~~~~~~~~

CHAPTER 11

Suppressing Market Realities

Conventionally, monopoly and monopsony are the chief economic forms of market suppression, and government control is the chief political form. Monopsony was discussed at the end of chapter 5 in terms that brought out its partial similarity to the production market mechanism; monopoly was briefly mentioned at the beginning of chapter 9 along with the upstream orientation; and chapter 12 will examine both as to exploitation. This chapter has a different argument.

The first section probes the dynamics that are implicit in "pure" competition. This is a limiting case, which Frank Knight termed "perfect competition" (see chapter 1). It is an ideal type, which ostensibly describes a market but which invokes competition across firms without regard to their market membership. Thus it is akin to the models of the second section, which sketches some models that simply elide markets.

Then we examine how theory of pure competition infiltrates econometric analyses that are ostensibly more general. Next comes an examination of how and why orthodox economic theory remains so committed to this ideal type. The patterns in entries and exits supposed for pure competition is the focus, which suggests possible reconfigurations between markets and their member firms. Such reconfigurations can lead to, as well as come from, an alternative, hierarchical organization, as analyzed in the final section.

"PURE" COMPETITION

Orthodox economics still largely works outward from a limiting case that it labels as "pure" or "perfect" competition. Economists are using pure or perfect competition to provide a framing and the norm for markets. "Imperfect" should thus be the economists' term for actually observed markets, those for which the $W(y)$ model is designed.

This practice is pernicious in distracting attention from the construction of quality across a particular set of firms as the central concern in and around a market. Perfect competition should be renamed "flawed" competition, despite its serving as a useful foil. That is the thesis of this and the next three sections.

Subsequently we construe pure competition as a special sort of $W(y)$ market, but first, let's examine this "pure" competition more closely in its own terms. The objections begin with the lack of attention to quality and thus to differentiation of product. In "pure" competition the buying side recognizes no distinctions in quality among the producers. This will introduce an issue of buyer unravelings. Both these and the producer unravelings described in chapters 2–4 suggest alternative arrangements that market participants may well try building, such as guild and monopoly forms. But in this "pure" competition of economic theory, no network relations of any sort are recognized. This is a paradox.

Think about actual market situations that seem to approach pure competition. Commonly they will be sites of rigid intervention by the state. For example, the oft-cited example of a commodity market in winter red wheat of, say, grade number 5: A whole elaborate apparatus of state and nonprofit, and perhaps monopoly trust, regulation is prerequisite to maintaining its purity. The whole drive of market situations is toward differentiation, albeit within joint discipline that softens uncertainty.

Economic theory, by contrast, denies the fact of regulation being requisite to enforce this uniform common quality. It instead stipulates free entry, which it makes the central support of pure competition. If existing producers are making a profit, so the argument goes, new entrants can and will come in and cause the price to go down. Pressure on this common price is said to arise as the market is flooded with more producers who supposedly can produce a commodity identical in quality in buyers' eyes. Uniformity of price for this homogeneous product is then enforced by the possibility and practice of arbitrage, wherein a producer can double as a broker in sales, according to economic theory. What is said to happen, thus, is induction of changes in the common competitive price until there is equilibrium between supply and demand, which are being both defined and generated by free entry.

Such a story must be incomplete even as a textbook solution for pure competition, however, because it suggests no basis for limiting which firms and how many will be accepted altogether as the market supply by the buyers' demand downstream. The second level of substitutability, that between whole markets, is not addressed. Phenomena modeled in chapter 6 with the introduction of gamma are elided. Indeed, that is the nub, because the assumptions of perfect competition are hard to square with the existence of markets that have distinct identities.

Rather than being natural or common, pure competition comes to seem an odd and extreme form of market. But it can exist, and it deserves to be taken seriously as a model to be applied rather than as a convenient foil in rhetoric. More precise analysis is difficult without some choice of definite framing from among the multitude of frames that have been or could be used to specify pure competition for economic theory.

The discussion of subcontractors in the last section of chapter 5 suggests one way of modeling pure competition. Pure competition can be seen as coming from the breakup of a preceding monopoly or trust, in which case n^b might be interpretable as a measure of capital (see chapter 12). Chapters 8–10 refer **V** for a market directly to markets in downstream layers, which may or may not themselves be in pure competition: see figures 8.1 and 9.4. Such a breakup could lead to, as well as come from, vertical integration (see Eccles 1985, and chapters 4 and 11 in Schmalensee and Willig 1989). We return to this in the final section, and chapter 14 shows it also fits with ecology modeling.

Next we take a different track: We try to analyze pure or perfect competition exactly as a special case of the $W(y)$ mechanism for production market. The products from all the firms in such a perfect market appear to the buyers downstream to have the same quality. Perfect or pure competition requires that b be zero. The production firms need not have the same cost schedules. But it seems likely that their schedules will have similar shapes, justifying the use of the same C formula as in previous chapters.

Let us turn to the market space for the $W(y)$ model. Since $b = 0$, pure or perfect competition maps into one or more points along the horizontal axis in figures 5.1, 7.2, and 9.2. The same buyers' taste schedule applies to all products, since S no longer varies with n. So the observed offer schedule, the $W(y)$ profile, is from equation (2.3) expected to be proportional to this S schedule. But that means that different producers would earn different unit prices for their output streams of different volumes, entailed by their different cost structures. Such a schedule could not maintain itself because, with products being indistinguishable, anyone could broker purchases at a lower price. In this special case, arbitrage would take over. Every producer receives the same price per unit volume, whatever the volume y that its cost schedule is motivating it to offer. So in this special case of $b = 0$, the aggregate buyer valuation schedule is itself restricted to the particular formula having $a = 1$.

Even in the case of pure competition, where b must be zero, each producer would still be choosing from an observed $W(y)$, now known to be linear, its own optimal niche of volume $y(n)$ that maximizes its net revenue, $W - C$, given its distinctive cost structure. But note that the choice of y now could have *no use as signal,* there being no basis from differences in product quality for signaling. Every producer receives the same price, whatever volume y its cost schedule is motivating it to offer. The buyers downstream would not veto any particular producer's volume offer with all being at the identical competitive price.

One can derive a $W(y)$ solution for this pure competition with any assumed set of n's and cost schedules, and r and q, and thereby predict equilibrium revenue, price, and so on. But the crux is now the degree of substitutability, the parameter gamma. No longer can this be unity, so that plane of the state space cube is excluded. Instead, variation in context for a pure competition market is restricted to the plane of figure 7.1 but not including $(1/gamma) = 1$ even when this is the $b = 0$ plane.

Allowed contexts in this plane for pure competition are restricted by $(1/c) < 1$. (There is, of course, no degree of freedom, such as k, for path dependency.) There are solutions with different forms in the two triangles within the square such that $1/\gamma$ also is less than unity.[1] And in this normal range of $(1/\gamma) < 1$, there are solutions for revenue and for price that resemble those with b not restricted to zero.

Pure competition has remained a textbook notion that *misses the central point:* Each production market requires, and thus must engender, *repeated* commitments by some set of producers. Commitment always is subject to true risk, Knight's third form of uncertainty. So it requires the support of a frame such as market profile. This mechanism of production market centers not in the aggregations found in pure competition myths but rather in equilibrating pressures on the market profile being interpolated between observed terms of trade. These pressures arise exactly from dispersions, not from averages, more exactly from dispersions on cost and on appeal dispersions across both volume and quality. Each market comes to offer an interdigitated set of footings to existing producers who have established themselves with products differentiated in buyers' eyes. Commitment by a producer except to such a market would be so risky and uncertain as to be foolhardy.

The existing theory of pure competition has producers exposed to any number of new entrants, to a panoply of interventions. But this would erode their commitments. To stay in such a pure competitive market is to cede all control elsewhere, especially to further along stream. Production markets have constructed themselves in what has to be an interactive social process, a history into which entrance by newcomers is costly, slow, and thus implausible (except by acquisition: see chapter 12). Triggering a new market is more likely.

Survival is the first and overriding requirement. Only then is a producer free to do the best it can for itself. Survival comes with establishing footing in some particular market jointly with other producers, but it also is shaped by the presence of other markets. Pure competition theory fails to explain market sources for its "new entrants" and thus to explain the intervention regime that must discipline pure competition.

POPULATION COUNTS AND SIZE DISTRIBUTIONS

In this book, firms are treated as atoms in industries as molecules, and with firms more constrained by network settings than in any microeconomic theory. Consider three population-modeling approaches that evade the distinct molecular level and that also overlook social networks and are reminiscent of pure competition. All focus on counts of firms, one over time and two by distribution in size. At the end of this section, one model for populations of molecules is considered.

A group sparked by Michael Hannan (Hannan and Freeman 1977) studies the dynamics of various populations of firms under the labels of "population ecology" or "organization ecology" (see also Carroll 1988, and for recent overviews Barron 1999, Baum and Mezias 1992, and Haveman and Rao 1997). Such a population of firms may derive from a whole sector or from a large, and especially from a newly emerging, industry. One construct emphasized by this school is density, but since there is no operationalization of a space, density reduces to the number of organizations, the population size. From hypotheses about birth and death parameters they derive, usually with motivation from biological ecology, shapes for the trajectory of population size over time; see also our discussion in chapters 13 and 14. This group also tests a variety of subsidiary hypotheses that we bypass.

They use stochastic modeling and econometric techniques. The fits to data have been good from a variety of case studies. These include microbreweries, restaurants, local telephone companies, and semiconductor start-ups. Presumably the $W(y)$ molecular models will not do well in these cases. None are for a small number of producers, and none are looking for equilibrium, self-reproducing configurations. There is only the one level, rather than a population of firms clustered across a population of industries, as here.

A next step is to examine the sizes of firms. There is a long tradition in studies of size distributions, which have dealt not just with firms but also many other sorts of populations (Zipf 1949). Stochastic models pioneered by Simon (1957) have generated good fits. Ijiri and Simon (1977) is an authoritative presentation of results for populations of firms. Their monograph is of particular interest in that it models size distributions not only of total populations of firms in an economy, but also of the firms in an industry—or, more accurately, what corresponds in present terminology to an industrial sector, such as is designated by a three-digit SIC code or European Union industrial code. These authors' principal conclusion is that their stochastic model applies at both these levels—neither of which considers structuring of small numbers of firms such as in the market molecules of $W(y)$.[2]

Ijiri and Simon (1977) uses a bare-bones model. They assume that the firm follows a stochastic growth process with a rate proportional to its present size, rather than having changes in a firm's size depend on its market position and decisions. And, also unlike microeconomics, they have small firms appear in the economy at some fixed, exogenously determined rate. They make no use of contagion dynamics, whereas typical in the Hannan approach is a birthrate varying with the square of the density of firms. As in the $W(y)$ models, dynamics in the Simon-Ijiri models are not studied directly but rather are inferred from distributions in equilibrium.

Conversely, the Hannan group passes over the sizes of firms and also over any exogenously fixed injection of new firms, but it does probe identity and boundary of the given industry with more care (e.g., Polos, Hannan, and

Carroll 1999). Their approach is maximally social in that new firms are triggered by interaction, albeit unspecified interaction, among existing firms,
and their approach thus should be called a demography. By contrast, Simon
and Ijiri (and one later strand of Hannan ecology) develop an asocial model
in which a firm grows by exploiting a generalized environment, with success
proportionate to its size to date, but they do model the death process too,
and their model can also be considered a demography.

Yet both groups report good fits. A possible implication is that neither
time profiles of sheer counts nor equilibrium distributions in sizes permit
much discrimination as to the underlying mechanism. This conclusion is
also suggested by a survey of earlier results such as the series reported by
Hamblin and associates (1973).[3] The $W(y)$ model, like the Hannan group's
model, deals with interactions among firms, but these interactions have to do
with a measure of size, namely revenue, rather than existence or duration per
se. And the $W(y)$ model focuses specially on the interaction between firms
and markets rather than on the interactions within a population of firms.

Flaherty (1980) combines features from the Hannan and the Simon approaches. She examines the evolution of a size distribution of market share
among a given set of firms (still other evolutionary economic models will
taken up in chapter 14):

> Firms here are units that can produce a non-storable, homogeneous product at
> some constant marginal cost and that can invest to reduce that cost. Firms face a
> stationary industry demand, have perfect foresight expectations about the future
> actions of all firms, and behave non-cooperatively. . . . Marginal cost can vary
> both among firms and over time. . . . The investment function relating expendi-
> tures to reduction in marginal cost is the same for all firms for all periods. . . .
> Positive investment is required to maintain cost levels because input costs, such
> as labor costs, are assumed to be increasing over time. . . . The expense of a
> given unit of cost reduction achieved through cost-reducing investment [taken
> from the firm's profit] is invariant to the amount of output produced using
> it. . . . This model . . . is concerned with the configuration of firm sizes that can
> be sustained in an industry. (Flaherty 1980, 1187–92)

She has R&D rather than physical plant investment in mind. She proves that
there exists at least one industry equilibrium path and investigates steady
state industry structures that can result.

Under some reasonable conditions, only industry structures in which
firms have different market shares can be stable with respect to even small
perturbations (with which the Hannan approach does not attempt, and the
Simon approach is not equipped, to deal). These Flaherty findings are compatible with the $W(y)$ analysis but are limited in purview, like the Hannan
approach, to a single industry. This means, in practice, eliding actual molecular markets within the industry. For example, she, like the Hannan

group, would take the entire Scot knitwear industry (see the first section of chapter 6) and perhaps more as the frame of analysis, within which only firms need be recognized.

Like the $W(y)$ models, the Flaherty approach finds multiple equilibria and path dependence. Her results are informative about over-time dynamics. But her assumptions are much more specialized than ours:

Constant returns to scale, corresponding to $c = 1$.

All firms start with the same cost structure, corresponding to $d = 0$.

All firms are equally attractive to buyers, corresponding to $b = 0$.

The last assumption defines pure competition. Thus, Flaherty is able to derive a pure competition configuration in equilibrium by invoking differential investment to provide the necessary divergence in cost schedules among firms. Her results remain restricted to constant returns to scale and undifferentiated products, so they are applicable to very few of the market contexts surveyed in this book. More than illustrative special cases are needed.

Now, finally, consider a size distribution approach for a population of molecules. Miller McPherson in a series of works (e.g., 1997), studies a population of groups of persons. He uses hypotheses that are richer than Simon-Ijiri's but are keyed to a more limited class of populations. He has three levels, too: The population is of voluntary organizations, and these are explicitly modeled in terms of entry and exit by persons to memberships. So McPherson, like Simon-Ijiri, develops results on size distribution and finds good fits with his data sets.

Molecular models invite and must supply more specification in more aspects of phenomenology, but this is phenomenology of interactions in tangible ties among tangible actors. The principal difference of McPherson's from the $W(y)$ model is in the lack of any larger asymmetric flow process such as production. There is no persistent distinction of upstream from downstream as in a production economy. So each of McPherson's groups is a properly walled-off molecule rather than the elusive bidirectional warp in network action that the $W(y)$ market was shown to resemble in the previous chapter.

Another difference is that McPherson imposes uniform hypotheses. These are social-psychological, on molecular activity, which consists in membership change across the whole population. The principal difference is exactly that McPherson looks only at moves of members between molecules, whereas the $W(y)$ molecule is constituted to sustain its membership. But McPherson does visualize the population as locations in an abstract space, somewhat akin to the $W(y)$ market space.

What all of these schools are emphasizing is changes in members, seen as independent of constraints exerted by the sort of tangible molecules modeled here. That difference in basic strategy leads to different approaches in applications. (Chapters 13 and 14 return to this issue.)

PURE COMPETITION AND ECONOMETRICS: NERLOVE

Econometrics is economic measurement guided by economic theory made tangible. Taking experimental control to be impossible, it turns to procedures of statistical inference that were initially developed for applied biology and that have since been elaborated further by specialists not necessarily committed to or deeply informed in any specific realm of science. The point below is that, although ostensibly econometricians are not confining themselves to pure competition, they are lured by its fictions into substituting ex post speculations by economists for the real-time mechanism of market pricing.

So the theme of this section is that econometrics, as applied to industrial organization, has been misled by orthodox economic theory. This section begins with two early works in econometrics of industry and ends with a recent one, all of high repute, but all of which abandon the search for market mechanism. We use three variant approaches to better develop the intricate issues, although work by one econometrician, Marc Nerlove, will figure in all three.

First Approach

Eighty years ago Frank Knight (see chapter 1) issued a powerful warning that orthodox theory had leached out uncertainty, that is, pure uncertainty of his third kind, the kind most crucial to economic action, the only kind from which profit ensues. This becomes especially critical for microeconomics, where overlooking the third uncertainty corresponds to, and induces theory based on, the admitted fiction of pure competition.

Early work on returns to scale by Marc Nerlove is still cited as classic in chapter 1 of the 1989 *Handbook of Industrial Organization* (Schmalensee and Willig). Nerlove bundles early lecture notes with several related works in a subsequent book (Nerlove 1965) that takes pains to lay out the approach in detail and with numerous variants. Nerlove uses in early chapters the same functional forms of schedules, referred to as Cobb-Douglas, as were introduced in previous chapters, so comparison is straightforward. (In later chapters, Nerlove introduces more elaborate forms, on which see somewhat later overviews by Christensen, Jorgenson, and Lau 1975 and Griliches and Ringstad 1971.)

Nerlove focuses on there being three and not just two roles involved in the minimal unit of decision for pricing across production flows, the basic fact emphasized here from chapter 1 on. Nerlove, too, is trying to understand a system of flows rather than just some isolated nexus of exchange. But thereafter he follows orthodox theory. In the first variant, he explicitly assumes pure competition, the approach just critiqued.

Then Nerlove explicitly introduces differentiated competition, in several varieties. Careful reading shows, however, that he dispenses with any positive, ex ante account of how market prices are established for the differentiated producers. Instead, somewhat as in the elaborate model by Rosen (1974) introduced in chapter 2, price outcomes for transactions in differentiated products are just postulated ex post. Nerlove is invoking a response function whose parameters are to be estimated but not predicted.

Rosen (writing somewhat later) attempts to infer what response functions would emerge from individual maximization attempts on two sides of a market interface such that they could as a set be consistently enacted. This maximization problem is difficult to solve, even from the mathematician's armchair, and Rosen does not tie his approach to explicit cues in participants' behavior. Nerlove had taken a different tack. As an econometrician, he does not even attempt to theorize interaction of response functions across an interface of differentiated competition.

Nerlove instead puts himself in the role of the producers in-stream *between* suppliers and buyers—the same commitment to a three-role analysis as in $W(y)$ models. Functions are stipulated for estimation of prices that the producer is counting on both upstream and down, and the possibility is allowed that the size of its own commitment affects those prices. What is then the problem remaining to give the econometrician a challenge? It is the involuted, technicist problem of how to optimally choose and combine an array of procurements sufficient to generate product flows for deliveries.

Turn back to figure 8.1, which diagrams flows to set up for the (approximate) derivation of $W(y)$ parameters in that chapter. The crucial assumption there was that the cost valuation of what is produced was a determinate function of the amount of *that* product y_j—without reference to the actual volumes of various inputs, x_i. That is the conventional logic that leads to cost functions. The $C(y, n)$ of chapter 2 is proposed to capture the understandings of executives and their rules of thumb about cost variation with different choices of output size. The proposal there is that the executives making commitment decisions are overwhelmingly concerned with and oriented to the Knightian uncertainty downstream, around which evolves the market profile for the interface.

Nerlove, however, in lieu of examining market interface, chooses the task of internal optimization within one's own firm. He treats that as the strategic or governing choice of an executive—whose role Nerlove is usurping as econometrician. The uncertainty of the market interface has been suppressed. Nerlove has the executive turn away from Knight's challenge and instead carry out elaborate estimations of how to squeeze down cost a bit by varying proportions of particular inputs.

Before proceeding to implications for broader analysis, in the rest of this and subsequent chapters, let's pause to assess commonalities between the $W(y)$ approach and that of Nerlove. Both insist on a sequence of three roles as minimal unit, but *Nerlove considers only upstream orientation.* He conceives neither of commitment making nor of enacting a distinct level of market action, so he is trapped within the ex post straitjacket of before-after in causation that David Hume warned against.

Indeed, Nerlove has no market as such and in particular no market molecule of a particular set of producers. Instead Nerlove is, implicitly, treating producers as caught up in networks akin to those of putting-out economies. That is why Nerlove comes up with a determinate solution, as opposed to the path-dependent solution of $W(y)$ summarized by the span of values for k, the historical constant.

Second Approach

Another way to say this is that Nerlove comes up with a separate solution for each differentiated producer, one that does not depend on mutual perceptions and comparisons. In the $W(y)$ model, these perceptions begin with indeterminacy as a set, though of course with a determinate $y(n)$ solution for each producer individually once the market profile has established itself. It is instructive to compare the respective solutions. Figure 11.1 is a reproduction of figure 2.1 in the second chapter of Nerlove (1965, 27). That chapter begins, "We shall be concerned only with the model that results when output and inputs are measured in physical units."[4] This figure is the focus of a section titled "The Meaning of a Statistical Relationship between Inputs and Output" (Nerlove 1965, 22). Note the use of singular and plural.

> To illustrate this situation, consider an industry composed of firms producing a single product with only one factor of production. Suppose that each firm buys the factor in a single competitive market so that the factor price is the same for all firms, but sells its products in a local market. In each local market we suppose that the demand for the commodity differs only in level and not that elasticity of demand differs from market to market. We also suppose that managerial ability differs from firm to firm. (Nerlove 1965, 22)

(The book then goes on to develop solutions for a wide variety of more general cases.)

Extensive quotation of Nerlove's solution is appropriate both because he is a lucid writer and because important issues are involved:

> Figures 2.1a–c illustrate the relationship between the production function for the "average" firm and the observed combinations of output and input. By "average" firm we mean one for which both managerial ability and the level of product demand are at their mean values for the group of firms as a whole. Figure 2.1a

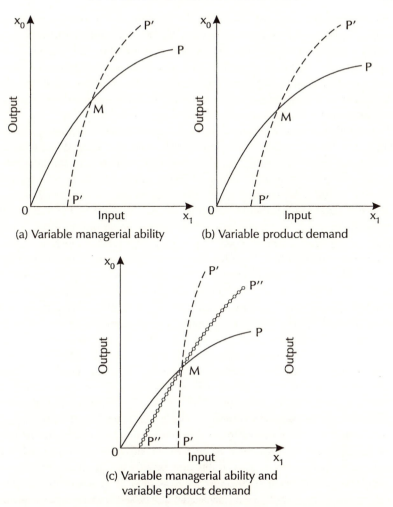

FIG. 11.1. Nerlove production functions: (*a*) variable managerial ability; (*b*) variable product demand; (*c*) variable managerial ability and variable product demand

(here figure 11.1a) shows the relation of the observed input-output combinations to the production function for a firm with mean managerial ability, where all firms in the group considered face the same demand schedule, that is, for a group of firms in which managerial ability varies, but the level of demand does not. Since above average managerial ability is associated with high levels of both output and input, the observed input-output combinations for such firms lie above the production function for a firm with mean managerial ability. Similarly, the observed input-output combinations for firms with below average managerial ability lie below the production function for the firm with mean managerial ability. The curve OP represents the production function for the firm with average managerial ability; the curve P′P′ represents observed combinations of input and output in a group of firms with varying degrees of managerial ability. The two curves cross, of course, at the point at which the observed input-output combination lies for the firm with mean managerial ability.

In exactly the same way, we can show that the observed input-output combinations for a group of firms with varying levels of product demand, but constant managerial ability. . . . Figure 2.1b [here figure 11.1b] illustrates this situation.

The net result of variable managerial ability and a variable level of product demand on the relationship between the observed input-output combinations and the production function for the "average" firm depends on the relationship between demand level and managerial ability in the sample of firms under investigation. It is reasonable to suppose that high demand level and high managerial ability will tend to be found together; i.e., firms supplying the larger markets will tend to have the best management. . . . This case is illustrated by the curve P′P′ in figure 2.1c, in which the slope of the observed input-output combinations is much steeper than the production function for the "average" firm, and steeper than the slope of the observed input-output combinations when only one of the two factors (managerial ability and level of product demand) is allowed to vary. On the other hand, if managerial ability and demand level are completely uncorrelated, the observed input-output combinations will tend to lie along a curve somewhere between P′P′ and the production function for the average firm, OP. This is illustrated by the curve P″P″ in figure 2.1c. If managerial ability and demand levels are negatively correlated, which is most unlikely to be the case, it may happen that the observed input-output relation will coincide with the production function. But this would be an accident, in general, and we would expect the observed relation, even in this case, to have a slope either less than or greater than the production function. Since the most likely possibility is a positive or zero correlation between managerial ability and demand level, it would seem that the most likely possibility is that the observed relation between output and input will tend to overstate the true effect of increased input levels upon output. (Nerlove 1965, 26, 28)

Let's translate the gist of this into terminology for the $W(y)$ model in order to ease comparison and discussion.

The x_o in Nerlove's figure 2.1 corresponds to y in $W(y)$, managerial ability corresponds to $(1/n^d)$,[5] and level of demand corresponds to n^b. But *nothing in $W(y)$ directly corresponds to* the x_1 in any of figure 2.a–c in figure 11.1. It is true that Nerlove orients back upstream, but comparing instead to the chapter 9 dual model for $W(y)$ would not help. And although he does choose the upstream orientation, this is not out of worry about connections and terms with the suppliers. So, since it is less familiar, the upstream $W(y)$ model will not be used here as baseline.

Instead, Nerlove is concerned about which set of multiple types of inputs, in what volumes, will maximize output x_o. Nerlove is thus solving a different problem, and surely not the problem that executives focus on. And what about Nerlove's "production function," which is his central vehicle? There is no direct analogue to it in $W(y)$, just as there is none to his x_1.

The next point to notice is that, like Spence a decade later, Nerlove presupposes that the situations likely to be found correspond to the PARADOX variety of $W(y)$ market: thus the use of $(1/n^d)$ above. It seems to me a bit of the individualist machismo favored by many economists. Surely it is more plausible that higher quality (as calibrated by buyers) comes out of higher tangible expenditures in production than that it corresponds to more efficient managerial operation per se (and see the earlier discussion of the PARADOX market and the Spence model in chapter 5). Perhaps the most basic point is that even this avowed econometrician asserts rather than turns to empirical study, and thereby does not come to set up an explicit framework for all possibilities such as in the $W(y)$ market space.

Third Approach

Let's reiterate the central point. Nerlove claims there is a unique determinate solution. Now let's turn to discuss this in comparison to $W(y)$ results. The nearest thing to Nerlove's production function in $W(y)$ is a cost function $C(y, n)$. Indeed, if the x_1's are each multiplied by a price, presumably a standard off-the-shelf price, then that axis is turned into cost. Thereby a "production function" such as those exhibited in Nerlove's three figures transforms into a cost function (or rather to the inverse form, with cost along the abscissas). The "production function" need not and usually will not correspond to $C(y, n)$, however, even when Cobb-Douglas parameters are matched.

It is clear what Nerlove has done. He has by fiat abolished the veil of uncertainty hanging over demand. The satisfaction schedule of chapter 2, reexpressed as satisfaction per unit y, matches the demand function of volume by price that he stipulates. Nerlove's unique solution, his x_o, is the volume at which there is the greatest distance between that fixed demand schedule and the cost schedule resulting from the transformation of his "production function." So the demand and supply schedules each can be equated across the two models. Each of the values of k, that is, each profile, yields a unique $W(y)$ volume, but no one of these need correspond to the unique solution propounded by Nerlove.

For Nerlove's illustrative case, direct comparison with the $W(y)$ solution seems appropriate since, in both models, supply prices are not affected by the volume the producer acquires. His solutions for cases where the supply side also is not a purely competitive market—or his consideration of such other complexities as substitutability effects analogous to gamma not being unity—are in the same mold, simply more intricate. Such variants cannot even be calibrated to stipulate the same context as assumed in a $W(y)$ model.

The model Rosen proposed (1974), which I discuss in chapters 2 and 12, is different again. None of the three models need have a solution that agrees with any other model's solution. The multiplicity of solutions offered by $W(y)$ thus seems appropriate. And this multiplicity follows from the $W(y)$ model's insistence that firms derive their commitments from tangible perceptions of what peers are doing.

Nerlove emphasized that his modeling approach follows that given in a paper by J. Marschak and N. H. Andrews (1944), which he then "explored in detail" in his own chapter 3. That early paper introduces a space of parameter values akin to that for $W(y)$ in chapter 3 earlier. Marschak and Andrews, however, are seeking to *limit* the ranges in parameter space that need be considered. They do so by assuming various limitations in managerial ability to optimize. Their attempt at greater realism does not, however, carry over into some mechanism by which these managers, optimizing or not, guide themselves and each other toward estimates of what lies behind the veil of Knightian uncertainty.

Nerlove (1965) himself is not attempting to exclude parameter ranges. But neither is he welcoming wider ranges, nor is he working toward arrays of predictions in terms of parameter subranges. In one possibly significant respect, Nerlove enlarges the range of parameters beyond that in $W(y)$, as regards quality. He does keep the equivalents of exponent ("elasticity") of demand, a, and exponent c for cost the same across firms. He has "managerial ability" as a restrictive label, but does use it just as n^d is used in $W(y)$, and similarly he allows for each firm to have a different multiple in demand schedule, corresponding to n^b. Nerlove also is asserting that each "quality" is unidimensional, but he does not build in any correlation between managerial ability and product attractiveness. He does not stipulate any common base indexes such as the n's in $W(y)$. So to have a complete comparison, one would return to the fourth phase of parameter estimation, in the first section of chapter 8, and carry out estimation without asserting equation (8.3).

Nerlove does make the ad hoc assertion that managerial ability and product attractiveness are likely to be positively correlated. So Nerlove thinks that the likeliest context for a market corresponds to the PARADOX region. For tangible comparison, let's turn to a solution for a market in PARADOX. Turn back to figure 5.3, which reports curves for $y(n)$, one such curve for each of the market profiles that are indexed by the value of k, for the given combination of parameters in that point of the PARADOX region. As noted above, there need be no agreement between his solution and any of the $W(y)$ solutions. But in fact there is one, a point y, on each of the curves with distinct k values that nest together to fill out the region in figure 5.3 between the boundary for positive profit and the boundary from the second-order condition on maximization.

Nerlove often, however, retreats to the use of pure competition assumptions, and other econometricians do likewise. This is not surprising in view of the problem of pulling out of the air demand schedules, and/or supply schedules, of amounts forthcoming according to proffered price. This seems to have remained the state of affairs, since Nerlove's work was again cited as classic in the 1989 *Handbook* (Schmalensee and Willig) in its foundational chapter 1. That chapter's author was John Panzar, whose collaborative work with Baumol is reviewed in the next chapter and shown to suffer from a similar lapse into pure competition.

Nerlove resorts to pure competition in his chapter 6, which is a revision of the original paper that is cited in the *Handbook*. This work models the electricity-generating industry. There are indeed manifest reasons, in particular government regulation of rates, not to assume a competitive market for output, and yet also some plausibility to an approximation to pure competition in some input markets. (Also, and ironically, regulated industries are among the few where academic economic analyses find eager external audience, viz., antitrust lawyers.) The issue of so-called natural monopolies comes up in the present work too, but discussion is postponed until Panzar's work is taken up in the next chapter.

This section of Nerlove's chapter carries three other important implications. The first is its qualitative support for a stance entirely compatible with the $W(y)$ approach. To use Nerlove's words again: "Thus, the particular amounts of factors which a given firm employs and the output it produces are determined solely by the discrepancies of conditions in its factor and product markets from average conditions, and the amount of managerial ability it possesses" (1965, 24). However, the second implication is that Nerlove, and other econometricians, will not be able to identify the important parameters except as they too recognize some perceptual and behavioral interaction, such as in $W(y)$, as framing the market for executives' choices of commitments. Entertaining pure competition within one's analytic framework pulls one toward neglecting the molecular structure of markets.

The third implication ties in also with the proclivity for pure competition assumptions noted earlier and serves as introduction to the final section of the present chapter, and to generalizations in subsequent chapters, because it illustrates econometric work finding itself drawn into considerations of network structure and how that intercalates with markets of one sort and another.[6]

Economic Orthodoxy: Hicks

Economic institutions on the ground are fascinating not only in their richness and suppleness, but also in their exactitude. It is perhaps not surprising how inadequate current social science portrayals of them remain. Current microeconomic theory, summarized in the *Handbook* (Schmalensee and Willig 1989) surely is inadequate.

Economic theory has other concerns than, and is broader than, microeconomics. The latter's *Handbook* itself contains as the last chapter in its volume 1 an overall assessment by a macroeconomist of theory, titled "The Theory and Facts of How Markets Clear: Is Industrial Organization Valuable for Understanding Macroeconomics?" In it, one reads, "Much of industrial organization [economics] seems fixated on answering how the behavior of markets differs as industry concentration [in market shares of producers] changes. Although this is certainly an interesting question . . . heterogeneity of product, variability in demand and supply . . . are also interesting characteristics" (Carlton 1989, 911). "*It is the development of new theories of market clearing that should receive priority* in explaining the pricing anomalies and that could have some impact on macroeconomic thinking" (925; emphasis added). "In the standard theory, we usually assume that there is *a fictional Walrasian auctioneer* adjusting prices to clear markets. But in fact there is no such person" (936; emphasis added). "Since product heterogeneity within an industry is an endogenous characteristic, the industrial organization economist should be able to *predict which markets are likely to be sufficiently homogeneous so that an organized market can exist*" (938; emphasis added).

The $W(y)$ model may fill Carlton's call for a market-clearing mechanism, but with the reversal that the mechanism depends on sufficient *heterogeneity* rather than on homogeneity. The market mechanism depends both on discrimination according to jointly perceived quality, and on embedding into dispersed networks. Such is the argument of the present book, which has been derived in conformity with perceptions and practices of participants in the business world. What is the economists' perspective that is being challenged by the $W(y)$ story? Is not it, too, compatible with those perceptions and practices? Is not economics also a business discourse, thrown up in the evolution of business culture in rather the same fashion as accounting? Certainly, economics penetrates into and influences business practice also, though to a lesser extent than accounting. Why does it remain so wedded to pure competition?

Let's turn to the master trope of this discourse, which is general economic theory, upon which the many specific economic discourses depend. In his masterwork *Value and Capital* (1946, chap. 10) the economist Sir John Hicks supplies a trenchant framing of the economy:

The whole material equipment of the community, as it exists when the market opens on Monday morning, including the finished goods now ready for sale, the half-finished goods and raw material, the fixed plant of all sorts and the durable consumers' goods, must be taken as given. . . . An entrepreneur's plan includes decisions about the quantities of products he will sell in the current weeks and future weeks, and about the quantities of inputs. . . . The degree of disequilibrium marks the extent to which expectations are cheated, and plans go astray. (Hicks 1946, 130–32)

Perhaps it was from Marshall's work a half-century before (1930) that Hicks derived some sense of the in-stream siting of production markets such that they participate in a system not of exchange but rather of successive sales, with value added in each melding and transformation by successive producers. And Hicks does explicitly single out production markets, "markets for intermediate products, which are products for one firm and factors for another, so that supply and demand both come from firms." He does slip in a misleading tautology, however, as the next sentence: "In all kinds of markets, however, supply and demand are determined, once the price-system is given" (Hicks 1946, 101).

In one footnote Hicks points in just the right direction:

In the general case, of a firm employing several factors, we have to take into account the possibility of monopsonistic exploitation of factors as well as monopolistic action in the sale of product. We may have to think of the firm gathering its (perhaps necessary) surplus from the percentage by which it squeezes the buyers of its product on the one hand, and from the percentages by which it squeezes the suppliers of factors on the other. (1946, 84n)

Hicks also is well aware of a limitation imposed by the conventional view: "In the theory of production there is a third condition, which corresponds to nothing in the theory of subjective value, . . . that average cost must be increasing [with volume]."

This limitation is lifted in the $W(y)$ model.

And there are other, more general problems. Hicks's use of the term *entrepreneur* conflates firms with individuals, as do his remarks on consumers in chapter 6: "A certain parallelism which exists between the case of the firm and that of the private person . . . will enable us to put the laws of market conduct of the firm into a similar form . . . and ultimately to extend the theory of exchange to take account of production as well" (1946, 78). Hicks is here referring to earlier chapters where he derives valuations from a theory of economic exchange among individual persons:

We have discovered how the total demands and supplies of a group of persons will react to price-changes, assuming that the scale of preferences of each member of the group remains fixed. . . . The objects bought and sold . . . should be objects of desire, which can be bought and sold, and which can be arranged in an order of preference (an indifference system) *which is itself independent of prices.* (1946, 55).

Hicks's emphasis on order of preference corresponds to emphasis in the $W(y)$ model on a quality order, except that the latter has two faces.

Missing in Hicks is the differentiation of two levels of actor in the transferals through production markets: the firm and the persistent grouping of firms as an industry. This differentiation is without parallel in his theory of consumers, and it provides the basis for establishing terms of trade, $W(y)$, according to relative quality across the market.

Missing also is a focus by producers on deciding commitments in terms of their *aggregate* revenues so as to coordinate transactions with both upstream and downstream such that prices become secondary by-products of transactions across interfaces among networks of production flows.

These elements missing in Hicks are central to the consistency between the $W(y)$ story and observable practices in the business world. But the lucidity and precision of Hicks's account eased the further evolution of theory.

Hicks dismissed the monopolistic competition approaches that Chamberlin and Robinson (see chapter 2 earlier) derived a few years before he wrote, and his formulation also did not incorporate the insights of Knight (see chapter 1). Hicks reverted to a theory of perfect competition that was rarely given explicit empirical specification and was subject to the distortions laid out in some detail in previous sections. Hicks did so to support the larger project of a general equilibrium theory, which economics continues to regard, in its later mathematized form (Arrow and Hahn 1971), as a scientific rather than a rhetorical accomplishment.

This general theory of equilibrium for market systems passes over distinctions and networks among markets (see Favereau 1989).[7] This theory, in effect, slights monopolistic competition. It does so in favor of over-time discriminations that are key to financial markets. It yields, in the hands of Arrow and Hahn (1971), penetrating analysis of the temporal disequilibria that must attend establishment of market profiles, which are not treated in the present book. The resulting picture is referred, nonetheless, to the current world and so encompasses production markets as well as markets focused on time spreads, such as financial markets. But this very abstract and general picture has little to say about the market mechanism despite paying close attention to time spreads in market clearing.

This general theory also ignores network connections, which is equivalent to invoking a totally connected network.[8] Yet there is some consistency with the picture of $W(y)$ markets, once one introduces decoupling, as in the previous chapter. In fact, decoupling suggests enlarging the very abstract approach of general equilibrium theory with a stochastic argument. Since particular pair ties need not be permanent, then even though only a small fraction of all possible pair ties is being enacted at a given time, when averaged over time there is an approximation to fully connected networks. One can push this argument further with "small world" simulation models (Watts 1999a, 1999b) such as that discussed at the end of the previous chapter. Distinct from all these visualizations is the fixed network of input-output theory.[9]

What the $W(y)$ model does not do with its network ecology is specify or predict scale. (The so-called scale factors q and r are just placeholders, as was shown by the normalization procedure introduced in chapter 3.) This is an issue on which general economic theory can be invaluable. The $W(y)$ model is invariant with (indifferent as to) overall scale, whereas Ricardian and other classical economics do give insight on scale. On the other hand, the $W(y)$ approach builds path dependence in, together with local variability as efficient cause. Combinations are worth pursuing. A key issue is how to accommodate a distribution of values for parameters such as a, b, c, d, gamma, and tau.

The main tension between general economics and an economic sociology approach such as that represented by $W(y)$ is as to social construction. Keynes mainly spoke in psychological terms, although his formulations call for and imply the significance of social networks. Other economic theorists such as George Akerlof (whose work was used in chapter 5) introduce social constructions, but as auxiliary to usual economic principles. Another economic theorist develops a sophisticated model of social construction in a market (Ryall 1998), only to denounce the resulting market behavior as suboptimal—a strange view of science.

HIERARCHY FROM PURE COMPETITION

The underlying basis for a $W(y)$ market is a quality order that differentiates peer firms, along with their products, from one another. This is a kind of pecking order (Boorman and Levitt 1980; Wilson 1979). Such a pecking order is enforced by onlookers (Chase 2000) as well as among the producers themselves. Pecking order can be seen as deriving from a search for comparability, which is akin to structural equivalence (White 1992a). But pure competition can be represented as an extreme form of structural equivalence in networks; so it can be studied as an extreme form of the $W(y)$ market model in still another sense from that used earlier in the Nerlove section.

Distinguishing upstream from downstream in market networks also concerns structural equivalence. We can put this hint to work: Comparisons of downstream with upstream equilibria in the $W(y)$ model will shed light not only on this ideal type of production market designated "pure competition,"

but also on when this type shades over into the scalar order found in hierarchic organization. Scalar organization is commonly used as a hierarchical
stereotype for authoritative organization, whether governmental or not. (For
recent canvases of alternatives to scalar forms of authoritative organization
see Fligstein and Freeland 1995; Gulati and Gargiulo 1999; Ocasio 1994;
Powell 1990; White 1992a.)

Pure competition is invoked in economic discussions almost entirely in
pursuit of market aggregates under the influence of orthodox theory, as discussed in the preceding section. And indeed, the sizes of aggregates, and the
price common at all volume levels and thus common to all producers, are all
there is to look for with perfect competition! One can derive how the market
profile model of $W(y)$ yields, through terms of trade, aggregate predictions
that reduce into results predicted by pure competition. The reduction occurs
as b/d approaches zero asymptotically; see table 3.3.

"Pure competition" can be seen as including a whole set of special cases,
only some of which were discussed in the first section of this chapter. Consider first the downstream mode of markets. Within the $W(y)$ framing, "pure
competition" becomes assigned as the label for contexts with $b = 0$, across
some range of values for a/c; see the line segment marked $p.c.$ in figures 5.1
and 7.2, although that first section established that the value of a itself had
to be unity. Note also that in these cases the allowed range of k shrinks to
$k = 0$.

Indeed, in the ORDINARY region that abuts pure competition on one side,
zero is an allowed value for k. Figure 3.4 illustrates this for the point marked
in this region of the plane of figure 5.1. This figure gives a transformation of
each market profile $W(y)$ for various values of k to a plot of this observable
volume y according to the value of the quality index n.

Observe that the PARADOX region lies just the other side of the $p.c.$ line
segment. And observe that, as reported in figure 5.3 (which parallels figure
3.4), the historical constant k can be exactly zero for one viable market
profile for the PARADOX region also, which is separated by pure competition from the ORDINARY region. (Figure 5.3 corresponds to the point
marked as iv in the market plane of figure 5.1.)

But it is well known that any special case of a general mathematical model,
such as pure competition here, will not be found robust and usable for
applications unless other nearby special cases also are robust and viable (see,
e.g., Hofbauer and Sigmund 1988). Market locations in the ORDINARY region abut familiar kinds of examples of pure competition. But one must
search out and prove the feasibility of markets in contexts from this PARA-
DOX region also in order to justify the use of pure competition as an ideal
type for markets in downstream mode.

So now turn to the upstream mode. On the one hand, there are viable
market solutions in this mode too for the PARADOX region side of the line.

(In upstream mode, this line is for $d/b = 0$, as explained in chapter 9). On the other hand, in the triangular region of figure 9.2 that corresponds to the triangular region labeled ORDINARY in figure 3.1, there are no viable upstream markets in general (no robust values of k; thence the triangle is crosshatched). So there could be no switching into upstream mode from downstream markets exactly in this ORDINARY triangle, which is perhaps the most common location for observed downstream markets.[10]

Just two sections ago, pure competition was analyzed in terms of its being a special case of the $W(y)$ mechanism. Note the change. In upstream orientation, the $W(y)$ market mechanism is not stable across a region of state space surrounding the ideal types of pure competition, and so pure competition will not be found for the upstream or dual mode. This suggests a reason for the curious asymmetry in microeconomics texts, which lean on pure competition, whereby they focus almost entirely on sales markets rather than on procurement markets. The text by Mansfield (1975), an exception, does include a whole chapter on pure competition in procurement markets, but according to the present analysis there are no procurement markets that are purely competitive.

What is being taken as given in applying the $W(y)$ model is some concrete context for production work that is being summarized by parameters. These parameters are inputs to the $W(y)$ model, not results from it. On the contrary, the parameters used in the $W(y)$ model derive from a given context. This context will be partly technology, geography, and the like, but as these are transmuted into social organization, which is coded as networks of relational ties.

Even though a market does not sustain itself for given parameter values, work on those products will nonetheless continue under the pressures of a production economy. The work will be managed through some other form of business transactions. This could be an enlarged form of older putting-out arrangements, discussed in chapter 1, at the end of chapter 5, and again in chapter 15. Another candidate is some form of hierarchical organization (Bradach 1998; Eccles 1985; Williamson 1989, 1992).

What does appear is *not* a matter of unconstrained choice, nor need it even be consciously shaped by participants, and efficiency and optimality may be of little moment. What counts is robustness, the survivability of mutual social arrangement under manipulations and impacts typical of that sociotechnical context. Intervention itself is constrained by viability of alternative forms.

Rather than pure competition contexts (the line segments indicated by *p.c.* in the market planes of figures 7.2 and 5.1) being the furthest from usurpation by hierarchies, they may instead sustain hierarchies more commonly than other regions of market space. At least that seems to be the case when the market orientation is upstream (fig. 9.2).

Consider a set of producers that is especially eligible to emerge as a market because they are structurally equivalent in their continuing networks, as discussed earlier (and see Burt 1987). The $W(y)$ model suggests that when for some reason—either general, like inflation, or local, like a supplier bottleneck—its chief dangers seem upstream, then this set is oriented upstream. And then it is exactly when they are least differentiated in quality spread that emergence among them of hierarchies is the likeliest rather than some sort of pure competition. Instead of keeping an upstream market, against likely unraveling interventions, the undifferentiated set of producers will tend to coalesce as, or be seized in, a hierarchy. The mastery of a putting-out factor or merchant is extended rather than being replaced by a market form.

Possible Examples

One example could be when cement plants in a region, faced with inflation or government imposition, shift into some basing-point formula of pricing that in effect turns them into divisions within one firm (e.g., Scherer 1970, 262–72). Basing-point pricing can be seen as the freezing of a $W(y)$ market into a hierarchical organization. The monopsony analysis of chapter 5 is similar.

A second example might be Bill Gates and Microsoft. They have been very successful with a new technology situation that has sociotechnical contexts remote from pure competition. But the situation that they were facing, of packaging computer programming, had some unusual properties. In particular, they could merchandise predictably any package that proved reliable to users. Their controlling problems, and thus their orientation, arguably, were upstream. And although highly differentiated in their own eyes, would-be programmers were difficult to discriminate reliably, either for Gates or for buyers. One wonders if Microsoft is not best thought of as "the" (almost single) hierarchy into which a nascent upstream market for programming packages came so near pure competition as to be unable to reproduce itself as a sustained social form. Perhaps a similar argument could be made about other famous examples of dramatic centralization of emerging industries, such as Rockefeller's of oil in the Midwest in the nineteenth century.[11]

Instead of resorting to conspiracy or imperialist theories of how some putting-out situations led to competitive markets while from others emerge authoritative organizations, we can apply a stochastic theory for outcomes of maneuvers in network context for given industrial equipment, as called for recently by Waechter (1999). In addition to spelling out the process, one needs to bring in explicit models of formal organizations as the alternative frame to market outcomes. Leads from natural science can provide only partial guidance.[12]

 PART

Markets and Firms over Time

An over-time perspective will now supplement the equilibrium perspective that dominates the preceding chapters. These final chapters bring a change in emphasis from cross-sectional toward historical. Strategic perspectives are given as much attention as analytic perspectives were earlier.

Chapter 12 brings in external influences such as financing, as well as longer periods. It examines a further level of market competition involving networks of financial accumulation across compound firms, multidivisonal firms. It sketches several ways to apply the $W(y)$ model to investment flows.

Chapter 13 looks to the trajectories of markets, chapter 14 pauses to sketch alternative diagnoses, and chapter 15 turns to evolution of the accompanying business cultures.

CHAPTER 12

Investing across Markets

Strict hierarchy and market profile are not the only forms of control of production flow, and these next chapters survey some of the others.[1] One common devolution of market mechanism comes with the spinning out of chains of control-ties in contexts around boundaries between markets and their surrounding social context, as discussed in chapter 10. Such devolutions were featured in chapters 4 and 5, and more sophisticated forms are the topic of this chapter.

Other competitive forms and processes that occur in place of, and also as supplement to, production market mechanisms often are triggered by efforts at change. We have already uncovered and pointed to some eruptions of agency, of entrepreneurship, from within role structures around quality orders, which led to new competitive forms (chaps. 4, 5).[2] But there are other effects from the larger field of production markets and from outside that field. The production market mechanism is subject to mobilizations and changes effected through whole institutions distinct from those of production markets, notably via the financial system. This chapter begins to extend the preceding theory for production markets to further ranges of agency and scope.

Guild and monopsony forms are seen (from those sections of chapters 4 and 5) to be directed largely toward defense, toward safeguarding and controlling a line of business and niches within it. This chapter goes on to examine proactive mobilizations from outside the production market streams. These are directed toward profit on a new scale and with a longer time horizon for investment. The ubiquity of multidivisional firms (abbreviated MDF) will be seen as one result.

Entrepreneurial mobilizations are the prime vehicles of business mobilization that is mediated by finance, whatever its scale. Mobilization suggests deliberate seeking of those actions that have the largest cumulative impacts, whether the level be firms, markets, or whole sectors. Such mobilizations are typically either smaller or larger in scope than defensive interventions. Entrepreneurial mobilizations are of at least equal moment with, and also dovetail at some points with, deviations from roles by participants within particular markets that count as interventions.

Financing and Investment

The division between mobilization and intervention is fuzzy, with the former exhibiting more explicit articulation and quantitative assessment, both in plan and in prognostication. Both mobilization and intervention invoke folk theories that are at least partly divorced from academic theories (the contrast between chapters 15 and 14). Investments themselves derive, to a greater extent than the interventions sketched at the end of the previous chapter, from explicit and quantitative theory.

Entrepreneurs are alert to fortuitous opportunities for improving footing and/or performance. Entrepreneurs also can develop conscious strategy. And there is a vast zone in between of essays at helping contingencies materialize by something more than witchcraft.

In entrepreneurial mode, one seeks out all possible advantage from social mores and rules. The options include violating and ignoring them—accounting rules among others (see chapter 15). What remains in common across all variants of entrepreneurship and attempts at change is some need for financing. Financing is required even for routine commitments to production operations in a market. Financing provides leverage toward some control of operational decisions and commitments, leverage often calibrated to longer time horizons and thus called investment.

Well-developed monetarization is already presupposed in the account of production markets from which the $W(y)$ models derive. There exists a distinct network of financial relations with and among banks and other such actors, as well as state agencies, which come to cohere as a socially constructed system of finance. Such financial relations are at right angles with the relational networks taken as the source and basis of production networks and their markets: perpendicular yet connected (for background see Eccles and Crane 1988; Uzzi and Gillespie 1999; Baker 1987).

Normal business operations are geared usually to volume of continuing loans obtained for working capital. These bring with them routine monitoring by commercial banks, which tally accounts receivable and payable.[3] Thus the commitments central to the $W(y)$ production models are monitored externally. Such routine banking shades over—differently in different national economies—into risky investment, where longer-term finance is involved and indeed supplies the measures of postponements and anticipations.

The risks in each particular footing in a production market can be shared through the institution of fractional ownership. Quite separately, unease with robustness of the context, with exposure to incalculable risk—the uncertainty proper of Knight (1971)—can fuel diversification in footings. Footings also can be sought and constructed outside of and in a sense above the production markets, in other auxiliary networks as well as those of finance.

The production market field thus can be seen as having a shifting boundary with respect to a financial flows system at right angles to it. Finance institutions evolved such that the investment function could be left to separate markets. These may recruit investors, some anonymous, relying on discourse through accounting, rather than retaining investments in-house. So financial flows of investment fit with a distinct institutional system with its own species of fiscal or exchange markets in networks of their own. Even without explicit modeling, it is clear that time framings are central. Evaluations of delays and other displacements in time are what drive financial flows, through interest rates and like features of finance.

The underlying issue is control over the future. The rivalry profile for the production market is constituted in monetary terms. The very terms of trade for a production market interface depend on a fiscal frame. This frame, fiscal flows to and from firms over time, is tangibly rooted in social organization quite separate from production markets and their firms. This frame is the envelope resulting from competing efforts for control over the future, which play out over large stretches of time and of sector, as they coalesce into an order of borrowing, lending, investment, and ownership.

Use of W(y) Models

Commercial banks specialize in certain sectors because informed views of likely and possible contingencies depend on familiarity with that market's tangible context and its history. Business pressures will have induced in bankers and some businessmen overviews reaching beyond particular markets into comparisons and clusterings in industrial sectors and the like.

Data agencies, state and private, will have followed and reified them further, as in SIC classification codes for industries. Some such overview constantly is invoked to guide efforts at investment and other entrepreneurship. Use of the $W(y)$ model may well, however, uncover variations that can be shown to be real but that have long been covered up by routine business parlance and whose significance is noticed neither in these institutional surveys nor in economic theory. See the section of the next chapter on switches.

As an investment scenario plays out, impacts may be perceived downstream on the qualities of many producers, and, usually differently, producers may perceive shifts in their cost schedules. There also will be implications from possible segmentations of network relations, on either the supply or the demand side. For example, when should one seek to group demand-side outlets in multiunit chains, franchised or owned (Bradach 1998; Porter 1976b, chaps. 2 and 3)? Financing arrangements will be part of the search.

The $W(y)$ models can provide an overview even more general and penetrating, as to production markets, than those available to bankers, and do so in explicit mathematical form. Adaptations will often be required: Several illustrations have already been given. One prediction is that heralded new forms of production organization (see Page and Podolny 1998; Perrow 1993; Stuart 1998) still will come to function through this same market mechanism, but with variations in the embedding in finance networks.

The production market models are, in compensation for their greater abstraction from contextual and historical details, subject to numerical fitting and test. Five parameters suffice for most comparisons. The master parameter is gamma, for overall substitutability. Like a, b, c, d, this gamma is a saturation exponent, but on a higher level.

In practice, market footings such as those established in the $W(y)$ models in terms of quality index values will be pulled apart in business inquiries. Those making production commitments will have estimated their present cost schedules. They and others considering investment on a longer horizon will desire some picture of how changes in quality will affect costs, and also possibly redound on the quality perceived for other producers.

It is the production regime customary across all the firms of that industry, however, rather than the quality locations of specific firms, that will be the primary broker. The bigger changes are at industry level in technology and customary patterns of organization (Penrose 1959; Nelson and Winter 1982). A production market often gets established around some distinctive new cluster of products, such as fiber optics in the 1980s or the bottled water industry in the 1990s. Importance and thence valuation of perceived quality ranking, the b parameter, in such an industry may well show a strong trend, upward or downward, as is elaborated in the next chapter. That trend may owe little to equipment investment and much to rule promulgations, or it could be to taste epidemics, which can then elicit broadening investment to include lobbying and advertising.

Observers such as bankers and investors also will wish to develop independent estimates of the qualities of producers such as fit with perceptions by buyers. This again pulls apart market footing, with the demand schedule of each producer estimated independently. Here, too, it is an overall quality regime perceived for the industry as a whole that will be primary broker. For example, established practices in marketing in that industry, such as those regarding buyer segmentation, can affect the abilities of all producers to shift position on the buyers' quality index.

From the $W(y)$ schedule for a market, one can develop estimates of how much outcomes, in profits and so on, for a particular firm could be improved by various increments in quality. One would then also seek business estimates of the investment required to bring about such a shift in cost schedules or in buyer valuation schedules. One scheme developed within the business world itself is taken up in the PIMS section below.

Figures 5.1 and 7.2, joined by figure 7.1, are maps giving an overview of downstream production markets that can be extracted from the $W(y)$ models. One can discuss possible entrepreneurial strategies as if the actors were thinking in terms of this map instead of the mélange of distinct, specialized, and often conflicting framings that they must in fact draw from their diverse business backgrounds. The important point, as, for example, Porac and his associates make clear in the study summarized at the beginning of chapter 6, is that industries are being constructed around a commonly negotiated phenomenology, not around some exogenous technology.

The $W(y)$ model provides explicit solutions when all circumstances—all parameters and indexes (k, n's, tau)—are known. The solution framework, around figures 5.1 and 7.2 of market planes, also can help guide estimations even with only partial information: Begin with equations (2.10–2.11, 3.4–3.7) and note the procedures developed in chapter 8 in the initial section on estimation.

Note that the process of investment in itself may disturb the market parameters as well as profile even of a long-established market. A change in one firm's perceived quality will result in some shift of market aggregates such as **W** and also may affect the deal criterion **tau** for all. The new shape of profile could correspond to a change in the historical constant k.

And there is no provision for fixed costs in the earlier formula for cost schedule, equation (2.1); these are costs that continue to be borne, even in a period with no ongoing production, and so with zero volume of sales. The manager choosing the level of commitment for the next interval can ignore that as a sunk cost. But external sources of investment will be concerned with a longer time horizon and go beyond operational ratios like profit rate. Fixed costs require absolute amounts for their amortization, amounts that need not correlate well with current operational volumes.

PULL/PUMP INVESTMENT MARKETS

Special markets for banking get constructed among these continuing and diverse borrowing and repayment histories between investors and production firms. One impetus for such separate financial markets is the great exposure of a firm to risk when retaining and investing profits in-house. A pool of arms-length investors can spread the firm's risk widely. The greatest difficulty for investors is assessing the quality of the options that the firm sees and that fuel its requests for financing. For this reason, particular sets of investors will tend to concentrate on particular sectors of related markets.

Possibly the $W(y)$ mechanism can be applied afresh, quite separate from its application to the underlying production operations. Other investigators have brought related ideas to the study of banking markets. Eccles and Crane (1988), Uzzi and Gillespie (1999), and Podolny (Podolny 1995; Podolny and Castellucci 1999) have interpreted banking in terms of networks and roles. Podolny (1993) has particularly emphasized the structuring of a banking market around quality ranking.

A producer can estimate the amounts by which it will improve its earnings through upgrading the levels of the present infrastructure with external investment flow. The producers use continuing ties with a variety of contractors to implement the upgrade, so they can assess costs besides reliably estimate the resulting improvement in net income stream over time. It is in the procurement of investment dollars that the set of producers perceives most uncertainty. They face contingencies as to sources and amounts, and especially terms, for obtaining the investment.

Let us seek an analogy between such investment market and the *upstream mode* of the production market. We may view the investment market as a market in the production of subsequent, perhaps much later, improvements in operations of the production firms being invested in. Their subsequent cost and profit structures are to be the basis for assessing the investment. Cash flow of investment now in current dollars is provided by investors in return for commitments from the operating firm to a subsequent stream of paybacks to be made out of their improvements from the said investment. Two possible correspondences will be examined in this section.

First Correspondence

The arm's-length investor will want to spread its interests across some variety of firms and products. But to facilitate information assessment, each will tend to confine itself to some particular industrial sector. The resultant focus is a definite set of firms, possibly just those in some one production market.

Let y stand for investment flow for this year being sought by a producer in present dollars, and let $W(y)$ stand for promised repayment in later dollars from the producers to the investors.

Thus, the producers are seen in the commit role of a $W(y)$ mechanism. This is a commitment to convert an amount of present dollars for making improvements into a stream of future dollars as repayment via improved infrastructure of the producer. This can be diagramed as in figure 12.1.

The promises of repayment are contingent on the future course of events. Investors must assess the believability, the degree of certainty of fulfillment that attaches to the payback offers $W(y)$ from the various producers. Conversely, producers fashion their offers of payback commitments with an eye to each other's and investors' perceptions of their position in a pecking order of reliability. This reliability is likely also to correlate with how much benefit in improved later performance that firm will be able to achieve from a given level of investment.

Thus let n index the underlying reliability of promises from the various producers. There can emerge a market profile only if there is some underlying agreement on the rank order of these reliabilities, presumably highly

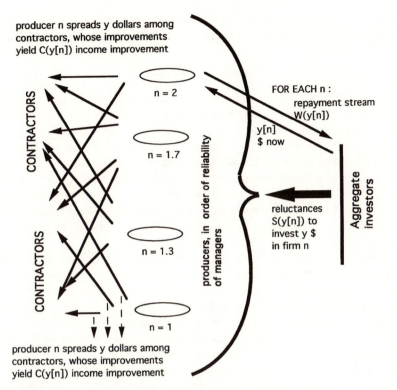

producer n spreads y dollars among
contractors, whose improvements
yield C(y[n]) income improvement

CONTRACTORS

n = 2

CONTRACTORS

n = 1.7

n = 1.3

n = 1

producers, in order of reliability
of managers

FOR EACH n :
repayment stream
W(y[n])

y[n]
$ now

reluctances
S(y[n]) to
invest y $
in firm n

Aggregate
investors

producer n spreads y dollars among
contractors, whose improvements
yield C(y[n]) income improvement

FIG. 12.1. Financing as an upstream production market

correlated with the ability of their managements and thus of how much improvement they get from a given investment.

Downstream, y becomes the current dollar flow to various contractors and specialists to upgrade the plant. The upgrade is known to be able to generate an array over future times of additional profits from operations then. Designate this by $C\{y[n]\}$; it must be at least as large as the committed future array of paybacks $W(y)$.

The $S(y[n])$ is the (unobserved) array of reluctances, in aggregate for bankers to that investment market. These are reluctances to be parted from current investment flows of various sizes y to a producer of reliability n. Summed over producers and escalated by gamma, the resulting aggregate $\mathbf{V}$ must be *less* than the $\mathbf{W}$.

The parameters c and d will reflect how the payback array of enhanced profits from improved infrastructure increases with the size of investment (in current dollars) and with the quality of producer management of contractors, with this indexed along the same dimension n as investor reluctance. Analogously, a and b reflect how the reluctances of investors in aggregate vary.

Second Correspondence

Let the banks become the committers, playing the role of producers in the $W(y)$ model. On the opposite side of the bank from the producers will now be some collection of financial contractors, market factors along with other specialists. No direct account is taken by bankers of what set of contractors and equipment providers the producers will draw upon. This bank committer model can polarize either upstream or down. This market orients in push or pull mode according to the banks' perception of whether the greatest uncertainty is from the players in its financial background or from the unpredictability of the terms producers will settle for in obtaining this year's capital budget.

Indeed, one can turn back to the first correspondence, to producers as committers, and see that then, too, there can be a push market for investment. This would be when the local banking scene seems predictable as to the size of investment dispersed this year according to terms of payment—with temperamental contractors being the principal concern.

In models for the product market, y and W are flows of entirely different sorts, the one a volume of a distinctive product and the other a volume of money. By contrast, in any of these investment markets both y and W are money flows, but they are flows at different dates. And thus the substantive interpretation of n as a tangible present quality of product/service from that source firm must be converted into the more abstract level of assessment of degree of contingency—of the promise from that source firm of repayment from performance as enhanced by the present investment.

MULTIDIVISIONAL FIRMS

Analysis of finance markets can shade over into discussions of organizational forms that center around authority. One common form of attempting mobilization in markets for enhancing financial performance does so by combining local with global perspectives (see Jacquemin and Slade 1989). Conglomerates and other acquirers and spinners-off of producer firms are concerned with bringing distinct actors from different markets under some sort of common control through investment. They hope for catalytic effects (Eccles and White 1986b, 1987, 1988). Franchising (Bradach 1998) is a variant of this move.

The investment strategy most directly keyed to the mechanism of production markets, however, is the practice of joining under common executive direction, as well as ownership, producer divisions from distinct markets:

these are the multidivisional firms (MDFs) that became common during the early twentieth century. Outside investors cannot pierce the veil of ownership to invest in particular operational units, that is, in particular divisions of the MDFs. Economists complain about the difficulty of obtaining information separately on operational divisions of an MDF. Two analysts of British business write in their conclusion: "The ideal would be to seek to replicate this study with a much greater number of sectors. This will not, however, be easy, not only because of the normal problems of market definition, but also because of the lack of information about the allocation of investment between different firms by large diversified firms that are often the key competitors in industrial markets" (Hay and Liu 1998, 97; see also Buzzell and Wiersema 1981).

Can one model these investments? The $W(y)$ mechanism may be invocable in still another way. Take the investment banks and brokers as competing, as to some economic sector, to attract and hold downstream buyers of equity and debt.[4] Equity positions are not and cannot be taken or offered in different production markets as wholes, but instead investment can be diversified beyond any single producing division across the set of markets an MDF is represented in via its divisions. The MDFs of some sector are now themselves set analogous to independent producers; y is the rate of return offered on the next periods borrowings for innovation; n is the (unobservable) viability of that MDF; W is the volume of investment supplied; and $C(y, n)$ is the cost of operational improvement that is forgone because of efforts diverted to courting exogenous investment.

A chief executive office, call it CEO, is akin to an investment bank, while the divisions are what have been called production firms above. The central office of the MDF itself controls investment for upgrading of its divisions, since it may use retained earnings from the firm overall for investment in this division or that. The CEO may screen and examine its particular producer divisions in various markets from much the same perspective as outside investors.

Potential advantages of the CEO as investor include closer knowledge of contexts in its sector of markets and quicker responses to perceived opportunities. These combine with the same advantages that an outside investor can get, especially the spreading of risk between distinct particular markets, each exposed, even when within the same sector, to differently incalculable contingencies. When context changes and erodes the stability of the market that affords protective footing to some division, there are more cues and experience available to guide the transition away from that market to some other organizational embedding in that economy. This is the payoff from the greater complexity in the nonmarket organization of the MDF with its multiple levels. Broader knowledge of context will enable better insight (see Eccles and White 1986a, 1986b; Leifer and White 1988).

Let the multidivisional firm constitute the boundary of a particular investment market. Each division always is in competition with the others with regard to the CEO's assessment of its package of financial performance. One aspect is competition for investment flows through the CEO, whether these derive from retained corporate earnings or from external investors. Let divisional managerial ability be n, and signal y be the size of the innovation proposal submitted to the CEO, who becomes the analogue to the aggregate of downstream buyers. Then $W(y)$ is the immediate investment flow offered a division with signal y, that is, the size of investment plans. Each cost schedule comes from that division's estimates of the losses from the distractions of planning a project of scope y, from the interference with internally achieving optimal operations. (This melds first and second correspondences from the previous section.) Now again the producers, here divisions, are the committers. And it is downstream orientation, the push mode.

But there is a further level of competition across CEOs. Since each CEO or CEO surrogate will be oriented upstream, not downstream, such a market for financing production firms will not, by the analysis in chapter 11, exhibit any approximation to pure competition among the production firms over capital infusions. Even to a first approximation, such investment markets can establish themselves only in contexts marked by considerable differentiation in reliability. Investment markets presuppose product differentiation, where the "product" is the assessed reliability of promised repayment from out of the investment-enhanced capacities of production firms.

Evolution and Context

The history suggests that this MDF form developed initially around problems of control (Chandler 1962, but see Freeland 1996 for a dissent). The central executives' logic of control is to group, at the next level down, subordinates into parallel, comparable units as opposed to the specialized, complementary units of functional departmentalization. Thus performances can be directly compared and contrasted. The possibility of favoritism simply induces still more competitive striving by producer divisions. This control logic has been well worked out in an extensive literature. An incisive account is offered by Vancil (1979).

Maximal parallelism, for further enhancement of control, would require that divisions be within the same product market, just positioned quite differently on the quality index in that market. Such is not the case. Antitrust considerations factor in, here as in the previous section. Yet the main considerations are ones of business performance.

Enhanced control is useful to the central executive only to the extent the overall business results are not only on the average good but are also ensured against failure. The risks would be highly correlated across divisions operating in the very same product market, however, and the multidivisional firm's ownership would thereby be exposed to unacceptable aggregate risk. Instead, divisions are spun off into or as production units in distinct markets, even if these are chosen to afford some commonality in underlying infrastructures, so as to enhance the effectiveness of the overall operations of the multidivisional firm. This business logic presumably evolved from a prior stage that relied on push/pull banking to diffuse in-house risk.

Neil Fligstein gives an account (1990) of the social construction of the modern American production economy that focuses on the control of firms. These are seen primarily as corporations, local polities, rather than as members of markets. Their fates are shaped directly by management talent. Fligstein's derivation emphasizes eras, each marked by the diffusion of a distinctive new paradigm for organizational control within firms. He speaks of diffusion through an organizational field rather than diffusion through the networks among production markets specifically.[5] He also notes influence from the state. Earlier chapters suggest contexts where authoritative organization may be triggered as a modifier or replacement to the market even without political intervention; so the $W(y)$ market analysis can supplement Fligstein in this regard. For recent canvases of such alternatives to pure market forms see Davis and Stout 1992; Eccles and Crane 1988; Evans 1995; Fligstein and Mara-Drita 1996; and Uzzi 1997.

Baumol's Dreamworld

An extreme reduction of industrial competition to isolated cognitive process is found in a series of contributions by Baumol, Panzar, and Willig (1989) that are intended as an economics of multidivisional forms. They refer to their contribution as an economics of scope. Like the $W(y)$ approach, theirs seeks out the determinants of industry structure rather than taking it as exogenous. But they do so by taking the ideal of pure competition one step further: "Contestability theory offers an analytic framework . . . via a process of simplification; by stripping away through its assumptions all barriers to entry and exit, and the strategic behavior that goes along with them both in theory and in reality" (Baumol, Panzar, and Willig 1989, 487).

The $W(y)$ model also strips away influences, fixed costs for example, and it segregates effects of strategic interaction. But fixed costs were disregarded because of the *fixity* of membership in the industry. The focus is on joint reproduction of an observable market profile, whereas the Baumol team calculates how some hypothetical decision-maker would compute the array of industries to enter into. As in Panzar's *Handbook* article (1989), and in Nerlove's econometrics sketched in the previous chapter, costs themselves have become cognitive projections. "Costs" become inferences by the analyst, from fragmentary public data on that industrial setting, as to how to minimize total costs across hypothetical menus of production.

The most bizarre assumption is there being no barriers to entry and exit. This is a sure sign of fixation once again on pure competition as theory guide. Yet, as just discussed, the whole point of acquisitions and divestitures, the reason they are the predominant means for large firms to enter new markets, is exactly that getting established in a different market, which is to say a different line of business, is difficult even for the large and well-financed firm. It is reasonable to assign importance, as Baumol, Panzar, and Willig do, to technological innovation as a motive for entry and exit. But they turn this into a rationale for substituting technological determination of hypothetical production functions for study of the perceived cost structures that actually sway business commitments, *including* those of entry and exit.

From there it is an easy step to doctrines of supposed "natural monopolies"—natural only to the analyst's imagination. Technological transformation transmutes into a utopian justification for dispensing with any tangible markets, which would be disfigurements of the elegance these authors see in arabesques of "pure competition." They go so far as to define away profits, the sign of Knightian uncertainty and the reward that is a by-product of a tangible system of markets that copes with it. There is an eerie overtone of planned economy, a sort of stateless socialism, about the Baumol, Panzar, and Willig dreamworld. The Nelson and Winter model that ends the next chapter is a more believable approach to investment in technological innovation, and perhaps even the Flaherty model, discussed in the second section of the previous chapter.

EXPLOITATION WITHIN A MARKET

Monopsony offers favorable strategic ground for exerting control, and indeed within this option the distinction between ownership and managerial control becomes blurred. Monopsony can serve as a surrogate for control struggles going on *within* a firm. And, with respect to control of a set of lesser entities, monopsony also can serve as a prototype and surrogate for the central office of the multidivisional firm riding herd on its distinct and parallel product divisions.

Monopsony has been treated already. The last section of chapter 5 offered a scenario. The essential point of that first scenario was that substitutability with other industries was assumed to be minimal, so the key parameter gamma was taken to be unity. Thus the distinction between **tau** and theta disappeared and, along with it, the whole conundrum of feedback laid out in chapters 6 and 7.

Now in a second scenario for this monopsony, substitutability is no longer ignored. The parameter gamma is not unity. Return to the GM example from chapter 5. Operationally, in any version of this opt-out, GM enforces equation (2.3), but also with gamma capturing GM's degree of involution/substitution: see equations (6.5, 6.6, 6.9, 6.10). Dispense with the consideration of shape of offer schedule $W(y)$ that was carried out in the first scenario.

One obvious criterion for GM to adopt, as in the first scenario, is maximizing its net profit. But there is another criterion that may appeal to GM, namely, maximizing total production from the suppliers completely committed to it. Then GM presumably would want to keep all its suppliers in play, and so would avoid choices of k that would lead many or any to opt out. These k values could be computed for the relevant context (a, c, b, d) according to the spread of the producers on n and, of course, on GM's strategy, influenced by its own valuations.

Turn now to take instead the subcontractor perspective. They are especially concerned with how their revenue compares with their cost, the markup they receive. This is W/C, for which an explicit formula was derived, in the case $k = 0$, equation (3.4).

And refer back to figure 3.2, which reports rays in niche space along which markup is constant, as well as buyer ratio tau. One can also elide the broker role of W to express V directly in terms of C. We now can compute what might be seen as the degree of exploitation by GM in our monopsony example. The market size W, and thus net income to producers, can be expressed for $k = 0$ most simply as a multiple of its value for no net income to GM, breakeven, designated W_e, which occurs for tau $= 1$. That is,

$$V - W = (\text{tau} - 1)W = W_e(1/\text{tau})^{1/(1-(a\gamma/c))}. \qquad (12.1)$$

Maximizing net income for GM, for $k = 0$, therefore means choosing the value of **tau**,

$$\tau_{\max} = c/a\gamma. \qquad (12.2)$$

As noted in the previous treatment of feedback in chapters 6 and 7, enlarging the buyers' net income means lowering the aggregate market size.

When GM is thus maximizing its net income, is there exploitation? It would seem likely if only because the aggregate market volume, and hence the volume per firm on which producers are earning a profit over cost, is being shrunk. Substantively, in short, the interests of the two sides seem opposed, so control by one side can reasonably be construed as exploitation of the other side.

The verdict of exploitation is easy to establish more formally. One needs a base line for comparison. Let that base line be that the producers know the value of their production for GM, exactly as it depends jointly on volume and quality, and that they are able to insist on that valuation schedule being in fact the offer schedule, the $W(y)$. (That means, however, that c must be greater than a; otherwise, the volumes chosen by producers would explode.) Under those conditions one has

$$y^{c-a} = (ar/cq)n^{b-d} \qquad (12.3)$$

and further

$$W/C = 1 - (a/c). \qquad (12.4)$$

Patient manipulation will verify that, in allowed contexts, equation (12.4) indeed yields a larger ratio than one finds from equation (12.1), so producers do better. Against this latter as a formal base line, it is suitable to label the market $W(y)$ profile as indeed yielding exploitation of little producers by the surrogate aggregate buyer, GM.[6] This competitive market mechanism is compatible with exploitation. Note that the economist Michael Spence, who introduced a core mechanism that has been adapted for the $W(y)$ model (see chapter 5), missed the possibility of exploitation such as is illustrated here.

An *upstream dual* for this bypass option to downstream markets has been identified at the beginning of chapter 9 using the obvious dual label to monopsony, *monopoly*. The guild (see chapter 4) was an early form of monopoly. In the monopsony, the aggregate buyer (possibly a single organization like GM) can insist on a particular price structure in paying the producers their revenue. In the monopoly, as dual form, it is the aggregate supplier that is enforcing a structure of payments on itself. A state could be such an aggregate supplier, but so could a large firm.

PIMS Data Analyses

Profit Impact of Management Strategies (PIMS) is a cooperative research program among, and targeted at interventions by, multidivisional firms in the United States that was initiated in 1960 by staff at General Electric Corporation (Anderson and Paine 1978). PIMS expanded under staff of its own as the Strategic Policy Institute, which was loosely affiliated with the Harvard Business School. Through the 1970s it grew to include reporting, at least annual, from about 2,000 units from 200 corporations (Hambrick, Mac-Millan, and Day 1982, 515).

Business unit is "congruent with the term *strategic business unit* (SBU) and is defined as an operating unit that sells a distinct set of products to an identifiable group of customers in competition with a well-defined set of competitors" (Anderson and Paine 1978, 603). These SBUs are mostly divisions of the two hundred *Fortune* 500 MDFs that joined. An overview of the PIMS studies by Buzzell and Wiersma (1981) is consistent with predictions and stipulations developed from the $W(y)$ model, now applied to divisions of multidivisional firms.

The PIMS story can be suggestive of how and how not to study and model production markets. Studying and analyzing production markets requires observations that are much harder for outsiders than for participants to make. The Census Bureau relies on self-reports. A variety of state agencies such as the Securities and Exchange Commission require both regular and occasional reports from all larger firms, but often there is little detail by constituent SBUs. The Justice Department has subpoena power to gain information from all producers in a given industry, especially in aid of antitrust investigations (Baker and Faulkner 1993). The more complete the information, the more confidentiality restrictions limit access by investigators.

PIMS offered some relief from these conundrums (as have, since then, openings of research access to staff of some investment advisory firms). Firms chose to participate voluntarily with each other and with an institute divorced from state agencies and supported by the substantial contributions required. The benefit was reports on situation and performance of a large set of peers, with accompanying analysis to supply assessment and advice to each contributor. They could anticipate more benefit the more completely they as well as their peers reported.

The irony is that reports from these SBUs were never, so far as the public record shows, placed together in a market-level report. Firms themselves wanted confidentiality, and this became a guarantee by PIMS. The research staff would only report results for SBUs grouped by attributes. Sector and market share were covered in the hundred and more items measured, but you could not know how many of the set of SBU with which you were compared had footing in your actual market.

PIMS had grown from a base in marketing research, and its operationalization of the market was skewed toward buyers, so "the PIMS database is particularly deficient in data on task or structure related variables" (Ramanujam and Venkatraman 1984, 138, 146). Even so, findings are useful checks on assumptions of the $W(y)$ model. Later use of PIMS was, for example, enlivened by comparisons to the qualitative diagnoses put forward by the Boston Consulting Group, which centered on an experience curve that relates to cost schedules such as $C(y, n)$.

More generally, PIMS's collection of a portmanteau containing more than one hundred measured variables had the somewhat paradoxical effect of making investigators more skeptical of the importance of most of them. A longtime participant commented that "many of the variables. . . . are *not* controllable by management. . . . [H]e must accept them as inherent in the type of business he operates" (Buzzell and Farris 1977, 143). This fits social constructionist views that underlie the $W(y)$ model. PIMS asked many qualitative, subjective items, not least the bounds of the respondent's market, and its staff were available for dialogue with a respondent to clarify meanings.

Turn to more specific findings from analyses by business school faculty (e.g., Hambrick, MacMillan, and Day 1982, 515) of accumulated PIMS surveys, coordinated with reports by PIMS staff. One of the most basic findings is that increases in market share are modest indeed, even though that is one of the criteria most emphasized by PIMS and business consultants. This fits the $W(y)$ framing of stable niches. Other findings have to be pieced together. Tables normally separate firms by role attribute without grouping them into a market. Firms of different quality level, in $W(y)$ terms, are often put in opposition rather than being seen as locked into a mutual profile. Useful indications can be gleaned, however.

One PIMS measure is relative product quality: "the percent of sales from products and services that, from the perspective of the customer, are judged 'superior' to those available from leading competitors *minus* the percent of those judged 'inferior'" (Gale, Heany, and Swire 1977, 18). In the Hambrick, MacMillan, and Day study (1982, table 8, p. 527), the results are not inconsistent with the $W(y)$ claim that generally market share declines with quality, where, however, the distinct types of firms are being treated as in the same market. A complication is that in this study there appear to be many large SBUs that fit the PARADOX region: high market share going with both high prices and low costs.

Another PIMS measure is immediate customer fragmentation: "the proportion of the total number of immediate customers accounting for 50% of total sales, expressed as a percent" (Gale, Heany, and Swire 1977, 16). The Hambrick, MacMillan, and Day study (1982, table 6, p. 525) points out that there are almost no differences in this measure across the types of firms (which corresponds to differences in a quality index in the $W(y)$ model). This is consistent with producers not discriminating there among customers.

Let's finish with one market diagnosis, for one multidivisional firm that was a longtime participant in PIMS, coupled with an account of its experience with PIMS diagnosis for one of its divisions. Seeking to diversify into areas related to its long-standing core business in acrylic resin, Sterling Industries[7] had set up a rubber division, producing some emulsifier chemicals but primarily cis-polybutadiene (CPB) and related synthetic rubbers used not only in tires but in beltings and other products subject to high-stress use. CPB was a high-value-added product, raw materials accounting for only 20 percent of the selling price, with only about half of that being purchased from other firms.

The total U.S. market for CPB was not small: half a billion dollars a year in 1974, which was about half the total world market. Even in the U.S. market, however, Sterling still had less than 10 percent market share ten years after it had entered through investment in technology licensed from the largest producer, the non-U.S. firm NEKO. The rubber division had regularly consulted PIMS for diagnosis and strategy recommendations. However, NEKO had itself entered the U.S. market for CPB in 1970, and in 1973 it constructed its own U.S. plant, about the size of Sterling's. In 1975, both the diagnosis and the strategy recommendation from PIMS were grim.

Even this beginning sketch of a story is much more complex than the simple framing of the $W(y)$ model, but the question is whether essential aspects of this market's workings nonetheless are captured by this model. Apply the model just to a market for the United States, which was quite decoupled from any world market by tariffs (a reason for NEKO's building a plant in the United States). Even there, the largest producer, a U.S. tire manufacturer, should be excluded because it used in-house all its production, about half the national total.

Four principal producers, then, are claimed to be eying and keying to each other and thereby delimiting this CPB market (aside from several large overseas producers who altogether had less than 10 percent of this U.S. market). The largest, Union Chemical, was also the oldest in the CPB business (and had itself started European production in 1975, thought to be a signal of riposte to NEKO). The second largest was another tire company that, although keeping much CPB for its own use, was attentive to market conditions and perceived by Sterling to never be selling less than 2 percent on the open market. NEKO (U.S.) was third and Sterling fourth in market share.

CPB production of each of the four was subject to substantial economies of scale, $c < 1$, whereas customer response to volume was nearly linear, $a = 1$, so that, if this market fits the model, its location is on the right in market space, figures 3.2 and 5.2 with $a/c > 1$. There was a substantial spread in product quality, with Sterling at the top with its expensive new equipment, and the others following in inverse order to market share. This ordering was the same both for cost schedule and for customer satisfaction schedule. The sensitivity of customers to quality seemed comparable to the sensitivity of cost to position on quality index.

The final piece in parameter fitting is substitutability, gamma, of other sorts of product from other markets for CPB. This is substantial on technology grounds and is so perceived by participants. So gamma is well under unity: The test, thus, should be whether the CPB market behaves as predicted for CROWDED region of state space: see figures 7.2 and 7.3. Aggregate market size could well decrease when more firms gain footings, and this seems to have happened. That is the main prediction for CROWDED markets.

Table 7.1 shows that this prediction holds for the whole panel marked CROWDED in figures 7.1, 7.2; and it also holds for upstream orientation. And from figure 7.4 in the lower part of the panel firm revenue is positively correlated to position on the quality index, but in the upper part the correlation is negative. In this respect, the lower part behaves like PARADOX, whereas the upper part behaves like ORDINARY. Sterling CPB commanded a substantial price differential, but that does not ensure that aggregate revenue goes up with quality. It seems that the CPB market may well have been some approximate fit to the $W(y)$ model, but for different locations in the CROWDED panel over time (see the "Tracks" section of chapter 13).

PIMS advice was given with caution because the previous experience of Sterling in the CPB market lay outside the statistical bounds of observations accumulated over the other thousand or so divisions participating in PIMS. Sterling had invested far too much given the relatively small share of the market it had obtained when the entry of its licensor NEKO sandbagged Sterling. This financial issue is not represented in the $W(y)$ model since it need not alter optimal choice of operating volume. Finance ties rather to the demography of entry and exit, a business demography more tuned to the network environment than to internal attributes of company "health."

Analysts of Sterling's planning department kept working and developed additional options for the next ten years besides those pumped out by the PIMS program. PIMS could be repeated for successive periods, but it did not have a representation of how managers of one's own and competing companies strategized. That is more natural to do within the $W(y)$ model framing with explicit representation of market positions of peers.

Crucial to use of $W(y)$ for such purpose is the use of numerical computations. Both in observable fact and in strategic intentions, firms have different profit rates even when these are referred as in the model just to operating costs. So the simple analytic results available for profiles with $k = 0$ are not germane.

The largest domestic competitor of Sterling's had a very good profit rate, only partly because its sunk costs from its older plant were lower. How is such a premium for a longtime market leader to be captured in the $W(y)$ model? By not only investigating displacement of profile, with k, that favors the largest firm, but also by noting there are strong interaction effects between k and levels of tau and of gamma, as Bothner (2001a, 2001b) is in the course of laying out.

ECCLES ON TRANSFER PRICING

The central issue of both intervention and mobilization is interdependency. Exploiting interdependencies is the method of social mobilization generally, so we turn to that literature for guidance (cf. Tilly, McAdam, and Tarrow 2000). Mobilizations around market forming surveyed in this chapter, and earlier in chapters 4 and 5, integrate markets and hierarchies views of interventions. Let's examine in more detail the contradictions that accompany these economic mobilizations, which appear policy-guided to some participants and as interventions to others.

The examples drawn on concern transfer pricing within multidivisional firms in a number of industries. These examples are woven around markets, and they underline the basic claim of this work: that competitive production markets are constructed out of and in order to reproduce the inequality order into which mobilization dependencies are transmuted.

Transfer prices within companies are akin to children's and spouse's allowances within the household economy of a traditional family (see discussion of alternate moneys in Zelizer 1989, 1998). Transfer prices are neither fish nor fowl, neither market nor administered. In a multidivisional manufacturer often one division can be or is the source or destination for some product flow from another division of that firm. How are such amounts and the accompanying revenues to be determined? One tension is that the "parent," the CEO, assesses and then compares the contribution of each division in net revenue, and yet also is concerned for the synergies of the company as a whole.

Eccles (1985) gives a thorough review of alternative views of transfer pricing in industry—together with the rather few previous studies—and reports his own extensive field studies in thirteen MDFs in three industrial sectors: electronics, machinery, and chemicals. From this, together with analysis of one major survey, he goes on to develop his own theory for practice.

The analogy to family suggests just the sort of erratic, unbalanced changes and misunderstandings that Eccles reports from his field interviews with top managers across each of his thirteen MDFs. Eccles quotes on his first page a leading authority on managerial control systems, the author of the major survey Eccles used: "My disappointment in this study is that I have been unable to say anything definitive—or even mildly useful—on the subject of transfer prices. . . . The issue remains a perennial puzzle for academicians, while practitioners continue to cope" (Vancil 1979, 142).

The basic finding in Eccles' report is that multidivisional firms do not settle down to any one form of transfer pricing but erratically bounce between options and/or settle into one arbitrary formula, which in no case is accepted without cavil. Indeed not the formula but the means by which the transfer pricing is decided, under the aegis of the CEO, is the best predictor for low level of contention.

Eccles reports that managers' concerns typically were more involved with status and their own personal perceptions of what was a just price than with accounting and optimization arguments: The managers he studied seem just the players to staff a $W(y)$ mechanism, context permitting.

An overall conclusion Eccles came to is that division managers preferred doing business through the market to doing internal transactions within the MDF. This directly contradicts the assertions of transaction cost economics (Williamson 1975, 1985, 1989)—which do not derive from systematic fieldwork or surveys. It supports the present view of the market as a social construction within which the manager finds primary footing, as to discourse as well as decision making.

The central difficulty in applying the $W(y)$ model when the market members include divisions from MDFs is that volume y may no longer serve as a signal, breaking its role of mediating between quality differentiation and revenue. One can predict, therefore, that other media than volume (see the last section of chapter 4) become commoner in signaling in markets with MDFs present. But there is further evidence for the centrality of volume.

Eccles went beyond his extensive comparative fieldwork to draw on the Vancil survey of 250 firms. Like Vancil, Eccles searched for causes of transfer pricing policy in the strategy of the MDF as well as the concerns of the general managers of its divisions. The size of transfers was substantial enough, even at the 5 percent level found in all but a fifth of the cases, to affect production unit costs and divisional performance measures.

In order to overturn Vancil's negative verdict, quoted earlier, Eccles had to discriminate MDF strategies differently. Are internal transfers between divisions mandated? In the third of the firms that were diversified into unrelated business lines, no, but otherwise mostly yes. The other question: Is the selling division (in accounting terminology a profit center) treated by top management as a freestanding business? Only with this new dissection of strategy in two dimensions at once, diversification and vertical integration, was Eccles able to find significant variation of transfer pricing policy with strategy.

His findings (table 4.3) are clear.[8] The predominant policy in MDFs with diverse businesses that were not vertically integrated was negotiation, whereas when they were vertically integrated, the predominant policy was market price. Full cost was the predominant policy when there was vertical integration but not diversified businesses. These results are consistent with the view that the main concern of division managers is with cutting the feedback loop between price or revenue and volume, for in the MDFs with unrelated businesses, a division is too remote from the market discourse of the other divisions to be knowledgeable about "market price." Mobilization is generated and contested among divisions.

The present analysis of production markets through $W(y)$ models points to a possible major gap in the analyses by Eccles and by those he draws upon. The $W(y)$ model forces attention to how the market establishes itself as a distinct level of actor. Without such a model, Eccles does not recognize a distinct upstream polarization for market.

Which polarization obtains is central to transfer pricing phenomenology. For example, Eccles discusses dual pricing as a significant variant among the transfer-pricing regimes that he observed. In dual pricing, the upstream division applies the pricing rule it favors and so too does the downstream division. Eccles examines how these preferences held by selling and buying divisions change over stages of the product life cycle (see chapter 13). He goes on to argue that the two views rarely coincide (Eccles 1985, fig. 9.2). Indeed, the underlying issue bedeviling transfer pricing can be seen as conflict about which polarization to take—confused by the specificity of trading partner. This also fits with the fact that an MDF will typically have not one policy on transfer pricing but rather different rules for different pairs of divisions. Usually, however, the central office will not long support the distortions in its control and assessment systems that result from the use of a dual-pricing rule.

~~~~~~~~~~~~~~~~~~~~

CHAPTER 13

Strategic Moves and Market Evolution

What are the larger, longer-term implications of the continuing patterns of investment just treated? Interventions affect and reconfigure markets and sets of markets as much as they do the member firms. This chapter goes beyond impacts within markets upon firms to track also impacts on markets as wholes. Viability of a potential market as well as performances by its firms depend on location in market space; so this market space can serve not only to array a population of markets at a given time but also to trace subsequent movements.

First comes the demography implied, and then switchings of orientation are taken up as major market moves. Next, more explicit attention is given to distinctions between the strategic interventions of the previous chapter and the role perspective that was favored in earlier parts. Both these perspectives are needed in the next section on technological changes familiar from product life cycles. The chapter ends by comparing the $W(y)$ story with another institutionalist story of evolution for a system of production markets.

DEMOGRAPHIES IN NETWORKS

The environment for dynamics of firms and markets, for their careers, is mostly the other life courses in streams of interacting firms and markets. There are births and deaths. And note that Eccles used a life cycle scenario to frame his results on transfer pricing policy (1985, figs. 9.1, 9.2) discussed in the previous section. Exact theory becomes very hard in such evolving populations in interaction, harder even than trajectories of interplanetary wanderers, which to this day remain too complex for exact solution despite completely specified gravitational theories.

Big firms live a long time, partly by engrossing smaller firms, and usually longer than the markets in which their divisions compete for business footing. Look back at the business census of 1920 and you will not find many five-digit (detailed) industries that ring a bell for you. Yet a new firm always is seeking a business footing in some market that at any given time is bigger, better known, and more stable than those firms seeking a footing.

Conversely, a new market typically appears in the train of a new firm, some entrepreneurial organization that is proselytizing for a product reconstrued enough to be considered new. Take, for example, Melvin Hershey, who labored for two decades of the 1800s, with mixed results, in the confectionery industry. He cashed out his caramel company for a million dollars, but only in order to create what was a new industry: chocolate candy. He transformed chocolate from an esoteric luxury good, transforming a freak specialty into a broad industrial market. A whole city, Hershey, Pennsylvania, grew up around his enterprise and so did a host of imitators, often split off from previous long-term competitors of his in various regional confectionery markets. Hershey created the first national confectionery market, moving his product from the status of perishable and thus local to that of long shelf life.

Any number of "life stories" can be told of this and other examples, but perhaps there are at least some overarching patterns. The disposition of potential buyers can be as crucial as the entrepreneur. Some new markets, such as chocolate, will be shaped by an initial refusal by consumers to do more than taste the new product. That is, the parameter a and thence a/c will start off small. Yet b is likely to be large, in that some varieties of the new product may suit aggregate taste much better than others. What will be up in the air initially is the size of the cost parameter d for quality.

If d is negative, we have the Spence signaling model. In the case of products, this seems likely to hold only for an initially dominant producer such as Hershey in the chocolate industry. Market revenue would grow initially only through engrossment of hitherto separate market cachement areas. There would be few surprises as a stable market evolved around the dominant firm.

If d is positive, we have a fragmented small-producer mode found among the economics of convention. A producer will tend to attract buyers only for a taste of its particular variety. The producers also may have reliability difficulties in production so that a/c will tend to be small. From table 3.1 and figures 3.2 and 3.5 one sees that these attempted start-up industries will tend to be in the UNRAVELING region. In this region few of the markets can stabilize, save possibly with state assistance or joint connivance.

Consider other initial and subsequent locations of new markets within the market space. Many will tend to exhibit large ratios of b to d. The new product may be complementary to existing products, such that a will be large from the beginning, as in, say, fiber optic cable. Such new markets are likely to appear with downstream orientation: hence the designation ADVANCED could well be changed to NOVEL in figure 3.1. These are cases where the new product catalyzes additional desire for other products complementary to it.

Now consider gamma. A new market is likely, with either polarization, to be in a novel line of service or product with little substitutability with other markets. This will tend to support the preceding scenarios, according to figures 7.1 and 9.3.

Examples could be multiplied. What is needed is a demography of a population whose actors change even in type, not a demography of some fixed species. Indeed, it is a double, coupled population of firms and markets. The most difficult question is when different tracks—or planned trajectories—are consistent with one another.

Chapters 9 and 11 showed that switching a market's orientation in production stream can yield stability; contrast figure 9.2 with figure 5.1. One would expect a tendency there for b to decline while a increased as the new product became institutionalized. The producers could function together as monopsonist with respect to upstream, with each having predictable sales downstream. The projection would be a movement over into the TRUST region, the other stable region for upstream market mechanism.

Switches

Switching as a term induces notions of agency and disruption. So switching is entirely suitable as a label for the complex and messy maneuvers that must transpire between what we see now as a downstream and then, perhaps, later as an (only partly overlapping) upstream market. Switching a production market between a mode of orientation upstream and one downstream requires extensive intervention in the previous operation of a market or sector of markets. Its occurrence constitutes a major market move.

Some general guidance can come for examining the dual solutions, for markets as wholes, with the dual framings in terms of context parameters given in figures 5.1 and 9.2. Chapter 9 already pointed out striking contrasts between the outcomes in corresponding regions of these two figures (consult figures 9.7 and 9.8). Now these discussions can be reconstrued to suggest differential opportunities and constraints for maneuver by market participants.

First, stand back from particular instances to consider switching more generally as a process. Clearly it places heavy demands on communication among peer firms and their customers, suppliers, and observers. This may require change, indeed a switch in discourse. An inflationary register replaces a deflationary register, or the reverse, or new technology induces and requires adoption of new frames of perception. What is required, put generally, is an intervening period of suppression of particular registers in favor of some bland public discourse.[1] A business panic provides such an occasion. So does the abrupt arrival of wholly new competition, say from abroad.

A switch of orientation in common for all or most processor markets together may be triggered, exactly from the arrival of inflation or from a business downturn with deflation. But from time to time, a switch of one or more markets may be triggered by local disturbance. Hardest to understand and discuss in generalized terms are these localized cases in which the common orientation in just one market switches by itself.

Consider a particular scenario for a switch in orientation. Perhaps a huge market leader, a dinosaur that is in trouble in a downstream market (IBM?

GM?) might deliberately cut off procurements from along some major lines of suppliers for long enough to throw into turmoil for all the members of that downstream market their upstream procurement process. Some subset of members, together with producers from heretofore independent markets, thus might be joined together into a newly active upstream market. This latter might prove more advantageous (say, in its effects on return on investment, ROI) to the dinosaur than the previous downstream market—or at the least might be on the path back to a more felicitous composition for a downstream market.

Switches in orientation, reversal of polarization in a market, also may often accompany technological changes. Such changes relate to restructurings of industries that are heavily influenced by substitutabilities observable at a given time, which are reflected in the parameter gamma. Gamma equal to unity is the extreme found in populations where there is no interaction between valuations of productions from one industry and those from another.

Consider a market with producers facing downstream. There, gamma less than unity corresponds to considerable substitutability, probably the predominant everyday expectation. There should be a trend as one moves from brand-new to long-established industries, a trend toward smaller gamma. Movement would be toward the origin along the direction of the $1/\gamma$ axis, figure 9.3.

Also, one might expect gamma to tend to be higher the further upstream toward raw-material stages that one looked, and also higher for markets facing upstream. Yet gamma may also exceed unity for downstream markets. Aggregates behave differently with large gamma—see the earlier discussion in chapter 7.

Examples

When fiber optics—or Frisbees, hula hoops, or Rollerblades, for that matter—came in as new products, no substitutes would do and demand seemed insatiable, which corresponds to the product of gamma times a being large. But then even after only ten or fifteen years, fiber optics transformed into an established industry whose products are seen as substitutable with alternatives from other industries. Soon they may approach being mere commodities. Turn to figure 13.1, which repeats the market space of figure 5.1 with tracks added.

Diffusion theory suggests several possible scenarios for this example (see Abrahamson and Rosenkopf 1993), but these have to be fleshed out. The track X-X-X could be for fiber optics. And it may be that fiber optics could then, its market profile being subject to unraveling, switch into upstream mode and appear as the X in the cognate region of figure 13.2, where it is not subject to unraveling: refer to figure 9.2.

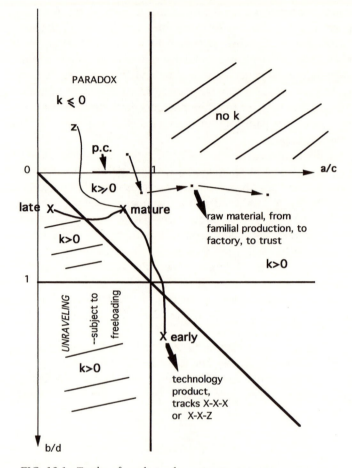

FIG. 13.1. Tracks of markets, downstream state space

But the track for a new product might also evolve according to X-X-Z track in figure 13.1. Perhaps T-shirts once were an exciting new product that then decayed into the ORDINARY region, but subsequently entered a new phase of extreme specialization. In this latter mode, which was examined under the label *Domestique* in chapter 7, various ad hoc production arrangements spring up, which often are tied to another social organization, such as family or community, in which perceived quality is lower when cost of production is lower. Some may amount to switching.

Consider now a possible scenario for deliberate switching between orientations. Suppose an ordinary industrial downstream market located in the ORDINARY triangle finds itself caught up, perhaps because of technological change, in a situation where these traditional producers' markets are coming

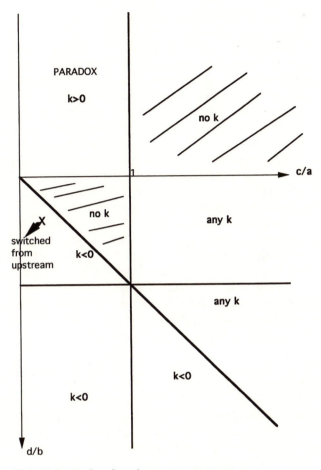

FIG. 13.2. Tracks of markets, upstream state space

to be seen as obsolescent. This would correspond to a sharp lowering of the parameter *a*, and hence of *a/c*. Thus, the ordinary market might shift into a context where it is subject to unraveling. But the responses to this might well be such as to enable some sort of joint switch to emphasize and focus on the upstream side, to the dual form of market that is not subject to unraveling.

This talk of moving along trajectories in a niche space has been ad hoc. No one process has been proposed whereby a market observed as one variety, as one location in niche space, "moves" to another location, nearby or not. And the processes that may be involved in switches between the two orientations are hard to anticipate and model. Indeed there can be no simple or clean mechanism of such changes, because by hypothesis the market profile gets established by a trial-and-error process with any of a wide variety of implementations.

So far, the membership of a market has been argued to be stable, because of processes of identification by selves and others as some industry or other entity. Yet until a process is specified, it is not clear that all firms in a market will switch orientation together, that "the" market will maintain some sort of continuing identity. Perceptions oriented upstream may be very different from those oriented downstream, and switching is a severe enough disjunction to jolt perceptions anyway. To take an example from academic experience, what it seems natural to group as "the education industry" from the buyer (student) side will differ significantly from what seems natural from the producer (administrator, teacher, and staff) side, or from investors or other outside observers (donors and governments).

The model's parametric description (a, c, b, d, r, q, gamma) of context for the market as a whole, then, is not sufficient. Observers must look also inside markets at their constituent producer firms, with their quality index values n. What is perhaps the most intriguing and difficult question follows at once: What is the relation between a given producer's quality index in a downstream market and its index in an upstream market? On this could hang the scope of opportunity and hence temptation for one or more market actors, or outsiders, to try disrupting a given market by throwing it into a dual form.

Switching from downstream to upstream market by a particular industry not only requires wholesale reappraisal of their ties by producer firms, but also may well induce them to look to changes in their organizational form. Such reappraisal is likely to bring reconsiderations of and speculation about investments, such as were sketched in the previous chapter. These may be investments in upgrading, possibly supported just from the firm's own retained earnings. The upgrading may lower costs but usually it is also expected to enhance the quality of producer and product in its own and others' eyes. Proprietors thus can be seeking to upgrade the quality of their firm's position within a market otherwise unchanged. Thus switching and investment for upgrading may be interwoven in the perceptions of firms.

ROLES VERSUS STRATEGY: BOTHNER

Human agency, and thus in particular business strategy, comes into existence only with behavior constituted and shaped in and as a role system, here a production economy. A role system is a transposable realization of a culture, the earliest and most basic instance being the system of kinship relations (White 1963). Most of the talk in previous chapters has been of business firms filling roles whose interactions produce a market profile that reproduces itself out of itself, disciplining the firms. The key puzzle of roles is how any actor exhibits agency over time while yet its identity and thus role is embedded into social networks.

Previous chapters developed some answers. The interplay of decoupling with embedding is what establishes roles, which are what permit strategy and other agency in actions. Decoupling processes such as those discussed in chapter 10 can dissolve the contradiction between such human agency and the determinism, albeit stochastic, of other ecologies. Chapter 12 just postulated intentional agency and planning by actors.

Roles also beget deviation. Sometimes this deviation is endogenous, and sometimes it is traceable to impulses and resources from outside that role framing. The whole set of parameters for the $W(y)$ model reflect the perceived and interpreted impacts of context, including network ties. Insides and outsides of the given market both contribute to such parameter values. Entrepreneurship (see end of chapter 4) is also a role. In business behavior one speaks of entrepreneurial urges as sources of changes, great and small, intended as well as unintended.[2] Turn to the individual firm and its executive. The issue is not the freedom of some independent actor, but, on the contrary, how an entrepreneur detects, nurtures, and exploits degrees of structural autonomy (see Burt 1992). There are subtle issues of mobilizing network ties in triads that offer indirect leverage for gaining control (Gargiulo 1993, 1999).

As a process market continues in operation, there may come periods when all the transactions, both inflows and outflows, are unproblematic and so come to seem habitual. Little regard is being given to any profile. However, the claim is that subsequently, additional problematics may soon resurrect the earlier profile in perceptions such that processors will again turn inward toward the results being achieved by peers within a profile for that market. But there are other possibilities.

Carlton (1989) argues, in an assessment of microeconomics (for an excerpt see chapter 11) that typically the dynamics of price changes in particular transactions do not correlate highly across different purchasers in an industrial market. In plain English, some buyers get much sweeter deals in price change from certain producers than are available to other buyers.[3] Thus Carlton is arguing for ties as overriding market discipline. Most economics discourse is couched in terms of "the market" and thus asserts, on the contrary, high correlations in such price changes. So, apparently, does the $W(y)$ mechanism for the market. But another central result of the $W(y)$ model, a result that can be traced back at least to Chamberlin's 1933 doctoral thesis on monopolistic competition, is that different producers obtain quite distinct prices from the *equilibrium* shape of the market profile.

Strategy emerges from identity through agency. Henry Mintzberg (1987) gives us a lucid parsing of "business strategy" into five usages (with illuminating contrasts with public administration and the military). The familiar business notion of "setting key decision variables" sounds like a combination of his second and third meanings: a consistent pattern in a stream of action that yet is crossed with tactics or ploys in dynamics. Mintzberg's first usage or meaning is the explicit plan. It simply is unavailable except by interview or some other source for accounts of any conscious, intentional conception that can constitute a plan that precedes decisions and actions, within or across firms.

How can one get at strategic change that has some considerable time profile, apart from at least some data on intentions? One can argue for Mintzberg's fourth usage as the core vision. This is strategy for a niche, strategy as mediator between the "organism" and its environment. This shades over into Mintzberg's fifth usage: ingrained, inward perspective, as of IBM for marketing and Hewlett-Packard for engineering. Strategies, or in longer perspective careers, are precipitated out by dynamics; see, for example, Ocasio and Kim 1999. The master parameter for strategy is surely the historical constant k, which reflects the leeway left even with market discipline obtaining.

Trajectories and Tracks

In analyzing interventions and elaborations, the previous chapters mix interpretive moves with observations of regularities. A distinction should be drawn between track and trajectory. *Trajectory* refers to a forthcoming or planned path of movement, whereas *track* refers to a path already accomplished.

Strategies can be reflected in trajectories in niche space, while at the same time shaping and contributing to the trajectories. Viewed personally, trajectory becomes career or, in shorter perspective, strategy. The coupling of identity with trajectory in this sense is as true of compound social actors like firms and markets as it is for persons. Trajectory is not the record or track of an identity but, on the contrary, a major means of building, recovering, and adjusting identity.

Different observers will bring competing ways of parsing these interactions. Strategies come out of the perceptions of and thus are shaped by perspectives of participants in the market situation. The point is that strategy is available only from basis in an identity shaped by roles, which in turn are shaped by the identity of the market that is embedded. One can work back from possible trajectories to identify strategies.

Strategies are constrained by market context, so let's begin with that. Turn back to figure 3.2, the three examples or rays through niches in market plane that each share a common performance outcome. The main point is that the exponents a, b, c, and d so powerfully determine performance that, as long as a/c moves in step (read linearly) with b/d, representative firms from all the niches along its ray will continue to achieve the same outcome even though moving across different regions in state space, different types of market. Strategically speaking, what does this imply? It implies that an equation to guide state-space movements must be such that a/c is some *nonlinear* function of b/d. *Then* a representative firm can enjoy better performance along the track, together with different performance from its peers in that market (for $k = 0$ see equation 3.5).

Niche space is a good framing for assessing strategy. It is this structure of parameters that remains invariant as scaffolding for specifying markets, sets of markets making up a production economy as it evolves over time. Tracks rather than trajectories in niche space are the subject of the next subsections. The discussion of asymptotics in chapters 3 and 7 shows how to gain insight both for strategic moves and for tracks without complete or exact knowledge of context parameters and constants. Moreover, as shown in chapters 5 and 11, firms and various other contracting arrangements and interventions can also be located in this niche space.

Assume we have located various industrial markets in the state space, as illustrated earlier in the plane of figure 3.3. Quite aside from switches of orientation, a market may drift in its location because of several sorts of lesser changes in its context. Some will be just tracks. Some of these changes will be the intended results of strategic moves by individual firms making investments. Many or all of the producers in a $W(y)$ market may innovate in parallel just as they set their prices in view of those achieved by peers. A particularly important class are changes in product associated with technological innovation (Nelson 1994; Nelson and Winter 1982).

Such analysis is complicated by the presence of multidivisional firms, which chapter 12 described as a focus of investment and innovation. From his study of transfer pricing within multidivisonal firms, Eccles (1985) concluded both that internal transfers were substantial and that policies tended to be erratic. So it is not clear what interactions are thereby induced between the distinct $W(y)$ markets in which different divisions of various firms are engaged. One might expect some instability in the market profiles, so the tracks of particular markets may be erratic, even discontinuous, whether or not the actual product innovations centered in those divisions.

Product Life Cycle

Yet Eccles' other main finding was a strong correlation between the form of transfer pricing used and the strategy of the company. These strategies were, it seemed to him, predictable from characteristics of that industry that could be summarized by position in a "product/process life cycle." So tracks might be regular, in part because they followed from trajectories envisioned by some or all the top managements who touched on a given market.

One can also expect to derive guidance especially on the sheer appearances and disappearances of markets—on market demography—from the ecological perspective that was opened up in the second section of chapter 11 and is further discussed in the first sections of chapter 14. Natural history can be as apt as strategy for appreciating how markets evolve. Markets corresponding to points in the CROWDED region will presumably extrude firms and spawn new markets. Markets in UNRAVELED region (see figs. 5.1, 7.2) presumably either tend to split up into further markets or merge into some collusive form of organization. Markets along the principal diagonal ray through (1, 1) may do the same. Markets in TRUST may tend to conglomerate together, combining into some collusive organizational form. Markets in the PARADOX region may tend to shed smaller firms but thereby increase the total number of markets. It makes sense to check these expectations for consistency with the historical background to current production market systems.

One needs to examine both the strategic and the institutional impetuses to see how they fit together. Substantive scenarios need to be explored, not just abstract tracks. Product life cycle is a favorite topic in management literature (Lawrence and Dyer 1983) and with consultants (Porter 1980). It is a good focus for such combined examination of technological innovation generally.

The Boston Consulting Group (BCG) gained prominence largely through expositions on product life cycle. In particular, they emphasized a "learning curve" effect in which costs of production decrease over time after a new product is brought out. A prominent case was semiconductor production, and their prototype firm was Texas Instruments. The point is that BCG had to emphasize the natural and inevitable quality of this effect in order to be convincing, and yet of course they were selling advice about how to gain advantage. But there is a natural reconciliation, since getting in early, with BCG advice, would get you ahead in sliding down this universal curve, as your company accumulates experience and makes adaptations. This scenario is more apt for a track than for a trajectory; it structures commentary rather than providing a causal mechanism.

Consider product life cycle more generally. The convention is four stages: introduction, growth, maturity, and decline. It may be possible by use of $W(y)$ models to develop various causal accounts to replace BCG's scenario. The goal is to turn an exogenous and ad hoc explanation into an endogenous by-product of the operation of a causal mechanism.

TRACKS

One advantage of the $W(y)$ approach is that it enables analysts to compute for themselves detailed numerical results suitable to particular scenarios of interest to them. The technical background needed for studies of change—or investment programs for change!—besides explicit models of process, are assessments of sensitivities. These are sensitivities to various levels of, and small changes in, parameters and constants of the cross-sectional $W(y)$ models. Some of this has been carried out in tables A.1–A.5 in the appendix. Other leads are found in the discussion of the figures. The main leads are the results of asymptotic analyses introduced in chapter 3 (see equation (3.8)) and some reported in table 3.3. Needed, in addition, are assessments of how these sensitivities impinge upon one another.

Such sensitivities should be computed for the market profile $W(y)$, as well as for the various market aggregates and shares that have been introduced. For this analytic purpose, included among the parameters should be the locations hypothesized for some number # of producers on the n index. The historical constant k should not be treated as one of the parameters. This k is an ex post description of how things turned out in a successful try at $W(y)$, rather than a parameter that could be independently measured and might be subject to manipulation. What is important about k has already been pointed out earlier: The size of the allowed *range* in k will be a measure of the vulnerability of that market variety.

Let's turn to a more general and abstract measurement perspective. From some initial population of firms connected in production networks emerge role structures across interacting levels of firms and the markets being parameterized. Explicit modeling of these dynamics would be prohibitively difficult, so we turn to a view in terms of successive cross sections in time, in the market space.

What evolution can be expected? Certain locations in the market space already have been seen to be unstable for a $W(y)$ market, as a hilltop is for a ball. But it is something of a tour de force to attempt more general predictions on continuing evolution from a modeling framework of comparative statics. This is especially true since this $W(y)$ framework includes dependencies, endogenous relations among the parameters, the exploration of which has only been begun in chapter 8.

Market space arrays all possible contexts of a production market. One can hope to trace evolution by a market as a track of its location in niche space. But this depends also on consideration of a possibly changing spread on the quality index in the market, on path dependency, which is to say the bricolage of incident in business life, and on the mores of relative advantage across the interfaces in a sector, the level of tau.

Suppose all this is accomplished. Even so, this tends toward a passive, ex post stance. But it does offer a rich menu of possible action, including the switches of orientation between upstream and downstream discussed earlier. This section will take an estimation stance to focus on track, whereas the preceding two sections took interpretive approaches, focusing on trajectory.

What are possible tracks of change for markets, and with them firms, within this space, and how are they bases for action? Let's begin with a focus on tracks that run through points near the origin in state space. The interest may, but need not, be in a particular substantive context, such as technologi- cal change. Interest could be in what sort of deviation from $W(y)$ market form might be set off by the dynamics implied by that class of tracks, giving underpinning to the discussions of the previous two chapters.

Let the market start in upstream mode. As and if the given market resettles in to production streams, it may well be switched by its participants to downstream. Subsequently, as its product or service loses prominence, it may well become more and more oriented to recruitment of the buyer side so that it may once again adopt an upstream stance, now through preoccupation with distribution. Other likely tracks can be investigated both from modeling and from case study perspectives (for those see, for example, Lawrence and Dyer 1983; Porter 1980).

The niche space for $W(y)$ markets is a space in three dimensions, which adjoins the spaces of table 3.1 and figure 7.1. Figure 13.3 diagrams a track in the resulting space. There is, however, also the market space for upstream polarization. Since it is a dual space, the same diagram can serve with but a different mapping of coordinates.

Conjecture: A market over its life course moves in one of the tracks exemplified by the dotted line in figure 13.3.

This is a turn to a more general portrayal of evolution in market population. It is akin to visions in demography and in population ecology. The search is for regularities in time paths of individual markets without making reference to a particular historical period, much less to particular strategies and im- pulses.

Sensitivities to parameter changes can help indicate more and less likely and more and less profitable directions of change in variety for a market. They can also help suggest, from just how that variety of market profile is most vulnerable, just what exogenous occurrences are most likely to trigger a move. The end goal is to show explicitly what mediations might make real some hypothesized track, perhaps one "caused" by an independent techno- logical innovation. Several possible such trackings of a market's moves through its state space were sketched in figures 13.1 and 13.2. They were described as trajectories, but they may in fact be by-products of actions not strategized.

A study of cross-derivatives of various orders and contents in solutions of $W(y)$ models would be useful. The difficulty is that closed mathematical formulas are achievable only for boundary varieties. The $W(y)$ model frame- work has been chosen to be just complex enough to capture main interac- tions and show them as an emergent level. The balancing goal was simplicity such that outcomes could be traced analytically. The results remain too com- plex, however, to yield closed formulas applicable across all regions and parameter configurations.

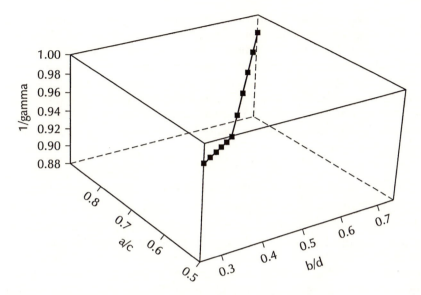

FIG. 13.3. A track in the three-dimensional space for markets

Numerical solutions are required, such as are illustrated in tables A.1–A.5 of the appendix. But the number of parameters is large, and thus so is the dimensionality of the exploration. Searches for results are too complex to be resolved by arbitrary series of cases such as in these appendix tables. What will eventually be required is higher-level programming for choosing and scanning series of cases in terms of assessment criteria built into the program, just as is done in many modern laboratory investigations (e.g., Watts 1999b; Boorman and Levitt 1980).

Such programming should be guided by leads from paradigmatic case studies that suggest sets of scenarios with important substantive implications. Some promising beginnings by Matthew Bothner are reported separately in accounts of simulation computations (Bothner 2000a, 2000b; Bothner and White 2000). They take the form of qualitative guidance as to what kinds of changes in performance go with changes in one or another configuration of parameters.

Now let's return to the discussion of asymptotics in chapters 3 and 7: for example, equation (3.13). Consider two incarnations of the same market—profile 1, where k is close to zero, and profile 2, where k is far from zero, all other parameters being the same in the two profiles. In profile 1, the parameters that, if tweaked, induce the most change in global outcomes (such as market concentration) are the exponents a, b, c, and d. The Herfindahl Index of market concentration and the profitabilities is, in contrast, little affected by changes in r, q, and gamma (Bothner 2000b). So, it is for profile 1 that two-dimensional trajectories such as in figures 3.1 and 9.5 matter most.

Conversely, in profile 2, small percentage changes in the exponents—a, b, c, d—induce only minimal shifts in outcomes like concentration. Numerical computations show that for profile 2, it is r, q, and gamma that exert the preponderant effects. So for profile 2 one must turn to the full three dimensions of state space (figures 7.1 and 7.2 adjoined, or figure 13.3). The third axis is, of course, 1/gamma. The substantive importance of certain state-space movements—whether (1) moving out along b/d, but holding gamma constant, or (2) rising in gamma, but holding a/c fixed—depend very much on the level of k.

High-Art Market

Consider an unconventional, brief example: a subeconomy or small separate economy in a contemporary high-art oil painting.[4] There is enormous emphasis on individual genius and distinctiveness, which may translate into a market profile with very low value for the parameter a. But the only such profiles that will be stable for every distribution of producers on the quality index n will be those in the PARADOX region (see figure 5.1). This requires that painters perceived as offering higher-quality works suffer *lower* costs in creating a painting.

Otherwise, the market profile can establish itself only subject to the constraints of the UNRAVELING region. Here, the presence of low-quality painters will shake the stability of any market profile. An observer could expect to see signs of the guild option being invoked through joint intervention by better painters. Perhaps lesser painters would become redefined as amateurs and excluded. More generally, one would expect to see signs of devolution as well as of investments across these arrays of painters.

Think about types of vectors in the three-dimensional state-space. Strategies that shift perceptions of quality distinctions (move 1) matter most—that is, induce the greater differences in market shares—when vendor profitability positions are equal, that is with $k = 0$. Strategies that better position the industry *as a whole* (move 2)—such as organizing for lower q or collectively advertising for higher gamma—induce the largest intramarket differences when producers are dissimilarly profitable and efficient (k not zero). This portrayal is too tidy, however, to be realistic. Multidivisional firms are common and, according to the discussion of transfer pricing that ended chapter 12, each division has a role as constituent in an MDF in addition to a footing in the market particular to its product.

Two Evolutionary Stories

The practical business of living gets done in many ways. Organizations and specializations of various sorts enhance flows of production of goods and services and thereby get institutionalized in an era. Money flows enable degrees of calculation and planning for production flows in our era such that more and more of ordinary business gets included in a system of production economy. Business is now mostly subsumed in such economies, and for two centuries it has centered around markets of a new species, production markets.

Comparisons can be ventured between the $W(y)$ approach and explicit evolutionary work by economic theorists Nelson and Winter (1982), who pay attention to institutions. These theorists emphasize, as the $W(y)$ framing does, how evaluations and information that are uncertain induce comparabilities via processes of satisfying. This comparison will bring the analysis back to the focus on quality in chapter 4.

Products, being social, can be thought of as social mores. Taste is contingent, being socially constructed, and mores change, sometimes in broad patterns. For each product, the accepted cultural boundaries can shift along with the perceptions induced, for example, by groupings of products in advertisements for various producers and/or industries. This is a universal process (for instructive fieldwork see Urban 1991). Thus "products" are mutually determined with "industries," through the market groupings that persist. This process continues within the smaller compass of a market profile, and thus yields the phenomenology around what becomes labeled as quality, defined as valuation that is socially constructed.

The account Chamberlin sketched in 1933 of evolution in a modern economy continues to ring true as regards many later developments. Growth in amount and scope of advertising was central, according to Chamberlin, in increasing product differentiation so that "monopolistic competition" would become more and more the rule. Consider possible explanatory stories of the burgeoning of monopolistic competition, articulated in terms of the $W(y)$ model.

Story 1

Growth in advertising has system-level effects and improves the perceptions of quality for particular firms. The latter might be interpreted in the $W(y)$ model as growth in the range of n for a given market, whereas growth in the exponent b would correspond to the impact on the level of market from the growth of advertising. Effects across, at the level of, the economy would correspond to a secular trend upward in the median value of b among markets.

Nelson and Winter suggest that the diffusion of technology and of forms of business organization leads to increasing parallels between different firms in how they produce. That suggests that one might also expect the value of d to be going down, on average, over the same era, along with the spread in perceptions of quality indexed by n. Thus one would expect a long-term secular trend upward in the ratio b/d; whereas on the spread in n opposing tendencies would tend to cancel out.

Sensitivity of valuation to volume produced by a firm, the exponent a, would on similar grounds be increasing. Indeed many observers (see Oster 1982) note that alongside advertising to differentiate products come forces for standardization, including other aspects of advertising itself, such that larger and larger volumes are demanded from the relatively few producers who survive for a product that is becoming no longer differentiated by locality. But sensitivity of cost to volume produced by a firm would tend to decrease sharply through the effects of standardization. Thus the ratio a/c, the other axis in the state space for the $W(y)$ profiles, would be increasing sharply.

The upshot, according to story 1, could be a wholesale movement of locations for markets in the niche space (e.g., figs. 3.2, 3.5, 7.1) along the main diagonal away from the origin. This would predict a secular trend away from ORDINARY markets on out toward ADVANCED or CROWDED region for markets. In particular, there would be movement away from any approximations to the pure competition of neoclassical economics.

Story 1 could be continued. In the CROWDED region, there tend to be fewer producers per market, and even so smaller markets. But there is continued growth in population, as well as continued exogenous pressures to maintain real total volumes of production. So one would expect great opportunities for new markets to be founded and split off, which would reinforce some of the underlying trends.

So much for story 1. Exactly the wrong things to do are to polish this story, to try to fit the story to some existing historical descriptions, to "test" it with multivariate correlational techniques applied to some available set of data. Instead, the underlying hypotheses should be probed. Specific new phenomena should be teased out of the analytic scheme.

The $W(y)$ model helps one articulate and pull apart all the many assumptions going into such a story. But computation is required to assure accuracy in even the qualitative conclusions about system performance. For example, even if the elements of story 1 are validated, computations might show that it was the TRUST region, discussed mainly in chapter 9 on the upstream orientation, that was the destination of the drift of most markets in state space.

Story 2

Consider an alternative. In story 2, advertising is in the long run the great leveler, putting an outside agent in the position of offering to enhance the visibilities of different producers. Omitted from both story 1 and story 2 is the parameter gamma, which reflects substitutability between industries. Absolutely critical to aggregate market outcomes, on the $W(y)$ model, are the relative sizes of (a/c) and γ. If this were computed to be less than or near unity in median value across a population of initial markets, the predicted outcome of market drift could be the EXPLOSIVE region (see figs. 7.1, 9.3)

Despite and indeed because of its parts and subprocesses being simplified to the point of caricature, the $W(y)$ model permits one to sketch scenarios for complex evolutions. Particular stories such as 1 and 2 must be compatible with the model. But they also should fit into narratives recruited in part from sources of explanation that fall outside the present $W(y)$ model. These include analytic approaches focused on dynamics, found in Nelson and Winter 1982, and methods appropriate thereto (e.g., Abbott 1983, 1984, 1990; Abbott and Barman 1996; Tuma and Hannan 1984; Western 1995). Germane also are the contributions of Arthur (1985), discussed in the next chapter, and Schlicht (1998), and see the survey in Maki, Gustafsson, and Knudsen 1993. Other sources are interpretive historical ones, such as that offered by Lazonick (1991), already discussed in chapter 1.

~~~~~~~~~~~~~~~~

CHAPTER 14

Contrasting Research Perspectives

In this chapter, different pairs of approaches to studying market moves will be contrasted with each other as well as with the $W(y)$ perspective. All can be seen as partly derivative from business cultures themselves, examined in the next chapter, as well as from ideologies specific to science as an institution.

ECOLOGY AND FLOWS

The self-consistent field approach introduced in chapter 8 can be extended into an ecology by introducing some sort of spatial infrastructure. Space, ordinary metric space, is the central vehicle for modeling in natural sciences, from DNA work in molecular biology (Pollack 1994) and cell growth to the chemical physics of matter (de Gennes 1979). Even the combinatorial calculations of statistical mechanics are wrapped into this spatial frame, which indeed is the principal basis of the self-consistent field motif. *This* space seems to come, in a sense, free to researchers, at least since the geometric discoveries of the ancient Greeks. Social science, by contrast, must derive its space, must conceive it as being induced and shaped in the very processes that social science claims to be applying.[1] So, in large part, do the parts of biology concerned with organisms (Wilson 1979), under the rubric of ecology.[2]

The obvious entry to social space is networks. We want to formulate as an ecology how markets emerge in network settings. This is to be an ecology with special degrees of freedom for action. And it is an ecology of continuing flows rather than of populations under reproduction.

One can list a population of markets, along with a population of firms, but they appear only together as an ensemble across these two discrete levels of actors getting socially constructed out of networks. Therefore, many constraints affect the distribution across a network space of all markets from a sector or economy. One can frame this market population as a statistical ensemble (see Abbott and Barman 1996). Or one can use *field* as a framing term to avoid confusion with some determinate "system" from technology or even from bioecology.

Production networks somewhat resemble feeding chains in networks of predation among species of animals competing in a territory, to the extent that both ecologies are unplanned, emergent outcomes of diverse competitive efforts. Competition is hard to distinguish from cooperation, however, since both realize coordination and rest on establishing comparability. A different analogy for production networks is to the ecology within some cooperative species of ants, with its coordination of specialized efforts into continuing flows of production sustaining the community (Wilson 1970).

Both analogies are needed in accounting for the intricacies of a market system. Social ecologies differ from biological ones in sustaining and making use of transposable structures for choices, and thus of culture. But parallels remain between social and biological. In each, ecology weaves niches.

Many biological paradigms of ecology are as yet underspecified, so application of mathematical models to specific data there is often elusive (Hofbauer and Sigmund 1988) and depends on the particular substantive focus. The key constructs of niche, environment, and resource also remain elusive in the usage of the population ecology school of organization studies discussed early in chapter 11 (Hannan and Freeman 1989; Barron 1997). Their usage of niche seems to derive from resource-dependence models of organization (Pfeffer and Salancik 1978), and it proves hard to specify in substantive terms (e.g., Brittain and Wholey 1988).

The central insight from the population ecology studies of the economy to date is that interaction effects favoring population growth are in proportion to the number of ties among the growing number of firms, which is to say roughly proportional to the square of population size. One might adapt that to the $W(y)$ approach, since here, too, firms are basic units in the process of social construction, but with the wrinkle that their market constructions exert some control over them as member firms. But it is hard to discriminate the underlying mechanism merely from examining a graph of counts in time. A precursor in such search was the Hamblin, Jacobsen, and Miller book (1973, especially chapter 5), whose main point is that very diverse sorts of populations can yield similar profiles.

Let's bring in what proves to be a related contrast, that between the $W(y)$ story (see end of chapter 3) and orthodox economic theory (see chapter 11). Particularly at issue in that contrast are conceptions of boundaries and levels, which is to say ecological thinking. According to the $W(y)$ story, boundaries cannot be chosen independent of continuing processes of social construction and reconstruction from social networks in the array of markets. These continuing processes of social construction and reconstruction also reach across distinct levels to include firms, with decoupling between them and their markets as distinct identities. Chapter 10 spelled this out, and chapter 11 spelled out how the theory of pure competition should accordingly be reconstrued. Variants of pure competition theory are included in population ecology.

The $W(y)$ approach looks for the appearance of clusterings of firms from early on in the evolution of production. Markets are an important format but not necessarily the only one, for such clusterings. The dependent variables thus go much beyond sheer number of firms or their rate of change, or even their sizes, and they call for analysis of systemic interaction. A market is not some empty box of pure competition into which firms can be drawn and from which they can disappear, subject only to environmental pressures, but instead a market is an ongoing production of tangible relations among firms oriented to each other as well as to the environment, itself largely made up of markets and firms. Some attempts to broaden population ecology toward institutionalist views of organization move in this same direction (Singh, Tucker, and Meinhard 1991; Barron 1999; Haveman and Nonnemaker 1996).

The $W(y)$ network model thus offers a view of environment in market ecology that differs from the one in much of the population ecology school's work. Environment is seen as largely endogenous, from embedding into the production flow networks. Evolution is not in one but in two levels of actor. Market evolution must affect evolution of constituent firms and the reverse; so the evolutionary context is complex. The $W(y)$ approach in these respects resembles biological ecology (Boorman and Levitt 1980), but with a different focus, on processing flows of production rather than on reproduction and multiplication of population.

The $W(y)$ view is that the firm, even early on, is seeking the cover afforded by membership in an established market, which indeed may have caused it to grow to its present size from a small firmlet. Population ecology has demonstrated with careful quantitative studies that early stages of evolution in some sectors may well include proliferation of firms according to their maxims, but the $W(y)$ argument is that thereafter markets become the principal basis of evolution. This evolution can be in size of firms and it can also be in their number within a market, but it is as much or more in firms' interactions and the course of births and deaths of markets.

What most urgently needs study is the evolution not of firms but of markets in number and in gross size. What aspects of endogenous dynamics lead to splits of markets? Are they associated with spin-offs by constituent firms? The state space for markets can provide some guidance on such questions, as developed at the end of chapter 11, where evolution of markets was seen in terms of their locations in market space, as well as in networks. This evolution cannot, however, be seen as just the drift of a cloud of unrelated points in a market space, since the evolution of one market influences the evolution of other markets among locations seen as niches.

The multilevel approach by $W(y)$ can help clarify how to apply the seminal ideas on graininess of environment, following Levins, which were the focus of the founding paper of the population ecology school (Hannan and Freeman 1977) and subsequently were applied to the genetic evolution of altruism by Boorman and Levitt (1980). It seems likely that firms should be regarded as normally within a fine-grained environment. Markets, on the other hand—at least in the approximation used by the present model, with but a single parameter for substitutability—will be in a coarse-grained environment unless they are part of a historically close-knit sector such as the knitwear industry studied by Porac and his collaborators (see beginning of chapter 6).

Population ecology models can help with, as well as be helped by, $W(y)$ models. The population ecology school offers an extensive set of documented empirical studies as well as a number of thoughtful commentaries informed by literature in biological ecology. And there surely will be many sectors, such as restaurants, where the population ecology model will be sufficient not just for the initial period but for the steady state.

INDUSTRIAL ORGANIZATION AND BUSINESS STRATEGY

Let's examine possible gains from interrelating the $W(y)$ model with the applied studies, some institutional and some built around statistical testing. These include but go beyond Industrial Organization and business strategy studies. The research culture around statistical testing has been largely bypassed so far in this book, even in the citations.

It is useful to distinguish ten directions within assertions in applied work across several disciplines. The first direction is the population ecology of organizations just discussed (Hannan and Freeman 1989; Carroll and Hannan 2000). Here the levels of population and industry are conflated, in the interest of focusing on over-time evolution of some large set of firms, responsive to changes in environment.

A second direction concerns political interventions, interactions between state and economy. Fligstein (1996, 2001) has recently provided a comprehensive overview of studies done and to be done, qualitative as well as quantitative, in this direction. Padgett is finishing a monumental case study (based on Padgett and Ansell 1993) of these interactions over several centuries of the Florentine republic. This again is remote from the focus of the $W(y)$ approach, although possible overlaps with the $W(y)$ approach have been pointed out in chapter 12. Certain parameters and constants in the $W(y)$ model are more relevant here than others: Interventions will show up particularly in the distributions and averages of the scaling factors in valuations, namely r and q, and of substitutability gamma, as well as of the historical constant k and the buyer pressure tau. The 1989 *Handbook* by Schmalensee and Willig, which was cited often in previous chapters, surveys a large number of empirical studies, many in this second direction, but misses the first and several of the remaining directions.

Quality is a core construct in the $W(y)$ model. Indeed the punch line of the $W(y)$ model is its state space, which distills the interaction between quality order and local context in actual production flow. Chapter 7 identified the economics-of-convention work of French economists, much of it qualitative, as the studies most relevant to the $W(y)$ model, and this work centers around quality. Call it the third direction. Striking parallels were shown between the respective findings from these independent lines.

The fourth direction is applied economic studies centered around quality. The focus in my chapter 4 was on the social construction of quality within a given industry. That chapter spelled out resemblances between the $W(y)$ model and a fifth direction, various hedonic pricing approaches within economic theory (Terleckyj 1976). But it is only the economics-of-convention studies and the $W(y)$ approach that point to distinctly different sorts of field and archival studies of quality. Only these latter two approaches conceive quality as an institutionalized interaction pattern across a market, with dual buyer and producer facets. Chapters 6–12 showed how bound up such a quality ordering within a given market is with parallel social constructions in other industries, distinct but interconnected, upstream and downstream. These subsequent chapters concern still broader interrelations, which are the other half of $W(y)$ theory.

The directions remaining, from my list of ten, intertwine in complex fashion. Disentanglement is only partial and with many overlaps. Michael Porter (1980) identifies major issues faced by practitioners in two U.S. traditions in empirical business studies. He emphasizes the split between these two, which I designate as my sixth and seventh directions. Earlier Porter (1976a) had explicitly proposed a new melding of these two, industrial economics with pragmatics of business strategy.

Business strategy practitioners themselves are mostly not economists and include many sociologists. They are concerned primarily with the individual large firm, whereas industrial organization (IO) practitioners, mostly economists, are concerned primarily with the industry as a whole and usually take more of a naturalist than an advocacy position. External attention to strategy scholars comes primarily from upper business management, while IO is attended to primarily by various agencies of the state—judicial, regulatory and legislative. The former are concerned primarily with what particular firms can do, whereas the latter are primarily concerned with how particular industries circumscribe what particular firms can do.

Neither of these last two traditions has much theory with which to explicitly site and to explicitly string together their unending supplies of cases, on the one hand, and their extensive statistical tabulations, on the other. Nor has anyone produced theory that brings their two divergent strings together under one conceptual roof in order to derive larger and more general implications. Recently, however, Porter's associate Rivkin (1997) appears to be calling for some such theory.

The $W(y)$ approach offers a modeling framework in which it may prove possible to integrate with, as well as test findings from, these two traditions identified by Porter. The $W(y)$ model also bears on various regularities proposed and statistically tested by Porter in his own studies. Porter emphasizes the importance of demand characteristics in shaping industry structure and performance, in contrast with the supply-side focus of the pioneer work of an earlier IO generation led by Joe Bain and Edwin Mason.

So just within the IO approach, Porter is pointing out a further split. The approach through $W(y)$ forces the analyst to integrate these two. Market orientation, or polarization (as analyzed in chapter 9), indicates which is predominant in a given case, without suppressing the contribution of the other, and so can help integrate the older line in IO with Porter's. Designate this as the eighth direction.

The $W(y)$ approach also induces attention to how different configurations in relations between three adjacent positions in a stream shape the role of the next position in the stream, all being required to characterize the market as a whole. (Chapters 8–10 point the way.) This parallels another thrust in Porter's work. Porter argues the importance of distinguishing between convenience outlets and other sorts of retail outlets. Designate this as the ninth direction.

Porter and later Oster (1982, 379–80) offer empirical tests but no theory for this approach. Such statistical tests from fits of multivariate models cannot offer positive direction for extension and elaboration such as is made possible by explicit theory as mechanism.

Porter more generally argues for special standing of the final market interfacing to ultimate consumers. Economic theorist Kelvin Lancaster (1970) had earlier argued, instead, for assimilating consumers themselves to roles as producers (of final satisfactions obtained from the use of particular goods acquired—see hedonic pricing earlier). The $W(y)$ perspective supports the latter view. The $W(y)$ mechanism for the market as a distinct level results in a decoupling such that positions for markets are relative to one another in a transposable framing rather than being fixed. This is a role theory of markets, which is transposable to various locations in chains of inflows and outflows among industries.

Porter's privileging of the "boundary" market thus is dissolved. Instead of ultimate buyers (or ultimate suppliers) having special status as "edge" markets, *every* market is seen as in some sense an edge market. The practical impact on analysis is great. Auxiliary markets, such as of legal services, temporary workers, or advertising, are assimilated on an equal footing into the $W(y)$ approach. Studies of such markets can be seen as a tenth direction.

Another sense of boundary is with respect to deviation. A second main fault line that Porter has discerned within business studies lies between structural constraint and entrepreneurship. The former, characteristic of IO work, emphasizes how the structure of a market constrains and shapes the performance of firms in it. This is captured in the paradigm

$$\text{Structure} \rightarrow \text{Conduct} \rightarrow \text{Performance}.$$

Firms become mere enactors of roles, for example, according to market-share position. The second paradigm, business strategy, focuses instead on the individual firm, and by bringing in a much larger variety of contextual effects it loosens the effect of constraints featured in IO. This amounts to an analytic restatement of the split between the sixth and seventh directions designated earlier. Porter proposes a melding of these two paradigms, as does the present chapter.

What can become and remain central is position in the market space, in its planes with regions and rays, along with the dual niche space for the upstream orientation. This is what theory should do: designate on its own terms the major regularities to be expected from observation. Otherwise, one is left with an unending series of special, ad hoc groupings as the primary distinctions sought in observation, without any path of theory for generalization and refinement, without mechanism to be tested. Distinguishing convenience outlets from others no doubt will prove useful, as Porter argues, but that usefulness can be greatly enhanced when the distinction is operationalized with parameters, such as those of the $W(y)$ state space, which also operationalize very different examples of markets. The same can be said about Porter's other substantive arguments, such as that regarding contextual influences on retail price maintenance. Of course, there have been many other contributors of empirical work parallel with Porter's, ranging from Oster (1981, 1982) through Rivkin (1997).

This is not a conflict but rather a call for extension and generalization. This argument for improvement also runs in the reverse direction. How does the $W(y)$ modeling approach build on and how can it inform and be informed by existing empirical work on business economics? The phenomenology of the $W(y)$ mechanism has been left open in a number of respects. Bringing the model with its state space to bear on the tangible, yet general, problems suggested in Porter's early empirical work will help to improve Porter's analysis just as it can help to test the proposed mechanism. Collaboration is in order. What the $W(y)$ model hopes to do for business economics, to sum up, is synthesize the contributions of Joel Dean and Michael Porter. The former was Mr. Cost, whose trenchant analyses of the production side of a market set its frame for half a century. The latter is Mr. Distribution, whose seminal work seems to me to have set that later frame.

What $W(y)$ does is to show how each is incomplete, how each has torn excellent analysis from the minimal, tripartite frame (procurement, transformation, distribution) necessary to understanding dynamics in context. It is exactly that tripartite interaction that throws up the *abcd* planes and thereby distinguishes varieties of markets. Observations of the volume and price outcomes realized by their other peer producers, the market profile, provide producers with only part of the basis for estimating payoffs from their choices. The $W(y)$ market mechanism articulates the position of that industry among three, not two, layers of players.

Attributes and ties of supplier, of producer, and of buyer all figure in the interactions that set the concrete terms of trade across the focal producers. The market mechanism must derive ultimately from all three, rather than just from some two roles of buyer and seller, as for an exchange market. Strategy can only be enacted from within a role framing even though its aims include subversion. Agency in production market contexts comes with, and only with, distinct levels of roles for firms and markets. Agency is lubricated by decoupling of their role framings. Agency combines deviation from, with reproduction of, roles, whence strategy.

Always the central puzzle in social science is how action is fresh even though embedded in subcultures, languages, and stories. There is a unique interpretive moment for social processes that has no analogue in other self-organizing systems. Polymers may indeed spontaneously seek out one rather than another, on some scale of interaction, and hence one rather than another form of organization, but this "spontaneity" does not go beyond chance, nor is the "self" aware. Strategies, and social action generally, are interpretive accomplishments made possible by autonomy in interaction that is sustained only by a culture that can define deviation.

In this book, Erving Goffman (1974) is being combined with Gary Becker (1976). The model assumes actors who are boundedly rational in that they are striving, within their joint framing of perceptions, for best results within constraints that are taken for granted. Optimality is taken as the principal concern, since that is built into business culture more commonly than any other modality, but it is constrained optimality that relies on habit as default for those choices not framed as problematic and urgent. Optimality is a modality for dealing with the pressure to choose *both* within a context that is obscure to the chooser *and* where the consequences are perceived as major, with resort to habit otherwise.

EVOLUTIONARY ECONOMICS—YOUNG AND ARTHUR

Developments in microeconomics itself have continued, despite the strictures of orthodoxy, and provide many of the tools and ideas used in these chapters (see citations of Spence, Porter, Williamson, Rosen, Akerlof, and others in earlier chapters). Much of the credit might well go to Allyn Young, who early in the century supervised the doctoral theses of both Frank Knight and Edwin Chamberlin. These are the two directions disdained by orthodoxy à la Hicks (see chapter 11).

Although he did not develop and publish positive models of his own, Young was prescient in the critiques he offered his two pioneering students. If they, or their associates, had been able to absorb and implement his suggestions, the hegemony of pure competition might be much less and the development of microeconomics more coherent. The understanding of industrial economies might be much further advanced now.

Among the several new developments in general economic theory that bear on microeconomics, a school of evolutionary theories comes closest to the approach of the present book. W. Brian Arthur is not only a prolific author but also a chief marshaller of a branch with an American lineage. This is evidenced most recently in a symposium from the Santa Fe Institute (Arthur, Durlauf, and Lane 1997).

Earlier, Arthur (1994) published a collection of his own essays under a revealing title: *Increasing Returns and Path Dependence in the Economy*. He is picking up themes from Young that vitiate framings in terms of pure competition, as Kenneth Arrow emphasizes in the foreword. Arthur touches on many aspects of economies but much is applicable to industries in themselves. Yet there is no modeling of tangible markets. He remains focused on analysis of cognition, citing Spence's works (1974b, 1981) repeatedly, which fits with his effort to track nonlinear feedback processes over time, in contrast with the cross-sectional equilibrium analyses for $W(y)$ models.

The Santa Fe symposium volume contains some specific applications to market models. Mazzucato (1997), for example, has traced how market share of firms is affected by economies of scale. She also draws on the size distribution models discussed early in chapter 11. There is no modeling of explicit mechanism, however, no social construction of the market. Instead, forms of equations are borrowed from biological evolution (see Boorman and Levitt 1980; Hofbauer and Sigmund 1988; and the preceding section on ecology). As in $W(y)$ models, multiple equilibria are obtained, but, in the static case, only for decreasing returns to scale—just as in orthodox microeconomics. The interest is in dynamics, feedback, which in Mazzucato's simulations can lead to multiple solutions even for decreasing returns to scale. An important direction for future work is introducing some such dynamics into the explicit mechanism supplied in the $W(y)$ model.

The contributions in this evolutionary school by Nelson and Winter (e.g., 1982), which develop concrete analyses of effects around particular technological innovations, were taken up separately in the last chapter. Here the focus is kept on the more explicitly programmatic statements found not only in the symposium above, but also in its predecessor (Anderson, Arrow, and Pines 1988), and in a compatible more recent collection (Dow and Earl

1999) that derives inspiration from a British pedigree in evolutionary economics bracketed by Alfred Marshall and Brian Loasby.

First, let's consider the striking overlaps and similarities between evolutionary economics and the present approach, and then follow that with an account of important differences. Arthur and his collaborators point out "six features of the economy that together present difficulties for the traditional mathematics used in economics: Dispersed Interaction . . . No Global Controller . . . Cross-cutting Hierarchical Organization . . . Continual Adaptation . . . Perpetual Novelty . . . Out-of-Equilibrium Dynamics" (Arthur, Durlauf, and Lane 1997, 3, 4). These expositions, except for the last one, could well have appeared in the present book.

They go on to discuss "Cognitive Foundations and Structural Foundations and What Counts as a Problem and as a Solution." A good deal of what they write there also would find a natural place in the present book, notably: "Recurring patterns of such social interactions bind agents together into networks. . . . Standard theory typically . . . treats agents' values and information as exogenous and autonomous. In reality, agents learn from each other. . . . These processes of learning and influencing happen through the social interaction networks in which agents are embedded" (Arthur, Durlauf, and Lane 1997, 6–10). Network sociologists Granovetter and Baker are prominent in this account.

Along with these basic similarities come several crucial differences: In the $W(y)$ models

> Causation among actions is local among the particular producers who are the sources. Its cumulation yields a market as social construction whose local discipline is induced as a quality array, a pecking order subject to vetting by bystanders, so that there is *no preestablished lattice* of influence positions.
>
> Emergent from networks of relations among firms, this market is thereby *also decoupled* from those networks and thus is exposed to maneuver and entrepreneurship in these actions (see the survey in Thornton 1999); strategy joins with ecology.
>
> In testing the larger setting of a market, these actions outline said setting in the form of constraints and of guides to perceptions of inducements. By parameterizing these, one derives *explicit solutions* within one fixed, simple framework for markets within a network context.
>
> Thus the present approach asserts *separate and tangible levels of actor*. And it does so from sociocultural construction instead of merely socially situated cognition: Decoupling is as central as, and complementary to, embedding, so that markets are actors within a setting that is fluid, as is necessary to account and allow for human agency and its disruptions

and innovations—a goal that is, of course, shared with evolutionary economics.

One can be purely qualitative but very incisive, like Frank Knight, so that it should be no surprise that, conversely, mathematical packaging and computer simulation can be dressings for inane ideas. Much of evolutionary economics is content with existence theorems, or just broad speculations. Many contributions do not exhibit mastery of the analytic machinery they invoke that is sufficient to enable computation. This tension is partially resolved by extensive use of computer simulation runs, as is also done in the present book.

In some respects, the schools of evolutionary economics resemble older institutional economics in that they are more concerned to raise objections, counterexamples, and warnings of complexity than they are to propose positive models of their own for explicit solution. There is little evidence that our vaunted social sciences have yet contributed much either to disciplines or to inventions in social life, aside from rhetorical packagings. Why expostulate about nonequilibrium, nonlinear processes, dynamic learning, and the like, which are already second nature to participants in the economy?

Think of surfing as a metaphor here. Surfers are not helped by pronouncements of the undoubtedly enormous complexity of turbulence—even in water coming from a faucet, much less in salt water pounding as waves on some beach of a particular shape. The surfer can benefit from some rules of thumb, which usually take form as comparative statics. He or she is forewarned to ride waves differently on Southern California beaches bordered by caverns than on broad Hawaii beaches.

The best forewarning is riding in with a cohort of denizens of that beach, where surfing is being subjected to an implicit discipline of mutual construction. What they could make best use of is insights from models of the formation of such disciplines. Surely more tangible contributions to human organization will come through modelings that are explicit and also simple enough to be soluble. To be soluble means using techniques presently mastered, and which thereby are able to uncover the unexpected and to predict effects not already recognizable in the lore of participants.

In the British collection, Birner (1996) develops out of ideas in F. von Hayek a qualitative account of making markets that fits well in most respects with the present book, especially as to critique: "The assumption of 'perfect competition' in standard economic theory usually stands for homogeneous goods, atomistic markets with free entry and exit and perfect information. But this *denies the existence of competition,* as competition only works where all these circumstances do *not* obtain" (Birner 1999, 38). Yet Birner does insist on tracking back to an individualist cognition in his table 3.1. There the emergent market becomes translated into implicit information that is transmitted by the "price system," which, alas, once again is left a disembodied affair, presumably run by Maxwell demons.

Birner nonetheless is calling for a differentiated competitive market: "How markets emerge, why they continue to exist, and how they function are problems about which economists know surprisingly little. Brian Loasby is one of the few economists who have put the working of markets onto his research agenda" (Birner 1999, 36).

And he is on track toward a mechanism like $W(y)$:

> A process of *calibration* has to take place in which individual plans are adapted to the environment, which consists in the observed behaviour of others, that is the outcome of their plans. And for calibration to be possible, there has to be a *structure of interaction and communication*. Here we have the basic building blocks of a theory that may enable us to understand markets (and other social institutions). . . . As Hayek emphasizes, markets create value by bringing together dispersed knowledge into a whole that far transcends the possibilities of a single individual. . . . Social institutions are stable if the rules of behaviour which constitute them have been internalized by individuals without giving up their diversity. This is the case where individuals are integrated in intermediate groups (social cohesion, Durkheim) . . . A natural framework for this type of analysis is network theory. . . . It appears that the image of the market system as a network of weak ties must be supplemented by that of clusters or sub-networks that are held together by strong ties. (Birner 1999, 44, 51)

The role of institutions is also emphasized by Arena (1999) and several other contributors to this volume, as well as by some in the Arthur volume (e.g., Kirman 1997).

The solutions proposed in the present book should prove useful to evolutionary economists at least as foil, or as null model on which to base elaborations and generalizations. Perhaps this book also can embolden them to shake loose from the hold of methodological individualism, which they confound with cognitivism. They need to face the facts that the primary shapings of economic, as of other social, action are twofold: (1) mutual disciplines such as were mapped here in chapter 4 as quality arrays; and (2) organizational inventions by the participants, such as chapter 12's multidivisional firms and Granovetter business groups (1994, 1995).

Arthur urges recasting economic theory so as to be able to fit observed phenomena of the economy, as the present text does for production economy. He invokes positive-feedback mechanisms to explain economic growth and technical change especially, as Kenneth Arrow emphasizes in his 1994 foreword. The work of Arthur and kindred spirits is able to naturalize path dependence and multiple equilibria for an economic orthodoxy grown stolid. Yet the present book achieves much the same without requiring explicit introduction of feedback and probability modelings. Its simpler methods permit more explicit application to a broader swath of the economy; they also focus attention on parameters that are widely applicable rather than on special fitting constants (see White 2000a).

Despite Arthur's originality in other respects, he and his colleagues remain trapped in the now-antiquated individualist phenomenology of the Enlightenment: nonlinear and multitrack techniques of novelty and power, yes, but still all used, in the end, to tell the story, the myth, of the Competitive Individual in a Hostile World.

RATIONALITY AND NETWORKS

What basis in perceptions of participants is there for the $W(y)$ model? How are these perceptions and accompanying choices formed? How do substantial fractions of market participants arrive at estimates equivalent, when taken together, with values predicted from parameters in the $W(y)$ mechanism?

Chapter 8 already derived mappings between network context and market parameters, but these mappings took for granted framings in common cultures, to account for which requires some sociocultural calculus of learning. The previous chapter began with the foundation in demography for identities, around which grows culture (see chapter 15). But these identities in forming networks are also concerned with rationality in choices. Let's turn to these competing views of presuppositions.

To sociologists, market relations are intrinsically and explicitly social relations. For example, exploitation is expected to be common. Whereas Anglo-American economists, who commonly construe market actions as due to individuals guided by their own cognitions, see no structural basis for exploitation in a market. By contrast, the $W(y)$ model has built in at least one parameter, tau, that can reflect the degree of one form of exploitation, as was laid out in a section of chapter 12. The economics literature, by contrast, tends to offer models that presuppose purely cognitive and individual bases for perception and learning. This tendency may explain why the economist Michael Spence (see chapter 5) missed spotting most of the contexts that allow a $W(y)$ mechanism to sustain itself.[3]

Networks are central. Information gets constituted only as an aspect of flows of social interaction, and so only from this origin does it have an impact on action, on markets, or elsewhere. For some developments of this theme see works by the sociologists Ronald Burt (1987), Arthur Stinchcombe (1990), and Emmanuel Lazega (1992). Whereas even economic theory of information focused on signaling (see the survey by Stiglitz 1989) treats these as essentially cognitive matters.

In particular, rationality is treated as an individual matter.[4] The whole edifice of economic theory is then raised on this narrow foundation. But rationality is, after all, a collection of habits derived from and ensconced only through interaction. These habitual practices were long in development, though perhaps they have become even more prominent through reinforcement in production market action.

Proper modeling of modern social behavior of almost any sort would be vitiated by overlooking or downplaying rational modes, among other modes of action. And the sociological analyst will seek to build around rationality in whatever variety and extent it is present, since modeling is eased thereby (see Lindenberg and Frey 1993). The $W(y)$ mechanism depends centrally on assumptions of rationality.

The issue is not rationality but how to construe information and signaling, notably, for example, with respect to meanings and measures of quality. Spence's own approach was not extreme in its cognitivism. Nonetheless, Spence's preoccupation with signaling as individualized phenomenon may have contributed to his oversights. And, second, Spence's approach to information obscures issues about control. This remains true in his other influential piece (Spence 1981), which focuses on individual learning as the key to market process.

The broad assessment of economics as a discipline by a prominent microeconomic theorist, David Kreps (1997), reinforces how crucial this issue of information is.[5] Kreps argues that information is the focus of the revolutionary opening of economics to other perspectives that he sees under way. Yet the approaches to information Kreps cites are almost entirely cognitive and do not recognize the centrality of networks in the interpretation and indeed the very construction of this information. Much the same observation can also be made about a parallel assessment by an avowedly institutionalist economist (Bowles 1997). Yet individual rationalities derive, just as do particular market memberships, as cultural patterns from learning that is embedded within social networks. The point is that construing "information" in "decision making" is part and parcel of living in a subculture, which sprawls well beyond the narrowly cognitivist formulations of present studies of behavioral decision making (e.g., Hardie, Johnson, and Fader 1993).

Analyzing subcultures and their discourses requires specification of social setting and in particular its networks (Milroy 1979; Mische and Pattison 2000; White 1992a, 1995b, 1995d). That is the claim. There is very much still to be learned about just how perceptions cluster in accordance with network connections. Some form of initial seeding of markets was required, such as the putting-out systems sketched in chapter 1; that is, some initial formations that approximated markets around some sort of profiles, in the perceptions of participants. The participants then come to build institutions out of their perceptions as these congeal into rational habits and constructs that guide actions both several and joint.[6] Diverse others in business could then learn from these prototypes, at first hand and also indirectly.

The expectation is that industrial sectors and general lines of business will be identifiable by specific practices within the business culture of some given economy An important component of the distinctions will be the different ways in which material objects are incorporated within the workings of the sociocultural calculus (see Boltanski and Thevenot 1991; Sverrisson 1994). This material culture will permeate the stock of stories in terms of which accountability and thus relational ties in that sector are derived.

The working assumption has been, and will continue to be in chapter 15, that regions or subregions in the market spaces indicate ranges of parameter values that correspond to such subcultural commonalties, which also reflect tangible network commonalties. That is, industrial sectors will often have subcultures that can be mapped onto particular regions of $W(y)$ state space, as well as particular locales in networks of flows of intermediate goods. Processes of learning are at work. This is the theme pioneered by the French originators of the economics of convention (see the last section of chapter 7).

Cross-sectional views of such processes of learning aided by experience can be obtained from the outcomes of simulations. These were pioneered by Carley (1991) in models of adaptive actors (persons and others) who learn from embedding in a network comprised both of actors and of tasks. With various associates, she has developed a series of increasingly realistic computational models together with statistical assessment procedures (see Banks and Carley 1994, 1996; Carley 1992, 1993; Carley and Krackhardt 1996). Carley's models have universal applicability, though they have been used primarily for particular groups. They can be adapted and indeed given more power for the delimited set of business production contexts in $W(y)$ models. Participants there react not as general social beings, but to business settings and in business terms that also are socially constructed but within much tighter constraints. Carley and her associates in these works have provided one series of algorithms for simulation and assessment of such sociocultural calculus, which is shaped by network topology in how perceptions can be summarized through parameters of a model.

Systematic interrelations across levels and sectors will also cumulate from the interplay of incidents with context. This is pursued in the section of the next chapter on modeling evolution of valuations from network dynamics. Note here just one vivid example, from an industrial study by Stuart, of the hegemony that practices may exert: "One potentially confounding feature of the semiconductor business is that alliances in the industry were sometimes formed to develop devices that would succeed commercially only if they were adopted as standards" (Stuart 1998, 696). How ridiculous it is to construe these as individualist, purely cognitive processes.

~~~~~~~~~~~~~~~~~~~~~~

CHAPTER 15

Business Cultures

Against orthodox views, production markets have been seen in this book as molecules that arise in and depend on business subcultures shaped in networks of relationships. There are many other distinct species denoted by this same English word *market* whose mechanisms, including how they embed in networks, are unlike those of industrial markets. Potlach markets in ceremonial circulation of goods for displaying and earning status have long been familiar both from anthropological accounts (e.g., Strathern 1971, following up Franz Boas) and from our own social history. This species has declined to leave only remnants and echos. Yes, Veblen continues to be right about the importance of conspicuous consumption, but it remains consumption obtained through market institutions centering around industries (contra arguments in Collins 1988; Blair 1995). The same is true of auctions. Yes, tobacco is still "auctioned" in North Carolina, but in fact as a smoothly running part of a whole interlocking network of production markets. Much the same can be said about the famous seafood auction market across the world in Tokyo (Bestor 1996).

The foundation of this chapter is that business activities are sustained within and across production markets only as common discourses are generated and shared in common histories, retained and propagated in some business culture with many facets. Drives toward identity and control interact with network topology and information flow to shape these industrial markets and subcultures. This was already sketched in sections of chapter 1 and was illustrated by Porac's case study in chapter 6.

The market mechanism for producer firms is an emergent pattern in sociocultural interaction whose continuing authority distills out of threats and confusions in ongoing business life among producers who are committed for long periods to particular intermediate roles within extensive networks, so that there is common ground on which terms of discourse and trade can evolve. Not just operation but change in production markets is mediated by these social networks. As analyzed in chapter 12, investment processes are sociocultural primarily and cognitive only secondarily. Investment is a process that derives from and depends on the interactive construction and validation of frames and estimates.

This chapter takes accounting practices as central to discourse across most business worlds, a specific basis for business culture that is rooted in the history. It goes on to speculate about the foundational principles of discourse that can generate such shared practices. The chapter begins to derive from sociolinguistics tangible processual accounts of the emergence of levels and profiles that have so far only been inferred ex post from cross-sectional patterning in behavior. Then it goes on to speculate about the emergence of valuations as well as identities. This chapter ends with a case study exploring how a wholly new business institution, professional sports, gets fashioned both as to valuations and as to identities.

Various observer views from academic disciplines are not only reflections but also influences on and within business cultures. This chapter could have been enlarged accordingly and merged with the previous chapter. Although accounting may be the most universal business discourse (Baecker 1992), the economics discipline does make efforts to provide and even insert discourses of its own into business practice. Six of these discourses have been surveyed already in previous chapters, two orthodox (chaps. 2, 11) and four heterodox (chaps. 5, 7, and 14), along with more pragmatic disciplinary accounts of business in the latter chapter.

Accounting and Other Business Discourses

Institutions, including those in the economy around markets, are formed in the interpenetration of history and culture across social networks, as expressed and embodied in distinctive discourses. That is the claim: Every social mechanism is mediated by discourse in reproducing itself. Any discourse activates particular topics in *some* cultural domain and, equally, is thereby activating particular pairs and paths of accustomed interaction among actors in *some* social networks.

The business context of production markets calls forth a discourse of accounting that is shared across all varieties of them. Specification of acceptable sorts of goals—good business—and performances are the conventions that are least restricted within particular business worlds; see the discussion by Eccles (1985, 27–35), as well as essays by Favereau (1997) and Waechter (1999). So production businesses have a common discourse around accounting (see Parker 1969). Let's examine this rhetoric of and by business as a prime register of discourse.

As in any rationalized activity, there has always been some keeping of records in business. Even in its early phases of putting-out, units in the production economy were associated with the use and hegemony of accounting. Double-entry bookkeeping had come in still earlier with merchant and banking networks. Further development followed on the elaboration of large firms with ownership and investment separate from management. It was no longer a matter of keeping or even accumulating counts and records on topics of immediate interest. Accounting became primarily concerned with accountability (Ijiri 1975; Kaplan 1982; Power 1997). A system of detailed records of all transactions was set up, not primarily for the use of managers nor for measures of performance. Rather, the accounting system is for the benefit of those to whom accounts were due, outside the management.

Accounts were due in four senses, at three different scopes. Most generally, in the words of two French business economists:

> General bookkeeping was the symbolic procedure by which the actual firm could become one with the way that free-market society saw it as an atom in the structureless social space by claiming that the "unique economic operation (was) the purchase and sale of an exchange value or utility, that is, exchange according to natural law," whereas "the operational cost accounting of a firm must be exactly suited to its organic structure and to its special operational activities." (Laufer and Paradeise 1990, 43, 62)

Third, accounts were also due to the owners. The goal was not just measures that were unbiased, but rather a system of measures that was unbiasable because of its intricate ballet for checking internal with external records of the same transactions.

Fourth, the sociocultural construction of quality order within a production market legitimates its constituent firms for their broader setting, upstream of suppliers and downstream of purchasers. Discourse is central for these interlocking processes of market enactment exactly because it is constitutive of quality positions in markets. This discourse is maintained yet also constrained as the invidious idiom of quality.

What also must underlie any production economy is a broader political system able through feedback enforcement to make sustainable various sets of rules or laws, and, in particular, ones operative in money and banking within the economy. Production market footings go, as we have seen, well beyond such exogenous rules, but they do rely on and interpenetrate with operation of such rules. The most notable rules are for various categories of ownership and its assignment and fractionation (see chapter 12). They are the rules that enable the kinds of financing observed, and thus division of rights to income streams, aided through equity markets as well as banking, and sustained by accounting discourse. Pause to recapitulate the historical background.

Historical Background Sketch of the Production Economy

This is a new genus of markets evolved through history such as that recounted in the first chapter, which began with a differentiation of markets by city that could be extended to other cities. More generally, business in putting-out forms interacted with a shifting matrix of more general social connections to supply the basis for an institutional system around flows shaped by network relations. The result was already sketched in figure 1.1. Agents seeking footings within the Knightian uncertainty of business life coalesced out in production markets with distinctive identities of their own from transactions with other actors in the economy.

Let's extend the American vignettes of the first section of chapter 1 to some longer-term historical sketch of how production came to be assimilated into business networks. Work in the sense of physical transformations for human use has been with us for eons and has taken many organizational forms (e.g., Udy 1970). Out of trading among distinct tribes and/or among cities, in the products of their work, traders and routes first became established. This went along with exchange markets evolving as mechanisms in sites and occasions of collective activity in those networks (Swedberg 1994, 256). On the other hand, production, storage, and disbursement within a city-state engendered the first bureaucracies. In these, consciously designed trees of authority relations, quite unlike exchange markets, now accompanied calendars for interrelated schedules. Money and taxes, along with prices and assignments, were, respectively, the economic outcomes and the means of accountability along these two evolutionary paths, which both contributed features to later business among markets.

Lines of business emerged before production firms and their markets. They get socially constructed as productive activity burgeons and specializes during an era of domestic manufacture expanded by various putting-out systems. But first, luxury trade and war loans had to engender banking and finance with monetary flows of sufficient scope to sustain the entrepreneurial reorganization of traditional production into lines of business in an economy and thence into markets. The past half-century has seen intervention in new forms across such markets that yield control and financial advantage. A production economy, in the view developed here, is a distinctive business institution that evolved from the bottom up through networks of production markets.

In the era around 1800, industries evolved especially from various "putting-out" systems of piecework, notably in textiles.[1] The distinct new mechanism labeled "production market," within a new business system often labeled "industrial," supplanted many much older species of exchange markets, with their own distinctive mechanisms. Loose networks of ties with workers became transmuted into distinct firms, each bounded by ownership and itself disciplined by some particular production market.

Such networks and firms, and the market mechanism, can have developed only on the basis of broader changes in configuration of social ties, as Adam Smith argued two centuries ago. In the high Middle Ages of Europe, new visions of social relations did develop, which induced and permitted novel sorts of social ties in new configurations and thence networks. In earlier precommercial society, person and social station were less separable:

Prior to commercial society, the space between friend and enemy was not occupied by mere acquaintances or neutral strangers, but rather was charged with uncertain and menacing possibilities. . . . Unlike the prevailing conditions in other settings, strangers in commercial society are not either potential enemies or allies, but authentically indifferent to each other—an indifference that enables all to make contracts with all. . . . The exclusivistic bonds defined by custom, corporate group, station and estate are dissolved. (Silver 1997, 52–55)

Silver's version of Smith's argument is that this new order permitted a sphere of private relations, which gave a basis for the trust needed in commercial calculative connections, whereas older orders had limited relations to inbred logics of kinship, honor, or collegial formations. In other eras and continents also, sophisticated business systems independently evolved on this basis, but none of these were integrated with production in an industrial business system (see Hamilton 1996, part 1; Udy 1970).

SOCIOLINGUISTIC REGISTERS AND MARKET REGIONS

The underlying network relationships in business, as in kinship and other realms, maintain themselves through discourses. The perceptions and computations essential within a production market rely on some accounting idiom, even though it is peers rather than owners who are the accountees. But idiomatic discourse for some particular market variety evolves out of anecdotes and longer picaresque narratives. Just as for dialects and jargons elsewhere, observers and participants alike discriminate various business registers (see Gramley and Pätzold 1992; Gumperz 1982; Halliday 1976; Swales 1990).

These business registers of discourse evolve and are maintained by mutual social pressures within that industry. At the executive level in firms, where production commitments are decided through observations of business flows, the registers may be common across a whole industrial sector. (For a thoughtful overview of cognition and norms in organizations see Powell and DiMaggio 1991, chap. 1, esp. notes pp. 34–38, whose scope is broader than accounting discourse.)

Memos and announcements as well as face-to-face talk should play a role. Think now of discourse analysis in an inclusive sense, which encompasses, but goes beyond, parsing the utterances of individuals. Analogously, one may speak of family discourse as well as of daughters' discourse, though clearly they are mutually referential.

The $W(y)$ model generates regions in niche space that may correspond to distinctive idioms. Markets and firms are no more inhuman than your family or than cliques or clans. Markets and firms both are equally actors. Their interaction is specifiable by a mechanism with actors on distinct levels that are nonetheless mutually constitutive. Discourse here is being generalized beyond the personal, the oral, and the occasional but still retains its essentially interactive nature.

The actors are themselves theorists of a pragmatic sort (Cicourel 1989, 1992; Levinson 1983); so what constitutes a mechanism for the observer—in Stinchcombe's sense, quoted in chapter 1—corresponds to pragmatic rules of thumb from, and their recognition by, the participants. It should, in short, be possible to validate at least some aspects of the mechanism being hypothesized for markets from statements and interpretations by participants, quite aside from the usual routes of prediction and test.

Useful and more novel is coding aspects of market function from sociolinguistic analyses of speech in various modalities as well as of other communicative practices. Sociolinguists' analyses of how assessments of context are produced in interaction offer one scholarly template, and the results can in turn contribute to those analyses. Verbal forms suggesting novelty may prove characteristic of discourse around markets in PARADOX contexts and analogously for CROWDED region contexts.

Crowding can occur within a market across producers seeking distinct niches along a given market profile. But crowding also applies across distinct markets that are in structurally equivalent positions, which is to say within a layer of other markets with similar packets of connections to their various suppliers and purchasers in the production networks. The one parameter gamma subsumes both the substitutability of the given industry vis-à-vis all other, even distant industries, and its firms' crowding along a profile. Note that each of the firms' valuations S is equally subject to the external substitutability, so that gamma is a master parameter.

Chapter 8 presented a heuristic model that mapped the size of gamma onto the degree of overlap between the buyers of goods from two substitutable industries. A parallel overlap measure can be computed from Venn diagrams of the overlap between characteristics of the products of respective industries subject to substitution. Gamma will map to the tone and form of discussion regarding products, as to how special and distinctive they are, in discourse of that sector of markets.

In discourse terms, setting the value of gamma for various industries and sectors derives from and, when tested, makes claims about boundaries of linguistic registers. Gamma discriminates: The lower the value of gamma, the greater the overlaps in discursive style. This is manifest from equation 8.23: since omega has been equated with the Venn overlap measure w, it is clear that substitutability, parameter gamma, is inverse to the overlap.

More generally, consider market orientation. The three sorts of discourse by members of a given market—with peers, with upstream, and with downstream—always are concretely different, of course, in the particular others being dealt with and in the tangible topics regarding products and characteristics. There is a deeper distinction, however, a distinction between the *tone* of discourse by members depending on whether their mechanism is oriented up- or downstream. In the former, producers are taking a coaxing stance, overcoming the reluctance of suppliers to work to the order of this or that one of the producers, overcoming by the terms they offer from the dual market profile that applies. And in the former, producers are taking downstream buying for granted in the sense of being covered by formula, whereas with the downstream orientation, it was the suppliers who were taken for granted as formulaic. Here, the subtleties laid out by Comrie (1983) in the use of tense can suggest operational criteria for polarization.

Discourse thus takes on a very different form in a production market oriented back upstream as the direction perceived by producers as their main source of uncertainty, the focus of attention and yet also veiled in obscurities. One example is in an inflationary era, say after a major war, when upstream is where to be most on guard against uncertainty, in the eyes of most manufacturing industries. The discourse sign for which polarization obtains, for that market at that era, is about whom the producers are exchanging tall tales.

A second example is an industry whose members are powerful intermediaries or brokers to downstream purchasers, retailers, or consumers dispersed widely. There it is normal to face back upstream toward the major uncertainties facing you and your peers, say Home Depot, Target, and Wal-Mart, along with other huge wholesalers. Each of you may have your downstream marketing codified down to an applied science. You focus instead on exerting Galbraith's "countervailing power" against big manufacturing industries. Whereas in an industry with a downstream market orientation, procurement is back-room, boring stuff with no audience for tales, by contrast, in upstream market, say Detroit automakers just after World War II, attention is upstream on unions, suppliers, and so on.

The extensive literature on discourse in sociolinguistics supplies leads for coding the stigmata (for overviews see Gumperz and Hymes 1986; Hopper and Traugott 1993; Mische and White 1998; Milroy 1979; Perinbanayagam 1991; Tannen 1993). These can be supplemented by investigations of the prestige and standing within a firm of those responsible for upstream versus those responsible for downstream transactions. Is it the advertising manager or the procurement vice president who has the big office? And similarly for priorities in cultural content: Predominance of institutional advertising over product advertising suggests a polarization back upstream, oriented to the perceived reluctances of the firm's suppliers. Another difference is that some approximation to pure or perfect competition in market operation is robust *only* when the market mechanism is oriented downstream. So the higher the attention devoted in business discourse to advertising, the less one would expect to find upstream orientation.

DISCOURSE DIALECTICS: SILVERSTEIN

The present treatment of interaction also, unlike Arthur's individualist perspective, calls for interpretative constructions of meaning. Interpretive activity is foundational for the commitments and competitions that constitute economic action. All patterns of meaning are social constructions as much as, but different from, interaction patterns. Linguistics has done much to elucidate how social context is co-constituted with discourse, as in the work of M. A. K. Halliday. Chapter 10 discussed some of his work. The desired result is a Halliday view of economic interaction necessary to full understanding of terms of trade. Much work is required, and only some speculations are offered in this section.

The Porac study (chap. 6) interpreted what managers said and wrote to reveal membership and personae of various markets that the various participants and informants agreed in hypostatizing. Also, Porac drew on reports of all sorts by external observers such as the business press and government officials. But detective stories and taste for gossip alike teach us to seek eyewitness accounts and real-time reconstructions. That requires turning again to sociolinguistics, but to the different face that watches the actual emergence of chicks from eggs. Reporting of naming and labeling practices, as in the Porac study, is not sufficient. Social sciences and linguistics thus must open up to each other.

Change of a market from one orientation to the other requires switching in idiom (and conversely). Perhaps also some particular industrial contexts are such that production markets there are subject to chronic switching. A possible analogue in language is diglossia, in which speakers who are masters of two languages switch back and forth between them. (Gumperz 1982 and Gal 1979 provide guides.)

Switching may be brought on in part by some increase in crowding, which depends crucially on gamma. So the size of gamma, discussed above for crowding, also will affect discourse for switching. Indeed, gamma and tau and k together as a triad affect market viability and performance and thus the tone and content of discourse, with or without any switching.

Subsequently, anthropological linguistics has brilliantly opened up, through comparative grammar as in the work of Silverstein and kindred, the actual mechanisms by which new levels of meaning emerge. They move beyond individualist preconceptions through deep analysis of the tie, a dyad, thereby inducing phenomenology such as required to fill in the outer husk of von Neumann's game theory. Such analysis has been extended by William Hanks and Erving Goffman to the anonymous realm of the public. But the key step remains of integrating this depth into the reality of social space as networks among actors embedding in distinct levels such as are modeled explicitly in the text above.

Reflexivity through indexing captures the aspect of discourse that illuminates the emergence of market identity, both in its vagaries as market profile and in its agentive standing. Every social construction is reflexive in reproducing itself as enactments, and it is indexical in providing an order that guides perceptions and thus destination for an interaction. Reflexive indexing is what enables the transposing of a discourse, such that what I say here now can become what you say there then, depending on our mutual positioning in a role frame. This may be the deep structural frame of kinship, à la Lévi-Strauss, or the superficial Goffman frame for everyday urban encounter (Burns 1992), or it may be the business context that frames a production market.

Insights on how reflexivity in language (see Lucy 1993) builds context, more particularly deictic analysis, are to be assimilated here to a theory of role structures (see White 1992a). Deictic terms—such as *here, now, this*, and the pronouns—effect the transposability assumed by roles, but they require a base in agreed footings, the positions that deictic terms fill in. Here (note the deictic usage!) the footings of the various producers take tangible form in market discourse in the coin of network stories, whose recountings establish reflexive indexicality. Much the same processes can be uncovered in completely different sociocultural contexts. For example, Hanks deploys his insights on deixis (1992) to establish how a neighborhood of significant locales is constantly reproduced in linguistic practices shaped in terms of such locales (Hanks 1990).

The parallel, though more abstract, analysis of production markets here has two goals: first, to show how a market profile imposes itself; and second, to show how the agentive stature of a market—its emergence on a new level of actor—can establish itself. Goodwin and Goodwin (1992) provide a closer parallel than Hanks in that they show the constituting of a group (of black city kids over a year) as bound up in the kids' collaborative building of events in their lifeworld through talk. This penetrates deeper than the interview approach of the Porac team (but requires very much more investment of time). The two goals require pushing all these sociolinguistic approaches beyond their explicit focus on speaking human persons, with a claim that much the same causal texture obtains when higher-level actors such as firms and markets are interacting via perceptions of talk and memos issuing from persons variously perceived as agent and representative.

Theoretical depth is required to support such extrapolations. Michael Silverstein, a teacher of several sociolinguists to be cited subsequently, has been the master analyst of reflexive indexicality since a 1976 paper.[2] His presuppositions about the sociality of cognition are those of the present book.

[Beliefs of the speaker range over] any propositions about anything that, when invoked as an inferential chain, make text "logical" to have been communicated in that context. Most neo-Griceans simply gloss over what is obviously an arm-chair pseudo-psychology that is nothing more than Western ideologies of auton-omous mind and agentivity essentialized as some kind of mental stuff, its own brand of picture-theory of social cognition if not based on, then at least *compati-ble with microeconomic models of rational market behavior*—because both emerge from the same sociocultural system in which such social-scientifically ignorant but intelligent "natives" as Grice live(d). (Silverstein 1997, n. 1; emphasis added)

Using his insights does require extra extrapolation to encompass network context, because Silverstein focuses so intently on how a single tie is being constituted.

Back to hypostasis: Already this book has established some sense for the standing of the market profile as a cognitive construct, a construct that is, however, also at the same time a joint social construction. First consider the traditional level of person: "Verbal deixis is a central aspect of the social matrix of orientation and perception through which speakers produce con-text. . . . The relationships that are encoded in deictic usage make up what might be called an implicit playing field for interaction—a set of positions in deictic space, along with expectations about how actors occupy these posi-tions over the course of talk" (Hanks 1992, 44). Now producer firms become the actors, the playing field is flows through the economy, and positions are the footings on a market profile.

Ranking in quality as producers is a compressed form of reflexive index-icality, one that is rigid as compared with the flexibility of deixis. Such rank-ings are local grammars for discourse for, by, and about markets and their members (Urban 1991, chaps. 2, 8). One can expect them to be opera-tionalized, and thus their reality verified, in complex patterns of reference and deference specific to relative locations (upstream, downstream) and topics (money, goods, delivery) perceived by various participants. One para-digm is the investigation of political discourses by Duranti:

> The use of respectful terms cannot be simply predicted on the basis of referent or addressee, but must be related to the kind of activity and the kind of social relationships and social personae that the lexical terms are used to activate. In other words, linguistic choices are shown to be both context-defined and con-text-defining, while the status and rank distinctions they presuppose are consti-tuted in the constant struggle to reassert or challenge the existing social or-der. . . . Respectful words are activated not only to defer to another's authority but also to coerce, or to oblige the recipient(s) or target(s) of the speech act to behave according to the expectations dictated, through tradition, to the social persona indexed by the honorific term. (Duranti and Goodwin 1992, 78)

Porac and his team could have used some translation of this scheme to estab-lish guiding of market flows in terms of quality indexing of various firms.

Other examples of phenomena to be "emerged" are impacts from market crowding (see CROWDED section in chapter 7) and the possible inversion of orientation of the market mechanism (see chapter 9 and "Switches" section of chapter 13). It is important to establish a firm theoretical basis for these explorations of emergence. For this we turn to Silverstein.

Having examined an earlier version of my project of dissecting social form with sociolinguistic tools (White 1995b, 1995d), Silverstein comments:

> The work gets done, in your paper, by transforming the very sense of the concept of "network" into such a doubly-functioning descriptive tool: both as an extensional concept . . . and as something that, once gelling into a structure of network relative "inequalities"—of access, of usage, of effectiveness of usage-given-access—gets invoked intensionally as the measure against which usage in the token instance must be described. . . . Sociocultural . . . normativities that are routinely, if however misguidedly relied upon by people in their instances of usage, say with a new interlocutor drawn from a conceptualizable different sub-population . . . have . . an ontic necessity for your account . . . and yet don't have a clearly theorized concept. (1998b, 1)

Such a concept, necessary to establishing emergences of profile and of actor, can be developed from Silverstein's recent works.

> "Indexical order" is the necessary concept that shows us how to relate the micro-social to the macro-social frames of analysis. . . . For any n-th order indexical that *presupposes* a contextual schematization of some sort, there will tend to be an *entailment*—a "creative" effect—regularly produced by the use of the $n + 1$st order indexical system as a direct (causal) consequence of the degree of (institutionalized) ideological engagement with the n-th order indexical meaningfulness. . . . Such ideological intervention functions characteristically as a cultural construal of the n-th order usage, an ethno-metapragmatics of it.
>
> However, this effect can itself also be conceptualized as an $n + 1$st order indexical fact, that is as a coterminous indexical form *presupposing* a transcendent and competing overlay of contextualization possibly distinct from the n-th order one at issue, a "virtual" contextualization. . . . [The] n-th and $n + 1$st order indexical values are, functionally, in "dialectic" competition with one another. (Silverstein 1996, 266–67)

This, exactly, is the phenomenology of market as one level above but equally real as, and in dialectic alternation with, disaggregative perceptions of separate producer firms and their actions. Intensive investigation, no doubt invoking new procedures, will of course be needed to develop this; fortunately, the examples and figures of this article offer many leads.

Silverstein later develops further the unfolding of these processes:

> This fact of recurrence manifests an order of types of events of social action realized by genres of performed texts-in-context, even if these are, in each in-

stance, characteristically "improvisational" in nature. . . . Let us recognize not one but two types. . . . *denotational* coherence—propositional organization of conceptual information . . . underlies our notions of grammar as a perduring order of language-as-structure. . . . [The other type] is *interactional* coherence, . . . the mapping of the "presupposed" social situation, the one thus far established by defaults and by any prior social action, into the "entailed" one. . . . Observe that insofar as this takes place with a certain balletic multiparticipant consistency (or at least relative non-inconsistency) over a span of interactional realtime, we have a coherent, intersubjectively accomplished interactional text, the interpersonal achievement of a "doing" of something. (1998a, 266–69)

A market rivalry profile $W(y)$ is just such an accomplishment. Silverstein sums up:

Text as a set of relationships constituting a developmental structure in (real) time is a function of establishing complex *indexical relationships*, just as are relationships of text to context. All interaction rests on indexicalities "all the way down"; and thus, indexically invoked, culture turns out to be the decisive component for achieving the text/context divide in a discursive interaction, however improvisational such interaction may be. By understanding the logically autonomous nature of events of indexicality . . . we will understand the necessity for relating those two planes of textuality. . . . For as structures of cohesion, texts are nothing more than by-degrees complex and multiply overlaid patterns of *co-occurrence* of (token) sign-forms one with respect to another. . . . One particular sign "points to" (indexes) the other under the principle of textual co-occurrence. . . . *Cotextuality* . . . is thus a special, text-internal form of indexicality. . . . Both text-internal cotextuality and indexes pointing to aspects of context can be seen to be either *presupposing*, where a sign-token points to a co(n)text that is already an intersubjective reality at the interactional moment of its occurrence, or the indexical sign-token is "performative" or *creative* or (as I rather call them) *entailing*, where a sign-token points to a co(n)text that may become an intersubjective reality—and thus subject to further or other indexical presuppositions—precisely as a causal consequence of the occurrence of that particular sign. . . . The realm of indexicality is merely a complete congeries of "pointings-to." (Silverstein 1998a, 270–71)

A market assumes an identity as actor on a distinct level just as entailing merges with presupposing in constitution of a market rivalry profile.

Economic Valuations from Network Embeddings

One challenge is to show how the sorts of valuations central to business may emerge from and thus may be derived from studying the dynamics of markets in business networks. Markets derive from agency expressed through social roles, built in network relationships. The production market is a social construction of considerable sophistication, beyond that coming from non-human species (Wilson 1970) but akin to the marriage sections of systems of classificatory kinship in preliterate tribes (White 1963; Bearman 1997). This construction includes, but goes much beyond, cohesion from shared ties (Burt 1987) and beyond comparability in linear pecking order (Chase 2000; White 1992a).

Generalized exchange underlies all differentiated social organization of humans. This section takes up the challenge of generating economic valuations as network by-products of market organization. The argument is neither simple nor easy.

This book has examined how production markets embed into relational networks. But it takes economic valuations for granted rather than seeking their roots in social network processes. It was only quality positions whose construction was examined (chap. 4). Now the focus is on valuations themselves, the coin of the profiles and schedules of the $W(y)$ model.[3]

Generalized exchange derives from and generates mores and practices sustained by common discourse in social networks. It derives historically from settings in much earlier economies, such as feudalism (Rader 1971), where valuation is hard to disentangle from power. The generalized form of power is influence; so we turn to models of influence generation and accumulation in social networks generally (see Bonacich 1987; Knoke and Burt 1983).

Rueschemeyer (1986) can be seen as an alternative search for influences of larger configurations of power and the political on the economic. He by-passes markets and does not get down to detailed specification at a level of process in concrete network relations, however. Let's turn from his focus on power to a focus on economic valuation.

Valuation must invoke cultural as well as perceptual and cognitive aspects. Guidelines come, as in the Porac study, from DiMaggio's calls (1994, 1997) for integrating cultural with cognitive perspectives. We also follow DiMaggio's earlier injunction to bring nodal attributes back into network relational analysis, Porac's research offering one paradigm.

Economic valuations build regarding both nodes and flows: that is the axiom. Valuations of nodes, including quality ranking, are influenced by flows. There can be effects from nodal attributes that cannot be accounted for in flow terms. Turn back to Stuart's study on the semiconductor industry: "Technological prestige is a positional variable because it is engendered by flows of deference between firms and so it has relational foundations. . . . But the reason for these flows of deference is, at least in part, that an organization has contributed an ongoing stream of notable innovations. . . . this ability must be considered an attribute of an organization" (Stuart 1998, 695).

But flows are the crux.

Production flows derive from social ties in the $W(y)$ model. If we reexamine the nature of a social tie (Burt 1990; White 1992a; White, Boorman, and Breiger 1976), we see that it exists in, and only in, a relation between actors that catenates, that is, that entails (some) compound relations through other such ties of those actors. Thus, there can be no social tie unaccompanied by some network. A social tie generates and is warranted by other such ties in one or another network. This is most evident in what are presumably the oldest and most basic social ties, those of kinship. Although a social tie often carries much affective intensity, its essential message is not particular content but rather implicature in further connection.

So much for general perspective concerning social effects from ties of very long duration. Their specifically economic effects have been traced for production economies in earlier chapters through discussions of putting-out systems. The theory traces to Durkheim on division of labor (see Rueschemeyer 1986, chaps. 1–3) and, of course, thereby to Adam Smith. But valuation itself, the existing theory of economic value, remains outside the account; instead, valuation is derived from closure of the macro system, as in general equilibrium theory, and from subjective desires of persons, with monetary system as midwife (Arrow 1981; Davidson 1981; Hahn 1981).

Generalized exchange depends on legitimation (Bearman 1997), and therefore legitimation is essential to any social organization that reproduces itself, including in particular production markets today, as noted by Eccles (1985, chap. 5). Modeling legitimation requires understanding perceptual and evaluative frames not only of "subjects" but of subjects serving as observers (Barth 1993). But such frames coevolve along with relations among these subjects. Mathematical modeling is indispensable with such complexity.

Studying legitimation and thence valuation protocols requires building out beyond the local cultures exemplified in the second section. Combine a cognitivist approach with the consideration of relational networks urged in previous sections. The intent is to derive valuation as a by-product of interaction as formed in social networks among the markets they induce.

The production market institutionalizes structural equivalence in networks as common membership that enables mutual signaling and thence individual agency. Embedding and decoupling are the requisite complements in the flow processes that are induced. The packaging of actors at one level, firms, into a second level of markets resembles social constructions in other domains and at other scopes, for example, role systems for persons in their kinship relations, as just noted.

Now, we may open out from the focus on economic valuation specifically. Let's explore deriving valuations as by-products of network influence processes in general. Social psychology has been groping for 50 years toward how to construe and model processes in and positions from flows of influence among sets of persons, across quite various levels of closure, size, and continuity of population. This has been brought together by Friedkin (1998) in a recent monograph, which can be fit in with the Porac work, since both focus on relations of attention. The argument, in short, is that economic valuations arise in much the same way as assessments of influence in continuing discussions among a human group.[4]

This tradition concerns much shorter time frames than in the modeling of previous chapters. It sticks with natural persons as actors and within that rubric has accumulated considerable bodies of experimental and observational data. Even early on, it was not entirely separate from larger-scale and more general social theorizing (see Parsons, Bales, and Shils 1953).

Let's turn away from Friedkin's confusing language of exogenous and endogenous causes in "influence process" to bring two other, interrelated calls to bear on his modeling. DiMaggio's (1992) call for bringing attributes of nodes back into network relational analysis has been cited earlier. And Winship and Mandel (1984) urge us to seek the more abstract role-equivalence, as distinct from the ordinary structural equivalence used in blockmodeling networks. Friedkin fits with both calls. He thinks of his configuration of reciprocities, transitivities, popularities, and the like around ego as a measure, admittedly quite abstract, of qualities of ego, and argues that these may well reflect more ordinary attributes, such as wealth and gender. But one can also see this network configuration around ego *relationally*, as describing ego's transposable role such as that of doctor or uncle. And surely, role, thus abstracted from the particularities of the larger network that must be made up from all the egos, is intimately related to attribute—at least if one thinks of deeper attributes that characterize identities.

Let's restate this. Friedkin has devised a new way to assess structural equivalence. It yields a continuous measure, a cardinal degree, between each pair. Only then does Friedkin trace out the whole system of interconnections, in blockmodel or sociogram derived from his measure.

Embedding means, and obversely derives from, a whole being greater than the sum of its parts, which is to say, such wholes are discernible to be acting on a level distinct from that of constituents' acts. Examples are market and firm, firm and department, family and person, or, as here, shaper of research direction and scientist. To be in an invisible college is to lock in with notations and standards and concrete momentums all perceived and taken by you as external to, and vindicating, reality framing.

Embeddings are subtle, not simple, and so various that distinct varieties evoke their own terms. But embedding is pervasive, as Granovetter (1985) has eloquently argued. Not to recognize its distinction of level is as silly as treating a street as a sidewalk.

The embedding formation is characterized exactly by how actors on the lower level tuck in to it. One candidate here could be triad census profile. Yet more perspicuous is Friedkin's invention, the attachment profile. Any embedding induces differentiation, even linear ordering, of constituents. Popularities, reciprocities, transitivities will be shaped through such ordering and hence are a basis for portraying it and its level. Friedkin can so induce various spaces of transaction profiles.

The issue is how ongoing actions get shaped not just by nestings of particular members but by the overall curvatures and involution of the space characterizing the embedding formation. Let market replace clique, firm replace person, and ongoing flows of production correspond to continuing discussions. Valuations can be reflections of cumulated influence coordinate with perceived weight of ties to the person. Economic valuations need not be referred to some macrosystem of unknown etiology; they need not be treated as exogenous to multilevel network process.

Identities

Interactions among trajectories for firms and markets must be assessed from observation and records. This requires some universal operational context, or space, such as proposed in the market planes and space of previous chapters. It also requires theoretical and interpretive context, especially as to identities of actors, at distinct levels.

Consider these parallel assessments:

> Self-formation is conceived as a continual process in which moments of selfhood are arrayed in a strongly memory-endowed sequence. . . . An individual actor, acting in and as the present moment of self, engages *intra-biographically* in intertemporal transactions that are arguably analogous to an actor's transactions with other persons and their perceived biographies at any given moment. One interacts retrospectively with one's younger selves . . . and interacts prospectively with one's older selves. (Hazelrigg 1997, 118–19)

And bracketing firm and market from the other extreme of size:

> Since at least the nineteenth century, scholars and politicians alike have recognized the fundamental connection between memory and the nation. While political elites invented and propagated legitimating traditions, historians objectified the nation as a unitary entity with a linear descent. . . . Theorists of postmodernity, however, . . . have problematized the role of memory as [but] one component in a complex and shifting amalgam of perceptions that form the pervasive and permanent, though ever changing historicity of the world. . . . Scholars from a wide range of disciplines have begun to examine aspects of social memory. (Olick 1998, 377, 380)

Business study needs to turn in such direction. A significant beginning is the probe of change in institutional logic, and its impacts, within one industry by Thornton and Ocasio (1999).

Corporate identities of scope between the individual and the national are of most relevance for dynamics of market fields. Cohorts of individuals themselves become actors as they cohere enough around events, in both their own and others' perceptions, to be called generations. A generation is a joint interpretive construction recognized from outside as well as from inside itself. There are generations in business and its sectors and industries and firms. Firm and market each can be seen as an analogue to person with respect to identity (White 1995a, 1995c, 1992a; Waechter 1999). Chapter 13 offers as an example the growth of a chocolate industry around Melvin Hershey.

Generations are recognized through behavioral as well as interpretive aspects. Cohort can turn into generation only if there is some previous generation, and then only as previous generations—and the concerns they wrap around—are moved out of the way. Generation is a cumulation of choices that depends upon opportunity and succession as well as interpretation. The opportunity for a new generation in a business sector is events not gathered in and signified already by a previous one. A generation is thus a contingent construct; it emerges as an identity expressed across social networks among social molecules of many sorts and sizes, which are embedded into some larger population and its culture.

Creating a Business Institution: Leifer

Another set of contradictory dependencies in mobilization concern the operation of professional sports leagues in the entertainment sector of the economy and can in part be assimilated to transfer pricing. In contrast to the Eccles focus (chapter 12) on strategies of managers for each other, Leifer focuses on relations to buyers in aggregate from a complex of organizations, in his case professional sports teams, that also are oriented to increasing net revenues. Like divisions of the MDF, each team in a sport seeks to do better and to best the others. Like divisions, teams cannot survive without each other. Indeed, the ostensible purpose of each team is to beat others, so they certainly meet the $W(y)$ stipulation of eyeing each other for cues. But more explicitly and consciously than MDFs in long-established sectors, the teams work jointly to create and cultivate a base of committed customers.

Leifer studies histories and analyzes extensive data series for each of the four major professional sports in the United States, baseball, football, basketball, and hockey. One league is as different from another as MDFs in heavy chemicals, say, are from others in electronics. There are not literal transfers of revenues accompanying product flows from one team to another, of course—though "tradings" of players comes close. As in the MDFs, there is a host of conflicting perceptions of whether there are implicit subsidies of one unit by another.

Even a disinterested observer is hard pressed, either for divisions or for teams, to find a convincing basis for allocating revenues and costs to MDF and divisions separately. This is the riddle solved by the $W(y)$ mechanism for peers in a production market. The sports leagues face the same paradoxes as firms in a market but perhaps find them more transparent, less confounded by economic doctrine.

It is especially clear that one team cannot survive without the others in that their products are games between them. To hold customer interest, the games and thus the teams must be relatively even. Yet customers are drawn to the sport in large part to identify with some team, which in this culture means to insist on the team's winning.

A professional sports league is thus an extreme, even caricature version of the production market mechanism of chapters 1–5. Teams are vitally concerned with preeminence, what corresponds to quality n, and yet the essential is maintaining a footing as a peer in that league, whatever a team's specific ranking at a given time. Leifer argues that these league organizations have explicitly confronted these paradoxes and mobilized to overcome them through a host of specific arrangements meant to stabilize each team, as well as thereby to increase the overall public for their sport.

The analogy suggests that industrial production markets, too, can well be thought of as mobilizers, social mobilizers trading off contradictions. And sports teams also have some form of market profile, in the sense of perceiving and mutually monitoring positions in the operational space of revenue for production. It is also clear that the $W(y)$ mechanism is not transparent even to those as familiar with it as Eccles and Leifer.[5] The crux is inducing a culture.

~~~~~~~~~~~~~~~~~~~~~~~~~~~~~~~~~~~

CHAPTER 16

Conclusion

The most important chapters for theory are chapters 8, 10, and 15 and for applications are chapters 7, 9, and 13. The most important section in the present chapter is the final one: "Challenges." Economic sociology is moving toward supplanting many existing views on both organizations and markets, views that really are just conventions within economics or sociology. Fieldwork is one key to accomplishing this, and I have drawn on such to focus on the other key, which is modeling that can be transposed across particular instances and cases, modeling that identifies and uses social spaces.

Both these keys presuppose and draw on historical vision. Long-term specializations within production activities evolved early from loose networks for putting-out, of materials for dispersed processing leading to subsequent gathering for sale.[1] From this stage of development evolved production and service firms with paid staffs. Such organizations can grow large and yet continue to figure as atoms relative to market molecules with which they nest in networks of relations.

These molecules that bind firms are called *production markets* here in recognition of their being distinct from commonplace markets of swap meet, lawn sale, and auction (see, e.g., Smith 1993). Their distinctness is not mainly in size of transactions, since even gigantic companies sometimes engage in barter and auction, for instance in the oil industry, and similarly governments have been known to hold lawn sales. Also, conversely, a start-up firm with ten employees may achieve significance in an industrial market, say in textiles or plastic diving boards. The main distinctions concern commitment to repeated production. This induces a competitive structure of rivalry around quality among peers who have to incorporate upstream supply-side considerations as well.

My view is that theory should provide explicit models. Markets constructed among firms in networks are here mapped into a space of settings with interpretable parameters. A multilevel system is then traced in flows, embeddings, and decouplings.

Some say fundamental transformations are under way that will yield quite a different field of economic action, and in a matter of years, not generations. This suggests obsolescence for existing practices in industrial organization research. My analytic model $W(y)$ continues to apply for most sorts and sizes of processor markets, so the approach in this book is coming to be applicable, I argue, to more and more of total productive activity, exactly as more and more is subcontracted and spun out from within the boundaries of hierarchies.

This book has sought new ways of construing a production economy over time as dynamics among firms and markets on separate but interacting levels of population that are bound together in networks of relations. Most of the flows that link these firms and markets are of intermediate goods and services, as distinct from end-products and raw materials. So interfirm relations of procurement and supply constitute the principal network setting for business practices in these production markets fueled by rivalry among member firms.

Existence and continuance of markets can be seen to require endless interpretive work. Business cultures are the deposit and also the ground of such work. Across a whole economy, the whole population of markets, there will be common understandings derived in and as some envelope across distinct, but overlapping linguistic registers from particular sectors. These are the hegemonic notions of that business culture as a whole. Among the most important are exactly the recognitions of further levels of actor. Most social scientists, including economists, have taken this for granted—and thus they have given inadequate attention to just how such distinct levels of actor can be sustained amid the confusions of business activity and to just how the resulting paradoxes can be kept manageable (for some notable exceptions see Burt 1992; Granovetter 1985; Hamilton 1996; and Uzzi 1997).

The claim is that a field of action of a new sort has been socially constructed over the past century and more, around markets as a new level of social actor. Very different overall balances in outcomes can result. This competitive market mechanism is compatible with exploitations either of buyers or of suppliers—or of the producers as a set, in a monopsony situation. It also is compatible with a range of particular organizational forms for its producers.

This model of market structuring, this $W(y)$ mechanism, is transposable to yield approximate fit across all sorts of varieties of context and local quirks, as has been exemplified in sections of each chapter. And of course participants themselves develop new approaches to exploiting these markets, as is exemplified by the invention and dissemination of multidivisional firms (chap. 12), whose distinct divisions participate in different production markets. Many such new forms are in the business headlines today.

Change is being heralded by many organization analysts. One early example (Powell 1990; Powell and DiMaggio 1991) was cited in chapter 1, and to that should be adjoined work from economics (e.g., Piore and Sabel 1984). One interesting recent invocation of change (Stark 2000) is marked by introduction of a new term, *heterarchy*. Another (Baecker 2000) invokes instead network and system.

Some journalistic cries of crisis prove to be hype (Eccles and Nohria

1994), analogous to that in regards developments in art (Rosenberg 1969, 1982; White 1993a, chap. 4; White and White 1993), but one or more of the current cries may be validated by reinstitutionalizations taking place over the next decade. But even then, beneath the surface somewhat the same mechanism may be at work. One way to see recent developments is as an extension of and even acceleration in the incorporation of still more human productive activity into an industrial system changed in cultural overlay but not in fundamental sociocultural dynamics. And whatever the changes in human social organization, the building blocks remain identity and control (Bourdieu 1995; Luhmann 1995; White 1992a), and the only reliable guide is explicit theory.

THE BASIC IDEA, WITH ANALOGIES

The basic idea is to catch up market existence and properties as interactional regularities that reinforce each other to keep reproducing the market as a social construction. Setting and context matter, of course, but only as they filter through the infrastructure of interaction. The plausibility of this idea I have now established, surely, although verification/refutation will come only with extensive use and, no doubt, elaboration, adaptation, and specification of exclusions. Each of the four parts of this book includes discussion of alternative approaches.

The market model itself identifies contexts where such markets are not viable. This book points, in chapters 4, 5, 11, 12, and 14 particularly, where to look for substitute forms. And chapters 5–9 develop major, natural extensions and generalizations of the core model from chapters 2 and 3. Chapter 12 argues that prominent parts of the observed economy around us, notably multidivisional firms, are superstructures erected around $W(y)$ markets as continuing scaffolding, and chapter 13 pursues other such evolutions.

This basic idea has an abstract skeleton that it should be possible to fill out for social situations not obviously related to markets and of very different scope. Consider analogies and metaphors. Members of a high-kicking chorus line also are keying on each other to regulate what each is presenting to an audience in aggregate—but, except metaphorically, the dancers are not transferring materials or services procured upstream into their output of kicks. And of course they are, in a sense, aiming at perfect competition, where each kicks just the same. Radio City Music Hall shows demonstrate that the number of producers in such molecules can extend greatly in vivid realization of the linear molecule variant of chapter 5.

A related analogy is a choir, where also each member gets guiding discipline from the product of their fellow singers. The "a capella" species of choir is an apter metaphor still for the $W(y)$ market, in that each member has to seek his or her own niche by quality, whereas an ordinary choir points toward perfect competition, so it is no surprise that it needs a choir director, analogous to the auctioneer implicit in the orthodox Walrasian vision of markets.

A different analogy for the basic idea is to conversation, where participants as a set tend to keep each person in line with one-at-a-time or other conventions that constitute themselves out of the very talk and gestures that they guide (Gibson 1999) within some given language institutions (Lucy 1993). All the while the analogue of chapter 5's substitutability (parameter gamma) is being enacted. But this conversation market differs in being "inbred," such that the "buyers" are also the "producers" and simultaneously the suppliers, as of topic and address. Nor does a conversation "economy" provide so convenient a metric as money for valuations, though certainly a hick or vulgar accent will generate cold shoulders.

That brings us up to chapter 10, not invoked in the scan from the introductory paragraphs of this section. The last section of chapter 3 does set up most of this scan in summing up the core model. But chapter 3 leaves merely implicit the embedding of market among thousands of such along streams, often long, of hand-offs. For analogy to chapter 10 turn to the relay race, or rather to some interacting ensemble of relay races in some complex decathlon, wherein referees would monitor switch in orientation of molecules of runners between downstream and upstream.

Summary

Markets and firms are reaching through production streams primarily to other markets and firms. These markets and firms may be sited or national; they may be manufacturing or professional. Some production markets are edge markets, but most are intermediate in input-output flow networks. It is through gaining general recognition of its embedding into these flow networks that a production market comes to take on a life of its own as a distinct actor, a separate identity on a level of other such identities (chap. 1).

Rivalry among a particular set of producers yields a market interface. The member firms of production markets commit to particular volumes of flows. Such volumes act as signals that reflect the ordering of firms in that market—an ordering by quality that is itself constructed in the very course of being signaled. The commitments of production firms thereby come to nest within a market profile of revenue by volume, as each locates an optimal niche conditional on its costs of production.

Prediction for a particular market derives from the sensitivities and substitutabilities within its networks of relations, but historical contingency also claims a place. Commonplace notions of supply and demand become contingent and relativized. A $W(y)$ market mechanism thus transmutes a continuous range of possible signals into an array of discrete footings, one per producer. Each such signal comes from and at the same time reconfirms a choice of commitment that each producer finds optimal for itself from within the menu, a choice that maximizes the gap between revenue and cost. That is the view from the producers' side of the interface. The set of volume and price signals comes to be associated with distinct levels of quality, with differentiated products. From their own downstream perspective, buyers in aggregate veto any commitment by any one producer that appears less favorable than those being made by the rest (chaps. 2 and 3).

In contexts that vary widely as to dispersions in technology and taste, signaling other than by volume can also sustain itself and thus produce the same variety in profitability and output profiles across producers and products. In certain contexts, this market mechanism is especially vulnerable to unraveling from maneuvers by would-be producers (chap. 4).

Competition thus is disciplined, according to the $W(y)$ model, around substitutability. There is an inner face of substitutability between outputs of differentiated products within the given market. Paradoxically, the quality as seen by buyers need not increase with the degree of producer's pain evidenced by its cost, but then it must vary in the exact inverse order, the case stipulated by the mechanism's inventor, economist Michael Spence (chap. 5)

There is an outer face of substitutability between whole markets as well. The model can fit whatever degree of substitutability is estimated between markets parallel in their accessing of procurement and of buying (chap. 6). And the model comes with two polarities, upstream and down, with respect to that flow of accessing (chap. 9).

"The" market can exist, in fact, only in the plural. Each industrial market becomes a player in its own right—semiautonomous, with demand and supply being as much effects as causes. But it is a market already established by a set of firms amid and connected with other such markets (chap. 7). Locating boundaries in tangible phenomena is distinctive in the present model. This is as subtle an issue as quality and relates to asymmetry in production flows. It requires deriving distinct levels of actor from processes of embedding and decoupling in the networks of market relations (chap. 10)

The market emerges from competition as a social form amid struggles by firms to secure footings. These footings require achieving recognition in and as a line of business, whether in manufacturing or in service. Uncertainty of and within these lines may be reduced through this partition into market memberships (chaps. 1 and 10), which is not always feasible, however (chaps. 4 and 11). Building markets is enabled only by communication within shared genres in discourse (chaps. 14 and 15) and action (chaps. 12, 13).

Social construction of the market is a fact. Neither technology nor inherited tradition sets the observed partition of firms among functioning production markets. A production market regularizes competition as a linear array of niches. To secure a niche is to win. The underlying impetus is gaining shelter from uncertainty. Within a competitive economy, seizing the top niche in particular is a luxury that may result partly from historical accidents. Much the same is true of the market as a whole: History and agency shape its profiles, but only within ranges set by contingencies of its network context. Very different varieties of markets can be distinguished in terms of this array of possible contexts, the state space for markets.

Possibilities for change, and often for survival, across such a population of firms and markets involve seeking financing and/or securing capital through other networks, those of banking and finance. Chapters 12, 13, and 14 especially draw implications for membership of firms and for trajectories of their markets across a niche space according to likely investment scenarios. These market creations and breakdowns can guide and be guided by political as well as economic mobilization, again only within particular genres.

Some answers were developed for questions that should be more widely asked. For example, why and when is the sales function housed and treated so much better within industry than is the procurement of products, even when procurement accounts for half the value of the output? Corey (1978) opens up a perspective on this using only the largely interpretive and linguistic procedures of case studies. Instead of probing such questions, many analysts portray business flows either in terms of perfect competition (chap. 11) or in terms of an earlier genus of market, the pure market of exchange, the labile memberships in which accord with individualist preconceptions.

We encountered surprises and paradoxes. Production markets can operate with increasing returns to scale (chaps. 3 and 7), contrary to the mechanism required for pure competition but in line with new evolutionary theory in economics (chap. 14). Supply and demand come to seem a bromide for a world of joint maneuver where, in fact, the most decisive feature is the matching of local variabilities. One-half of the state space in which markets are arrayed is referred to as the PARADOX region because of a counterintuitive relation between perceived quality and the costs of production (namely, the most valued goods are actually the cheapest to make). Firms create markets, but also market failures generate or enlarge firms and other authoritative forms of organization. Many markets, moreover, prove to be smaller than the firms involved in them (chap. 12).

I offered guides to explicit testing. Chapter 8 gave directions for seeking explicit predictions, with a quantitative basis, concerning individual markets. And the last part of chapter 13 did the same at the level of major parts or all of an industrial economy. The chapters in between offered ways to bridge these two levels as well as to probe beneath the market to include its basis in firms, entrepreneurs, and their relationships.

THEMES IN COMMON

The two academic disciplines of sociology and economics are melded in the present modeling approach, which is intended as a framing for a new economic sociology. Two of the key new ideas are signaling as expounded by the economist Michael Spence (1974a, 1974b) and embedding as expounded by the sociologist Mark Granovetter (1985) and generalized here (chap. 10). The argument thereby melds optimization derivations from neoclassical microeconomics with social constructions from network sociology. It rejects both system-perfectionism from economics and case-exceptionism from sociology.

At its base, however, the present approach is sociological. It insists on a mechanism traceable in observed social construction rather than imputed to individuals' imaginings. And yet it also insists, in common with economic theory, on insights that can be transposed across empirical instances and that can be generalized across distinct scopes and realms, as is required for dealing with, or even just assessing, Knightian uncertainty. Economic valuation is seen to come from melding comparability for domination with complementarity from effectiveness—as in clan and family. The production market and its analogues can be described as role structures. Systems of roles exist in tension with deviation, which in business is called entrepreneurship and which must figure in any realistic efforts at modeling.

A market's membership emerges as a structurally equivalent set within networks of production relations in the course of joint social construction of a quality ordering across the set. Since markets are analogues to the positions generated from structural equivalence in role relations, one can adapt algorithms for computing roles and positions, such as blockmodeling (Pattison 1993; Wasserman and Faust 1995), to predict likely sortings out of firms among markets. Common membership in a market by firms thus derives from similarities in what ties they have had with all the other sets (markets) in this partition more than upon their being connected with specific other firms as such.

Several other themes and principles in this modeling approach cannot be disentangled from features specific to the production economy. The central feature of a production economy is that there are always both sources and sinks bracketing a market, whence derives the designation as upstream or downstream. A production market is always a construction embedded among ties of flow of goods and services both into and out of the market. Directionality in persisting flows of products as intermediate goods among industries is a by-product of the overall commitment by an industrial economy to production, as well as of the commitments by individual producers in an industry to volume for next period. Interaction through three, not just two, layers of actors is thus the irreducible framing required to model choices in production markets.

Relatively irreversible stances are taken by industries and firms in their business networks, which is to say in their social relations. Typically, for each period a manufacturer commits itself and thence its supplier channels to a volume of production some of which may have to go into storage. The pattern of commitment is what establishes upstream and downstream in networks for industries, as orientation or polarization of the market profile. One can predict some correlation between polarization of a market and its being near raw supply or final demand in production streams.

Economic theory for the most part slights this feature of directionality, along with the asymmetry in commitments that results, although applied economists do not (chap. 14). There are not just the two "sides" of actors envisaged in theories of exchange markets. In its problematic direction, a production market's members turn inward to each gauge its own footing from among the footings perceived for its peers, but these footings are disciplined by assessments from further along that direction, whereas production firms are price-takers in the other (nonproblematic) direction through habitual relations there.

The population ecology school discussed in chapter 14 also largely slights this feature, but not all other sociological and institutionalist theories of markets and organization do. In particular Williamson (1975) deals with it in his discussion of markets and hierarchy, but with particular attention to state intervention. A major sociological account of markets is supplied by Burt in a series of contributions (Burt 1979, 1983, 1988a, 1992; Burt and Carlton 1989). This alternative, like the present model, derives from network analysis and sidesteps state intervention. But Burt is focused less on role patterns and their reproduction and more on autonomy and entrepreneurship. Burt (1992, chap. 6) compares his approach with both population ecology and my $W(y)$ approach.

Still another sociological alternative does center on roles, addressing status and justice aspects. It came out of analyses of banking cited earlier. Several of their coworkers have helped Eccles and Podolny each to refine and apply their role and quality perspectives in several contexts beyond the original ones of investment banks. Podolny (1999) assesses commonalities with Burt's perspective, and, together with Park (Park and Podolny 1998), also with respect to the population ecology approach, to which Podolny has also contributed directly (Podolny, Stuart, and Hannan 1996). These approaches all combine qualitative institutional considerations with explicit modeling, and so also count as mathematical sociology.

The market interface integrates three phases in clock time into a perceived template of action. Indeterminacy within the market mechanism indicates the scope of agency remaining even when the market model fits well to the observable situation. And agency implies potential for disruption of the market mechanism. Even this can be addressed within the $W(y)$ model. Over longer periods, producers may, for either polarization, commit by investment to new qualities of production processes and thus of product and service. Chapter 4 discussed this and also showed differential vulnerability to unraveling maneuvers from within, and chapters 11 and 12 from without, the market, according to context, both engineering and social. Contexts and histories wherein market mechanisms change or are vulnerable—where they fail to get started or to continue or to restart—may be starting points for, and shape changes to, other organizational forms built from within the attempted market (Sverrisson 1993).

Generalizations

The two abstract terms *reflections* and *contexts* used above are shorthand for the cumulation of market operations in and by the jointly interpretive processes that yield subcultures and shape culture. An economy emerges only as marked by common understandings derived in and as some envelope across distinct but overlapping registers of discourse. Each register, in turn, marks the more or less definite boundaries of a sector of activities, on a large scale as for banking or locally as for some particular manufacturing industry. The common understandings are hegemonic notions for that business culture as a whole.

Social scientists have taken these recognitions for granted as common sense, whereas instead models should be judged in terms of accounting for the mechanism generating such notions. Among the most important are recognitions of further levels of actor, such as firms and also markets. Especially in this respect, the production market mechanism has analogues in realms other than the economic. Industrial firms may be said to "own" their markets in much the way that academics from various universities can be said to own their particular subdisciplines or invisible colleges, or in the way that divorce lawyers in a community are thought to jointly own the local divorce business. In all three realms, a pattern of self-selection emerges alongside joint monitoring around some status ordering by quality. Such an ordering is perceived not only by producers—whether firms, professors, or lawyers—but also by relevant audiences upstream or downstream.

One can seek to formulate principles still more general, applicable as theory for all social constructions and their cultural embeddings. These should be informed by anthropological as well as sociological and economic traditions. All themes in the $W(y)$ modeling approach can be seen as deriving from a search for comparability, given commitment to production flow. One can rephrase more abstractly to say that the $W(y)$ market modeling derives from interaction between a commit principle and a comparability principle to yield distinct levels of actors spread in networks—and also, within each market as actor, a quality ordering among peer firms. By-products in the particular case of production markets are persistence of positive profits and inequalities in them.

Distinct levels are both a general principle and a concrete feature. The $W(y)$ approach requires recognizing markets as a distinct level, each market being seen as an actor in its own right. The market's identity emerges along with cultural recognition of a product genre for that industry. Its flows are partially substitutable for those from other industries, just as its terms of trade schedule renders one producer's flow partially substitutable for flows from its peers in that market.

The underlying axioms of mechanism, introduced in the early chapters, suggest the project of learning how the formation of a new level of actor, the production market, requires and supplies an embedding into social networks that is, at the same time, a decoupling from their continuance as a routine of habit and precaution (chap. 10). An actor is any social presence that is taken by participants on all levels as being a source of commitments subject not only to observation, but to observation observed so as to elicit and maintain warranties and entailments. This requires joint participation across levels, which is embedding. Embedding implies and requires decoupling: The two are duals. Commitments by producers, being at the market level, are decoupled from underlying networks of concrete relations among firms, which, however, do guide transactions across the back of the interface. Such duality between embedding and decoupling is a principle as well as a pervasive theme.

This duality, together with the principles of comparability and commitment, can be seen as just a reflection of the search for *identity* and *control* that triggers and fuels all social action (White 1992a). So there must also be indeterminacies and vulnerabilities with markets. These induce identity and control. Indeed, a distinctive feature of the $W(y)$ mechanism is indeterminacy. This is reflected in the range of market profiles, indexed by the range of the historical constant. The prize for theory is articulating just how, from out of the mess, emerge social forms that reproduce themselves in relational networks and thereby instantiate an economy. Reproduction is the sine qua non, which translates in modeling terms into comparative statics, and just this emphasis is the main difference from the economic sociologies of Burt and Granovetter.

INNOVATIONS AND CHALLENGES

Three general directions should have priority. One is developing explicit measures and models of discourse, and of culture more generally, for operationalization of the mechanism. Some beginnings can be found in earlier writings that point to new lines of inquiry that have opened up in the past generation; see chapter 15.

Second, the market mechanism can be generalized. The signaling mechanism of chapters 2 and 3 will not prove to fit all instances of production, much less of service and professional markets. This remains true even when one invokes such extensions as the alternative signals of chapter 4, the street-length molecules of chapter 5, and the upstream polarization of chapter 9. Applications to some markets may require alternative specifications of contexts, such as that in the Akerlof model (chap. 5), or different communication structure. Generalization of status-conformity theory by Phillips and Zuckerman (2000; cf. Hsu and Podolny 2001) can lead to relaxation of the $W(y)$ stipulation that every firm is equally locked into the discipline of a market profile; both highest- and lowest-status producers may be at least partially exempt; Bothner (2000a) is working toward similar relaxation of molecular boundaries.

This book that is so insistent on social infrastructure, as in networks, nonetheless presupposes perceptual processes. It does so without explicit articulation of them, so that individual cognition might be seen as crucial. Ezra Zuckerman (1999, 2000) offer a generalization. He introduces social brokerage roles into market perception and provides convincing evidence that one such role, investment analyst of an industry, contributes significantly to enforcing the discipline of molecular markets. This surely bridges back to the first direction for development, and other related work (Zuckerman and Kim 2000; Hsu and Podolny 2001) explicitly brings in the cultural aspect of bridging roles.

The third direction for innovation is developing a model of mechanism for authoritative or formal organization. One starting point is a sketch (of "council" discipline) in the earlier general theory (White 1992a), and the work of Burt (1992) and of Podolny (1999, 1994) contain many other leads.

One major challenge is calling forth questions and problems not previously formulated, but suggested by and/or fitting within the $W(y)$ framing, such as those already addressed in this book. Following up the existing modeling results poses a number of more specific and concrete challenges:

1. Bothner (2000b; Bothner and White 2000) is engaged in a variety of explorations with the model. He is using detailed simulations to uncover which parametric settings predict configurations within the market that suggest tendencies toward fractionation and maneuver among producers. He has done much the same with respect to the buyer side. Patterns of results are too intricate to be captured in rules of thumb, and this underlines the indispensability of guidance from models. These, in turn, can guide specific computations such as those in appendix tables A.1–A.5, which can be extrapolated using the many approx-

imation formulas developed in the text. These provide and receive guidance for simulations such as Leifer and Bothner have carried out.

2. Appraisal of orientations upstream and downstream for a wide array and large number of production markets should be top priority. The importance of orientation, with its impact on market outcomes and differential likelihood with context, are claims unique to the $W(y)$ model. Reassessment of existing studies should suffice for an initial test.

3. Interpretation and use of market measures will be affected by the kind of extramarket organization typically induced, which can differ greatly by region of market space, as previous chapters have shown. Consider, in particular, the CROWDED region for downstream markets. These are contexts in which the fewer the members, the better for aggregate size. The context is ripe for formation of trusts and cabals. For smaller values of b/d, one expects to find trusts and upstream polarization. For such markets at larger values of b/d, one expects to find Fortune 500 firms prominent, often through the multidivisional format spelled out in chapter 12. These are issues central in Bothner's work.

4. One can seek to use the models in this book to guide interpretation and prediction across whole realms of an economy. One reason the $W(y)$ model has been kept simple is exactly for the purpose of being able to trace intricate and extensive ramifications in ways that should prove useful qualitative guides on such broader scale. A first crude attempt was the evolutionary story at the end of chapter 13. Certain parameters will be key.

   a. Tau, the measure of counterpressure exerted on the choosing side, may stay the same across whole sectors. Aggregate sizes of markets in all regions of the space respond in proportion to tau for downstream polarization (see table 7.1). Government regulation as well as business association may be brought to bear on the level of this pressure. Upstream interventions include environmental protection measures and regulation of working conditions. Downstream interventions could include advertising and discounting policy measures.

   b. Policy concerning antitrust may need rethinking. According to the $W(y)$ analysis, levels of concentration are not exogenous but rather are endogenous variables that vary widely with market context and path of emergence.

5. There are also theory links to be forged to macroeconomics, as called for by Carlton in the quotation given in chapter 11. Turn back to table 7.1, which chapter 9 showed to be easily adaptable also to upstream markets This table on aggregates—supplemented by figures 3.2 and 7.4 on performance and quality discount in aggregates plus the up-

stream dual, figure 9.5—can suggest general themes and provide qualitative guidance for further study of macroeconomic implications.

6. The core signaling mechanism has been just stipulated and illustrated in this book rather than tested with analyses of particular industries and time periods that draw on details of such settings and periods. Casual illustrations now must be supplemented with more serious work, such as the investigation of the personal computer industry by Bothner (2000a). Numerous significant leads can be found in studies by the group around Porac (chapter 6), by the group around Favereau (chapter 7), by the group around Porter (chapter 13), and by the many other collaborations that have been cited.

7. The crux of modeling is deriving predictions and understandings of distinctive phenomena on the ground. Data may be available for some set of markets rather than any single one. Trying to locate the set on the market plane is a first step. There may be evidence for particular changes in context across that set, and the $W(y)$ model suggests outcome changes keyed to that region of market plane. For example, growth in buyer interest may for PARADOX region trigger hoisting of producer price structure that brings in low quality producers who unravel the market, possibly leading to boom/bust cycles.

The central impetus for a market is the difference between volume and quality sensitivity ratios, a/c and b/d, according to my model. That difference is indeed the kernel of the scaling for market sizes in equations (3.3) and (3.4) [also see equation (3.13)]. The producer deal criterion is inversely proportional to this kernel [equation (3.5) for W/C] so that as it improves, total market revenue will be slumping to an extent that depends on market variety and context. And that ratio also tends to scale the maximum range of sizes within the market [see equation (3.17)].

~~~~~~~~~~~~~~~~~~~

On Computations

OVERVIEW

Using Parameters and Constants in Fittings of Models (cf. chapter 8)

F ittings to empirical cases and interpretations for ideal types alike are eased by using a large number of parameters and estimates, as in the computer program below. At the same time the reporting and assessments of results is made more complex, as is illustrated by the following panels in the five appendix tables computed for market outcomes. So illustrative tables and figures do not provide sufficient guidance. Once a particular issue, or a range for parameters, is identified, a whole series of interrelated cases should be computed and then assessed or arrayed through a higher-order program such as described below.

Nonetheless, general overviews are feasible just from the illustrative results. Most significant in the theory are exactly the three parameters that supply the axes in the figures (e.g., 3.1, 5.1, 7.1, 7.2, 9.2, 9.3) of market state spaces. In substantive meanings: all three assess valuations and indeed compare distinct evaluations, and two do so as a ratio between the two sides making up a profile.[1]

1. Sensitivity ratio on the variable on which the producers commit to levels (which, in the text above, for convenience is called the production volume but need not be: see chapter 4). This ratio measures how much valuation by aggregate of buyers grows with choice level as compared to the growth of the corresponding (negative) valuation by a producer, its cost. *This is a/c.*

2. Sensitivity ratio on the index that is relatively unchanging and hence identifies the producer and its product (and which, in the text above, for convenience is called the quality, but need not be). This ratio is measured exactly parallel to number 1, that is, as rate of growth of aggregate buyer valuation compared to rate of growth of producer cost, but now with growth being in the index level. *This is b/d.*

3. Substitutability of generic product of that industry, measured as the deceleration of growth in aggregate buyer valuation as the product flows from more producers become incorporated into a summation across the industry. *This is γ.*

In the dual, upstream model taken up in chapter 9, deceleration may be replaced by acceleration of growth, which now concerns aversive aspect of flows.

The combinations of parameters are chosen so as to be decoupled from one another. This is a double decoupling. For example, *a* and *c* separately may exhibit values, such as 0.3 and 0.4, very different from unity and from values used for *b* and *d* even when both ratios are chosen to be near unity. The second decoupling is that the two ratios vary independently and thus define the market space planes of figures 3.1 and 7.2.

Fittings with Respect to the Historical Constants

Theta and tau are least like mathematical predictions. Yet neither will appear as direct estimates from observables, and such is also true with respect to the individual values of firms on the quality index *n*. This is also true with respect to the scale factors *r* and *q* since, as a section of chapter 4 shows, outcomes for various firms can be scaled directly to one another. These various terms have been introduced and retained in order to offer maximal transparency to the mathematical modeling.

Finally, the historical constant *k* is superfluous in making estimates by working backward from observed market profiles, as shown in detail in the first section of chapter 8.

COMPUTER SOFTWARE FOR $W(y)$ MODELS

Since (except when $k = 0$) only numerical solutions are feasible for the $W(y)$ models, availability of computer programs is of central importance.

Dr. Eric M. Leifer has programmed a full analysis of the $W(y)$ model for the downstream market. Appendix tables A.1–A.5 report illustrative results from this computer program for various sets of firms by quality index *n*, and for points in each of the major regions of the state space. Each of these tables is expounded in a section of the text above that is devoted to that region.

A complete and independent program for $W(y)$ models, including solutions for upstream orientation of the market, was prepared by Professor Matthew S. Bothner: a description is available from him (University of Chicago Graduate School of Business), and see publications by him in the References. It is not packaged for easy use.

Leifer's software is user-friendly.[2] It offers the user the option of using one or more of three modes: ANALYST/EMPIRICIST/MANAGER.

In ANALYST mode, used for appendix tables A.1–A.5:

Inputs are specified in two vectors. The seven standard parameters (*a*, *b*, *c*, *d*) and (γ, *r*, *q*) are arrayed into a nine-place vector around the buyer deal criterion theta, θ, and the historical constant *k*. The other vector supplies quality indexes *n* for the firms (ten or fewer) in the market.

Outputs are in four sections:

1. For each individual firm, five outcomes can be printed: quality (n), volume (y), revenue (W), price (ratio of W to y), and profit rate (W less cost, divided by W).

2. Results for the overall market, on each of these same five outcome variates, are assessed in five ways (easier to assess when there are many firms): as mean, as standard deviation, as coefficient of variation, as Gini index, and of course as market total.

3. For each firm, a graph of its cost function together with $W(y)$ for that market can be printed.

4. The program also computes and prints out the aggregate buyer valuation V, from which τ can be computed as the ratio of V over aggregate revenue W. The buyer valuations $S(y, n)$ for individual firms can also be recovered as products of theta times revenue, but τ does not equal θ.

The following points should be noted.

Because of the feedback loop concerning aggregate market size, a successive approximation search would be required to establish the value of θ that would yield a given size of τ. Instead the program inputs values of theta, but it does offer in addition the options of searching for either of two special values of theta: that which would yield $\tau = 1$ (breakeven at $V = W$) or else the θ leading to the value of tau yielding maximum buyer surplus ($V - W$). The program prints reports of when any such search does not converge with adequate fit or in few enough steps (< 20).

The program prints notices of failure or possible failure as to empirical viability—violation of any of the auxiliary conditions of maximization (chap. 2)—and as to volumes spanning the appropriate ranges, and so forth.

The convention in Industrial Organization studies is to use a measure of the predominance of the largest four producers in the market (sometimes more or less than four), as the measure of inequality, in place of the Gini index used here, which is a measure across all producers in the market.[3] These and other measures, such as the Herfindal index, can be computed from the coefficients of variation included in the second section of the output.

The EMPIRICIST mode requires input of at least partial cost schedule data for at least three firms, together with estimates of revenue W for firms in that market, and for their physical volumes y of production. A first example, for a frozen pizza market, was reported by Leifer (1985). (For equations on fitting to observed market profiles see the first section of chapter 8 above.)

The MANAGER mode is designed to permit managers in a firm to explore strategic options that may be available in their existing market or in other markets that may become relevant. Matthew Bothner has developed simulation programs to explore this more generally, suitable for strategy analysts (see Bothner 2000b).

TABLE A.1

Examples of Market Outcomes in PARADOX Region for Three Firms with Various n, Selected Values of Other Parameters, and $\tau = V/W$

Quality n	Volume y	Revenue W	Profit[a]
For $\gamma = 0.7$ and $k = +0.2$			
With $(a/c, b/d) = (0.773, -0.154)$ and $(r,q) = (10, 2)$ and $\tau = 1.356$			
1.0	.607	1.45	.206
1.5	2.13	4.41	.197
2.0	3.29	6.47	.269
Market total	6.03	12.33	2.91
With $(a/c, b/d) = (0.773, -0.154)$ and $(r, q) = (12,2)$ and $\tau = 1.070$			
1.0	1.31	3.36	.197
1.5	4.44	9.87	.197
2.0	6.57	13.94	.275
Market total	12.32	27.16	6.43
With $(a/c, b/d) = (0.682, -0.154)$ and $(r,q) = (12, 2)$ and $\tau = 1.260$			
1.0	.896	2.46	.278
1.5	2.16	4.95	.276
2.0	3.99	8.07	.276
Market total	7.05	15.47	4.27
With $(a/c, b/d) = (0.455, -0.154)$ and $(r,q) = (12, 2)$ and $\tau = 1.539)$			
1.0	.556	1.98	.472
1.5	.921	2.67	.473
2.0	1.32	3.29	.472
Market total	2.80	7.94	3.75
With $(a/c, b/d) = (0.455, -0.461)$ and $(r,q) = (12, 2)$ and $\tau = 1.406)$			
1.0	.723	2.27	.383
1.5	1.40	3.57	.375
2.0	2.22	4.90	.373
Market total	4.35	10.74	4.03
For $\gamma = 0.8$ and $k = +0.5$			
With $(a/c, b/d) = (0.1, -0.5)$ and $(r,q) = (10, 2)$ and $\tau = 1.208$			
1.0	.774	3.90	.6030[b]
1.5	1.53	5.11	.6010[b]
2.0	2.47	6.19	.6012[b]
Market total	4.77	15.20	9.15[b]

Note: For $\tau = V/W$, see equation (6.3).
[a] Unless otherwise indicated, $\theta = 4.5$.
[b] $\theta = 2.5$.

Examples of Market Outcomes in ORDINARY Region for $\gamma = 0.7$ and Three Firms
with Various $n = 1, 1.5, 2.0$; Selected Values of Other Parameters, and $\tau = V/W$

Quality n	Volume y	Revenue W	Profit
at $(a/c, b/d) = (0.681, 0.154)$ and $(r,q) = (10, 3)$			
$k = +0.05^a$ and $\tau = 1.188$ ($\theta = 2.3$)			
1.0	.225	1.42	.590
1.5	.192	1.31	.516
2.0	.165	1.20	.463
Market total	.582	3.94	2.07
at $(a/c, b/d) = (0.681, 0.461)$ and $(r,q) = (10, 3)$			
$k = -0.05$ and $\tau = 1.159$ ($\theta = 2.3$)			
1.0	.290	1.72	.552
1.5	.182	1.37	.562
2.0	.133	1.18	.565
Market total	.606	4.27	2.39
$k = +0.05$ and $\tau = 1.261$ ($\theta = 2.3$)			
1.0	.186	1.23	.617
1.5	.128	1.05	.613
2.0	.098	.938	.610
Market total	.412	3.22	1.98
at $(a/c, b/d) = (0.681, 0.385)$ and $(r,q) = (5, 2)$			
$k = -0.02$ and $\tau = 1.638$ ($\theta = 2.3$)			
1.0	.162	.555	.513
1.5	.101	.432	.514
2.0	.072	.362	.515
Market total	.336	1.35	2.39
at $(a/c, b/d) = (0.864, 0.385)$ and $(r,q) = (50, 25)$			
$k = -0.5$ and $\tau = 1.353$ ($\theta = 1.956$)			
1.0	.020	.648	.480
1.5	.016	.569	.379
2.0	.012	.460	.335
Market total	.048	1.68	.681

Note: For $\tau = V/W$, see equation (6.3).
[a]In the first panel, for $k = -0.05$, no $W(y)$ profile yields solution.

Examples of Market Outcomes in CROWDED Region with $(a/c, b/d) = (1.158, 2.6)$
$k = 0.2, \gamma = 0.7$

	Quality n	Volume y	Revenue W	Profit
For nine firms: uniform spacing on quality n from 1 to 2 with $(r,q) = (100,10)$				
		$\tau = 1.633$ ($\theta = 6$)		
Mean	1.49	.088	1.412	.250
Standard deviation	.32	.033	.385	.023
Gini Index	.121	.211	.151	.053
Market total		.791	12.71	3.10
		$\tau = 1.701$ ($\theta = 5$)		
Mean	1.49	.045	.809	.309
Standard deviation	.32	.015	.181	.027
Gini index	.121	.188	.124	.050
Market total		.403	7.28	2.21
For seven firms: remove $n = 1.25$ and 1.50 from the nine above, with $(r,q) = (100,10)$, $\tau = 1.767$ ($\theta = 6$)				
Mean	1.53	.087	1.394	.252
Standard deviation	.35	.037	.426	.025
Gini index	.128	.230	.165	.056
Market total		.607	9.76	2.39
For three firms: with $(r,q) = (200,20)$ $\tau = 2.12$ ($\theta = 5$)				
Firm a	1.0	.056	1.68	.229
Firm b	1.5	.028	1.04	.275
Firm c	2.0	.018	.773	.310
Market total		.103	3.49	.911

TABLE A.4

Examples of Market Outcomes in UNRAVELING Region with Three Firms and
$k = 0.75$; $\gamma = 0.8$; and Selected Values of $\tau = $ **V/W**

	Quality n	Volume y	Revenue W	Profit
	\multicolumn{4}{c}{For $(a/c, b/d) = (.789, 3.0)$}			
	\multicolumn{4}{c}{With $(r,q) = (40, 10)$, $\tau = 1.435$ $(\theta = 2)$}			
	1.0	.014	.883	.800
	1.5	.006	.770	.881
	2.0	.003	.725	.922
Market total		.023	2.38	2.05
	\multicolumn{4}{c}{With $(r,q) = (10, 2)$, $\tau = 1.373$ $(\theta = 2)$}			
	1.0	.073	.883	.810
	1.5	.038	.794	.861
	2.0	.019	.739	.901
Market total		.131	2.42	2.07
	\multicolumn{4}{c}{With $(r,q) = (10, 1)$, $\tau = 1.490$ $(\theta = 2)$}			
	1.0	.083	.774	.878
	1.5	.033	.714	.933
	2.0	.018	.691	.955
Market total		.134	2.18	2.01
\multicolumn{5}{l}{For $(a/c, b/d) = (1.0, 3.0)$ (border case), with $(r,q) = (40, 10)$, $\tau = 1.56$ $(\theta = 3)$}				
	1.0	.279	4.27	.302
	1.5	.065	1.83	.501
	2.0	.029	1.32	.624
Market total		.374	7.42	3.03

Table A.5

Examples of Market Outcomes in TRUST Region for Three Firms with Various n,
Selected Values of Other Parameters, and $\tau = V/W$

	Quality n	Volume y	Revenue W	Profit
For $(a/c, b/d) = (1.158, 0.667)$, $k = +0.2$, $\gamma = 0.85$; $(r,q) = (20, 4)$, $\tau = 1.312$ ($\theta = 2.5$)				
	1.0	1.39	11.45	.524
	1.5	.997	9.75	.446
	2.0	.766	8.42	.380
Market total		3.15	29.63	13.55
For $(a/c, b/d) = (1.00, 0.50)$, (border case), $k = +1.0$; $\gamma = 0.8$; $(r,q) = (10, 2)$, $\tau = 1.594$ ($\theta = 2$)				
	1.0	.119	.600	.600
	1.5	.083	.509	.511
	2.0	.061	.434	.435
Market total		.264	1.54	.809

Note: For $\tau = V/W$ see equation (6.3).

Glossary of Symbols

~~~~~~~~~~~~~~~~~~~~~~~~

DESCRIPTORS FOR PRODUCERS

y The choice to be made, usually on volume, by a producer.

\#   The number of producers in the industry.

n The quality index: so a vector of \# values of n identifies the set of producers.

MARKET PROFILE

$W(y)$ The schedule of payment W for volume y from the representative producer.

SCHEDULES DESCRIBING FIRMS' CONTEXTS

$C(y, n)$ The schedule of cost according to volume for a producer of quality n.

$S(y, n)$ Likewise a valuation of that volume and quality, by that industry's buyers taken in aggregate.

SUBPARAMETERS ACROSS THE INDUSTRY

See "Using Parameters and Constants in Fittings of Models" in the appendix.

a The exponent to which volume y is raised to project the expansion of buyer valuation.

c The same, but for producer cost.

b The exponent on quality n that projects to the expansion of buyer valuation.

d The same, but for producer cost.

SUBSTITUTABILITY PARAMETER AND MARKET AGGREGATES

V The superaggregate valuation by buyers in aggregate of all volumes shipped from that industry. It derives from the summation of aggregate buyer valuations $S(y, n)$ across every producer in the industry.

γ The exponent applied to that summation to yield V; a value of gamma less than unity indicates reduction of buyer valuation under pressure of substitutability from products of other industries.

τ The ratio, **V/W**, of summated valuation to summated revenue for the industry—must be at least unity to ensure buyer participation and thus market survival.

θ The like ratio for any one producer from just its $S(y, n)$, and so, unlike τ, it shifts according to a feedback loop with the aggregate market revenue, **W**.

k Adjusted within the revenue versus volume functional form predicted for a market profile to reflect its shaping by history (path dependence).

MARKET OUTCOMES

$y[n]$ The volume chosen by a producer with index value n.

$W(y[n])$ The payment to that producer.

W The sum of these across all the firms in that market.

C The aggregate of costs experienced by all the firms: substitute the $y[n]$ into the cost schedules $C(y, n)$ and sum across all firms.

π Profitability: aggregate revenue **W** less aggregate cost, C, as a ratio to **W**: an average of the profitabilities of the producers.

FITTING-CONSTANTS USED ACROSS THE INDUSTRY

r The monetary unit for buyer valuation.

q Same, but for producer cost.

AUXILIARY COMBINATIONS OF THE ABOVE FOR COMPUTATIONAL CONVENIENCE

Subscript i Used to label firms (chaps. 2, 5, and 8).

g, f, K to simplify $W(y)$ and clarify its form (chaps. 2, 3, and 9).

e, k' in table 3.2 to simplify computations of range of k (chaps. 3, 7, and 9).

W_o indicates that k is set to zero in a formula for **W**, and y and n are subscripted similarly (chaps. 3, 6, 7, and 9).

ε and its generalization, from equation (7.3), ε' Each discounts the exponent of the quality index (chaps. 3, 5, 7, 8, and 9).

Boldface **n** Denotes weighted average of quality across the set of producers (table 7.1, chaps. 7 and 9).

t, X, Y Transforms of variables to simplify equations for clines in state space of operating margin (chaps. 7 and 9).

SPECIAL SYMBOLS AND CONVENTIONS USED IN SINGLE SECTIONS

$y_o, n_o, R,$ and Q for base firm Chapter 3, third section.

S for the summation of S schedules Chapter 3, "Ratios of Aggregate Sizes" section.

A, to simplify $W(y)$ further   Chapter 3, last section.

h, markup margin for guild   Chapter 4.

q' as aggregate q, when the number of duplicate producers sharing given buyers is z Chapter 6.

Adapting notation to Akerlof's model   Chapter 5, last section.

m_i for ratio of quality index n to a base value, and a host of other conversions in deriving estimates; then notation for ecology and then for stream flow   Chapter 8, each section.

v and x for parameter ratios on axes of upstream market plane, figure 9.2   Chapter 9, section on split regions.

Notes

~~~~~~~~~~~~~~~~~~~

CHAPTER 1
INTRODUCTION

1. For a parallel assessment of Knight's importance by another sociologist see Beckert 1996.

2. This is evident whether events are seen contemporaneously (Marshall 1930) or in archives (Dobbin 1994; Herrigel 1996).

3. For a later statement see Stinchcombe 1998, which appears in a volume that also contains a compatible formulation by the economist Thomas Schelling (1998).

CHAPTER 2
PROFILES FOR A MARKET

1. This is the downstream market. In markets oriented upstream, to be introduced in chapter 9, producers instead contend in the establishment of a market profile as to flows from their suppliers.

2. Chapter 4 will sketch other forms of commitment signals besides volume that may be found in some production settings and for which much the same mechanism for signaling quality can be utilized.

3. Chapter 5 adds an option in which a market can be large—long as in a polymer molecule—yet observations need only embrace a subset near ego.

4. Only then would the supplier or the buyer come to consider making strategic threats, say, by differently "bundling" the goods it supplies (but see Katz 1989; Perry 1989). For a survey of mainline economic views of technological pressures on the firm in such matters see Panzar 1989, and for empirical studies see, in the same *Handbook*, Schmalensee 1989 and Bresnehan 1989. For a different economic perspective consult Nelson and Winter 1982 and Penrose 1959.

5. "Returns to scale" in economic parlance is judged by comparing growth in cost with volume with linear growth in revenue with successive volumes at fixed price. Textbook convention is that a market is not sustainable with increasing returns to scale, but see, for example, Beato 1982 and, more generally, Panzar 1989, 7. Chapter 8, below, attempts a derivation of the size of c from the larger pattern of network connections.

6. For an alternative formulation of these conundrums see Leifer and White 1987.

7. Then a representative market will, analogously, be the focus later, in chapters 6–10.

8. One can also formulate and solve this problem in terms of partial differential equations, as Spence did in his original work on signaling (1974b, appendix A; and see White 1976, 1978), but tracing the solution via ordinary differential equations gives better guidance to substantive intuitions.

9. This stipulation should be hedged with references to sunk costs, investment

strategy, and, hence, entry and exit of firms. See the surveys by Gilbert (1989) and especially Spence (1974b). Also see chapter 12, below. Explicit modeling of sunk costs in an earlier paper (White 1979, 54–58) suggests no change in major conclusions in the $W(y)$ models.

10. The gambling imagery will be developed further in the chapter 4 section on alternative signals and in the last section of chapter 6.

11. Shapiro (1989) offers an authoritative survey, set against the historical backdrop of oligopoly theory, with special attention to a burst of papers published around 1985. Other chapters, in the same *Handbook*, survey product differentiation (Eaton and Lipsey 1989; Varian 1989), effects of dealership relations (Katz 1989; Perry 1989), and how markets clear (Carlton 1989).

12. Among such syntheses by economists are works by Baumol, Panzar, and Willig (1989); Dehez and Dreze (1987); Rosen (1974); Rothschild and Stiglitz (1976).

13. He was following the path opened by Kelvin Lancaster (1970; cf. Terleckyj 1976) with a theory of hedonic pricing, but Rosen did not turn to particular data, as did, for example, the econometrician Zvi Griliches (Griliches and Ohta 1976), who turned to explicit estimation of case studies, notably of sales for different makes of automobile.

14. Richard Nelson suggested that I rewrite an earlier version of this manuscript around a look at some of the sensible things said by Scherer (1970). This book is indeed remarkable as a compendium of observations about U.S. industrial organization, which is also knowledgeable about a great diversity of theoretical contributions that had been or could be brought to bear on the facts, and it has yet to be supplanted as a comprehensive overall guide. Chapter 14, below, discusses pragmatic business economics at some length.

CHAPTER 3
MARKET PLANE

1. Charles Tilly (personal communication) points to some kinship between this perspective and the "structuration" of Anthony Giddens.

CHAPTER 4
QUALITY AND UNRAVELING

1. Also see Scherer 1970, 216, for discussion under the rubric of fringe pricing.

2. Considerably more detail on these guild calculations appears in early working papers (White 1976, 1979), available upon request. And see the further discussion in the "Niche Plane for Monopsonist Subcontracting" and the "Exploitation within a Market" sections of chapters 5 and 12, respectively.

3. It is, of course, also true, and part of economic history, that established guilds even in such favorable configurations can be overturned by the incursion of entrepreneurial ventures. A superb account of one such transformation, which is well informed both as to economic and to social context, is offered by the art historian Baxandall (1980) in his account of Poland as the burgeoning frontier in art purchase that enabled evasion of German wood-sculpturing guilds.

4. Baxandall (1980), in his extraordinary monograph cited in the previous note,

indeed is tracing the *dissolution* of a guild organization by an incoming form of monopolistic competition. The $W(y)$ mechanism would fit the latter perhaps better than the standard microeconomics that Baxandall uses.

5. Extensive tables and qualitative descriptions can be found in a survey by Malcolm Salter together with a case report on Beech prepared by Tull Gerrald under Salter's supervision in 1969 (Harvard Business School, Intercollegiate Case Clearing House numbers 9-370-036 and 9-369-008).

6. The producers sell to dealers, not customers, except (1) in a few instances where a producer bailed out one or more dealers and packaged them as a higher-level, wholly owned subsidiary, and (2) the peripheral producers, who, however, were little attended to by the regular producers.

7. The principal business of each producer was selling new planes to diverse owners (corporate or personal) of single planes. Each had data and shared a consensus about the two keys to their market over time: (1) a more expensive new plane normally was bought as an upgrade from a previous plane, and (2) there was very high brand loyalty to the firm that had sold the customer the previous plane.

CHAPTER 5

SIGNALING AND PARADOX

1. The orientation of figure 3.5, with the b/d axis horizontal, is not used in the other market planes, just so that their page layouts could accommodate PARADOX region too.

2. One can see that, with this as the volume that all these firms with low n propose to offer, a "corner" appears in the dotted curve: The dotted curve for the putative market profile should be extended by a horizontal straight line on over to $n = 0$, at $y = 170$. Such "corner solutions" are familiar from linear programming and game theory as applied in microeconomics.

3. This section was doubled in size and given more prominence at the suggestion of an anonymous reviewer for Princeton University Press, to whom I am indebted.

4. Note that the sign convention for d is the reverse here to that in Spence's publications.

5. My own early exposure to Spence's model, in an interdisciplinary modeling RIAS seminar at Harvard in 1975, stimulated me to write RIAS Working Paper 1 (White 1976). It stayed mostly within Spence's framing and pointed out some imprecisions in the claims that Spence made in this fascinating and rich work—which yet I found obscure in conceptualization. Only in a subsequent working paper (White 1978) did I uncover the $d < 0$ half-plane (after introducing Cobb-Douglas parameterization) together with the viability there of increasing returns to scale, and also the unraveling phenomenon. Still later in RIAS Working Paper 16 (White 1979) I introduced the vision of molecular markets of small numbers of firms, and thus network phenomenology, including substitutability between parallel markets as operationalized by a standard CES demand function made compatible with Cobb-Douglas—see chapters 6 and 7—and also an early version of the upstream dual form—see chapter 9. In all three of these early unpublished papers, I followed Spence's economistic lead in developing abstract comparisons of institutions such as might be of interest to a philosopher-king.

6. The part with $a/c < 1$, excluding increasing returns to scale where the market mechanism is assumed not viable, as indeed it is not for Spence's generalization of the PARADOX region with $d < 0$.

7. The last section of this chapter will show that a subcontracting setup could also sustain low a even with d positive.

8. Castleman 1996 is a lucid and historically complete account of the Strip for a Fodor travel guide series; for the city more generally see Moehring 1999.

CHAPTER 6
SUBSTITUTABILITY EXTENDED

1. See Pattison 1993; Wasserman and Faust 1995; and Boyd 1991 for guidance on this. Bothner (2000a, 2000b) studies several particular industries.

2. In 1999 the sector was threatened by devastation from the banana subsidy war between the United States and the European Union.

The fieldwork of Porac et al. (1995) confirms Gulvin's (1984) evidence for separate registers of discourse and distinct subcultures correlated to network pattern in this long-standing set of industries; see the discussion of linguistics in chapter 5 above.

3. To restore the conventions of the production market model, one could, instead, conceive of skill in a gambling context as the reciprocal of quality n, and then both b and d are positive.

CHAPTER 7
MARKET SPACE

1. For a third sort of example, turn to an entirely different format of production activity, theater. See the figures in H. White 1998 for the system of theatrical performances in the United States. Dinner theater and off-Broadway productions are estimated also to fall along a ray in this region.

2. Matthew Bothner (1998) has explored these interconnections at some length.

3. This was defined earlier as the percentage by which total buyer valuation V exceeds total market revenue W (which also is total payments by buyers).

CHAPTER 8
ESTIMATING QUALITIES AND PARAMETERS

1. Checking second-order conditions for the optimizations is discussed in the fifth phase below; it is not a concern with observations of a functioning market. Also see the subsequent discussion of estimating the historical constant k.

2. For example, with $d/b = \frac{1}{2}$, the slope

$$dW/dy = Wy^{c-0.5a-1}cq(\theta/r)^{0.5}$$

and, for $d/b = 2$,

$$dW/dy = W^{-2}y^{c-2a-1}cq(\theta/r)^2.$$

3. For predator-prey interactions: see Hofbauer and Sigmund 1988, part 2, for a version accessible without extensive training and part 5 for a sophisticated version.

4. A pair of industries may offer symbiotic products—say staple gun and staples—in which case between them a substitutability measure gamma would be greater than unity. This corresponds to a negative value for omega, and thus for Venn overlap w, as one should expect.

5. For extended discussion see Bourdieu (e.g., 1995), Luhmann (e.g. 1995), and White 1992a. Neither Bourdieu nor Luhmann does any explicit modeling. But Bourdieu's field construct is substantively consistent with the idea of the self-consistent field (SCF).

6. A full technical account can be put together from Boyd 1991; Burt 1992; Pattison 1993; and Wasserman and Faust 1995.

7. These distinctions are simplifications of the real issue, which is the extent to which each possible parameter can contribute to mechanism models that are computable as well as insightful. The exponents b and d, for example, could be seen as derivative, though not to the extent of epsilon or pi. And similar distinctions can be invoked concerning what are called "variables" in the model mechanism. The "Entrepreneurship and Alternative Signals" section of chapter 4 points out how secondary variables have been folded into the volume variable y.

8. See, for example, the sections of chapter 3 on filling in, of chapter 4 on unraveling, of chapter 5 on linear molecules, of chapter 6 on Scottish knitwear and and of chapter 11 on size distributions.

CHAPTER 9
FACING UPSTREAM OR DOWN

1. A notable exception is Leontief 1966. Andrew Abbott (1994) first brought this indeterminacy of usage to my attention, in a review of an earlier work of mine (White 1992a).

2. Decoupling is elucidated by me at some length in *Identity and Control: A Structural Theory of Social Action* (White 1992a), both in general (12–13, 111–12) and also for production economies in general (181–84). And see chapter 10 below.

3. These are, in fact, just the two extreme and tidy cases where industries can be seen as stacked in a single channel of flow. The discussion of decoupling in the next chapter will argue against their likelihood. Decoupling is believable just because no one other market is dominant in perceptions of the focal market, either on its up- or its downstream side.

4. This will also prove key in the section of chapter 11 on econometrics.

CHAPTER 10
EMBED AND DECOUPLE

1. Both genres can be adapted to cover both locale in the sense of technology and locale in the sense of geographic address, although various metric weighting schemes would be required. Thus the historical divergence between address and nonaddress models of the market, which is emphasized by Eaton and Lipsey (1989, fig. 12.4, p. 762), could be overcome.

2. For further background on roles see, for example, Nadel 1957 on roles in general; Boyd 1991 and White 1963 on kinship role networks; Wellman and Berkowitz

1988 on phenomenology; and Pattison 1993 on models. White (1992a, chap. 3) supplies a more general overview.

3. Cf. White 1995a; Mische and White 1998. For examples of tracing this sort of evolutionary history for structural equivalence in networks see Anheier, Gerhards, and Romo 1995; Baker 1990; Boyd 1991; Breiger 1991; Faulkner 1983; Giuffre 1996; and Pattison 1993.

4. See the two previous notes. Any mapping of these terms into network constructs will be only approximate and stochastic.

5. Embedding and its distinct levels each exemplify self-similar constructs, which can also be applied to overlaps of larger scope between state and economy, as in Evans 1995; Fligstein 1996; and Fligstein and Mara-Drita 1992.

6. A number of examples can be found in Bothner 2000a. Still to be explored for each such case is which of the two facing profiles is more subject to disruption.

7. See, for example, Eccles 1981 on construction; Uzzi 1996, Lachmann and Petterson 1997, and Lazerson 1995 on textiles; and Romo and Schwartz 1995 on manufacturing. Also see Hamilton, Zeile, and Kim 1990 and Yoshino and Lifson 1988 for analyses of Asian firm-market systems where subcontracting seems central if not predominant.

8. One might investigate the plausibility of other topologies for quality array, for instance as a ring, with buyers' assessments conveyed by positioning either inside or outside the ring. Perhaps, for example, units in clothing fashion industries might develop mutual ordering in some sort of ring topology that reflected distinct approaches and uses in clothes worn that were not rankable, but which fit into a closed ring or a toroid according to degree of similarity.

CHAPTER 11

SUPPRESSING MARKET REALITIES

1. In this book, these are the only solutions for downstream models; contexts in the state space cube that have $1/\gamma > 1$ could refer to contexts for markets in radically new products.

2. But one could explore mappings of the scale parameters that they estimate for various industries onto results from the $W(y)$ model; see figure 3.3.

3. And the converse implication is that aggregated results from $W(y)$ models (see chapters 3 and 7) could be consistent with the Simon-Ijiri findings.

4. An attractive feature of the book, pedagogically, is that Nerlove generally works out his models in all four versions resulting from choices of physical versus valuation measures, for inputs or output. Scientifically, this is suspect, however, for the appropriate version is a matter of how committers, not econometricians, perceive the facts.

5. In his text, Nerlove imposes no a priori restrictions on how the effect of managerial ability (his w_{of}, e.g., in eq. (2.7), p. 24) differs from one firm to another, but in a long note (2, on p. 36) he suggests defining a measure of managerial ability for firm f, m_f—which is analogous to the quality index n for $W(y)$—and then equates w_{of} to m_f raised to the power γ.

6. Nerlove is, of course, fully aware of the difficulties of identifying parameters. Nerlove draws on other econometricians in producing the trove of ideas and procedures for overcoming these difficulties that can be found in his notes as well as the

text of the book. These ideas center around use of longitudinal data and sophisticated treatment of errors. Nonetheless, the claim of this section is that econometrics is not dealing with the central scientific issues: Knightian uncertainty and how the participants—not the econometrician—come to cope with it in a context inducing and requiring continued commitments.

7. Arrow recognizes, for example, in his foreword to Arthur's collected essays (1994) the limitations of this approach.

8. Note that this is an approximation akin to the blurring by the $W(y)$ profile mechanism of producers' perceptions of particularities in their ties with buyers of their products. Thus, this general theory also invokes decoupling, at an even more extreme degree of abstraction. But note that some equate general equilibrium theory not with fully connected networks, but rather with a star network in which each node is connected only to a master node for the Walras auctioneer (e.g., Kirman 1997, 493).

9. For recent formulations by economists on network framings see the survey by Birner (1996).

10. But then, as to makeup, although in the bottom left region of figure 7.2 for downstream mode there is a triangle in which market schedules are subject to unraveling and freeloading, in the upstream market plane of figure 9.2 there is no such area touching on the axis.

11. One can seek more abstract and general examples. Turn to settings remote from pure competition and/or upstream orientation and see if there too hierarchy can be a likely competitor with the processor or producer market. Developments in natural science can help with predicting which social formations are likely to construct themselves and how. Cascade models for evolution of altruistic behaviors provide one lead (Boorman and Levitt 1980, chap. 3 and 4). But more directly relevant leads come from design practices derived for polymers (Muthukumar, Ober, and Thomas 1997), where two analogies can be used: one from metric space into social network topology; the other from the "free energy" of statistical thermodynamics to social bonding (attractive energy) as weighted by combinatorics of network setting (entropy measure). For the most lucid treatment of thermodynamics in statistical mechanics context see Callen 1960, followed up by Balian 1991. A messy problem that offers some analogies to a system of markets and firms is that of spin glasses. For a lucid summary of the statistical mechanics see Ziman 1979, 468–71, and for an update and ties to varied experiments see Mydosh 1993.

12. Some basis for suitable abstract models is provided by early works by Herbert Simon on the employment relation and on pay hierarchies. The latter can be extended by new work on allometric scaling laws (West, Brown, and Enquist 1997). And Ijiri and Simon 1977, discussed earlier in this chapter, is a collection of models of the populations of such organizations.

CHAPTER 12
INVESTING ACROSS MARKETS

1. For an overview of corporate species of business organization see Fligstein and Freeland 1995 and more generally Powell and DiMaggio 1991.

2. For a cross-disciplinary survey of entrepreneurship see Thornton 1999; for an

evocative case study see Sverrisson 1994; for bearing on economic innovation see Nelson and Winter 1982; and for a sociological approach similar to the present one see Burt 1992, chaps. 1, 6, 7.

3. For background and history see the on-the-scene study by W. S. Jevons (1907) of the initial formation of commercial banking in Britain.

4. Gould and Fernandez (1989) supply an abstract model of brokerage in social networks; Eccles and Crane 1988 and Uzzi and Gillespie 1999 are two field studies of networks in banking.

5. Sociological and institutionalist theories of organization offer many more, and diverse, theories of markets. A broad survey of institutionalist views of the economy is provided by Smelser and Swedberg (1994), and Lie (1997) surveys economic sociology of markets more specifically. Studies of interactions between markets, both in their formation and in their operation, and other organizations are, for example, found in the collection of political science and sociology essays edited by Campbell et al. (1991).

Interaction with the state figures large in several subliteratures. One is comparative national studies of divisionalized organizations across markets, such as Evans 1995 and Hamilton 1996. Fligstein (2001) takes this approach in a monograph on economic sociology, as do several of the authors in Smelser and Swedberg 1994, who also reach out toward nonstandard components of economies, such as the nonprofit sector (on which see Anheier and Seibel 1990; Powell 1990) and socialist regimes (see Granick 1975; Stark 1992, 1996; Vlachoutsicos and Lawrence 1990).

A final alternative can be seen in the very large group of studies, overlapping somewhat with the above, that interpret a production economy primarily in terms of relational networks among and within firms. See, for example, studies by Eccles (1985), Lachmann and Petterson (1993), Uzzi (1997), and for Asian contexts Evans (1995) and Hamilton (1996).

6. Previous working papers (White 1976, 1979), which are available on request, report at greater length on a number of variants and explore other measures of outcome, including measures of social welfare and Pareto optimality that are traditional among economic theorists. Another approach is through models of clientage networks (Gibson and Mische 1995; Mische and Pattison 2000; White 1992a, 1992b).

7. The following account is taken from two case studies distributed by HBS Case Service, Harvard Business School: STERLING INDUSTRIES (A), (B), #9-178-163, 9-178-164. The names of companies and managers, as well as most of the numerical information and product descriptions, are disguised, in conformity with strict PIMS regulations. And unlike other HBS case studies, there is no identification of case writer, or of possible supervisor—who may have been the SPI director of research cited earlier, Bradley Gale.

8. The presentation here is simplified: see especially appendix B in Eccles 1985. Vancil in fact worked with 11 detailed types of strategy derived from work of Rumelt, and there are a variety of subtypes of the transfer pricing rules, some involving arcane issues of accounting. Many rules, including some so-called market price as well as cost ones, involve post hoc reassignment of prices by top management to suit various objectives.

CHAPTER 13
STRATEGIC MOVES AND MARKET EVOLUTION

1. For extensive discussion of this general approach to switching see Mische and White 1998; and White 1995b, 1995c, 1995d.

2. This is the approach emphasized by Matthew Bothner within our collaboration, which also drew on earlier contributions by Eric Leifer (1985, 1987, 1991). This section is but a sketch and draws heavily on his ideas.

3. The survey by Varian (1989) specifically on price discrimination, in the same *Handbook* as that by Carlton (Schmalensee and Willig 1989, chap. 10), begins with a vivid example.

4. Elsewhere (1998, fig. 9.3) I trace a state space for a larger artistic field, that of all varieties of American theater. This has been extended and generalized in a thesis on the French theater by Urrutiaguer (1997), who notes some overlap with a modeling approach by the American economist Henry Hansmann (1981). Hansmann cast the problem in traditional terms of price discrimination (for a trenchant account of which see Scherer 1970, chap. 10), which can offer a setting for the market profile model.

CHAPTER 14
CONTRASTING RESEARCH PERSPECTIVES

1. Geography is the discipline that tries to suborn physical space into service as social space. It is not much embedded into social science theory, with a few exceptions (e.g., Alonso 1964; Enelow and Hinich 1990; Gould 1995). Without *some* theory of social space, one is left with only theology, whose portrayals lie outside any tangible space; so it may be no accident that present social science, and notably economics (see discussion in Baker 1987; and Barber 1977), buries itself in normative approaches or sometimes proclaims a space without empirical referent (e.g., Peli and Nooteboom 1999).

2. In fact, conceptions of space have multiplied across the rest of the natural sciences, too, and these developments may suggest avenues for social science: decimal dimensionalities in cooperative phenomena of matter (see Ziman 1979 on K. Wilson); space-time conceptualizations as fields of virtual elementary particles; and so on.

3. Spence, as his work is laid out in chapter 5, supposed both that the quality of the producer was not an observable, *and* that this unobservable quality correlated *negatively* with the costs suffered by the producer. Thus Spence insisted that d was negative, $d < 0$, the PARADOX region in present terminology. This restriction to PARADOX and the cognitivist bias both contributed also to Spence's missing the possibility of unraveling, and this despite unraveling being related to the "corner solutions" long familiar to economists through game theory and linear programming (Dorfman, Samuelson, and Solow 1958). Spence also chose not to allow for a trade-off ratio in favor of the employer, that is, in present terms, he set the tau measure defined in chapter 6 as unity.

4. This can be maintained, but only when construed on another level. Elsewhere I have argued (1992, chap. 1; 1995) that a person becomes constituted, establishes self with an identity, only as a self-discipline is triggered for control. In recent centuries, as

the production economy emerged, such personal disciplines may have come to often resemble exchange market disciplines around rationality for selectivity profile (White 1992, chapter on interface and arena disciplines). You do not use rationality, but rather it uses you, embeds you as a person.

5. Kreps is unusual in his openness to other social science approaches. He both avows openness and exemplifies it in his own published work.

6. When this phenomenology is known and noticed by the participants, it is referred to in academic register as a subculture, but in a business context, it seems more suitable to refer to the rational habits distinctive of that sector.

CHAPTER 15
BUSINESS CULTURES

1. See, for example, a survey of early centuries in central Europe, Kriedte, Medick, and Shlumbohm 1981, and one in Italy, Lachmann and Petterson 1993. For surveys of later centuries see Bythell 1978 on Britain and Herrigel 1996 on Germany.

2. This is so even though this paper and those from the following decade are *nearly* indecipherable. He also exhibits some tendency to celebrate sheer intricacy (Silverstein 1992), like the evolutionary economist Arthur, but, like Arthur, he does develop many tangible examples in trenchant fashion (Silverstein 1997, 1998a).

3. This focus will be kept on economic value, as in Scitovsky 1993; for a survey on values more generally, see other chapters in that collection edited by Hechter, Nadel, and Michod (1993).

4. I am indebted to Ronald Breiger for helping me to understand Friedkin's work.

5. Who also spent time as sociologists on the same campus and knew each other's book, and yet neither has drawn parallels to his own book via an analogue to the production market mechanism.

CHAPTER 16
CONCLUSION

1. There is a recent survey by Lazerson (1993); for monograph treatments see Bythell 1978; Kriedte, Medick, and Shlumbohm 1981; for more general overviews see Udy 1970 on the theory; and Braudel 1986 on the history.

APPENDIX

1. This is why a modern economy is the apt choice for learning how to develop general system models of sociocultural construction. The empirical field itself generates a set of distinctive and commonly recognized evaluative metrics. Valuations are of course present in other systems, but they often revolve around grammars for justifications.

2. Dr. Leifer makes this program available as a software package in APL language (version 4), in floppy disk formatted for DOS operating system (address 56 Lyak Road, Hudson, New York 12534). APL is an IBM secondary language that is available in various operating systems besides DOS. Reliability was assessed by comparison to

computations from a second programming, also in APL, by H. C. White: agreement was found to better than 1 part in 1000. The Bothner programs all are in DOS.

3. The Gini index, G, is a measure of overall degree of inequality. Expand on the definition given in the text: Array the population from least to most favored on the attribute, say money. Starting from the poorest, for each successive member, plot on the abscissa the cumulative distribution of population from 0 to 1 against the cumulative distribution of the valued attribute on the ordinate. Draw a smooth curve through the points. With planimeter assess the area between the curve and the 45-degree diagonal as a fraction, $= G$, of the area ($= \frac{1}{2}$) of the triangle.

References

Abbott, Andrew. 1983. "Sequences of Social Events: Concepts and Methods for the Analysis of Order in Social Processes." *Historical Methods* 16:129–47.

———. 1984. "Event Sequence and Event Duration: Colligation and Measurement." *Historical Methods* 17:192–204.

———. 1988. *The System of Professions*. Chicago: University of Chicago Press.

———. 1990. "Conceptions of Time and Events in Social Science Methods." *Historical Methods* 23:140–50.

———. 1994. Book review: *Identity and Control. Social Forces* 72:895–902.

———. 1995. "Things of Boundaries." *Social Research* 62:857–82.

Abbott, Andrew, and Emily Barman. 1996. "Sequence Comparison via Alignment and Gibbs Sampling: A Formal Analysis of the Emergence of the Modern Sociological Article." Department of Sociology, University of Chicago, July.

Abell, Peter. 1987. *The Syntax of Social Life: The Theory and Method of Comparative Narrative*. Oxford: Clarendon Press.

Abolafia, Mitchel. 1996. *Markets and Opportunism*. Cambridge: Harvard University Press.

Abrahamson, Eric, and Lori Rosenkopf. 1993. "Institutional and Competitive Bandwagons: Using Mathematical Modeling as a Tool to Explore Innovation Diffusion." *Academy of Management Review* 18:487–517.

Adams, Julia. 1993. *The East India Companies*. Madison: University of Wisconsin Press.

Aitken, A. C. 1951. *Determinants and Matrices*. Edinburgh: Oliver and Boyd.

Akerlof, George. 1970. "The Market for Lemons: Quality Uncertainty and the Market Mechanism." *Quarterly Journal of Economics* 84:488–500.

———. 1976. "The Economics of Caste and the Rat Race and Other Woeful Tales." *Quarterly Journal of Economics* 90:599–617.

Alonso, William. 1964. *Location and Land Use*. Cambridge: Harvard University Press.

Anderson, Carl R., and Frank T. Paine. 1978. "PIMS: A Reexamination." *Academy of Management Review* 3:602–11.

Anderson, P. W., Kenneth J. Arrow, and David Pines, eds. 1988. *The Economy as an Evolving Complex System*. Santa Fe Institute Studies in the Sciences of Complexity, Proc. Vol. 5. Redwood City, Calif.: Addison-Wesley.

Andrews, Steven B., and David Knoke, eds. 1999. *Networks in and around Organizations: Research in the Sociology of Organizations*. Vol. 16. Stamford, Conn.: JAI Press.

Anheier, Helmut K., Jürgen Gerhards, and Frank P. Romo. 1995. "Forms of Capital and Social Structure in Cultural Fields: Examining Bourdieu's Social Topography." *American Journal of Sociology* 100:859–903.

Anheier, Helmut K., and Wolfgang Seibel. 1990. *The Third Sector: Comparative Studies of Non-profit Organizations*. Berlin: de Gruyter.

Arena, Richard. 1999. "Austrians and Marshallians on Markets: Historical Origins and Compatible Views." Chapter 2 in Dow and Earl 1999.

Arrow, Kenneth J. 1981. "Real and Nominal Magnitudes in Economics." Chapter 9 in Bell and Kristol 1981.

———. 1994. Foreword to *Increasing Returns and Path Dependence in the Economy*, by W. Brian Arthur. Ann Arbor: University of Michigan Press.

Arrow, Kenneth J., and Frank Hahn. 1971. *General Competitive Analysis*. San Francisco: Holden-Day.

Arthur, W. Brian. 1985. "Competing Technologies and Lock-in by Historical Small Events: The Dynamics of Allocation under Increasing Returns." Center for Economic Policy Research, Pub. no. 43, Stanford University, January.

———. 1994. *Increasing Returns and Path Dependence in the Economy*. Ann Arbor: University of Michigan Press.

Arthur, W. Brian, Steven V. Durlauf, and David A. Lane, eds. 1997. *The Economy as an Evolving Complex System II*. Santa Fe Institute Studies in the Sciences of Complexity, Proc. Vol. 27. Reading, Mass.: Addison-Wesley.

Baecker, Dirk. 1992. "The Writing of Accounting." *Stanford Literature Review* 9:157–79.

———. 2000. "Management out of Networks and Systems: A Workshop and Book Proposal." Management Zentrum Witten Universität Witten, Witten/Herdecke, Germany.

Bailey, Elizabeth D., and Ann F. Friedlander. 1982. "Market Structures and Multiproduct Industries." *Journal of Economic Literature* 20:1024–48.

Bailey, Robert W. 1984. *The Crisis Regime: The MAC, the EFCB, and the Political Impact of the New York City Financial Crisis*. Albany: State University of New York Press.

Bain, Joe S. 1954. "Economies of Scale, Concentration, and the Conditions of Entry in Twenty Manufacturing Industries." *American Economic Review* 44:15–39.

———. 1956. *Barriers to New Competition*. Cambridge: Harvard University Press.

Baker, Wayne E. 1984. "The Social Structure of a National Securities Market." *American Journal of Sociology* 89:775–811.

———. 1987. "What Is Money? A Social Structural Interpretation." Chapter 4 in Mizruchi and Schwartz 1987.

———. 1990. "Market Networks and Corporate Behavior." *American Journal of Sociology* 96:589–625.

Baker, Wayne E., and Robert R. Faulkner. 1991. "Role as Resource in the Hollywood Film Industry." *American Journal of Sociology* 97:279–309.

———. 1993. "The Social Organization of Conspiracy: Illegal Networks in the Heavy Electrical Equipment Industry." *American Sociological Review* 58:837–60.

Baker, Wayne E., Robert R. Faulkner, and Gene A. Fisher. 1998. "Hazards of the Market: The Continuity and Dissolution of Interorganizational Market Relationships." *American Sociological Review* 63:147–77.

Balian, Roger. 1991. *From Microphysics to Macrophysics: Methods and Applications of Statistical Physics*. Vol 1. Trans. D. ter Haar and J. F. Gregg. New York: Springer-Verlag.

Banks, David, and Kathleen M. Carley. 1994. "Metric Inference for Social Networks." *Journal of Classification* 11:121–49.

———. 1996. "Models of Social Network Evolution." *Journal of Mathematical Sociology* 21:173–96.

Barber, Bernard. 1977. "Absolutization of the Market." Chapter 3 in G. Tworkin et al., eds., *Markets and Morals*. Washington, D.C.: Hemisphere.

Barkey, Karen. 1994. *Bandits and Bureaucrats*. Ithaca, N.Y.: Cornell University Press.

———. 1996. "In Different Times: Scheduling and Social Control in the Ottoman Empire, 1550 to 1650." *Comparative Studies in Society and History* 8:460–82.

Barkey, Karen, and Ronan Van Rossem. 1997. "Networks of Contention." *American Journal of Sociology* 102:1345–82.

Barley, Stephen R., John Freeman, and Ralph C. Hybels. 1992. "Strategic Alliances in Commercial Biotechnology." Chapter 12 in Nohria and Eccles 1992.

Baron, James N., and Michael T. Hannan. 1994. "The Impact of Economics on Contemporary Sociology." *Journal of Economic Literature* 32:1111–46.

Barron, David N. 1997. "Organizational Ecology." *Annual Reviews of Sociology* 23:1–122.

———. 1999. "The Structuring of Organizational Populations." *American Sociological Review* 64:421–45.

———. 2000. "Organizational Ecology and Structural Analysis." Chapter 6 in Lazega and Favereau 2000.

Barth, Fredrik. 1965. *Political Leadership among Swat Pathans*. London: University of London and Athlone Press.

———. 1993. "Are Values Real? The Enigma of Naturalism in the Anthropological Imputation of Values." Chapter 2 in Hechter, Nadel, and Michod 1993.

Baum, Joel A. C., and Frank Dobbin. 2000. *Economics Meets Sociology in Strategic Management*. Stamford, Conn.: JAI Press.

Baum, Joel A. C., and Stephan J. Mezias. 1992. "Localized Competition and Organizational Failure in the Manhattan Hotel Industry, 1898–1990." *Administrative Science Quarterly* 37:580–604.

Baum, Joel A. C., and Christine Oliver. 1991. "Institutional Linkages and Organizational Mortality." *Administrative Science Quarterly* 36:189–218.

Baumol, William J., John C. Panzar, and Richard D. Willig. 1989. *Contestable Markets and the Theory of Industry Structure*. New York: Harcourt Brace Jovanovich.

Baxandall, Michael. 1980. *The Limewood Sculptors of Renaissance Germany*. New Haven: Yale University Press.

Bearman, Peter. 1993. *Relations into Rhetorics: Local Elite Social Structure in Norfolk, England: 1540–1640*. New York: Academic Press.

———. 1997. "Generalized Exchange." *American Journal of Sociology* 102:1383–1415.

Bearman, Peter, Robert Faris, and James Moody. 1999. "Blocking the Future: New Solutions for Old Problems in Historical Social Science." *Social Science History* 23:501–33.

Beato, Paulino. 1982. "The Existence of Marginal Cost Pricing Equilibria with Increasing Returns." *Quarterly Journal of Economics* 97:669–87.

Becker, Gary. 1976. *The Economic Approach to Human Behavior*. Chicago: University of Chicago Press.

Beckert, Jens. 1996. "What Is Sociological about Economic Sociology? Uncertainty and the Embeddedness of Economic Action." *Theory and Society* 25:803–40.

Bell, Daniel, and Irving Kristol, eds. 1981. *The Crisis in Economic Theory*. New York: Basic Books.

Bellman, Richard. 1972. *Perturbation Techniques in Mathematics, Physics, and Engineering*. New York: Dover.

Benjamin, Beth, and Joel M. Podolny. 1999. "Status, Quality, and Social Order in the California Wine Industry, 1981–1991." *Administrative Science Quarterly* 44:563–89.

Berk, Richard A., Alec Campbell, Ruth Klapp, and Bruce Western. 1993. "The Deterrent Effect of Arrest in Incidents of Domestic Violence: A Bayesian Analysis of Four Field Experiments." *American Sociological Review* 58.

Berkowitz, S. D. 1982. *An Introduction to Structural Analysis: The Network Approach to Social Research.* Toronto: Butterworths.

———. 1998. "Markets and Market-Areas: Some Preliminary Formulations." Chapter 10 in Wellman and Berkowitz 1998.

Berkowitz, S. D., P. J. Carrington, Y. Kotowirz, and L. Waverman. 1979. "Enterprise Groups." *Social Networks* 1:391–413.

Bessy, Christian, and Eric Brousseau. 1997. "The Governance of Intellectual Property Rights: Patents and Copyrights in France and the U.S." Paper presented at conference "The Present and Future of the New Institutional Economics," September 19–21, Washington University, St. Louis.

Bestor, Theodore C. 1991. "Visible Hands, Auctions, and Institutional Integration in the Tsukyi Wholesale Fish Market, Tokyo." School of Business, Columbia University.

Beth, T., D. Jungnickel, and H. Lenz. 1993. *Design Theory.* Cambridge: Cambridge University Press.

Bhagwati, Jagdish. 1965. "On the Equivalence of Tariffs and Quotas." Chapter 3 in R. E. Baldwin, ed., *Trade, Growth, and the Balance of Payments.* Amsterdam: North-Holland.

Biencourt, Olivier. 1995. "Théorie générale de l'enterprise." Ph.D. diss., Université de Paris X-Nanterre.

———. 1996. "Concurrence par la qualité dans le transport routier de marchandises: Normes ou réseaux?" *Revue d'Economie Industrielle* 75:211–22.

Biencourt, Olivier, and Daniel Urrutiaguer. 2001. "Market Profiles: A Tool Suited for Quality Orders? An Empirical Analysis of Road Haulage and the Theatre." Chapter 8 in Lazega and Favereau 2001.

Birner, Jack. 1996. "Mind, Market, and Society: Network Structures in the Work of F. A. Hayek." Working Paper 1996–2, CEEL Lab, University of Trento, Italy.

———. 1999. "Making Markets." Chapter 3 in Dow and Earl 1999.

Blair, B. 1995. *Elements of Social Theory.* Princeton: Princeton University Press.

Blau, Peter. 1964. *Exchange and Power in Social Life.* New York: Wiley.

Boltanski, Luc, and L. Thevenot. 1987. *Les économies de la grandeur.* Cahier du Paris: Centre d'étude de l'emploi, série Protee and Presse de l'université de Paris.

———. 1991. *De la justification: Les économies de la grandeur.* Paris: Gallimard.

Bonacich, Phillip P. 1987. "Power and Centrality: A Family of Measures." *American Journal of Sociology* 92:1170–82.

Boorman, Scott, and Paul R. Levitt. 1980. *Mathematical Models for the Evolution of Altruistic Behavior.* New York: Academic Press.

Bothner, Matthew S. 1998. "The Informal Workplace." Working Paper 225, Lazarsfeld Center, Columbia University.

———. 2000a. "Structural Position, Economic Performance, and Technology Adoption in the Global Computer Industry." Ph.D. diss., Columbia University.

————. 2000b. "Technical Aspects of Production Market Models." Working Paper 300, Lazarsfeld Center, Columbia University.

————. 2001a. "Contingent Contagion and the Adoption of a New Technology: The Diffusion of the Sixth Generation Processor in the Global Computer Industry." Working paper, University of Chicago, Graduate School of Business.

————. 2001b. "Structure, Scale, and Scope in the Global Computer Industry." Working Paper, University of Chicago, Graduate School of Business."

Bothner, Matthew S., and Harrison C. White. 1999. "Strategic Moves across Kinds of Markets: An Analysis of Consumer Perceptions and Scale Economies." Paper for Conference on Strategic Management, Graduate School of Business, Stanford University.

————. 2000. "Market Orientation and Monopoly Power." Chapter 2 in Lomi and Larsen 2000.

Bott, Elizabeth. 1955. *Family and Social Network*. London: Tavistock.

Boudon, Raymond. 1973. *Educational Opportunity and Social Inequality*. New York: Wiley.

Bourdieu, Pierre. 1984. *Distinction: A Social Critique of the Judgment of Taste*. Trans. Richard Nice. Cambridge: Harvard University Press.

————. 1995. *The Rules of Art*. Stanford: Stanford University Press.

Bowles, Samuel. 1997. "Endogenous Preferences: The Cultural Consequences of Markets and Other Economic Institutions." *Journal of Economic Literature* 36:75–111.

Boyd, John P. 1991. *Social Semigroups: A Unified Theory of Scaling and Blockmodeling as Applied to Social Networks*. Fairfax, Va.: George Mason University Press.

Boyer, Robert, and André Orlean. 1994. "Perception et changement des conventions. Deux modéles simples et quelques illustrations." Pp. 219–47 in Orlean 1994b.

Bradach, Jeffrey L. 1998. *Franchise Organization*. Boston: Harvard Business School Press.

Bradach, Jeffrey L., and Robert G. Eccles. 1989. "Price, Authority, and Trust: From Ideal Types to Plural Forms." *Annual Review of Sociology* 15:97–118.

Braudel, Fernand. 1986. *Civilization and Capitalism*. New York: Harper and Row.

Breiger, Ronald L. 1981. "Structures of Economic Interdependence among Nations." Chapter 12 in Peter M. Blau and Robert K. Merton, eds., *Continuities in Structural Inquiry*. Beverly Hills, Calif.: Sage.

————. 1991. *Explorations in Structural Analysis: Dual and Multiple Networks of Social Interaction*. New York: Garland.

————. 1995. "Social Structure and the Phenomenology of Attainment." *Annual Review of Sociology* 21:115–36.

Bresnahan, Timothy F. 1989. "Empirical Studies of Industries with Market Power." Chapter 17 in Schmalensee and Willig 1989.

Brittain, Jack W., and Douglas Wholey. 1988. "Environmental Dynamics and Community Structure: Competition and Coexistence in Electronics Manufacturing." Pp. 195–222 in G. Carroll, ed., *Ecological Models*. Boston: Ballinger Press.

————. 1990. Chapter 7 in Ronald W. Breiger, ed., *Structural Analysis*. Cambridge: Cambridge University Press.

Brown, Gillian, and George Yule. 1983. *Discourse Analysis*. Cambridge: Cambridge University Press.

Bryson, Arthur, and Yu-Chi Ho. 1969. *Applied Optimal Control*. Waltham, Mass.: Blaisdell.

Burns, Tom. 1992. *Erving Goffman*. London: Routledge.

Burt, Ronald S. 1979. "A Structural Theory of Interlocking Directorates." *Social Networks* 1:415–35.

———. 1983. *Corporate Profits and Co-optation: Networks of Market Constraints and Directorate Ties in the American Economy*. New York: Academic Press.

———. 1987. "Social Contagion and Innovation: Cohesion versus Structural Equivalence." *American Journal of Sociology* 92:1287–1335.

———. 1988a. "The Stability of American Markets." *American Journal of Sociology* 93:356–95.

———. 1988b. "Some Properties of Structural Equivalence Measures Derived from Sociometric Choice Data." *Social Networks* 10:1–28.

———. 1990. "Detecting Role Equivalence." *Social Networks* 12:83–97.

———. 1992. *Structural Holes*. Cambridge: Harvard University Press.

Burt, Ronald S., and Debbie S. Carlton. 1989. "Another Look at the Network Boundaries of American Markets." *American Journal of Sociology* 94:723–53.

Burt, Ronald S., and Ilan Talmud. 1992. "Market Niche." *Social Networks* 14:97–117.

Buzzell, Robert D., Bradley T. Gale, and Ralph G. M. Sultan. 1975. "Market Share—a Key to Profitability." *Harvard Business Review* 53:97–106.

Buzzell, Robert D., and P. W. Farris. 1977. "Marketing Costs in Consumer Goods Industries." Pp. 122–45 in H. B. Thorelli, ed., *Strategy + Structure = Performance*. Bloomington: Indiana University Press.

Buzzell, Robert D., and Frederik D. Wiersma. 1981. "Modelling Changes in Market Share: A Cross-Sectional Analysis." *Strategic Management Journal* 2:27–42.

Bythell, Duncan. 1978. *The Sweated Trades: Outwork in Nineteenth Century Britain*. London: St. Martin's.

Callen, Herbert B. 1960. *Thermodynamics: An Introduction to the Physical Theories of Equilibrium Thermostatics and Irreversible Thermodynamics*. New York: Wiley.

Cameron, Peter J. 1994. *Combinatorics: Topics, Techniques, Algorithms*. Cambridge: Cambridge University Press.

Campbell, John L., J. Rogers Hollingsworth, and Leon N. Lindberg, eds. 1991. *Governance of the American Economy*. Cambridge: Cambridge University Press.

Carley, Kathleen M. 1991. "A Theory of Group Stability." *American Sociological Review* 56:331–54.

———. 1992. "Extracting, Representing, and Analyzing Mental Models." *Social Forces* 70:601–36.

———. 1993. "Coding Choices for Textual Analysis: A Comparison of Content Analysis and Map Analysis." Chapter 5 in P. Marsen, ed., *Sociological Methodology*, vol. 25. Oxford: Blackwell.

———. 1999. "Extracting Team Mental Models through Textual Analysis." Chapter 5 in Andrews and Knoke 1999.

Carley, Kathleen M., and David Krackhardt. 1996. "Cognitive Inconsistencies and Non-symmetric Friendship." *Social Networks* 18:1–27.

Carlton, Dennis W. 1989. "The Theory and the Facts of How Markets Clear: Is Industrial Organization Valuable for Understanding Macroeconomics?" Chapter 15 in Schmalensee and Willig 1989.

Carroll, Glenn R. 1985. "Concentration and Specialization: dynamics of Niche Width in populations of Organizations." *American Journal of Sociology* 90:1262–83.

———, ed. 1988. *Ecological Models of Organizations*. Cambridge, Mass.: Ballinger.

Carroll, Glenn R., and Michael Hannan, eds. 1995. *Organizations in Industry: Strategy, Structure, and Selection*. New York: Oxford University Press.

———. 2000. *The Demography of Corporations and Industries*. Princeton: Princeton University Press.

Carruthers, Bruce. 1996. *City of Capital: Politics and Markets in the English Financial Revolution*. Princeton: Princeton University Press.

Carruthers, Bruce, and Wendy N. Espeland. 1991. "Accounting for Rationality: Double-Entry Bookkeeping and the Rhetoric of Economic Rationality." *American Journal of Sociology* 97:31–69.

Carter, Anne P. 1976. *Structural Change in the American Economy*. Cambridge: Harvard University Press.

Castleman, 1996. *Fodor Guide to Las Vegas*. New York.

Chamberlin, Edwin H. 1962. *The Theory of Monopolistic Competition*. 8th ed. Cambridge: Harvard University Press.

Chandler, A. 1962. *Strategy and Structure: Chapters in the History of the American Business Enterprise*. Cambridge: MIT Press.

———. 1977. *The Visible Hand*. Cambridge: Harvard University Press.

Charnes, A., W. W. Cooper, and A. P. Schinnar. 1976. "A Theorem on Homogeneous Functions and Extended Cobb-Douglas Forms." *Proceedings, National Academy of Sciences* 73:3747–48.

Chase, Ivan D. 1974. "Models of Hierarchy Formation in Animal Societies." *Behavioral Science* 19:374–82.

———. 2002. *Hierarchy Formation in Animal Societies* Cambridge: Harvard University Press.

Christensen, L. R., D. W. Jorgenson, and L. J. Lau. 1975. "Transcendental Logarithmic Utility Functions." *American Economic Review* 65:367–83.

Cicourel, Aaron V. 1989. "Elicitation as a Problem of Discourse." Pp. 903–10 in U. Ammon, N. Dittmar, and K. Mattheier, eds., *Sociolinguistics: An International Handbook of the Science of Language and Society*, vol. 2. Berlin: de Gruyter.

———. 1992. "The Interpenetration of Communicative Contexts: Examples from Medical Encounters." Chapter 11 in Duranti and Goodwin 1992.

Coase, Ronald. 1937. "The Nature of the Firm." *Economica* 4:386–405.

———. 1992. "The Institutional Structure of Production." *American Economic Review* 82:713–19.

Cobb, C. W., and P. H. Douglas. 1928. "A theory of Production." *American Economic Review* 18:139–65.

Coleman, James C. 1961. *Adolescent Society*. New York: Free Press.

———. 1964. *Introduction to Mathematical Sociology*. New York: Free Press.

Collins, Randall. 1986. *Weberian Sociological Theory*. Cambridge: Cambridge University Press.

———. 1988. *Theoretical Sociology*. San Diego: Harcourt Brace Jovanovich.

————. 1994. *Four Sociological Traditions.* New York: Oxford University Press.

Comrie, Bernard. 1983. *Tense.* Cambridge: Cambridge University Press.

Corey, E. Raymond. 1978. *Procurement Management: Strategy, Organization, and Decision-Making.* Boston: CBI.

Cuff, Robert D. 1973. *The War Industries Board.* Baltimore: Johns Hopkins University Press.

David, Paul. 2000. "Understanding Digital Technology's Evolution and the Path of Measured Productivity Growth: Present and Future in the Mirror of the Past." Chapter 13 in E. Brynolfsson and B. Kahn, eds., *Understanding the Digital Economy.* Cambridge: MIT Press.

Davidson, Paul. 1981. "Post-Keynesian Economics." Chapter 10 in Bell and Kristol 1981.

Davis, Gerald F., and Suzanne K. Stout. 1992. "Organization Theory and the Market for Corporate Control." *Administrative Science Quarterly* 37:605–33.

deBruijn, N. G. 1961. *Asymptotic Methods in Analysis.* Amsterdam: North-Holland.

Degenne, Alain, and Michel Forsé. 1999. *Social Networks.* Beverly Hills, Calif.: Sage.

Degenne, Alain, and Anne-Marie Lebeaux. 1994. Galois Correspondences: Software with annotations. Paris: LASMAS.

de Gennes, Pierre-Gilles. 1979. *Scaling Concepts in Polymer Physics.* Ithaca, N.Y.: Cornell University Press.

————. 1999. "Molecular Individualism." *Science* 276:299.

Dehez, Pierre, and Jacques H. Dreze. 1984. "On Supply-Constrained Equilibria." *Journal of Economic Theory* 33:172–82.

Dejoia, A., and A. Stenton. 1980. *Terms in Systemic Linguistics: A Guide to Halliday.* New York: St. Martin's.

De Vany, A. S., and T. R. Saving. 1977. "Product Quality, Uncertainty, and Regulation: The Trucking Industry." *American Economic Review* 67:583–94.

DiMaggio, Paul. 1992. "Nadel's Paradox Revisited." Chapter 4 in Nohria and Eccles 1992.

————. 1994. "Culture and Economy." Pp. 27–58 in Smelser and Swedberg 1994.

————. 1997. "Culture and Cognition: An Interdisciplinary Review." *Annual Review of Sociology* 23:301–20.

DiMaggio, Paul, and W. W. Powell. 1983. "The Iron Cage Revisited: Institutional Isomorphism and collective Rationality in Organizational Fields." *American Sociological Review* 48:147–60.

Dixit, Avinash K. 1982. "Recent Developments in Oligopoly Theory." *American Economic Review* 72:12–17.

Dixit, Avinash K., and Joseph E. Stiglitz. 1977. "Monopolistic Competition and Optimum Product Diversity." *American Economic Review* 67:297–308.

Dobbin, Frank. 1994. *Forging Industrial Policy: The United States, Britain, and France in the Railway Age.* Cambridge: Cambridge University Press.

Dobbin, Frank, and Timothy Dowd. 1998. "Was There a Market before Antitrust?" Chapter 13 in Joseph Porac and Mark Ventresca, eds., *Constructing Markets and Industries.* New York: Pergamon.

Donnellan, John. 1996. *Merchandise Buying and Management.* New York: Fairchild.

Dorfman, Robert, Paul A. Samuelson, and Robert M. Solow. 1958. *Linear Programming and Economic Analysis.* New York: McGraw-Hill.

Dow, Sheila C., and Peter E. Earl, eds. 1999. *Economic Organization and Economic Knowledge: Essays in Honour of Brian J. Loasby*. Vol. 1. Cheltenham, U.K.: Elgar.

Duranti, Alessandro. 1992. "Language in Context and Language as Context: The Samoan Respect Vocabulary." Chapter 3 in Duranti and Goodwin 1992.

Duranti, Alessandro, and Charles Goodwin, eds. 1992. *Rethinking Context: Language as an Interactive Process*. Cambridge: Cambridge University Press.

Eaton, B. Curtis, and Richard G. Lipsey. 1989. "Product Differentiation." Chapter 12 in Schmalensee and Willig 1989.

Eccles, Robert G. 1981. "Bureaucratic versus Craft Administration: The Relationship of Market Structure to the Construction Firm." *Administrative Science Quarterly* 26:449–69.

———. 1985. *The Transfer Pricing Problem: A Theory for Practice*. Lexington, Mass.: Lexington Books.

Eccles, Robert G., and Dwight B. Crane. 1988. *Doing Deals: Investment Banks at Work*. Boston: Harvard Business School Press.

Eccles, Robert G., and Nitin Nohria. 1994. *Beyond the Hype: Rediscovering the Essence of Management*. Boston: Harvard Business School Press.

Eccles, Robert G., and Harrison C. White. 1986a. "Concentration for Control? Political and Business Evidence." *Sociological Forum* 1:131–58.

———. 1986b. "Firm and Market Interfaces of Profit Center Control." Chapter 7 in Siegwart Lindenberg, James S. Coleman, and Stefan Nowak, eds. *Approaches to Social Theory*. New York: Russell Sage.

———. 1987. "Producers' Markets." Pp. 984–86 in *The New Palgrave: A Dictionary of Economic Theory and Doctrine*. New York: Stockton.

———. 1988. "Price and Authority in Inter–Profit Center Transactions." *American Journal of Sociology*, suppl. 94: S17–S51.

Emirbayer, M., and J. Goodwin. 1994. "Network Analysis, Culture, and the Problem of Agency." *American Journal of Sociology* 99:1411–54.

Enelow, James M., and Melvin J. Hinich, eds. 1990. *Advances in the Spatial Theory of Voting*. Cambridge: Cambridge University Press.

Evans, Peter B. 1977. "Multiple Hierarchies and Organization Control." *Administrative Science Quarterly* 22:364–85.

———. 1995. *Embedded Autonomy*. Berkeley and Los Angeles: University of California Press.

Eymard-Duvernay, F. 1989. "Conventions de qualité et formes de coordination." *Revue économique* 40:329–59.

———. 1993. "Conventions d'entreprise et marché du travail." *Les cahiers des relations professionelles* 9 (novembre), MRASH, Lyon.

———. 1994. "Coordination des échanges par l'enterprise et qualité des biens." Pp. 329–59 in Orlean 1994b.

Eymard-Duvernay, F., and Olivier Favereau. 1990. "Marchés internes, modéles d'entreprises et conventions de qualité: Matériaux pour une formalisation non standard du marché des biens." Paper presented at the Seventh Conference on Applied Microeconomics, Quebec, May.

Fararo, Thomas J. 1973. *Mathematical Sociology*. New York: Wiley.

Faulkner, Robert R. 1983. *Music on Demand: Composers and Careers in the Hollywood Film Industry*. New Brunswick, N.J.: Transaction Books.

Faulkner, Robert R., and Wayne E. Baker. 1996. "Ties of Firms with Ad Agencies." Paper presented at the Rational Choice session, Annual Meeting of the American Sociological Association, New York.

Favereau, Olivier. 1988. "Probability and Uncertainty: 'After All, Keynes Was Right.'" *Economia*, October, 133–67.

———. 1989. "L'économique des conventions." *Revue économique* 40:273–329.

———. 1994a. "L'économie doit définir le marché a partir de l'entreprise, plutot que l'inverse—une relecture du modéle de White en termes de conventions." Paper presented at a colloquium of the Society for Socio-Economics, Paris, July.

———. 1994b. "Régle, organisation et apprentissage collectif: Un paradigme non standard pour trois théories hétérodoxes." Pp. 113–37 in Orlean 1994b.

———. 1997. "Economics and Its Models." Manuscript, Université Paris X–Nanterre.

Feller, William. 1962. *Introduction to Probability Theory and Its Applications*. 2d ed. New York: Wiley.

Finley, M. I. 1973. *The Ancient Economy*. Berkeley and Los Angeles: University of California Press.

Fischhoff, Baruch. 1993. "Value Elicitation: Is There Anything in There?" Chapter 9 in Hechter, Nadel, and Michod 1993.

Flaherty, M. Louise. 1980. "Industry Structure and Cost-Reducing Investment." *Econometrica* 48:1187–1209.

Fligstein, Neil. 1985. "The Spread of the Multidivisonal Form among Large Firms, 1919–1979." *American Sociological Review* 50:377–91.

———. 1990. *The Transformation of Corporate Control*. Cambridge: Harvard University Press.

———. 1996. "Markets as Politics: A Political-Cultural Approach to Market Institutions." *American Sociological Review* 61:228–44.

———. 2001. *The Architecture of Markets*. Princeton: Princeton University Press.

Fligstein, Neil, and Robert Freeland. 1995. "Theoretical and Comparative Perspectives on Corporate Organization." *Annual Review of Sociology* 21:21–43.

Fligstein, Neil, and Iona Mara-Drita. 1992. "How to Make a Market: Reflections on the European Union's Single-Market Program." *American Journal of Sociology* 102:1–34.

Franzosi, Roberto. 1995. *The Puzzle of Strikes*. Cambridge: Cambridge University Press.

Freeland, Robert F. 1996. "The Myth of the M-Form: Governance, Consent, and Organizational Change." *American Journal of Sociology* 102:483–526.

Freeman, Linton C., Douglas R. White, and A. Kimball Romney, eds. 1989. *Research Methods in Social Network Analysis*. Fairfax, Va.: George Mason University Press.

Freeman, Linton C., and Douglas R. White. 1994 "Using Galois Lattices to Represent Network Data." *Sociological Methodology* 23:127–46.

Freyd, Jennifer J. 1993. "Five Hunches about Perceptual Processes and Dynamic Representations." In D. Meyer and S. Kornblum, eds., *Attention and Performance*, 14:99–119. Cambridge: MIT Press.

Friedell, Morris. 1967. "Organizations as Semilattices." *American Sociological Review* 32:46–54.

Friedkin, Noah. 1998. *A Structural Theory of Social Influence*. Cambridge: Cambridge University Press.

Fudenberg, D., and J. Tirole. 1991. *Game Theory*. Cambridge: MIT Press.

Furubotn, E., and R. Richter, eds. 1991. *The New Institutional Economics*. Tübingen: J. C. B. Mohr.

Gal, Susan. 1979. *Language Shift: Social Determinants of Linguistic Change in Bilingual Austria*. New York: Academic Press.

Galbraith, John Kenneth. 1967. *The New Industrial State*. Boston: Houghton Mifflin.

Gale, Bradley T., Donald F. Heany, and Donald J. Swire. 1977. "The Par ROI Report: Explanation and Commentary on Report." Strategic Planning Institute, PIMS Program, January, pp. 1–19.

Gargiulo, Martin. 1993. "Two-Step Leverage: Managing Constraint in Organizational Politics." *Administrative Science Quarterly* 39:1–19.

———. 1999. "Informal Networks, Social Control and Third-Party Cooperation." Working Paper 99/04/OB, INSEAD.

Geanakoplos, John. 1997. "Promises, Promises." Pp. 285–321 in Arthur, Durlauf, and Lane 1997.

Gerlach, Michael. 1992. *Alliance Capitalism: The Social Organization of Japanese Business*. Berkeley and Los Angeles: University of California Press.

Gibson, David. 1999. "Taking Turns in Business Talk." Preprint 225, Center for the Social Sciences, Columbia University.

Gibson, David, and Ann Mische. 1995. "Internetwork Encounters and the Emergence of Leadership." Preprint, Center for the Social Sciences, Columbia University, February.

Gibson, James J. 1979. *The Ecological Approach to Visual Perception*. Boston: Houghton Mifflin.

Gilbert, Richard J. 1989. "Mobility Barriers and the Value of Incumbency." Chapter 8 in Schmalensee and Willig 1989.

Giuffre, Katherine. 1996. "Social Networks in the Art World: Status, Style, and Occupational Success." Ph.D. diss., University of North Carolina, Chapel Hill.

Goffman, Erving. 1969. *Strategic Interaction*. Philadelphia: University of Pennsylvania Press.

———. 1974. *Frame Analysis*. New York: Harper and Row.

Gold, Bela. 1981. "Changing Perspectives on Size, Scale, and Returns: An Interpretive Survey." *Journal of Economic Literature* 19:5–33.

Goodwin, Charles, and Marjorie Harness Goodwin. 1992. "Assessments and the Construction of Context." Chapter 6 in Duranti and Goodwin 1992.

Gould, Roger V. 1995. *Insurgent Identities: Class, Community, and Protest in Paris from 1848 to the Commune*. Chicago: University of Chicago Press.

Gould, Roger V., and Roberto Fernandez. 1989. "Structures of Mediation: A Formal Approach to Brokerage in Transaction Networks." Pp. 89–126 in Clifford Clogg, ed., *Sociological Methodology, 1989*. Oxford: Blackwell.

Gramley, Stephan, and Kurt-Michael Pätzold. 1992. *A Survey of Modern English*. London: Routledge.

Granick, David. 1975. *Enterprise Guidance in Eastern Europe: A Comparison of Four Socialist Economies*. Princeton: Princeton University Press.

Granovetter, Mark. 1974. *Getting a Job: A Study of Contacts and Careers*. Cambridge: Harvard University Press.

———. 1985. "Economic Action and Social Structure: The Problem of Embeddedness." *American Journal of Sociology* 91:481–510.

———. 1994. "Business Groups." Pp. 453–76 in Smelser and Swedberg 1994.

———. 1995. "Coase Revisited: Business Groups in the Modern Economy." *Industrial and Corporate Change* 4:93–140.

Griliches, Zvi, and M. Ohta. 1976. "Automobile Prices Revisited: Extensions of the Hedonic Hypothesis." Chapter 8 in Terleckyj 1976.

Griliches, Zvi, and V. Ringstad. 1971. *Economies of Scale and the Form of the Production Function.* Amsterdam: North-Holland.

Groenewegen, Peter. 1999. "Perfect Competition, Equilibrium, and Economic Progress: That Wretched Division of Labor and Increasing Returns." Chapter 12 in Dow and Earl 1999.

Gulati, Ranjay, and Martin Gargiulo. 1999. "Where Do Interorganizational Networks Come From?" *American Journal of Sociology* 105:177–231.

Gulvin, Clifford. 1984. *The Scottish Hosiery and Knitwear Industry: 1680–1980.* Edinburgh: John Donald.

Gumperz, John J. 1992. "Contextualization and Understanding." Chapter 8 in Duranti and Goodwin 1992.

———. 1982. *Discourse Strategies.* Cambridge: Cambridge University Press.

Gumperz, John J., and Dell Hymes, eds. 1986. *Directions in Sociolinguistics: The Ethnography of Communication.* Oxford: Blackwell.

Guthrie, Douglas. 1999. *Dragon in a Three-Piece Suit.* Princeton: Princeton University Press.

Hage, Per, and Frank Harary. 1996. *Island Networks.* Cambridge: Cambridge University Press.

Hahn, Frank. 1981. "General Equilibrium Theory." Chapter 8 in Bell and Kristol 1981.

Halliday, M. A. K. 1976. *System and Function in Language: Selected Papers.* Ed. G. R. Kress. London: Oxford University Press.

———. 1994. *An Introduction to Functional Grammar.* 2d ed. London: Edward Arnold.

Hamblin, Robert L., R. B. Jacobsen, and Jerry L. L. Miller. 1973. *A Mathematical Theory of Social Change.* New York: Wiley.

Hambrick, Donald C., Ian C. MacMillan, and Diana L. Day. 1982. "Strategic Attributes and Performance in the BCG Matrix: A PIMS-Based Analysis of Industrial Product Businesses." *Academy of Management Journal* 25:510–31.

Hamilton, Gary G., ed. 1996. *Asian Business Networks.* New York: de Gruyter.

Hamilton, Gary G., William Zeile, and Wan-Jon Kim. 1990. "The Network Structures of East Asian Economies." Chapter 3 in S. R. Clegg and S. G. Redding, eds., *Capitalism in Contrasting Cultures.* Berlin: de Gruyter.

Han, Shin-Kap. 1991. "Unstable Firms in Stable Markets: A Paradox of Imperfect Competition." Department of Sociology, Columbia University, March.

———. 1992. "Churning Firms in Stable Markets." *Social Science Research* 21:406–18.

———. 1995. "Mimetic Isomorphism and Its Effect on the Audit Services Market." *Social Forces* 73:637–64.

———. 1996. "Structuring Relations in On-the-Job Networks." *Social Networks* 18:30–48.

Hanks, William F. 1990. *Referential Practice: Language and Lived Space among the Maya.* Chicago: University of Chicago Press.

———. 1992. "The Indexical Ground of Deictic Reference." Chapter 2 in Duranti and Goodwin 1992.

Hannan, Michael T. 1998. "Rethinking Age Dependence in Organizational Mortality." *American Journal of Sociology* 104:126–65.

Hannan, Michael T., and John Freeman. 1977. "The Population Ecology of Organizations." *American Journal of Sociology* 89:929–64.

———. 1989. *Organizational Ecology*. Cambridge: Harvard University Press.

Hansmann, Henry. 1981. "Nonprofit Enterprise in the Performing Arts." *Bell Journal of Economics* 12:341–61.

Hardie, Bruce B. S., Eric J. Johnson, and Peter S. Fader. 1993. "Modeling Loss Aversion and Reference Dependence Effects on Brand Choice." *Marketing Science* 12:378–94.

Hart, C., and A. Pilling. 1960.*The Tiwi*. New York: Holt.

Haveman, Heather, and Lynn Nonnemaker. 1996. "Competition in Multiple Geographic Markets: The Impact on Market Entry and Growth." Johnson Graduate School of Management, Cornell University, September.

Haveman, Heather, and Hayagreeva Rao. "Structuring a Theory of Moral Sentiments: Institutional and Organizational Co-evolution in the Early California Thrift Industry." *American Journal of Sociology* 102:1606–51.

Hay, Donald A., and Guy S. Liu. 1998. "The Investment Behaviour of Firms in an Oligopolistic Setting." *Journal of Industrial Economics* 46:79–99.

Hazelrigg, Lawrence. 1997. "On the Importance of Age." Pp. 93–128 in Melissa A. Hardy, ed., *Studying Aging and Social Change*. Thousand Oaks, Calif.: Sage.

Hechter, Michael, Lynn Nadel, and Richard E. Michod, eds. 1993. *The Origin of Values*. New York: Aldine de Gruyter.

Hedstrom, Peter, and Richard Swedberg. 1998. *Social Mechanisms: An Analytical Approach to Social Theory*. Cambridge: Cambridge University Press.

Henderson, James M., and Richard E. Quandt. 1980. *Microeconomic Theory: A Mathematical Approach*. 3d ed. New York: McGraw-Hill.

Herrigel, Gary. 1996. *Industrial Constructions: The Sources of German Industrial Power*. Cambridge: Cambridge University Press.

Hicks, John. 1946. *Value and Capital*. London: Macmillan.

Hirsch, Morris W., and Stephen Smale. 1974. *Differential Equations, Dynamical Systems, and Linear Algebra*. New York: Academic Press.

Hirsch, Paul M. 1972. "Processing Fads and Fashions: An Organization-Set Analysis of Cultural Industry Systems." *American Journal of Sociology* 77:639–59.

———. 1993. "Undoing the Managerial Revolution? Needed Research on the Decline of Middle Management and Internal Labor Markets." Pp. 145–57 in Swedberg 1993.

Hochberg, Julian E. 1990. "Gibson and the Psychology of Perception: After the Revolution." *Contemporary Psychology* 35:750–52.

Hofbauer, Josef, and Karl Sigmund. 1988. *The Theory of Evolution and Dynamical Systems*. Cambridge: Cambridge University Press.

Hopper, Paul J., and Elizabeth C. Traugott. 1993. *Grammaticalization*. Cambridge: Cambridge University Press.

Hotelling, H. 1927. "Stability In Competition." *Economic Journal* 39: 41–57.

Hsu, Greta, and Joel M. Podolny. 2001. "Critiquing the Critics: An Approach to Comparative Evaluation of Critical Schemas." Graduate School of Business, Stanford University, February 27.

Hubert, L., and Phipps Arabie. 1989. "Combinatorial Data Analysis: Confirmatory Comparisons between Sets of Matrices." *Applied Stochastic Models and Data Analysis* 5:273–325.

Ijiri, Yuji. 1975. *Theory of Accounting Measurement*. American Accounting Association, Studies in Research 10.

Ijiri, Yuji, and Herbert A. Simon. 1977. *Skew Distributions and the Sizes of Business Firms*. Amsterdam: North-Holland.

Ingham, Geoffrey K. 1970. *Size of Industrial Organization and Worker Behaviour*. Cambridge: Cambridge University Press.

Ingram, Paul, and Peter W. Roberts. 2000. "Friendships among Competitors in the Sydney Hotel Industry." *American Journal of Sociology* 106:387–423.

Ingram, Paul, and C. Inmar. 1996. "Institution, Intergroup Competition, and Evolution of the Hotel Population around Niagara Falls." *Administrative Science Quarterly* 41:629–58.

Jackson, Gregory. 1994. "Economic Sociology: Theories of the Economy as a Social Process." Department of Sociology, Columbia University, May.

Jacquemin, Alexis, and Margaret E. Slade. 1989. "Cartels, Collusion, and Horizontal Merger." Chapter 7 in Schmalensee and Willig 1989.

Jervis, Robert. 1970. *The Logic of Images in International Relations*. Princeton: Princeton University Press.

Jevons, W. Stanley. 1907. *Money and the Mechanism of Exchange*. New York: Appleton.

Johnsen, Eugene C. 1985. "Network Macrostructure Models for the Davis-Leinhardt Set of Empirical Sociomatrices." *Social Networks* 7:203–24.

Johnson, James Q. 1983. "Generalization by Analytic Continuity." Department of Sociology, Harvard University, spring.

Jorion, Paul. 1992. "Le prix comme proportion chez Aristote." *Revue du MAUSS* 15–16:100–110.

Kaplan, Robert S. 1982. *Advanced Management Accounting*. Englewood Cliffs, N.J.: Prentice-Hall.

Katz, Michael L. 1989. "Vertical Contractual Relation." Chapter 11 in Schmalensee and Willig 1989.

Kirman, Alan P. 1997. "The Economy as an Interactive System." Pp. 491–532 in Arthur, Durlauf, and Lane 1997.

Knight, Frank. 1971. *Risk, Uncertainty, and Profit*. 1921; rpt. Chicago: University of Chicago Press.

Knoke, David, and Ronald S. Burt. 1983. "Prominence." Chapter 9 in Ronald S. Burt and Michael J. Minor, eds., *Applied Network Analysis*. Beverly Hills, Calif.: Sage.

Kochen, Manfred, ed. 1989. *The Small World*. Norwood, N.J.: Ablex.

Kogut, Bruce, Weijian Shan, and Gordon Walker. 1992. "The Make-or-Cooperate Decision in the Context of an Industry Network." Chapter 13 in Nohria and Eccles 1992.

Kogut, Bruce, and Gordon Walker. 1999. "The Small World of Firm Ownership in Germany: Social Capital and Structural Holes in Large Firm Acquisitions—1993–1997." Wharton School of Business, University of Pennsylvania.

Kontopolous, K. M. 1993. *The Logics of Social Structure*. Cambridge: Cambridge University Press.

Krackhardt, David. 1987. "Cognitive Social Structures." *Social Networks* 9:109–34.

———. 1994. "Endogenous Preferences: A Structural Approach." Heinz School of Public Policy and Management, Carnegie Mellon University, September.

Kramer, Stella. 1927. *The English Craft Guilds: Studies in Their Progress and Decline*. New York: Columbia University Press.

Kreps, David M. 1997. "Economics—the Current Position." *Daedalus* 126:59–87.

Kriedte, Peter, Hans Medick, and Jurgen Shlumbohm. 1981. *Industrialization before Industrialisation*. Cambridge: Cambridge University Press.

Krugman, Paul R. 1980. "Scale Economies, Product Differentiation, and the Pattern of Trade." *American Economic Review* 70:950–59.

———. 1989. "Industrial Organization and International Trade." Chapter 20 in Schmalensee and Willig 1989.

Kuramoto, Y. 1975. "Self-Entrainment of a Population of Coupled Non-linear Oscillators." Chapter 29 in H. Araki, ed., *International Symposium on Mathematical Problems in Theoretical Physics: Lecture Notes in Physics*, vol. 39. New York: Springer Verlag.

Lachmann, Richard. 1987. *From Manor to Market*. Madison: University of Wisconsin Press.

Lachmann, Richard, and Stephen Petterson. 1995. *American Journal of Sociology*.

Lancaster, Kelvin J. 1970. "A New Approach to Consumer Theory." *Journal of Political Economy* 74:132–57.

Langlois, Richard. 1999. "Scale, Scope, and the Reuse of Knowledge." Chapter 13 in Dow and Earl 1999.

Larson, Magali Sarfatti. 1993. *Behind the Modernist Facade*. Berkeley and Los Angeles: University of California Press.

Laufer, Romain. 1990. "Marque, Marketing et Légitimité." Pp. 320–27 in Jean-Noel Kapferer and Jean-Claude Thoenig, eds., *La Marque*. New York: McGraw-Hill.

Laufer, Romain, and Catherine Paradeise. 1990. *Marketing Democracy: Public Opinion and Media Formation in Democratic Societies*. New Brunswick, N.J.: Transaction Books.

Lawrence, Paul R., and Davis Dyer. 1983. *Renewing American Industries*. New York: Macmillan and Free Press.

Lazega, Emmanuel. 1992. *Micropolitics of Knowledge: Communication and Indirect Control in Workgroups*. New York: de Gruyter.

———. 2000. "Rule Enforcement among Peers: A Lateral Control Regime." *Organization Studies* 21:1–22.

Lazega, Emmanuel, and Olivier Favereau, eds. 2001. *Conventions and Structures*. London: Elgar.

Lazega, Emmanuel, and Lise Mounier. 2000. "Structural Economic Sociology in a Society of Organizations." Chapter 2 in Lazega and Favereau 2000.

Lazerson, Mark. 1993. "Future Alternatives of Work Reflected in the Past: Putting-Out Production in Modena." Chapter 15 in Swedberg 1993.

———. 1995. "A New Phoenix: Modern Putting-Out in the Modern Knitwear Industry." *Administrative Science Quarterly* 40:34–59.

Lazerson, Mark, and Gianni Lorenzoni. 1996. "The Networks That Feed Industrial

Districts: A Return to the Italian Source." Department of Sociology, State University of New York, Stony Brook.

Lazonick, William. 1991. *Business Organization and the Myth of the Market Economy*. Cambridge: Cambridge University Press.

Leach, Edmund R. 1954. *The Political Systems of Highland Burma*. Boston: Beacon.

Leamer, Edward. 1978. *Specification Searches: Ad Hoc Inference with Non-experimental Data*. New York: Wiley.

LeBlanc, Greg. 1998. "Informative Advertising Competition." *Journal of Industrial Economics* 41:63–77.

Leifer, Eric M. 1985. "Markets as Mechanisms: Using a Role Structure." *Social Forces*. 64:442–72.

———. 1987. "Design a Market: Market Questionnaire." BPA Market Simulation Project, School of Business, University of Arizona.

———. 1991. *Actors as Observers: A Theory of Skill and Social Relationships*. New York: Garland.

———. 1995. *Making the Majors; The Transformation of Team Sports in America*. Cambridge: Harvard University Press.

Leifer, Eric M., and Harrison C. White. 1986. "Wheeling and Annealing: Federal and Multidivisional Control." Chapter 3 in James F. Short, ed., *The Social Fabric: Issues and Dimensions*. Beverly Hills, Calif.: Sage.

———. 1987. "A Structural Approach to Markets." Chapter 6 in Mizruchi and Schwartz 1987.

Leik, Robert K., and Barbara F. Meeker. 1975. *Mathematical Sociology*. Englewood Cliffs, N.J.: Prentice-Hall.

Leontief, Wassily W. 1951. *The Structure of the American Economy*. New York: Oxford University Press.

———. 1966. *Input-Output Economics*. New York: Oxford University Press.

Levine, Joel H. 1993. *Exceptions Are the Rule*. Boulder, Colo.: Westview.

Levinson, Stephen C. 1983. *Pragmatics*. Cambridge: Cambridge University Press.

Leydesdaaft, V., and P. V. D. Bessela, eds. 1994. *Evolutionary Economics and Chaos Theory*. London: Pinter.

Lie, John. 1997. "Sociology of Markets." *Annual Review of Sociology* 23:341–60.

Lindenberg, Siegwart. 1995. "Complex Constraint Modeling: A Bridge between Rational Choice and Structuralism." *Journal of Institutional and Theoretical Economics* 151:80–88.

———. 1996. "Multiple-Tie Networks, Structural Advantage, and Path-Dependency: Another Look at Hybrid Forms of Governance." *Journal of Institutional and Theoretical Economics* 152.

———. 2000. "It Takes Both Trust and Lack of Mistrust: The Workings of Cooperation and Relational Signaling in Contractual Relationships." *Journal of Management and Governance* 4:11–11.

Lindenberg, Siegwart, and B. Frey. 1993. "Alternatives, Frames, and Relative Prices: A Broader View of Rational Choice." *Acta Sociologica* 36:191–205.

Lindenberg, Siegwart, and Hein Schroeder, eds. 1992. *Interdisciplinary Perspectives on Organization*. Oxford: Pergamon.

Loasby, Brian J. 1993. "Institutional Stability and Change in Science and the Economy." Chapter 8 in Maki, Gustafsson, and Knudsen 1993.

Lomi, Alessandro, and Erik Larsen, eds. 2000. *Simulating Organizational Societies: Theories, Models, and Ideas.* London: Pergamon.

Lucy, John A., ed. 1993. *Reflexive Language: Reported Speech and Metapragmatics.* Cambridge: Cambridge University Press.

Luhmann, Niklas. 1995. *Social Systems.* Trans. John Bednarz Jr., with Dirk Baeder. Stanford: Stanford University Press.

Lumer, Erik D., and Bernardo A. Huberman. 1991. "Hierarchical Dynamics in Large Assemblies of Interacting Oscillators." *Physics Letters A* 160:227–32.

Macy, M. W. 1991. "Chains of Cooperation: Threshold Effects in Collective Action." *American Sociological Review* 56:730–47.

Maki, Uskali, Bo Gustafsson, and Christian Knudsen, eds. 1993. *Rationality, Institutions, and Economic Methodology.* London: Routledge.

Malerba, Franco, Richard Nelson, Luigi Orsenigo, and Sidney Winter. 1999. "'History-Friendly' Models of Industry Evolution: The Computer Industry." *Industrial and Corporate Change* 8:1–36.

Mansfield, Edwin. 1968. *The Economics of Technical Change.* New York: Norton.

———. 1975. *Microeconomics: Theory and Applications.* New York: Norton.

Mansfield, Roger. 1987. "Commentary on Chapter 7." Pp. 256–60 in Andrew M. Pettigrew, ed., *The Management of Strategic Change.* Oxford: Basil Blackwell.

March, James G., and J. P. Olsen. 1976. *Ambiguity and Choice in Organizations.* Bergen: Universitetsforlaget.

March, James G., and Herbert A. Simon. 1958. *Organizations.* New York: Wiley.

Marschak, J., and W. H. Andrews. 1944. "Random Simultaneous Equations and the Theory of Production." *Econometrica* 12:143–205.

Marshall, Alfred. 1923. *Industry and Trade.* London: Macmillan.

———. 1930. *Principles of Economics.* 8th ed. London.

Mattson, Lars-Gunnar. 1987. "Management of Strategic Change in a 'Markets-as-Networks' Perspective." Chapter 7 in Andrew M. Pettigrew, ed., *The Management of Strategic Change.* Oxford: Blackwell.

Matyas, A. 1985. *History of Modern Non-Marxian Economics.* New York: St. Martin's.

Maynes, E. S. 1976. "The Concept and Measurement of Product Quality." In Terleckyj 1976.

Mazzucato, Mariana. 1997. "A Computational Model of Economies of Scale and Market Share Instability." Chapter 11 in Arthur, Durlauf, and Lane 1997.

McAdam, Doug, Sidney Tarrow, and Charles Tilly. 1998. "Toward an Integrated Perspective on Social Movements and Revolution." Chapter 6 in Mark Irving Lichbach and Alan S. Zuckerman, eds., *Comparative Politics: Rationality, Structure, and Culture.* Cambridge: Cambridge University Press.

———. 2000. *Dynamics of Contention.* Cambridge: Cambridge University Press.

McGahan, A. M., and M. E. Porter. 1997. "How Much Does Industry Matter, Really?" *Strategic Management Journal* 18, summer special issue: 15–30.

McGuire, T., Mark Granovetter, and Michael Schwartz. 1993. "Thomas Edison and the Social Construction of the Early Electricity Industry in America." Chapter 9 in Swedberg 1993.

McPherson, J. Miller. 1997. "The Birth and Death of Social Forms." Memorandum, Santa Fe Institute, October 25.

———. 1983. "An Ecology of Affiliation." *American Sociological Review* 48:519–32.

McPherson, J. Miller, and Thomas Rotolo. 1996. "Testing a Dynamic Model of Social Composition: Diversity and Change in Voluntary Groups." *American Sociological Review* 61:179–202.

Ménard, C. 1995. "Markets as Institutions versus Organizations as Markets?" *Journal of Economic Behavior and Organization* 28:170.

———. 1996. "On Clusters, Hybrids and Other Strange Forms: The Case of the French Poultry Industry." *Journal of Institutional and Theoretical Economics* 152:154–83.

Menger, Pierre-Michel. 1999. "Artistic Labor Markets and Careers." *Annual Review of Sociology* 23:541–74.

Meyer, Marshall W. 1993. "Organizational Design and the Performance Paradox." Chapter 11 in Swedberg 1993.

Miller, Danny, and Ming-Jer Chen. 1995. "Nonconformity in Competitive Repertoires: A Sociological View of Markets." Ecole des Hautes Etudes Commerciales, Montreal, July.

Milroy, Leslie. 1979. *Language and Social Networks*. Oxford: Blackwell.

Mintz, Beth, and Michael Schwartz. 1985. *The Power Structure of American Business*. Chicago: University of Chicago Press.

Mintzberg, Henry. 1987. Chapter 18 in Glenn Carroll and D. Vogel, eds., *Organizational Approaches to Strategy*. Cambridge, Mass.: Ballinger.

Mische, Ann, and Philippa Pattison. 2000. "Composing a Civic Arena: Publics, Projects, and Social Settings." *Poetics* 27:163–94.

Mische, Ann, and Harrison C. White. 1998. "Between Conversation and Situation: Public Switching across Network Domains." *Social Research* 65:695–724.

Mischel, W. 1990. "Personality Dispositions Revisited and Revised: A View after Three Decades." Chapter 2 in L. A. Pervin, ed., *Handbook of Personality: Theory and Research*. New York: Guilford.

Mizruchi, Mark. 1989. "Similarity of Political Behavior among Large American Corporations." *American Journal of Sociology* 95:401–24.

———. 1992. *The Structure of Corporate Political Action*. Cambridge: Harvard University Press.

Mizruchi, Mark, and Michael Schwartz, eds. 1987. *The Structural Analysis of Business*. Cambridge: Cambridge University Press.

Moehring, Eugene P. 1999. *Resort City in the Sunbelt: Las Vegas, 1930–2000*. Reno: University of Nevada Press.

Mohr, John W. 1994. "Soldiers, Mothers, Tramps and Others: Discourse Roles in the 1907 New York City Charity Directory." *Poetics* 22:327–57.

Mohr, John W., and Vincent Duquenne. 1997. "The Duality of Culture and Practice: Poverty Relief in New York City, 1888–1917." *Theory and Society* 26:305–56.

Montgomery, James D. 1997. "Toward a Role-Theoretic Conception of Embeddedness." Institute of Management, London School of Economics, September.

Morrill, Calvin. 1995. *The Executive Way: Conflict Management in Organizations*. Chicago: University of Chicago Press.

Morris, Martina. 1993. "Epidemiology and Social Networks: Modeling Structured Diffusion." *Sociological Methods and Research* 22:99–126.

Mothe, J. de la, and Gilles Paquet, eds. 1994. *Evolutionary Economics and the New International Political Economy*. London: Pinter.

Muth, John F. 1961. "Rational Expectations and the Theory of Price Movements." *Econometrica* 29:315–34.

Muthukumar, M., C. K. Ober, and E. L. Thomas. 1997. "Competing Interactions and Levels of Ordering in Self-Organizing Polymeric Materials." *Science* 277:1225–32.

Mydosh, J. A. 1993. *Spin Glasses: An Experimental Introduction*. London: Taylor and Francis.

Nadel, S. F. 1957. *The Theory of Social Structure*. London: Cohen and West.

Nelson, Richard R. 1994. "New Directions in Technology Studies." Chapter 2 in Leydesdaaft and Bessela 1994.

Nelson, Richard R., and Sidney Winter. 1982. *An Evolutionary Theory of Economic Change*. Cambridge: Harvard University Press.

Nerlove, Marc. 1963. "Returns to Scale in Electricity Supply." Chapter 7 in C. Christ, M. Friedman, Leo Goodman, Zvi Griliches, A. Harberger, N. Liviatan, J. Mincer, Y. Mundlak, M. Nerlove, D. Patinkin, L. Telser, and H. Theil, eds., *Measurement in Economics*. Stanford: Stanford University Press.

———. 1965. *Estimation and Identification of Cobb-Douglas Production Functions*. Chicago: Rand McNally.

Newman, Peter. 1965. *The Theory of Exchange*. Englewood Cliffs, N.J.: Prentice-Hall.

Niebur, Ernst, Heinz G. Schuster, Daniel M. Kammen, and Christof Koch. 1991. "Oscillator-Phase Coupling for Different Two-Dimensional Network Connectivities." *Physical Review* A 44:6895–6905.

Nohria, Nitin, and Robert G. Eccles, eds. 1992. *Networks and Organizations: Structure, Form, and Action*. Boston: Harvard Business School Press.

North, Douglass. 1990. *Institutions, Institutional Change, and Economic Performance*. Cambridge: Cambridge University Press.

Ocasio, William. 1994. "Political Dynamics and the Circulation of Power: CEO Succession in U.S. Industrial Corporations, 1960–1990." *Administrative Science Quarterly* 39:285–312.

Ocasio, William, and Hyosun Kim. "The Circulation of Corporate Control." *Administrative Science Quarterly* 44:532–62.

Offe, Claus. 1985. *Disorganized Capitalism*. Ed. John Keane. Cambridge: MIT Press.

Ohta, Makoto, and Zvi Griliches. 1976. "Automobile Prices Revisited: Extensions of the Hedonic Hypothesis." Pp. 325–90 in Terleckji 1976.

Olick, Jeffrey K. 1998. "Introduction: Memory and the Nation—Continuities, Conflicts, and Transformations." *Social Science History* 22:377–87.

Ordover, J. A., and Garth Saloner. 1989. "Predation, Monopolization, and Antitrust." Chapter 9 in Schmalensee and Willig 1989.

Orlean, André. 1994a. "Sur le rôle respectif de la confiance et de l'intérêt dans la constitution de l'ordre marchand." *Revue du MAUSS*, 2ᵉ semestre.

———, ed. 1994b. *Analyse économiques des conventions*. Paris: Presses Universitaires de France.

Orr, Shepley W. 1995. "How Ties Are Used." Preprint 206, Center for the Social Sciences, Columbia University, June.

Oster, Sharon. 1981. "Product Regulations: A Measure of the Benefits." *Journal of Industrial Economics* 29:395–411.

———. 1982. "Intraindustry Structure and the Ease of Strategic Change." *Review of Economics and Statistics* 64:376–83.

———. 2000. "Is There a Future in Diversity: Essay on White (1981)." Pp. 352–58, 385–86 in Baum and Dobbin 2000.

Padgett, John F. 1981. "Hierarchy and Ecological Control in Federal Budgetary Decision-Making." *American Journal of Sociology* 87:75–129.

Padgett, John F., and Christopher Ansell. 1993. "Robust Action and the Rise of the Medici, 1400–1434." *American Journal of Sociology* 98:1259–1319.

Panzar, John C. 1989. "Technological Determinants of Firm and Industry Structure." Chapter 1 in Schmalensee and Willig 1989.

Page, Karen, and Joel M. Podolny. 1998. "Network Forms of Organization." *Annual Review of Sociology* 24:57–76.

Park, Douglas Y., and Joel M. Podolny. 1998. "The Competitive Dynamics of Status and Niche Width: U.S. Investment Banking, 1920–1950." Department of Management of Organizations, Hong Kong University of Science and Technology.

Parker, R. H. 1969. *Management Accounting: An Historical Perspective*. London: Macmillan.

Parsons, Talcott, R. Freed Bales, and E. Shils. 1953. *Working Papers in the Theory of Action*. Glencoe: Free Press.

Pattison, Philippa. 1993. *The Algebraic Analysis of Social Networks*. Cambridge: Cambridge University Press.

Pedersen, Jesper S., and Frank Dobbin. 1997. "The Social Invention of Collective Actors." *American Behavioral Scientist* 40:431–44.

Peli, Gabor, and Bart Nooteboom. 1999. "Market Partitioning and the Geometry of the Resource Space." *American Journal of Sociology* 104:1132–54.

Penrose, Edith. 1959. *The Theory of the Growth of the Firm*. Oxford: Blackwell.

Perinbanayagam, R. S. 1991. *Discursive Acts*. New York: Aldine de Gruyter.

Perrow, Charles. 1993. "Small Firm Networks." Chapter 14 in Swedberg 1993.

Perry, Martin K. 1989. "Vertical Integration: Determinants and Effects." Chapter 4 in Schmalensee and Willig 1989.

Peterson, Peter, ed. 1976. *The Production of Culture*. Beverly Hills, Calif.: Sage.

Pfeffer, Jeffrey, and Gerald R. Salancik. 1978. *The External Control of Organizations: A Resource Dependence Perspective*. New York: Harper and Row.

Phillips, Damon J., and Ezra W. Zuckerman. 2000. "Middle-Status Conformity: Theoretical Restatement and Empirical Demonstration in Two Markets." Graduate Schools of Business, Stanford University and University of Chicago.

Piore, Michael J. 1996. Review of *The Handbook of Economic Sociology*, ed. Neil Smelser and Richard Swedberg. *Journal of Economic Literature* 34:741–54.

Piore, Michael J., and Charles Sabel. 1984. *The Second Industrial Divide*. New York: Basic Books.

Podolny, Joel M. 1993. "A Status-Based Model of Market Competition." *American Journal of Sociology* 98:829–72.

———. 1994. "Market Uncertainty and the Social Character of Economic Exchange." *Administrative Science Quarterly* 39:458–83.

———. 1995. "Investment Banks." Chapter 11 in Carroll and Hannan 1995.

———. 1999. "Networks: The Pipes and Prisms of the Market." Graduate School of Business, Stanford University.

Podolny, Joel M., and Fabrizio Castellucci. 1999. "Choosing Ties from the Inside of a Prism: Status and Egocentric Uncertainty in the Venture Capital Markets." Chapter

5 in R. T. A. J. Leenders and Shaul Gabbay, eds., *Corporate Social Capital and Liability*. Boston: Kluwer Academic Press.

Podolny, Joel M., and Fiona S. Morten. 1999. "Social Status, Entry, and Predation: The Case of British Shipping Cartels, 1879–1929." *Journal of Industrial Economics* 47:41–67.

Podolny, Joel M., Toby Stuart, and Michael Hannan. 1996. "Networks, Knowledge, and Niches: Competition in the Worldwide Semiconductor Industry." *American Journal of Sociology* 102:659–89.

Pollack, Robert. 1994. *Signs of Life: The Language and Meanings of DNA*. Boston: Houghton Mifflin.

Polos, Laszlo, Michael T. Hannan, and Glenn R. Carroll. 1999. "Identities, Forms, and Populations." University of Amsterdam.

Porac, Joseph F., and José A. Rosa. 1996. "Rivalry, Industry Models, and the Cognitive Embeddedness of the Comparable Firm." *Advances in Strategic Management* 13:363–88.

Porac, Joseph F., José A. Rosa, Michael S. Sazon, and Jelena Spanjol. 1998. "America's Family Vehicle: Identities and Equivocality in the US Minivan Market." Paper presented at the American Sociological Association, San Francisco.

Porac, Joseph F., and Howard Thomas. 1994. "Cognitive Categorization and Subjective Rivalry among Retailers in a Small City." *Journal of Applied Psychology* 79:54–66.

Porac, Joseph F., Howard Thomas, Fiona Wilson, Douglas Paton, and Alaina Kanfer. 1995. "Rivalry and the Industry Model of Scottish Knitwear Producers." *Administrative Science Quarterly* 40:203–27.

Porter, Michael E. 1976a. "The Contributions of Industrial Organization to Strategic Management." *Academy of Management Review* 6:609–20.

———. 1976b. *Interbrand Choice, Strategy, and Bilateral Market Power*. Cambridge: Harvard University Press.

———. 1980. *Competitive Strategy: Techniques for Analyzing Industries and Competitors*. New York: Macmillan and Free Press.

Portz, John. 1991. "Economic Governance and the American Meatpacking Industry." Chapter 9 in Campbell, Hollingsworth, and Lindberg 1991.

Powell, Walter W. 1990. "Neither Market Nor Hierarchy: Network Forms of Organization." Pp. 295–336 in Larry L. Cummings and Barry Staw, eds., *Research in Organizational Behavior*. Greenwich, Conn.: JAI Press.

———, ed. 1987. *The Nonprofit Sector: A Handbook*. New Haven: Yale University Press.

Powell, Walter W., and Paul DiMaggio, eds. 1991. *The New Institutionalism in Organizational Analysis*. Chicago: University of Chicago Press.

Power, Michael. 1997. *The Audit Society: Rituals of Verification*. Oxford: Oxford University Press.

Rader, Trout. 1971. *The Economics of Feudalism*. New York: Gordon and Breach.

Rajan, Raghuram G., and Luigi Zingales. 1996. "Power in a Theory of the Firm." University of Chicago and NBER, October.

Ramanujam, V., and N. Venkatraman. 1984. "An Inventory and Critique of Strategy Research Using the PIMS Database." *Academy of Management Review* 9:138–51.

Rapoport, Anatol. 1983. *Mathematical Models in the Social and Behavioral Sciences*. New York: Wiley.

Raub, Werner, and Jeoen Weesie. 1993. "Symbiotic Arrangements: A Sociological Perspective." *Journal of Institutional and Theoretical Economics* 149:716–24.

Riley, John G. 1975. "Competitive Signaling." *Journal of Economic Theory* 10:174–86.

Rivkin, Jan W. 1997. "Reconcilable Differences: The Relationship between Industry Conditions and Firm Effects." Working paper, Harvard Graduate School of Business Administration, September 18.

Roberts, Peter W., and Ray Reagans. 2000. "Market Experience, Consumer Attention, and Price-Quality Relationships for New World Wines in the U. S. Market, 1987–1999." Working paper for SMS Conference, Graduate School of Industrial Administration, Carnegie Mellon University, October.

Romo, Frank P., and Michael E. Schwartz. 1993. "The Coming of Post-industrial Society Revisited: Manufacturing and the Prospects for a Service-Based Economy." Chapter 13 in Swedberg 1993.

———. 1995. "Structural Embeddedness of Business Decisions: A Sociological Assessment of the Migration Behavior of Plants in New York State between 1960 and 1985." *American Sociological Review* 60:874–907.

Rose, F. G. G. 1960. *Classification of Kin, Age Structure, and Marriage amongst the Groote Eblandt Aborigines*. Berlin: Akademie Verlag.

Rosen, Sherwin. 1974. "Hedonic Prices and Implicit Markets: Product Differentiation in Pure Competition." *Journal of Political Economy* 82:34–55.

Rosenberg, Harold. 1969. *Artworks and Packages*. New York: Horizon Press.

———. 1982. *The Anxious Object*. Chicago: University of Chicago Press, Phoenix Books.

Rothschild, Michael, and Joseph Stiglitz. 1976. "Equilibrium in Competitive Insurance Markets: An Essay on the Economics of Imperfect Competition." *Quarterly Journal of Economics* 90:629–49.

Rueschemeyer, Dietrich. 1986. *Power and the Division of Labor*. Stanford: Stanford University Press.

Ryall, Michael D. 1998. "When Competencies ARE NOT Core: Self-Confirming Theories and the Destruction of Firm Value." Simon School, University of Rochester, October 6.

Sachs, Harvey. 1995. *Lectures on Conversation*. Oxford: Blackwell.

Salais, Robert. 1994. "Incertitude et interactions de travail: Des produits, des conventions." Pp. 371–403 in Orlean 1994.

Salzinger, Leslie. 1998. "Gender under Production: Constituting Subjects in Mexico's Global Factories." Ph.D. diss., University of California, Berkeley.

Schelling, Thomas. 1963. *Strategy of Conflict*. New York: Oxford University Press.

———. 1978. *Micromotives and Macrobehavior*. New York: Norton.

———. 1998. "Social Mechanisms and Social Dynamics." Chapter 2 in Hedstrom and Swedberg 1998.

Scherer, F. M. 1970. *Industrial Market Structure and Economic Performance*. Chicago: Rand McNally.

Scherer, F. M., and David Ross. 1990. *Industrial Market Structure and Economic Performance*. Boston: Houghton Mifflin.

Scherrer, Christoph. 1991a. "Governance of the Automobile Industry: The Transformation of Labor and Supplier Relations." Chapter 7 in Campbell, Hollingsworth, and Lindberg 1991.

———. 1991b. "Governance of the Steel Industry: What Caused the Disintegration of the Oligopoly?" Chapter 6 in Campbell, Hollingsworth, and Lindberg 1991.

Schlicht, Ekkehart. 1998. *On Custom in the Economy*. Oxford: Clarendon.

Schmalensee, Richard. 1989. "Inter-industry Studies of Structure and Performance." Chapter 16 in Schmalensee and Willig 1989.

Schmalensee, Richard, and Robert D. Willig, eds. 1989. *Handbook of Industrial Organization*. 2 vols. Amsterdam: North-Holland.

Schwartz, Michael. 1976. *Radical Protest and Social Structure*. New York: Academic Press.

Scitovsky, Tibor. 1993. "The Meaning, Nature, and Sources of Value in Economics." Chapter 5 in Hechter, Nadel, and Michod 1993.

Shapiro, Carl. 1989. "Theories of Oligopoly Behavior." Chapter 6 in Schmalensee and Willig 1989.

Shoda, Yuichi, Walter Mischel, and J. C. Wright. 1993. "The Role of Situational Demands and Cognitive Competencies in Behavior Organization and Personality Coherence." *Journal of Personality and Social Psychology* 65:1023–35.

Shubik, Martin. 1984a. *A Game Theoretical Approach to Political Economy*. Cambridge: MIT Press.

———. 1984b. *Game Theory in the Social Sciences: Concepts and Solutions*. Cambridge: MIT Press.

Silver, Allan. 1997. "'Two Different Sorts of Commerce—Friendship and Strangership in Civil Society." Chapter 2 in Jeff Weintraub and Krishnan Kumar, eds., *Public and Private in Thought and Practice*. Chicago: University of Chicago Press.

Silverstein, Michael. 1976. "Shifters, Linguistic Categories, and Cultural Inscription." Pp. 11–55 in Keith H. Basso and Henry A. Selby, eds., *Meaning in Anthropology*. Albuquerque: University of New Mexico Press.

———. 1992. "The Indeterminacy of Contextualization: When Is Enough Enough?" Chapter 4 in P. Auer and A. di Luzio, eds., *The Contextualization of Language*. Amsterdam: Benjamin.

———. 1993. "Metapragmatic Discourse and Metapragmatic Function." Chapter 2 in Lucy 1993.

———. 1996. "Indexical Order and the Dialectics of Sociolinguistic Life." Pp. 89–102 in R. Parker et al., eds., *SALSA III: Proceedings of the Third Annual Symposium about Language and Society*. Austin: University of Texas Press.

———. 1997. "Commentary: Achieving Adequacy and Commitment in Pragmatics." *Pragmatics* 7:625–33.

———. 1998a. "The Improvisational Performance of Culture in Realtime Discursive Practice." Chapter 12 in R. Keith Sawyer, ed., *Creativity in Performance*. Greenwich, Conn.: Ablex.

———. 1998b. Letter to the author. September 17.

Simon, Herbert A. 1957. *Models of Man*. New York: Wiley.

———. 1981. *Sciences of the Artificial*. Cambridge: MIT Press.

Singh, Jitendra V., David J. Tucker, and Agnes Meinhard. 1991. "Institutional Change and Organizational Dynamics." Chapter 16 in Powell and DiMaggio 1991.

Smelser, Neil, and Richard Swedberg, eds. 1994. *The Handbook of Economic Sociology*. New York: Russell Sage Foundation, and Princeton: Princeton University Press.

Smith, Charles W. 1989. *Auctions: The Social Construction of Value*. New York: Free Press and Macmillan.

———. 1993. "Auctions." Chapter 8 in Swedberg.

———. 1999. *Success and Survival on Wall Street: Understanding the Mind of the Market*. Lanham, Md.: Rowman and Littlefield.

Somers, Margaret R. 1995. "Economic Sociology, Institutional Analysis, and Class Formation Theory: A Second Look at a Classic." *Social Science History* 19:591–630.

Spence, A. Michael. 1973. "Job Market Signaling." *Quarterly Journal of Economics* 87:355–74.

———. 1974a. *Market Signaling: Informational Transfer in Hiring and Related Screening Processes*. Cambridge: Harvard University Press.

———. 1974b. "Competitive and Optimal Responses to Signaling: Analysis of Efficiency and Distribution." *Journal of Economic Theory* 7:296–332.

———. 1975. "Product Selection, Fixed Costs and Monopolistic Competition." *Review of Economic Studies* 43:217–35.

———. 1981. "The Learning Curve and Competition." *Bell Journal of Economics* 12:49–70.

Stark, David. 1992. "Path Dependence and Privatization Strategies in East Central Europe." *East European Politics and Societies* 6:17–53.

———. 1996. "Recombinant Property in East European Capitalism." *American Journal of Sociology* 101:1993–1027.

———. 2000. "Heterarchy." Working paper, Department of Sociology, Columbia University.

Stearns, Linda B., and Mark S. Mizruchi. 1993. "Corporate Financing: Social and Economic Determinants." Chapter 11 in Swedberg 1993.

Stewman, Shelby, and S. L. Konda. 1983. "Careers and Organizational Labor Markets: Demographic Models of Organizational Behavior." *American Journal of Sociology* 88:637–85.

Stiglitz, Joseph E. 1989. "Imperfect Information in the Product Market." Chapter 13 in Schmalensee and Willig 1989.

Stinchcombe, Arthur L. 1983. *Economic Sociology*. New York: Academic Press.

———. 1988. "The Conditions of Fruitfulness of Theorizing about Mechanisms in Social Science." Paper presented to the American Association for the Advancement of Science.

———. 1990. *Information and Organizations*. Berkeley and Los Angeles: University of California Press.

———. 1995. *Sugar Island Slavery in the Age of the Enlightenment: The Political Economy of the Caribbean World*. Princeton: Princeton University Press.

———. 1998. "Monopolistic Competition as a Mechanism: Corporations, Universities, and Nation-States in Competitive Fields." Chapter 11 in Hedstrom and Swedberg 1998.

Stinchcombe, Arthur L., and Carol A. Heimer. 1985. *Organization Theory and Project Management*. Bergen: Norwegian University Press.

Strathern, Andrew. 1971. *The Rope of Moka*. Cambridge: Cambridge University Press.

Streeck, W. 1992. *Social Institutions and Economic Performance*. Beverly Hills, Calif.: Sage.

Strang, David, and Nancy B. Tuma. 1993. "Spatial and Temporal Heterogeneity in Diffusion." *American Journal of Sociology* 99:614–40.

Stuart, Toby. 1998. "Network Positions and Propensities to Collaborate: An Investigation of Strategic Alliance Formation in a High-Technology Industry." *Administrative Science Quarterly* 43:668–98.

Sverrisson, Arni. 1993. *Evolutionary Technical Change and Flexible Mechanization: Entrepreneurship and Industrialization in Kenya and Zimbabwe.* Lund: Lund University Press.

———. 1994. "Making Sense of Chaos: Socio-technical Networks, Careers, and Entrepreneurs." *Acta Sociologica* 37:401–17.

Swales, J. M. 1990. *Genre Analysis: English in Academic and Research Settings.* Cambridge: Cambridge University Press.

Swedberg, Richard. 1990. *Economics and Sociology: Redefining Their Boundaries—Conversations with Economists and Sociologists.* Princeton: Princeton University Press.

———. 1994. "Markets as Social Structures." Pp. 255–83 in Smelser and Swedberg 1994.

———. 1997. "New Economic Sociology: What Has Been Accomplished, What Is Ahead?" *Acta Sociologica«MDBI»* 40:161–82.

———, ed. 1993. *Explorations in Economic Sociology.* New York: Russell Sage Foundation.

Swidler, Ann. 1986. "Culture in Action: Symbols and Strategies." *American Sociological Review* 51:273–85.

Talmud, Ilan. 1992. "Market Embeddedness." Ph.D. diss., Columbia University.

Talmy, Leonard. 1995. "The Windowing of Attention in Language." Chapter 31 in M. Shibatani and Sandra Thompson, eds., *Essays in Semantics.* Philadelphia: J. Benjamins.

———. 1996. "Fictive Motion in Language and 'Ception.'" Chapter 11 in Paul Bloom, Mary Peterson, Lynn Nadel, and Merrill Garrett, eds., *Language and Space.* Cambridge: MIT Press.

Tannen, Deborah, ed. 1993. *Framing in Discourse.* New York: Oxford University Press.

Terleckyj, Nestor E., ed. 1976. *Household Production and Consumption.* New York: National Bureau of Economic Research and Columbia University Press.

Thornton, Patricia H. 1999. "The Sociology of Entrepreneurship." *Annual Review of Sociology* 25:19–46.

Thornton, Patricia H., and William Ocasio. 1999. "Institutional Logics and the Historical Contingency of Power in Organizations: Executive Succession in the Higher Education Industry, 1958–1990." *American Journal of Sociology* 105:801–43.

Tilly, Charles. 1995. *Popular Contention in Great Britain, 1758–1834.* Cambridge: Harvard University Press.

———. 1996. "Durable Inequality." Working paper, Center for the Social Sciences, Columbia University, September.

Tuma, Nancy B., and Michael T. Hannan. 1984. *Social Dynamics: Models and Methods.* Orlando, Fla.: Academic Press.

Udy, Stanley. 1970. *Work in Traditional and Modern Society.* Englewood Cliffs, N.J.: Prentice-Hall.

Urban, Greg. 1991. *A Discourse-Centered Approach to Culture: Native South American Myths and Rituals.* Austin: University of Texas Press.

Urrutiaguer, Daniel. 1997. "L'Analyse économique des organisations théâtrales." Working draft, LAEDIX-Paris 10, June.

Useem, Michael. 1982. "Classwide Rationality in the Politics of Managers and Directors of Large Corporations in the United States and Great Britain." *Administrative Science Quarterly* 27:553–72.

Uzzi, Brian. 1996. "The Sources and Consequences of Embeddedness for the Economic Performance of Organizations: The Network Effect." *American Sociological Review* 61:674–98.

———. 1997. "Social Structure and Competition in Interfirm Networks: The Paradox of Embeddedness." *Administrative Science Quarterly* 42:35–67.

Uzzi, Brian, and James J. Gillespie. 1999. "Interfirm Ties and the Organization of the Firm's Capital Structure in the Middle Financial Market." Chapter 4 in Andrews and Knoke 1999.

Vancil, Richard F. 1979. *Decentralization: Managerial Ambiguity by Design.* Homewood, Ill.: Dow-Jones Irwin.

Van Vleck, J. H. 1932. *The Theory of Electric and Magnetic Susceptibilities.* New York: Oxford University Press.

Varian, Hal R. 1989. "Price Discrimination." Chapter 10 in Schmalensee and Willig 1989.

Vaughan, Diane. 1998. "How Theory Travels: Analogy, Models, and the Case of A. Michael Spence." Paper presented at the Annual Meeting of the American Sociological Association, San Francisco.

Vlachoutsicos, C., and Paul Lawrence. 1990. "What We Don't Know about Soviet Management." *Harvard Business Review,* November–December, 50–66.

Waechter, Matthias. 1999. *Rational Action and Social Networks in Ecological Economics.* Habil. thesis, Swiss Federal Institute of Technology, Zurich, July 7.

Waldinger, Roger D. 1986. *Through the Eye of the Needle: Immigrants and Enterprise in New York's Garment Trades.* New York: New York University Press.

Wallerstein, Immanuel. 1980. *The Modern World System,* vol. 2: *1600–1750.* New York: Academic Press.

Wasserman, Stanley, and Kathleen Faust. 1995. *Social Network Analysis: Methods and Applications.* Cambridge: Cambridge University Press.

Watts, Duncan J. 1999a. "Networks, Dynamics, and the Small-World Phenomenon." *American Journal of Sociology* 105:493–527.

———. 1999b. *Small Worlds: The Dynamics of Networks between Order and Randomness.* Princeton: Princeton University Press.

Watts, Duncan J., and Steven H. Strogatz. 1998. "Collective Dynamics of 'Small-World' Networks." *Nature* 393:440–42.

Wellman, Barry, and S. D. Berkowitz, eds. 1998. *Social Structures: A Network Approach.* Cambridge: Cambridge University Press.

West, Geoffrey B., James H. Brown, and Brian J. Enquist. 1997. "A General Model for the Origin of Allometric Scaling Laws in Biology." *Science* 276:122–26.

Western, Bruce. 1995. "A Comparative Study of Working Disorganization: Union Decline in Eighteen Advanced Capitalist Countries." *American Sociological Review* 60:179–201.

White, Douglas. 1988. "Cites and Fights: Material Entailment Analysis of the Eighteenth-Century Chemical Revolution." Pp. 380–400 in Wellman and Berkowitz 1988.

White, Harrison C. 1963. *An Anatomy of Kinship: Mathematical Models for Structures of Cumulated Roles.* Englewood Cliffs, N.J.: Prentice-Hall.

———. 1970. *Chains of Opportunity: System Models of Mobility in Organizations.* Cambridge: Harvard University Press.

———. 1976. "Extending Spence's Market Models." RIAS Working Paper 1, Department of Sociology, Harvard University, fall.

———. 1978. "Markets and Hierarchies Revisited." RIAS Working Paper 11, Department of Sociology, Harvard University, March.

———. 1979. "On Markets." RIAS Working Paper 16, Department of Sociology, Harvard University, April.

———. 1981a. "Where Do Markets Come From?" *American Journal of Sociology* 87:517–47.

———. 1981b. "Production Markets as Induced Role Structures." Chapter 1 in S. Leinhardt, ed., *Sociological Methodology.* San Francisco: Jossey-Bass.

———. 1992a. *Identity and Control.* Princeton: Princeton University Press.

———. 1992b. "Markets, Networks, and Control." Chapter 7 in Lindenberg and Schroeder 1992.

———. 1993a. *Careers and Creativity.* Boulder, Colo.: Westview Press.

———. 1993b. "Markets in Production Networks." Chapter 6 in Swedberg 1993.

———. 1995a. "Social Networks Can Resolve Actor Paradoxes in Economics and in Psychology." *Journal of Institutional and Theoretical Economics* 151:58–74.

———. 1995b. "Where Do Languages Come From? Part I. Switching between Networks." Preprint 201, Center for the Social Sciences, Columbia University, New York City, August.

———. 1995c. "Network Switches, Actors, and Domination Grammar." Trans. E. Lazega as "Passages Réticulaires, Acteurs et Grammaire de la Domination." *Revue Française de Sociologie* 36:705–23.

———. 1995d. "Network Switchings and Bayesian Forks: Refounding the Social and Behavioral Sciences." *Social Research* 62:1035–63.

———. 1997. "Can Mathematics Be Social?" *Sociological Forum* 12:53–71.

———. 1998. "Varieties of Markets." Chapter 9 in Wellman and Berkowitz 1998.

———. 2000a. "Modeling Discourse in and around Markets." *Poetics* 27:117–35.

———. 2000b. "Parameterize! Notes on Mathematical Modeling in Sociology." *Sociological Theory* 18:505–9.

———. 2000c. "Does the Early Bird Catch the Worm: Essay on Oster (1982)." Pp. 359–66, 387–88, in Baum and Dobbin 2000.

White, Harrison C., Scott A. Boorman, and Ronald L. Breiger. 1976. "Social Structure from Multiple Networks: Part I. Blockmodels of Roles and Positions." *American Journal of Sociology* 81:730–80.

White, Harrison C., and Cynthia A. White. 1993. *Canvases and Careers: Institutional Change in the French Painting World.* Chicago: University of Chicago Press.

Wiley, Norbert. 1994. *The Semiotic Self.* Chicago: University of Chicago Press.

Williamson, Oliver E. 1975. *Markets and Hierarchies: Analysis and Antitrust Implications.* New York: Free Press.

———. 1985. *The Economic Institutions of Capitalism.* New York: Basic Books and Macmillan.

———. 1989. "Transaction Cost Economics." Chapter 3 in Schmalensee and Willig 1989.

———. 1992. Chapter 6 in Lindenberg and Schroeder 1992.

————, ed. 1998. *Industrial Organization*. Aldershot, Hants.: Elgar.

Williamson, Oliver E., and Sidney Winter, eds. 1991. *The Nature of the Firm: Origins, Evolution, and Development*. New York: Oxford University Press.

Wilson, E. O. 1970. *Insect Societies*. Cambridge: Harvard university Press.

————. 1979. *Sociobiology: The New Synthesis*. Cambridge Harvard University Press.

Winfree, Arthur. 1967. "Biological Rhythms and the Behaviors of Populations of Coupled Oscillators." *Journal of Theoretical Biology* 16:15–42.

Winship, Christopher. 1978. "The Allocation of Time among Individuals." Chapter 8 in K. Schuessler, ed., *Sociological Methodology*, vol. 10. San Francisco: Jossey-Bass.

Winship, Christopher, and Michael J. Mandel. 1984. "Roles and Positions: A Critique and Extension of the Blockmodeling Approach." Chapter 10 in S. Leinhardt, ed., *Sociological Methodology, 1984*. San Francisco: Jossey-Bass.

Winship, Christopher, and Sherwin Rosen, eds. 1988. Special issue on economics and sociology. *American Journal of Sociology* 94.

Winter, Sidney, and N. Phelps. 1970. "Optimal Price Policy under Atomistic Competition." In Edmund S. Phelps, ed., *Microeconomic Foundations of Employment and Inflation Theory*. London: Macmillan.

Yonay, Yuval. 2000 "An Ethnographer's Credo: Methodological Reflections Following an Anthropological Journey among the Econ." *Journal of Economic Issues* 34:341–56.

Yoshino, Michael Y., and Thomas Lifson. 1988. *The Invisible Link: Japan's Sogo Shosha in the Organization of Tradition*. Cambridge: MIT Press.

Zajac, Edward J., and Cyrus P. Olsen. 1993. "From Transaction Cost to Transactional Value Analysis: Implications for the Study of Interorganizational Strategies." *Journal of Management Studies* 30:132–45.

Zannetos, Zenon S. 1966. *The Theory of Oil Tankship Rates*. Cambridge: MIT Press.

Zelizer, Viviana A. 1989. "The Social Meaning of Monies: 'Special Monies.'" *American Journal of Sociology* 95:342–77.

————. 1993. "Making Multiple Monies." Chapter 8 in Swedberg 1993.

————. 1998. "The Proliferation of Social Currencies." Pp. 58–68 in Michael Callon, ed., *The Laws of the Markets*. Oxford: Blackwell.

Ziman, J. M. 1979. *Models of disorder: The Theoretical Physics of Homogeneously Disordered Systems*. Cambridge: Cambridge University Press.

Zipf, George K. 1949. *Human Behavior and the Principle of Least Effort*. Cambridge, Mass.: Addison-Wesley.

Zuckerman, Ezra W. 1999. "The Categorical Imperative: Securities Analysis and the Illegitimacy Discount." *American Journal of Sociology* 104:1398–1438.

————. 2000. "Focusing the Corporate Project: Securities Analysts and De-diversification." *Administrative Science Quarterly* 45:591–619.

Zuckerman, Ezra W., and Tai-Young Kim. 2000. "The Critical Trade-Off: Identity Assessment and Box-Office Success in the Feature Film Industry." Stanford University and Hong Kong University of Science and Technology.

Index

~~~~~~~~~~~~~~~~~~~~